Latin American Popular Culture since Independence

An Introduction

Second Edition

Edited by William H. Beezley and
Linda A. Curcio-Nagy

ROWMAN & LITTLEFIELD PUBLISHERS, INC.
Lanham • Boulder • New York • Toronto • Plymouth, UK

Published by Rowman & Littlefield Publishers, Inc.
A wholly owned subsidiary of The Rowman & Littlefield Publishing Group, Inc.
4501 Forbes Boulevard, Suite 200, Lanham, Maryland 20706
http://www.rowmanlittlefield.com

Estover Road, Plymouth PL6 7PY, United Kingdom

British Library Cataloguing in Publication Information Available

Library of Congress Cataloging-in-Publication Data

Latin American popular culture since independence : an introduction / edited by William H. Beezley and Linda A. Curcio-Nagy. — 2nd ed.
p. cm.
Includes bibliographical references and index.
ISBN 978-1-4422-1254-1 (cloth : alk. paper) — ISBN 978-1-4422-1255-8 (pbk. : alk. paper) — ISBN 978-1-4422-1256-5 (electronic)
1. Popular culture—Latin America. 2. Latin America—Social life and customs. 3. Arts—Latin America. I. Beezley, William H. II. Curcio, Linda Ann.
F1408.3.L2743 2012
980—dc22

2011018096

∞™ The paper used in this publication meets the minimum requirements of American National Standard for Information Sciences—Permanence of Paper for Printed Library Materials, ANSI/NISO Z39.48-1992.

Printed in the United States of America

Latin American Popular Culture since Independence

Contents

Acknowledgments

We thank the contributors above all for their help with this volume. Several people also helped in its preparation. Susan Deeds provided information on Indian resistance to missionaries in Mexico's far north. Betsy Brown indirectly guided us to the story of Doña Mariana Belsunse y Salazar of Lima and her portrait in the Brooklyn Museum of Art. The students in the undergraduate seminar on Latin American popular culture at the University of Nevada read the introduction and several selections and then offered us their criticisms and insights. On the same occasion, Mary Elizabeth Perry of UCLA shared her views of Hispanic popular culture with us. At the University of Arizona, research assistant Rachel K. Villarreal provided timely help on this project. At Scholarly Resources, we acknowledge the professional assistance of Rick Hopper, Carolyn Travers, Michelle Slavin, and our production editor, Janet Greenwood.

For the second edition, we have received encouragement and assistance from our editor at Rowman & Littlefield, Susan McEachern, and her assistant, Carrie Broadwell-Tkach. Other colleagues have made helpful suggestions and recommended authors to us. Monica Rankin at University of Texas-Dallas, for example, has provided us with comments from her classes that used the book and suggested changes to us. We also have benefited from the discussion of the first edition in the Theaters of Memory Seminar at the University of Arizona and the collective memory session at the Oaxaca Summer Institute. We thank these individuals and others for urging us to continue the study of popular culture in Latin America.

Revised Introduction

William H. Beezley and Linda A. Curcio-Nagy

What many call popular culture refers to the set of images, practices, and interactions that distinguishes a community and often serves as a synonym for national identity. More comprehensively, popular culture, as the term appears throughout this book, defines everyday culture. It identifies a set of behavioral practices with pervasive, ordinary character and acknowledges the general acceptance of these practices, their roots in common knowledge, and their frequent expression in nonwritten form. Because the literacy rate in most Latin American countries before the 1900s never exceeded 50 percent, reading and writing have not been the primary vehicles for expressing this prevailing culture. Rather, as the essays in this book reveal, oral traditions, music, visual imagery, dance, and family food represent the unique community character that forms much of popular culture. As with religion, a basic common pattern exists, but it is enriched and enlivened by the vernacular.

Furthermore, popular culture encapsulates the pleasure in everyday life—these experiences have been traced recently by William E. French.[1] Daily life offers moments of laughter (through jokes deriding political leaders regarding the economy, and mocking social betters, and simple foolishness); of delight in jobs well done (whether cooking or plowing, fixing a carburetor, or setting a table with flowers); of escape from dreary daily life (in festivals or drinking, romance, or dreams created by comic books and television); and of living well (by listening to current music, dancing the latest steps, or wearing the hottest fashions). As popular culture instills the pleasure in everyday life, it makes life memorable. It reorganizes the past and promotes the intriguing aspects of national culture. It creates local heroes accessible to everyday people—the best dancer, the best drinker, the best soccer player, the best cook, each of whom earns a place in the galaxy of neighborhood stars. As well, popular culture draws links to national heroes and attaches them in some way to the local community. The narratives connecting national figures to local affairs give texture and dimension to social interaction by becoming the references for anecdotes, expressions, and memories.

Often popular culture has a raw edge bordering on, or crossing into, vulgarity, with sexual innuendo, rich profanity, and ethnic slurs. Beyond its local character, widespread acceptance, and raucous humor, therefore, popular culture transgresses social, religious, and political boundaries. This insistent challenge to society's hierarchy finds expression by turning the world upside down during Carnival, in dancing the forbidden jarabe, tango, Charleston, or samba, and in repeating socially inappropriate, often profane, stories and gossip. Transgression hints at violence—which sometimes occurs. Its transgressive current makes popular culture at times a little daring and a little risky, giving people the delightful thrill of breaking the rules and of putting one over on authority.

I

Popular culture has served throughout Latin America as a means to display identity, as an activity to produce momentary and playful pleasure, and as a way to sing and joke. The identity can be expressed in individual, group, regional, or national terms; the pleasure can be enjoyed by participants and spectators; and the music and the humor become common weapons of the weak.

The humorous element of popular culture is the least known, perhaps because it has an ephemeral and elusive nature. Nevertheless, traces of historical humor survive that demonstrate the style and versatility of popular culture in its humorous forms. For example, missionaries in New Spain's northern marches (today the U.S.-Mexican border region) regularly reported that Indian neophytes repeatedly made mistakes in simple religious rituals. Their accounts stressed the childlike learning ability of indigenous peoples, but in their nearsighted and indulgent benevolence, the friars missed the treacherous and therefore subversive ways the Indians used these religious performances as occasions for sly humor.[2] The so-called mistakes or parody of rituals, especially religious practices, paralleled similar behavior in Europe and represented one form of popular satire.

Marginal peoples—the poor, the enslaved, women—historically have manipulated cultural forms to their own benefit, and in doing so they have sometimes succeeded in producing humorous incidents for the pleasure of an attentive audience. An example is the reaction of the willful Doña

Mariana Belsunse y Salazar of Lima (1775–1800?) to an arranged marriage to an old, wealthy count, whom she described as "uglier than an excommunication." Arranged marriages were not unusual, nor was the bride's disappointment, but Doña Mariana's action was. She demanded a year of grace before consummating the marriage. Once she secured her stipulation, she slipped into a convent. Her sulky defiance of the count's insistence that she fulfill her bridal duties delighted Lima's public. Wags soon suggested in ribald limericks that the count lacked the prowess to control and satisfy his young wife. The public insults laid to his masculinity and his honor drove the count to intense sexual indulgence that soon carried him to his death. The amused public then saw Doña Mariana emerge from the cloister a virgin, a widow, and a wealthy young woman.[3]

The humorous engagement of political satire has long been a part of Latin American popular culture. Holiday celebrations in particular offer opportunities for the sardonic review of officials. During the seventeenth century, Corpus Christi, the most important religious festival in colonial Mexico City, occasioned widespread antihierarchical satire. Masked groups took over sections of the city at night. They closed off the streets and performed parodies of colonial bureaucrats and high-placed clergy. Puppet shows operated well past midnight, with presentations lampooning these same officials. In the eighteenth century, agents of the Inquisition confiscated over 200 satirical poems aimed at colonial authorities. Most of the poems probably came from the ubiquitous taverns, where authors composed and read their works. Despite the bans against political and religious satire, authors continued to circulate them, and some of these verses even worked their way into popular music and dances of the day.[4]

During the last decade of the nineteenth century and the first decade of the twentieth, urbanization and immigration characterized life in Mexico City and Buenos Aires as well as other principal cities in the region. The established residents of these cities reacted to these new arrivals with sardonic humor, biting sarcasm, and blistering caricatures. Mexicans in theater reviews, puppet performances, and comic strips lampooned the rural arrivals such as Mamerto and Vale Coyote, whose ignorance of city life amused audiences, and their adroit dodging of many legal and administrative snares provided lessons for new arrivals. Mario Mareno created the character of the recent arrival, the downtrodden *pelado* Cantinflas, who became a movie sensation. Immigrants, especially from Italy and Spain, joined rural arrivals called *paisanos* in Buenos Aires. Angel Villoldo, known as the Father of Tango for his compositions, also wrote mocking scripts for stand-up comedy, such as "Testamento de un paisano," that pilloried both Italian and *paisano* arrivals to the city. Early recording companies made records of many of his tangos and some of his comedy routines as well.[5] These humorous patterns continued throughout the twentieth century.

An example of this popular satire followed the public exposure of the corruption and scandal in the administration of the former president of Mexico, Carlos Salinas de Gotari (1988–1994). Everyday Mexicans tendered public judgment by selling Salinas masks on street corners, T-shirts picturing the imaginary monster the *chupacabra* (the goat-blood sucker) with Salinas's head, and miniature statues of the former president in prison pinstripes. This ultimately resulted in a Salinas museum in the bathroom of a popular artist.[6] These incidents show humor used as a device for shaming brazen authorities, as a commentary on onerous cultural practices, and as a method of passing judgment on government figures. Humor invests popular culture with a wonderful sense of whimsy that turns from obvious jokes to more subtle, sardonic images and forms. Humor also appears in music, art, and handicrafts; it helps make popular culture pleasurable. At the same time, these expressions reveal the deep grain of humor that runs through popular culture in Latin America.

II

An enduring feature of popular culture is its incessant give-and-take with high or elite cultures. Art generally has been appropriated by high culture; nevertheless, numerous popular forms exist, and the reciprocity between elite and everyday forms can be illustrated using art. Cartoons and portraits provide examples. Latin American cartoonists have adapted high art styles and techniques to illustrate their comic books and caricatures. They have used the styles of art nouveau, art deco, romanticism, and realism (including photography); a few have even used the wild extravagance of Antoni Gaudí, the Catalan architect. José G. Cruz created montages of drawing and photography in his photo-stories (a kind of comic book) of El Santo, the Mexican professional wrestler, that owe an enormous debt to surrealism. Cartoons and caricatures in turn have inspired well-known Latin American artists, among them Fernando Botero of Colombia and Miguel Covarrubias of Mexico, who for a time drew stylish caricatures that appeared in *Vanity Fair*.[7] The language of comic books inspired such authors as Mario Vargas Llosa, who in *Los Cachorros* relies on the onomatopoeia of comic strip dialogue, while novelists such as Miguel Cervantes have supplied plot lines and adventures for cartoon characters. The interchange of forms and styles between high and low cultures enriches both.[8]

Elite culture rarely acknowledges its sources, nor does it draw on satire and irony to the same extent that popular culture does. Nevertheless, Latin American popular artists known and unknown have created images recognized throughout their nations and have devoted themselves to creating beauty in everyday life. This effort often takes subtly different forms for different people. Cooks, dancers, carpenters, and writers all see beauty slightly differently. And, even less apparent to many people, beauty exists for those who open their senses to the perfectly whistled song, the imaginatively whittled cane, the fresh smell of newly washed clothes. Often inspired by academic painting, popular art falls on a spectrum from ephemeral Day of the Dead grave paintings made from flower petals and colored sawdust to such utilitarian objects as furniture and cooking utensils. Even a cursory examination of art, both academic and popular, suggests that perhaps the most human activity is the attempt to create beauty in everyday life. In Latin America, this effort has often involved a reciprocal borrowing between popular and high culture.

This constant circular borrowing is evident not only in artifacts and forms but also in performances, during public celebrations, for example, and in everyday activities at home. During holidays, some people parody elite behavior, crowning kings and queens of Carnival, while elites go "slumming"—performing lower-class dances and dressing in what they regard as popular costumes. At home, food at times demonstrates this interaction. The well-known dessert *tres leches* offers a striking example of circularity. The Carnation Concentrated Milk Company wanted to boost its sales of canned milk. The company's home economists developed recipes, including one for a three-milk dessert, that appeared on can labels. During the 1920s, Carnation began exporting to Central America, especially Nicaragua, where housewives, wishing to introduce a foreign delicacy to the dinner table, began offering *tres leches* for dessert. Nicaraguans adopted the popular sweet as the national dessert. Today, chic Miami Caribbean-Central American restaurants offer it as a dessert to elites as Nicaraguan tiramisu. What might be considered an example of cultural imperialism at one time, as a popular food at another, and as elite cuisine later has also become the treasured recipe of a Sonora, Mexico, family that owns a Tucson restaurant.[9] Above all, the dessert illustrates the circulation of culture among social groups across international boundaries and the creative appropriation and reshaping by individuals of elements of that culture.

Popular music also reflects a pattern of cultural reciprocity between Latin America and the wider world. During the 1930s, Cuban musicians traveled to New York City, where they listened to jazz and then took home the instrumentation and improvisation they had heard. The exchange worked both ways, as Afro-Cuban music influenced rhythm-and-blues artists and jazz musicians, including Herbie Mann, George Shearing, and Cal Tjader. Israel López, renowned as the creator of the mambo, played with and influenced Eddie Palmieri and Charlie Mingus.[10] This new Cuban sound created a market for Latin American-inflected recordings in the United States. Tommy Dorsey's singer Helen O'Connell covered Mexican singles in English and Spanish, and Bing Crosby had a major hit in 1945 with "You

Belong to My Heart," based on Augustín Lara's popular "Solamente una vez." In the late 1950s the influence turned back to Latin America with the popularity of U.S. rock-and-roll.

III

Music production illustrates another reciprocal relation between technology, especially the technology of the mass media, and popular culture. The relationship between popular culture and mass or commercial culture raises troubling questions for theorists that will not be considered here.[11] Instead, the reciprocity between popular culture and the media-enhanced or media-affected culture can be addressed simply by tracing the history of the samba as this local form entered the technology age.

Samba began as neighborhood popular music, some would say as folk music.[12] Ernesto dos Santos, known as Donga, registered the first samba, entitled "Pelo Telefone," with the Brazilian National Library in 1917. He recognized the potential to make a profit if he protected his work. Other sambistas neither registered their songs nor worried about the songs' commercial character. By the 1930s the recording industry had improved its technology and, along with radio, had created a widespread market. Recognizing consumer interest, white Brazilian singers sent agents to the hillside *favelas* to buy Afro-Brazilian sambas to record, paying only a pittance for the material. Ismael Silva sold sambas to white recording stars at first, but, recognizing an opportunity, began recording himself and became an internationally known singer. Other sambistas recalled that unscrupulous record companies held tryouts in local bars. While the composers sang, a company employee would copy the words and music. Later the songs would be sung, recorded, and registered under someone else's name.

The technology of recording companies and the format of radio programs on which records were played greatly affected samba compositions. Recording companies and radio stations both wanted short musical selections that would fit on records (about three minutes a side) and allow enough broadcast time for advertisements during the program. Moreover, the radio and recording directors wanted sanitized lyrics, stripped of the vulgar, off-color, or socially inappropriate comments that gave samba so much pungency and vitality. By the 1960s the sambas, especially those used by the samba clubs, called schools, in the Carnival celebration, had lost their immediate connection to everyday life and its struggles. Sambas from this era dealing with the history of slavery, for example, stressed themes of racial harmony in which abolition was portrayed as a gift from whites to grateful blacks. Princesa Isabel and Ruy Barbosa were the heroes in these songs, not Zumbi, the black renegade leader of the Quilombo de Palmares. Curiously, the lyrics often were taken nearly verbatim from primary school textbooks. In this way a popular form became little more than an expression of official history set to music.[13] In the late 1960s younger composers began changing the nature of sambas, which entered a new phase as protest music.

IV

The history of the samba is only one example of the politics included in popular culture, which has a long history in Latin America. Some of the most striking examples involve the efforts of political leaders to justify their reign or to consolidate a national identity in support of their agenda. After the conquests, the Spaniards attempted to legitimize their colonial regimes by developing lineages of rule. In Peru, they collected popular stories of rulers and conflated them into an Inca dynasty. The purpose was to create a linear succession in which the Incas, recognized by popular tradition, were followed by the Spaniards as the legitimate rulers of the former Inca empire. Adopting European court practices, the colonial officials had portraits of twelve of the Inca rulers painted. The Inca emperor portraits represented composites of various popular examples of these individuals that became elite art intended to picture succession to the Spanish rule. (The twelve portraits today form part of the South American colonial collection of the Brooklyn Museum of Art.[14]) The entire episode illustrates the invention of traditions whose exact relationship to reality becomes blurred in popular memory.[15]

After 1870, popular culture increasingly formed part of the national character promoted by populist leaders. Politicians such as Getúlio Vargas, in Brazil, seized on well-known practices and publicized them as expressions of national identity, as a means of mobilizing a political following. Vargas built on the culture inspired by migrants from Bahia to Rio de Janeiro. In particular, he identified the samba and other Afro-Bahian practices as the true Brazil. Other Latin American populist leaders have made similar use of common practices of the humble population, giving national prominence to everyday culture.

V

Latin American popular culture has played a role in the social construction of middle-class self-consciousness, in the self-definition of elite classes, and in projections of national character. Both elites and emerging middle sectors identified popular culture as the traditions of the lower class. Although at times both groups enjoyed these activities, both also wanted to separate themselves from what they increasingly regarded as coarse traditions.

Latin American leaders and intellectuals after about 1870 struggled with the desire to define their elite character as both cosmopolitan (to demonstrate their place in the modern world) and patriotic (to express their ties to their nation). This dual goal led to a shifting back and forth between elite and popular culture as these individuals sought on the one hand to establish their identity in class, ethnic, and gender terms and on the other to hammer out their social, national, and cosmopolitan character. Their campaign can be seen as both imitation (of European or U.S. standards) and invention (of social and national traditions). Their efforts required decisions to be made about what customs, resources, and fashions expressed the nation in a positive way and what practices identified elite behavior.

Consumption became the sincerest form of imitation. Elites bought imports as a material expression of their claim to cosmopolitan identity. Foreign pianos, clothes, wine, education, and travel—material goods and fashionable practices—represented cosmopolitan society. Chic clothes, luxury home furnishings, and European wines all became status markers. The nature of these goods—their high cost, limited supply, and, often, their French origin—gave them social cachet.[16]

Ironically, France's failure to market general goods resulted in the popularity of French luxury items. The British, Americans, and Germans all managed to reach Latin American markets with cheap, mass-produced goods; the French did not. Addressed to a much smaller, exclusive market, French goods of limited availability and high prices appealed to Latin American elites and became the epitome of exclusive and refined products. Elite consumers eager to separate themselves from the people and culture of their homelands used imports to distinguish themselves. Beverages offer an example. During the mid-nineteenth century, beer became a popular drink, and soon breweries opened in most Latin American countries. Once German pilsner and British ale became widely available, they no longer conferred status on the drinker, and wine became a more important emblem of social standing. Even in Chile and Argentina, where vintners could produce wine, they could not produce champagne, so this sparkling beverage, available only by import from one district in France, became the most important social marker for celebrations.

Seeking recognition as a cultured, cosmopolitan people, Latin American elites wanted to avoid association with the barbaric reputation of their countrymen. Especially repugnant was the general public's potential for disorder, particularly as manifested in streaks of violence and in popular culture's notorious breaches of etiquette. Latin American elites attempted to separate themselves from the commoners by withdrawing behind the walls of their homes, the doors of exclusive clubs, and the ticket booths of expensive entertainment. They created cultural practices with limited access.

This desire to appear cosmopolitan resulted in strange behavior. Latin American elites disparaged the activities of their fellows as common, vulgar, even barbaric. But if these practices became the fad in Paris, London, or New York, they gained social acceptance at home. Music, dance, or food (today Aztec foods have become part of Mexican haute cuisine) became an emblem of national culture, once acceptance abroad invested the common practices at home with elegance. Brazil's upper- and middle-class society adopted samba after the French ambassador, accompanied by some one hundred chic Brazilians, visited the Imperio Serrano Samba School in 1955. When avant-garde Parisians took up the tango from the Buenos Aires underworld, then Argentine socialites quickly followed.

Elite culture established restrictions. The controlling factor might be a high-priced ticket to the opera, say, or the time and education required to gain an appreciation of classical music, golf (clearly a cultural practice, not a sport), or Impressionist art. In other cases, popular practices were abstracted into forms for exhibit in new national museums. Thus, popular knowledge of woodcraft and wildlife was distilled and rendered in the form of natural history displays, and mining skills were represented by a scattering of ore samples in geology exhibitions. Composers added instrumentation to traditional music and relocated it from street corners and cabarets to concert halls. Sanitized, popular culture served to create the national identity of Latin American peoples. Popular culture—appropriated by elites, refashioned, stripped of its vulgarity, and generally cleaned up—in the late nineteenth century became *costumbrismo*.

With the rise of programs to modernize Latin American societies in the second half of the nineteenth century, a small middle class began to emerge. Breaking away from popular culture became an act of self-definition for this aspiring group of middling persons hoping to be identified with progressive society. Members of this group sought to distinguish themselves emphatically from the lower classes by promoting, through legislative and moral force, the reform of what they considered the lazy, drunk, and sexually permissive behavior of the unredeemed masses. Punctuality, industry, sobriety, and abstinence became the ideals of the middle class's culture of progress. In local communities, proponents of these values passed laws against vagrancy and public drunkenness, and often restricted prostitution to special zones. Popular culture represented, in many ways, what the middle class said it was not.

Simultaneously, elites intended to put their unique nation on display. These nationalists seized every opportunity to express their identity as a nationality. At world's fairs, international exhibitions, and major, usually centennial, celebrations, civic and cultural leaders displayed the images of their nation and its peoples that they wanted to project to the world and to their fellow citizens. Bolivian musicians and Guatemalan marimba players were scheduled to perform, Mexicans sent archaeological artifacts, and Chileans established some kind of record by bringing an iceberg to the world's fair in Madrid. Each display or pavilion offered evidence of their unique national culture and economic capacity.[17] Rich agricultural potential, untapped mineral and natural resources, available workers—all represented ready themes for promotion at international exhibitions.

Other occasions were manufactured as opportunities to present national values as represented by great leaders. State funerals afforded a particularly impressive moment to make this display. The ceremonies surrounding the funerals of Benito Juárez in Mexico, Jorge Eliécer Gaitán in Colombia, and Che Guevara in Cuba all provided moments for the presentation of Liberal, labor, and revolutionary ideals personified in the dead individual. The state spectacle created for the burial of Evita Perón brought together the mass media, nationalistic pretensions, populist images and rhetoric, and Catholic ritual, reworked in personalistic display.

VI

The essays in this book examine different expressions of popular cultures, how such cultures and such expressions emerged, who used them, and what changed them. Neither the editors nor the authors have attempted to investigate inherited wisdom, the common knowledge that underlies popular culture and provides the wellspring for the wide-ranging references by which people construct an understanding of themselves. Instead, we focus on the expressions of people's preconceptions and passions. In other words, we examine the waves, not the water.

These themes all reveal to a greater or lesser extent, as do the high cultures of the Latin American nations, the effect of Roman Catholicism. Churchgoing and formal holidays are only the most obvious displays of the church's influence. More ingrained practices form part of the matrix of daily life. Crossing oneself to avoid bad luck, lighting candles with prayers for good luck, making offerings or leaving ex-votos for answered prayers, along with tattoos of the Virgin of Guadalupe, images of saints on the dashboard of trucks and buses, and naming children after saints merely scratch the surface of popular religion. Teaching and learning often draw on the forms of the church, in particular the catechism (for example, the catechism of Padre Ripalda remained the basic pedagogical tool used from 1791 to the 1940s in Mexico and most of Spanish America). In part, because the church fathers discouraged parishioners from reading the Bible before Vatican II (1962–1965), common knowledge of heaven and especially hell drew on Dante's *Divine Comedy* (translated into Spanish in 1428[18]). As a result, art, artisanry, parables, skits, parade floats, songs, operas, dramas, literature, and elite and popular culture made constant allusions, if not references, to these two sources. Pervasiveness of informal religion still awaits careful analysis, but its influence is apparent in all of the themes discussed in this volume.

In introducing the history of Latin America's popular culture, we have identified five threads that form the fabric of the chapters that follow. These themes are (1) the invention of traditions; (2) the creation of national identity, which some call the imagined community;[19] (3) the formation of gender roles; (4) the prevalence of ethnicity—a sharper designation than the category of race; and (5) the dynamic interplay between textual deconstruction and performance analysis that is neither one nor the other but the relationship of the two. Thus, while we might have offered a selection on the formation of the Argentine or Mexican imagined community, we chose instead to include a chapter on the Ecuadorian exhibit at the world's fair, an occasion used by national leaders to present their understanding of the Ecuadorian—that is, national—identity. The chapter discusses how these leaders invented the "Indian man and woman," expounding on their ethnicity, gender, and traditions in a changing series of exhibits that individually serve as texts and in their changes over time function as performance.

The chapters in this book show the humor, inventiveness, and determination with which people have used public events to effect more than the event sponsors envisioned. Sly individuals seized civic and religious rituals to mock authorities, elites joined popular celebrations for the amusement of masquerading as marginal peoples, and leaders attempted to teach political allegiance, religious orthodoxy, and patriotic virtues. Rarely did these simultaneous, contrary cultural practices result in conflict or in negotiation, to use an overused and misleading term. Rather, these multiple uses overlapped, with the practitioners and promoters of each approach oblivious to the others. Often spectators saw only part of what was intended. Each parade, celebration, funeral, and civic occasion reveals a cultural montage with its discrete elements forming a rich, varied collage. A wonderful, complex image resulted, it bears repeating, not from conflict or interaction (a synonym for the current usage of negotiation), but from the layers of intentions, behaviors, and meanings given to this composite. As a result, to a great extent people could experience what they expected, what they wanted, and what they knew.

Popular culture shapes memories. Because memory is an abstraction, it reduces, simplifies, and exaggerates. In doing so it allows for interpretation, invention, analogies, and retelling; it constitutes the stuff of popular culture. Recalling memories often relies formally on mnemonic systems, but informally it draws on associations to material and musical culture, especially the latter; so several chapters in this volume discuss music. And, most important, examining popular culture leads inevitably to the conclusion that ordinary people so often dismissed as ignorant and uncultured "are every bit as shrewd and perceptive as those who have been educated and lead a privileged existence."[20] Popular culture reveals the shared humanity of a community.

SUGGESTED READINGS

Anderson, Benedict. *Imagined Communities: Reflections on the Origin and Spread of Nationalism.* Rev. ed. London: Verso, 1991.

Arrom, Silvia Marina. *The Women of Mexico City, 1790–1857.* Stanford: Stanford University Press, 1985.

Beezley, William H. *Judas at the Jockey Club.* Lincoln: University of Nebraska Press, 1987; 2nd ed., 2004.

———. *Mexican National Identity: Memory, Innuendo, and Popular Culture.* Tucson: University of Arizona Press, 2008.

Beezley, William H., Cheryl English Martin, and William E. French, eds. *Rituals of Rule, Rituals of Resistance: Public Celebrations and Popular Culture in Mexico.* Wilmington, DE: SR Books, 1994.

Boggs, Vernon F. *Salsiology: Afro-Cuban Music and the Evolution of Salsa in New York City.* New York: Excelsior Music Publishing Co., 1992.

Chanady, Amaryl, ed. *Latin American Identity and Constructions of Difference.* Minneapolis: University of Minnesota Press, 1994.

Cooper, Donald B. *Epidemic Disease in Mexico City, 1761–1813: An Administrative, Social, and Medical Study.* Austin: University of Texas Press, 1965.

Curcio-Nagy, Linda. *Great Festivals of Colonial Mexico City: Performing Power and Identity.* Albuquerque: University of New Mexico Press, 2004.

Eicher, Joanne B., ed. *Dress and Ethnicity: Change across Space and Time.* Oxford: Berg, 1995.

Franco, Jean. *Plotting Women: Gender and Representation in Mexico.* New York: Columbia University Press, 1989.

Gillis, John R., ed. *Commemorations: The Politics of National Identity.* Princeton, NJ: Princeton University Press, 1994.

Gómez Avelleneda, Gertrudis. *Sab and Autobiography.* Austin: University of Texas Press, 1993.

Hall, Stuart, and Paul Gay, eds. *Questions of Cultural Identity.* London: Sage, 1996.

Hobsbawm, Eric, and Terence Ranger, eds. *The Invention of Tradition.* Cambridge: Cambridge University Press, 1983.

Jackson, Richard. *The Black Image in Latin American Literature.* Albuquerque: University of New Mexico Press, 1976.

Knight, Franklin W. *Slave Society in Cuba During the Nineteenth Century.* Madison: University of Wisconsin Press, 1970.

López, Rick A. *Crafting Mexico: Intellectuals, Artisans, and the State after the Revolution.* Durham, NC: Duke University Press, 2010.

Martínez-Alier, Verena. *Marriage, Class and Colour in Nineteenth-Century Cuba.* New York: Cambridge University Press, 1974.

Masiello, Francine. *Between Civilization and Barbarism: Women, Nation, and Literary Culture in Modern Argentina.* Lincoln: University of Nebraska Press, 1992.

McManners, John. *Death and the Enlightenment: Changing Attitudes to Death among Christians and Unbelievers in Eighteenth-Century France.* New York: Oxford University Press, 1981.

Mendoza, Zoila S. *Creating Our Own: Folklore, Performance and Identity in Cuzco, Peru.* Durham, NC: Duke University Press, 2007.

Messinger Cypess, Sandra. *La Malinche in Mexican Literature.* Austin: University of Texas Press, 1991.

Moore, Robin. *Nationalizing Blackness: Afrocubanism and Artistic Revolution in Havana, 1920–1940.* Pittsburgh: University of Pittsburgh Press, 1997.

Pérez, Louis A., ed. *Impressions of Cuba in the Nineteenth Century: The Travel Diary of Joseph J. Dimnock.* Wilmington, DE: SR Books, 1998.

Pérez Sarduy, Pedro, and Jean Stubbs, eds. *Afrocuba: An Anthology of Cuban Writing on Race, Politics, and Culture.* New York: Ocean Press/Center for Cuban Studies, 1993.

Poole, Deborah, ed. *Unruly Order: Violence, Power and Cultural Identity in the High Provinces of Southern Peru.* Boulder, CO: Westview Press, 1993.

Reis, João José. "Death to the Cemetery: Funerary Reform and Rebellion in Salvador, Brazil, 1836." In *Riots in the Cities: Popular Politics and the Urban Poor in Latin America, 1765–1910*, pp. 97–114, edited by Silvia M. Arrom and Servando Ortoll. Wilmington, DE: SR Books, 1996.

Roach, Joseph. *Cities of the Dead: Circum-Atlantic Performance.* New York: Columbia University Press, 1986.

Said, Edward W. *Culture and Imperialism.* New York: Knopf, 1993.

Samuels, Shirley. *Romances of the Republic: Women, the Family, and Violence in the Literature of the Early American Nation.* New York: Oxford University Press, 1996.

Scott, James C. *Weapons of the Weak: Everyday Forms of Peasant Resistance.* New Haven: Yale University Press, 1985.

Steele, Cynthia. *Politics, Gender and the Mexican Novel, 1968–1988: Beyond the Pyramid.* Austin: University of Texas Press, 1992.

Vaughan, Mary Kay, and Stephen Lewis, eds. *The Eagle and the Virgin: Nation and Cultural Revolution in Mexico, 1920–1940.* Durham, NC: Duke University Press, 2006.

Versenyi, Adam. *Theatre in Latin America: Religion, Politics, and Culture from Cortes to the 1980s.* New York: Cambridge University Press, 1993.

Vianna, Hermano. *The Mystery of Samba: Popular Music and National Identity in Brazil*, edited and translated by John Charles Chasteen. Chapel Hill: University of North Carolina Press, 1999.

Virgillo, Carmelo, and Naomi Lindstrom, eds. *Woman as Myth and Metaphor in Latin American Literature.* Columbia: University of Missouri Press, 1985.

Widdifield, Stacie. *The Embodiment of the National in Late Nineteenth-Century Mexican Painting.* Tucson: University of Arizona Press, 1996.

World Music: The Rough Guide. London: Rough Guides, 1994.

Sights

Buena Vista Social Club. 1999. Directed by Wim Wenders (Artisan).

Celilia Valdés. 1993. Directed by Humberto Solas (Cuban Studies).

Danzón. 1991. Directed by María Navaro (Facets Multimedia).
The Death of a Bureaucrat. 1966. Directed by Tomás Gutiérrez Alea (Facets Multimedia).
La Generala. 1970. Directed by Juan Ibáñez (Madeira Cinema).
María Candelaria. 1943. Directed by Emilio Fernández (Madeira Cinema).
El Otro Francisco. 1975. Directed by Julio García Espinosa and Sergio Giral (Lava).
Susana. 1950. Directed by Luís Buñuel (Facets Multimedia).
Tracing Folkore: All Culture Is Local. (Insight Media, no. EW357).
La Ultima Cena. 1976. Directed by Tomás Gutiérrez Alea (Facets Multimedia).
Yo, La Peor de Todas. 1990. Directed by María Luisa Bemberg (Facets Multimedia).

Sounds

Afro-Cuban All Stars: A Toda Cuba le Gusta. Nonesuch 79476-2.
Buena Vista Social Club. Nonesuch 79478-2.
Cuba, 1923–1995. Fremaux Associes.

Websites

Internet Movie Database: www.imdb.org
Latin American Curriculum Resource Center at Tulane University (a lending library): www.tulane.edu/~clas/CRChome.htm
Latin American Video Archive: www.lavavideo.org

Museum

East Harlem Salsa Museum, 2127 Third Avenue, New York, New York. Phone: (212) 289-1368; www.el-barrio.com/salsa.htm. (Located in the back of the "Made in Puerto Rico" store)

1

Piety and Public Space

The Cemetery Campaign in Veracruz, 1789–1810

Pamela Voekel

The Bourbon Reforms, Spain's official program of Enlightenment initiatives, have most often been discussed in terms of the institutional and structural changes enacted at imperial and colonial levels. Such accounts stress the drive toward centralization, efficiency, practicality, and secularization in both imperial administration and the economy. The Portuguese in the reforms of the Marquis de Pombal (after 1750s) and the British in the programs of Lord Granville (1763) initiated similar campaigns in their colonial systems. Because these campaigns helped foster the wars of independence that carried most of the European colonies in the Americas to independence by 1824, historians have for the most part ignored the impact of these Enlightenment reform campaigns on individuals. As Pamela Voekel demonstrates, the Enlightenment campaigns inaugurated remarkable changes in the daily lives of everyday people, leading groups from all social strata to question society's definitions of identity, how one related to God, and where one buried the dead.

In 1822, Lady Calcott (Maria Dundas Graham), the widow of a British naval officer, who at the time was living under the protection of Lord and Lady Cochrane, visited a suburb of Valparaíso, Chile. In this hamlet she saw "new burying ground" created by the government. "Separated from this [cemetery] only by a wall, is the place at length assigned by Roman Catholic superstition to the heretics as a burial ground; or rather, which the heretics have been permitted to purchase." As a result of prejudices, Lady Calcott felt, the new burying grounds were not being used as planned.[1] *All the concerns suggested by her report on Chile are carefully analyzed in the following selection. Pamela Voekel's chapter contributes to the current historical concern with the cultural origins of the sovereign individual as society's fundamental constituent.*

In 1787 the enlightened ministers of Spanish King Charles III prevailed over their conservative opposition. They ordered the end of church burials and decreed the creation of suburban cemeteries—a seemingly innocuous measure. The new burial grounds, however, threatened the elaborate visual display of social elites in church tombs and at well-attended funerals, and sundered the intimate relationship between the dead and the living that fueled traditional piety. Not surprisingly, the construction in 1790 of a suburban cemetery in Veracruz, Mexico, provoked impassioned debate between those with church burial rights and the city's cemetery *sensatos* (enlightened ones). Strictly speaking, the *sensatos* could not claim victory against their multiple foes: conservatives, state bureaucrats, some of the clergy, confraternities, and Church benefactors. At the time of Mexico's independence, in 1821, the projected network of verdant, hygienic public cemeteries still remained an ideal. The resulting cemeteries were few and shabby at best. However, unbeknownst to themselves, the *sensatos* had the last laugh.[2]

But the reality of suburban cemeteries is only part of the story. The background of this civic squabble was a definitive shift from an external, mediated, and corporate Catholicism to an interior piety, one that elevated the virtues of self-discipline and moderation and focused on a direct, personal relationship to God. Although reformers never argued for predestination as the path to God, they did stress the importance of God's prior gift of grace to the soul for salvation and challenged the efficacy of good works done without just intentions, without the presence of God's inner light. For these reformed Catholics, although the temptations of the world could never be entirely suppressed, those temptations could now be subjected—subjected to God's will through the identification of man's will with His, through the recognition of man's dependency on God, and through His grace in their hearts. Thus, for reformers, monastic separation from the world's temptations was no longer the loftiest path to God: the temptations of the world did not have to be entirely rejected in order to be subjected because God was inside human beings. Self-mastery could be wrought within, and the highest Christian virtue became godly moderation. Through numerous procemetery writings and sermons, New Spain's enlightened reformers attacked baroque display as a demonstration of unbridled "excess." In its place, they recommended an interior piety, for the path to God was now back into the self. Following this logic, much of the Church's mediating hierarchy between the soul and God, especially the saints, became less imperative for salvation. Reformers advocated an individual piety that helped to splinter the society of orders and estates into one of individuals.

In Veracruz this new piety constituted part of a larger movement propelling the city's enlightened to shun the church burials under the protection of the saints and the congregation in favor of the suburban cemetery. They also viewed the baroque theatrics that expressed the traditional divine sanctification of social hierarchy as displays of immoderation, and thus godlessness. Rather than make a spectacle of themselves—or make themselves through spectacle—Veracruz's *sensatos* created a different—but equally religious—justification for rule: by taking God's message to heart, they had prospered through individual effort and good conduct. They now looked down upon those who would not or could not receive the Word, those who therefore needed the enlightened to teach them the values of hard work and sobriety. Adherence to "enlightened" piety became both a marker of cultural identity and the critical justification for enlightened rule, a mechanism through which this emerging group distinguished itself from both the traditional elites it fought to displace and the popular classes it wished to rule.

At the end of this complicated route lay the postindependence Liberal dream of a nation of equal individual males. Many scholars define modernity as a society as one composed of atomized, autonomous men. They classify Mexican modernity as an import from Spain or as contraband smuggled in from the United States or France (New Spain, after all, did not undergo a Protestant Enlightenment, and Spain exported the seeds of modernity, voluntary associations, only in the wake of the 1808 monarchical crisis). These scholarly visions lack any sense of the local climate, shifts in piety, or the individuals who were to create a homegrown modernity in Mexico. The debate over the cemeteries of Veracruz offered precisely that fertile soil for the growth of individualism. Debating this issue, the Veracruzanos put forth their competing visions of society. The new piety with its stress on the individual made the political legitimacy of the people culturally conceivable.

The practice of burying the dead in parish churches, monasteries, and convents arrived with the Spanish, who had accommodated their dead in temples since at least the eighth century. Proximity to the saints was the most frequent goal of those who designated a particular burial location within the church, although some of the faithful requested burial near the epistle or near places frequented by the faithful, such as the font of holy water.[3]

But this complex web of spiritual functions did not exist in a vacuum. The combined elements of external display and communal mediation were simultaneously carrying out a social mission. New Spain's church floors and chapels mapped society's intricate caste and status categories, as the careful placement of the dead reiterated worldly honors and temporal distinctions. Only the colony's highest elites could be buried within the church, and many even established family chapels. Rather than charge a set fee, the Church required a "customary donation" to obtain a burial spot; in exchange for this gift, priests also prayed for the deceased's soul.[4] Ethnic and occupational groups had their own economic prerogatives, tax obligations, and even legal rights and court systems, and these juridically fixed privileges were manifested in the acquisition of church burial spaces. The clergy's sanctity and corporate status, for example, were demonstrated in the burial of clerics under the main altar, a privilege legally denied to the laity. In death as in life, the church sanctified the privileges of the traditional social structure. Its floors and chapels reproduced the social distinctions of the living in a fetid simulacrum.

Funerals provided the church with an opportunity to sanctify the elites' lofty social position. Although twelve was the usual number, hundreds to thousands of clergy regularly escorted the dead from their homes to the church and prayed at burial ceremonies. For example, in Mexico City the Countess Luisa de Albórñoz y Legazpi's 1653 funeral included the viceroy, the entire nobility, and every cleric in the city. An ornate carriage attended by twelve torch-bearing pages brought the body to the Franciscan monastery for burial in the sacristy.[5] In Veracruz, fewer priests were available for such processions, but Veracruzanos still managed to round up impressive funeral contingents. The wealthy even contracted *monigotes*, poor people who lived off their funeral appearances. Pious brotherhoods swelled funeral processions because these organizations promised their members a well-attended funeral.

Additionally, the religious orders in town did a brisk business by providing burial locations in their churches and chapels. For example, the Franciscans dealt in the town's most expensive burial locations, for which they charged at least one hundred times the daily wage of a Mexico City artisan.[6] Franciscan coffers also received revenues from the sale of their funeral shrouds, overwhelmingly the most popular of the available options. The monastery also housed the vault of the Franciscan Tertiaries, who boasted numerous city luminaries as members. The new cemetery threatened not only the friars' own time-honored right to interment in cloister but also their substantial burial earnings and their role in sanctifying the social status of Veracruz's elites.

Those of "enlightened" piety in Veracruz challenged the baroque opulence of traditional funerals as immoderate and rejected chapel burials under the protection of a particular saint as unnecessary to salvation. The most radical reformers elected moderate funerals and dreamed of a suburban cemetery with no markers of social distinction or saintly mediators—a physical testament to the godly moderation to which all should aspire. Thus, two different notions of the path to salvation were at loggerheads in Veracruz.

THE CEMETERY SKIRMISHES

Scandal and subterfuge rocked Veracruz after the cemetery's April 1790 inauguration and the subsequent ban on church burials. Led by the regular clergy, resistance began with foot-dragging and escalated into outright, if creative, disobedience. The Bethlehemites, for example, self-confidently declared that the Royal Cemetery Edict affected only the laity and not the religious themselves.[7] Alarmed by the friars' recalcitrance, Viceroy Revillagigedo immediately convened the clerical hierarchy in Mexico City to convince them to enlighten their wayward Veracruz brethren to the "utility and will of the King."[8]

Given the *sensato*-dominated state's unwillingness to brook opposition from the regular orders, it should come as no surprise that the leaders summoned by Revillagigedo enthusiastically pledged allegiance to the cause. Indeed, in language as brass as that deployed by the most ardent cemetery proponents, Mexico City's Augustinian provincial, Tomás Mercado, lectured his Veracruz subordinate on the mortiferous gases extruded by decaying corpses, reminding him that "true piety" and reason accorded with the cemetery and that "nothing was more important to the religious mission than encouraging subordination to both the secular and religious authorities." Rather than foment dissent, he said, the Veracruz Augustinians should disabuse the faithful of their belief that masses and orations worked better with the dead present, and should employ their authority in "sacred exhortations" in favor of the cemetery.[9] Supremely satisfied with the hierarchy's response, Viceroy Revillagigedo remained confident of the project's success.

Veracruz's embattled religious refused to go to the cemetery without a fight. News of the Augustinian hierarchy's adamant support for the new burial ground ricocheted through the city, prompting the priors of La Merced and San Francisco to hide their own superiors' procemetery instructions so as not to fan the "flames of sedition" flickering among their subjects.[10] A rattled José María Laso de la Vega, the city's mulatto parish priest, doubted he could enforce the measure without resort to violence, which Viceroy Revillagigedo had expressly forbidden in favor of "reason" and "prudence."[11] Further adding to the parish priest's anxiety was the rumor that "*sugetos visibles*" (well-known subjects) had colluded with the friars to bury young children in the city's monastic houses. Laso de la Vega feared that such actions, if true, would revive the antagonism to the cemetery that he had only recently begun to stifle.[12]

His trepidations proved well-founded. In December 1790, six months after the cemetery's opening, zealous Governor Intendent Miguel de Corral discovered that the Dominicans had surreptitiously buried Friar Mariano Cabeza de Vaca in their church's sacristy, an occasion attended by an impressive number of Veracruz's religious.[13] To make matters worse, the burial had been preceded by a secret session of the city's friars who had conspired to shun the new cemetery. Finger-pointing and backstabbing followed as the friars scrambled to justify their flagrant disobedience in the face of Corral's unrelenting investigation. Amid the excuses, accusations, and evasions, one point was clear: even if the majority of the religious would not publicly back the Dominicans, they had indeed attended both the funeral and the secret meeting, thus lending at least symbolic support to Cabeza de Vaca's scandalous burial.

Emboldened by the regular orders' defiance, Veracruz's traditional elites joined the friars to fight for the church burials so critical to their social status and their salvation. The death in April 1790 of Barbara Bauza, wealthy benefactress of the Third Order of Saint Francis and wife of the prominent and pious trader Don Francisco José de la Piedras, provided the opening salvo in the elites' defense of their burial rights.[14] Arguing that the law explicitly exempted church benefactors, Barbara Bauza's relatives demanded that her recently buried body remain in its Franciscan tomb. Similar cases followed in rapid succession.[15]

Other members of Veracruz's privileged set preferred to flee rather than risk burial in the cemetery or disinterment. Laso de la Vega's assistant reported that after he had confessed and administered the Eucharist to a wealthy widow, the woman abandoned her deathbed to summon a carriage, successfully escaping through the city's gates to nearby Boca del Río, where she insisted on and obtained a church burial.[16] The Veracruz city council reported that these actions confirmed most residents' belief that the site served merely as a dumping ground for paupers or as an overflow space for victims of epidemics, and thus was unfit for the town's more respectable residents.[17]

An alarmed Viceroy Revillagigedo convened Veracruz's religious to convince them that "utility, the will of the King, and the good of humanity" dictated support for the new cemetery. The beleaguered regulars eventually capitulated, but only on the condition that the burial ground displayed the same privileges and distinctions formerly represented in churches and monasteries—a compromise hammered out previously in Spain but conveniently overlooked by the Veracruz enlightened.[18] Viceroy Revillagigedo reluctantly sent instructions for the construction of burial vaults for confraternities, privileged families, the regular orders, and the secular clergy, and placed each group in charge of adorning its own tombs. This was seemingly a significant setback for the radicals' vision of a cemetery where elaborate displays of status would be eradicated.[19]

Although the cemetery could now visually display the corporate power of ecclesiastical institutions and confraternities and the inherited privileges of certain families, it was outside of town, where few could see it. This unfavorable location was not lost on contemporaries, who resented the severely reduced opportunities to display their status in the city's centrally located monasteries and parish church; their hatred for the cemetery intensified despite Viceroy Revillagigedo's concessions. To express their displeasure with the lack of "decency and pomp" in the new funerals and burials, Veracruz elites sought revenge against one of the principal proponents of the new cemetery, the mulatto parish priest Laso de la Vega. This priest perceived their goal as nothing less than "the ruin of the parish and its dependents." To combat his fervor, the elite resorted to a financial boycott. In 1790, in an elaborate maneuver, they conspired to request masses only from the regular orders and to "*fingirse pobres de solemnidad*" (pretend to be poor) to oblige the parish to inter their dead for free or at a reduced rate. This was a potentially ruinous measure, as elites had always paid the highest burial and funeral fees.[20] With most local and state officials and the secular clergy aligned against them, Veracruz's outraged elites knew that boycotting the parish was insufficient. They found a sympathetic ally in the conservative Council of the Indies, which functioned as an appeals court for American grievances. Prominent town personalities, such as members of the city council, in the interment wars petitioned for exemption from the cemetery and meticulously recounted the squabbles scandalizing the city.[21]

In the midst of the furor, the city council retracted its former support for the new burial ground, sheepishly noting that its members would prefer burial in the parish's San Sebastián Chapel, as had been the custom for decades.[22] At issue was the burial of councilman Esteve. His father insisted on burying Esteve in the new cemetery with an absolute minimum of funeral pomp. Some of the aldermen wanted to provide him with "the honors corresponding to a member of the illustrious body [the city council]" and placed guards outside his house to prevent a less than spectacular funeral.[23] This prompted a petition to the king in which they complained that inhabitants had been repulsed by the macabre sight of the hospitals' uncovered dead being trundled through the streets to the cemetery, where forced laborers discarded them nonchalantly at the gate or buried them in graves so shallow that buzzards could pick at their rancid remains.[24] These graphic complaints were mere justifications for the centerpiece of the aldermen's report to the king: documentation from the former bishop of Puebla and the parish itself demonstrating the city council's right to occupy the seven tombs in the parish's lavish San Sebastián Chapel.[25] Ignorant of the exact content of the council's report, Viceroy Revillagigedo confidently dismissed the protesters.[26] Nevertheless, the *cabildo* members hired an advocate in Madrid and conducted further investigations in Veracruz to cement their case for burial in the parish church.[27]

While the anticemetery petitioners awaited the crown's response, the battle intensified. Jocular, candle-bearing groups occupied the city's streets, engaging in mock funeral processions that spoofed the corteges shambling from the parish to the cemetery. In retaliation for appealing to his superiors, and to combat the opposition now spilling into the streets, Laso de la Vega took to haranguing his flock from the pulpit. To further underscore his point, the priest buried his own father in the cemetery rather than next to the bones of his long-dead mother resting beneath the Dominicans' church floor. The opposition remained unconvinced. After the *cura*'s third sermon appealing to utility and "true piety," an anonymous group of parishioners affixed a pasquinade to the church door declaring the cemetery to be little more than a glorified corral.[28]

These minor skirmishes set the stage for the mid-November arrival of the October 1791 royal order informing Revillagigedo that "in order to curb the excesses we are seeing," those with extant burial privileges in churches should not be impeded from enjoying them. As they had during the high-level cemetery debate in Spain, Bourbon bureaucrats divided over the cemetery issue. (This is further evidence that Bourbon cemetery reform is best viewed as a battle between a rising enlightened class and its popular allies, and traditionalists both inside and outside the state).[29] First and foremost, the edict rebuked Revillagigedo and his allies for acting precipitously in building the cemetery without respect for the 1789 royal order, which had merely solicited reports on cemeteries' feasibility, not ordered their construction. Furthermore, the enlightened had acted unilaterally, failing to consult either the religious orders or individuals and confraternities with extant burial privileges. Stung by this criticism but undaunted, the viceroy sent elaborate reports to the Council of the Indies and sought to influence the royal ministers.[30]

In the confusion that followed the decision to allow cemetery exemptions, it became apparent that some intrigue lurked behind the *cabildo*'s appeal to retain its seven San Sebastián Chapel crypts. Three councilmen had filed the complaints without the other members' consent, rendering the appeal legally invalid.[31] The procemetery city councilors claimed that a heated discussion had indeed occurred during an official meeting, but "those [aldermen] who coveted a distinguished burial" had been appeased by the compromise offer of burial rights in the San Sebastián hermitage, located outside the city, and the entire municipal council had consented to forward this request to the authorities. Only later did they learn that the anticemetery faction had instead sent the king a petition for parish—not hermitage—burial.[32]

The procemetery aldermen transformed the investigative hearing into a raucous forum, citing the cemetery's public health benefits and arguing that souls would continue to receive effective suffrages even if their bodies were not under parishioners' feet. The procemetery faction revealed its firm adherence to "true piety": "If a man who places himself at the feet of an altar to beseech his creator's favor cannot remember an obligation, he should expect very little from a mere oration."[33] In search of evidence to invalidate the royal order, Revillagigedo demanded a copy of city councilman Echeverría's clandestine missive to King Charles IV.[34]

Viceroy Revillagigedo opted for his own interpretation of the October 1791 burial edict. The cemetery would continue to welcome all of Veracruz's dead except those who had founded religious edifices or had officially been declared "saintly" by the Church. Revillagigedo's disobedience of an explicit royal order was motivated in part by his knowledge that Veracruz's popular classes, who generally were buried in the parish's exterior cemetery and who had been extras, never stars, in the city's baroque death dramas, relished the cemetery's explicit egalitarianism and would cease to support the site should the elites be exempted.[35] Puebla's Bishop Biempico y Sotomayor echoed Revillagigedo's sentiments, exhorting his fellow religious to embrace the cemetery and convince their flocks that "vain distinctions should not be carried on after death." Only martyrs and the saintly deserved to be sepulchered in churches. Finally, in a bold invocation, the bishop thundered that "all ecclesiastical rules [on burials] were nullified" by the order to restore the primitive discipline of the Church.[36]

It soon became clear that some aldermen were not Veracruz's only politically intrepid conservative group; other petitions belatedly surfaced as the Council of the Indies's cemetery exemptions trickled into Veracruz. The confraternities now took up the banner of resistance. Since the 1262 papal decree on the existence of purgatory, and in particular since its 1563 endorsement by the Council of Trent, the laity had organized itself in confraternities to ensure members' release from purgatory.[37] The Veracruz confraternities' anticemetery protests unfolded as high-ranking *sensato* reformers in Spain fulminated against confraternities' "exorbitant and vain expenditures" on liturgical celebrations and insinuated that their indiscriminate dedication to the charitable precepts of the Seven Acts of Mercy merely encouraged begging.[38] In 1776 these sentiments reverberated in New Spain in the form of a requirement that all confraternities obtain a crown license; later laws mandated a royal official's presence at every gathering and ordered all brotherhoods to submit their constitutions for review by the Council of the Indies, which often refused their licensing requests.[39]

When the Veracruz brotherhood of San Benito de Palermo accordingly petitioned the Council of the Indies to renew its constitution, their burial policy became a serious source of contention. Allocating substantial monies for the members' elaborate monastery burials, the clause was rejected by the council; henceforth, it ruled, dead confraternity members belonged in the general cemetery, which benefited public health.[40] The parish brotherhood of San Joséf joined the San Benito de Palermo confraternity in the anticemetery crusade, successfully petitioning King Charles IV to open a new crypt next to their chapel's main altar, a request that provoked the wrath of Viceroy Revillagigedo.[41] Thus, the new cemetery rattled the confraternities to their core by threatening the church burials that enticed both membership and the steady payment of the lifetime of weekly fees that ensured a decent interment.

Elite Franciscan Tertiaries provided the confraternities of San Benito de Palermo and San Joséf with additional anticemetery allies. Located immediately behind the Franciscan monastery's central altar, the group's chapel boasted both a sacristy and a large meeting room, and its adornment, as one traveler marveled, easily rivaled the glittering opulence of the Mexico City silversmiths' cathedral chapel.[42] Third Order members' wills further testify to their wealth and privilege, designating lavish bequests to family, Church, and charity. Powerful and prominent, Veracruz's Franciscan Tertiaries seemed stunned by the enlightened's aggressive cemetery offensive but quickly recouped, deploying their considerable cultural capital to whip off a series of written protests to secular authorities. To justify retaining their chapel tombs, the Tertiaries cited a 1753 ecclesiastical decision, ratified by the Council of the Indies, that granted burial jurisdiction to the regular orders. The group also emphasized its consistent upkeep of the chapel and a fifty-seven-year burial record (1733–1790) to support its claim to cemetery exemption. Unmoved, Veracruz's intendent governor warned Viceroy Revillagigedo that continuing the brothers' chapel interment privileges would incite an avalanche of petitions to join the order, mitigating the new cemetery's salubrious effects. Concurring with the governor's assessment, the bishop added that neither the religious themselves nor the Tertiaries merited exemption and that the Royal Cemetery Edict overrode all temple burial rights. Not surprisingly, Viceroy Revillagigedo invoked the dictates of public health to quash the prestigious Third Order members' petition for burial rights.[43]

SANCTIFICATION OF SOCIAL HIERARCHY AND ENLIGHTENED PIETY

The intensity of the sepulchral skirmishes that shook Veracruz in the early 1790s indexed a more profound social conflict. At stake in the burial battle was not only the traditional religious justification for rule and social hierarchy but also the dead's function as a critical mnemonic device to rescue purgatory's sin-ridden souls. Traditional elites' resistance to the cemetery is easy to understand: the suburban burial grounds directly and explicitly threatened one of their principal idioms of social distinction. Veracruzanos' fervent desire for saintly mediation, and their fear that exiling the dead would remove them from the community's prayers, are equally comprehensible. The *sensatos'* rejection of lavish funerals and their firm cemetery support is more difficult to account for, and it is to this dilemma that we now turn.

Critical to understanding the *sensatos'* rejection of funeral pomp and circumstance is the new enlightened piety that gripped some Veracruzanos in the late eighteenth century. The new piety rejected visual, external spurs to pious behavior, such as the dead's existence in public space and the community's tight bond with the departed that their presence encouraged. Linking this sentiment to the cemetery campaign, the "enlightened" bishops acknowledged that the dead in church provoked pious giving, but insisted that cemeteries would accustom the faithful to a purer, more interior religion independent of visual reminders.[44]

The rejection of the use of the dead as visual prods to pious giving was thus accompanied by the desire to foment a piety that focused on a direct, individual relationship to God and the Scriptures.[45] Pilgrimages, confraternities, devotion to numerous saints, flagellation, parades—all irked reformers. "It is a great offense against God," Josefa Amar y Borbón averred, "to believe that he is content with merely exterior practices and formulaic devotions, in which the heart plays no role, and the moderation of desires and subjection of the will does not occur." His statement echoed John Calvin's assertion that "there is nothing which God more abominates than when men endeavor to cloak themselves by substituting signs and appearances for integrity of the heart," as well as Martin Luther's belief that faith was "nothing else but truth of the heart."[46]

Critical to this shift to the heart was the 1783 Inquisition initiative to allow the Bible to be read in the vernacular and its 1789 permission for the publication of a Castilian Bible—decisions that unintentionally cracked the clerical monopoly on religious interpretation, opening the way to individual evaluation of doctrine.[47] Crown advisor Gaspar Melchor de Jovellanos, for example, regarded the Scriptures as the centerpiece of true piety, stating, "if this is the book of every Christian, if it should be read and thought about at all times, how could it not also be the most important book for theologians?"[48]

Equally important was the egalitarianism implicit in the new piety. City council and Junta de Policía member Juan Manuel Muñoz preferred "the general good of an entire people and the health of the most miserable beggar to the pompous and distinguished burials of a few . . . because marking social distinctions only leads to bad consequences."[49] Concurring with his counterparts in Spain, Puebla's Bishop Biempico y Sotomayor, who specifically requested a cemetery burial if he died while in Veracruz, satirized cemetery opponents' pretensions as motivated both by "the spirit of vanity and the desire to distinguish themselves" and by their stubborn suspicion that the new burial grounds could not accommodate the "odious distinctions" they so coveted; furthermore, the bishop continued, Veracruz's religious, rather than encourage such wrongheadedness, should remind the benighted that "death makes everyone equal and the vain distinctions of this world cannot be continued into the next."[50] Yet for all his eloquence and energetic advocacy, in Veracruz the real virtuoso of the new piety was not the bishop but mulatto parish priest Laso de la Vega, who seized every opportunity to sing the new piety's praises. In a characteristically controversial move, in 1793 the parish priest opened a special paen to the Virgin of

Guadalupe by warning his unsuspecting parishioners of the evils of lavish burials:

> What vain instructions the great and powerful of this world leave in order to win the esteem of their fellow men, building churches with elaborate tombs for the rest and repose of their cadavers. But does not all this, when examined with a strong light, reveal itself to be nothing more than a diaphanous cloud of smoke. . . . [A]s grand as their patrimony on earth may have been, they cannot make their remains last even one moment more than dictated by the rules of corruption and their bodies' own defective nature, nor can their earthly glory be locked inside their tomb along with them.[51]

Although perhaps more eloquently than most, Laso de la Vega expressed the heart of the enlightened's fears.

The individual, not the group or the clerical hierarchy, was the critical component of the new piety, and, like both Martin Luther and John Calvin, reformers found their prophet in Saint Augustine. "Do not go outward; return within yourself. In the inward man dwells truth," Augustine had declared, placing the individual at the center of epistemology. Thus, individual self-reflection was the first step on the road to God. But the Lord did not illuminate everyone: two churches existed, the invisible one, comprised of those predestined for salvation, and the earthly church, which included the damned among its members. Thus interventions could not influence the fate of the dead, and Augustine declared himself indifferent as to whether his dead body sank beneath the waves or was devoured by wild beasts.[52]

This doctrine of individual illumination and the irrelevance of the Church's intercession for salvation had potentially radical implications, as the Protestant Reformation demonstrated. But if Catholic reformism bore an eerie similarity to early Protestantism, the movement was tempered not only by a pragmatic fear of the Inquisition, but also by a sincere Catholicism; the clerical hierarchy, after all, provided the leadership of the reform movement. While the ultra-enthusiasts advocated a return to primitive Church simplicity, they rejected not the entire mediatory role of the Church but merely the bewildering array of exterior forms. For example, here is Laso de la Vega's assessment of the saint: "Augustine, reformer of the primitive faith, and the surest channel through which flows the crystalline water of its virtues . . . the very soul of Catholicism."[53] Augustinian theology animated Veracruz's enlightened, who rejected the dead's presence as a visual, exterior prod to piety as well as the need to maintain an army of celestial intercessors.[54] As Spanish Archbishop Francisco Valero y Losa succinctly put it, "What the saints truly esteem is the purity of one's intentions for giving . . . everything else is shell and body without spirit."[55] Thus, without embracing Protestantism's notion of predestination, from which logically followed Luther's scorn for funeral pomp and masses, the enlightened arrived at the same conclusion: elaborate funerals and in-church burials had little effect on salvation.[56]

Sensato intellectuals' opposition to worldly vanity and the visual display of social position did not fall on deaf ears, as the radical rise in the number of Veracruz wills requesting a moderate funeral illustrates. While only around 2 percent of all testators from 1740 to 1779 requested a modest burial, by the peak of the cemetery controversy, from 1790 to 1799, 20.3 percent of all testators demanded sparse funerals. More important, piety rather than economy motivated the modesty movement. Testators who chose modest funeral ceremonies rejected the numerous priests and confraternities that accompanied the dead to the church for burial, an elaborate funeral ceremony, or both. Imbued with the new piety, these propertied Veracruzanos spurned priestly mediation at the same time that they rejected the religious sanctification of their social position. Beatriz de Real, the widow of Laso de la Vega's wealthy father, was positively flamboyant in her modesty, insisting that her body be deposited in the Hospital of Our Lady of Loreto and illuminated only by four one-pound candles before interment in the suburban cemetery; she was especially adamant that her funeral be without a cacophany of church bells or any other "demonstrations of luxury."[57] Licensed medical practitioner Santiago Augie also called for "moderation" in his funeral and left the choice of his burial location entirely to his will's executors.[58] Enlightened piety, not economic necessity, dictated testators' election of a modest funeral. The new piety's fundamental tenets—rational individual judgment, self-control, hostility to elaborate display—were critical to the enlightened's sense of an "us" confronting a "them" who did not share "our" cultural sensibilities. Summing up the 1790s cemetery skirmishes that had polarized Veracruz, the 1806 city council claimed that "those of enlightened piety" had been the new burial ground's only consistent backers.[59]

The popularity of the "true piety" that gripped Veracruzanos in the late eighteenth century explains the city's numerous procemetery stalwarts. However, other important factors stimulated the rejection of elaborate displays of social status and the creation of new forms of group identification. As they did in Spain, doctors, enlightened members of the secular clergy, and government bureaucrats represented ascendant social groups whose status was firmly rooted in the social engineering projects so characteristic of the epoch in general and of post-1790 Veracruz in particular. In the port city, exploding numbers of new merchants joined these groups to constitute a critical mass of individuals whose occupations placed them outside the traditional social structure sanctified by religious display.[60]

Eight years before the official 1789 Free Trade Proclamation, Veracruz's merchant community came together to defend its interests, petitioning the crown for their own guild similar to that of Mexico City.[61] Nine of the twenty-six merchants who signed the 1781 petition played parts in the death disputes of the early 1790s. Six of them staunchly defended church burial rights, while three of them condemned those rights. Antonio Sáenz de Santa María surreptitiously buried his unborn child in one of the city's monasteries, pleading to Laso de la Vega that his distraught wife required the consolation of a church burial. Adrián Félix de Troncoso allied with several other merchants and insisted that the city's enlightened faction respect Council of the Indies and crown edicts allowing cemetery exceptions. Acting to protect the burial rights that they or their loved ones already held, and possessing the know-how and influence to gain the king's ear, these and other Veracruz traders joined the anticemetery efforts.[62]

By 1803 the Veracruz merchants' guild had not only officially advocated cemetery burial, it had also declared its intention to build a new cemetery with improved sanitary conditions.[63] Acting for "the good of humanity" and "the conservation of public health," the 1804 merchant-dominated city council renounced its burial privileges in San Sebastián Chapel and strongly urged others to do the same. Emboldened by a May 1804 royal order for cemetery construction, the twelve aldermen pledged that "no one, not even a viceroy, would be buried inside city walls."[64] Not to be outdone, an independent group of wealthy merchants publicly declared that neither they nor their families would accept church burial, hoping by their example to persuade the "common folk" to overcome their superstitions.[65] Thus, by 1804, the institutional voices of the merchant community had definitively declared for the cemetery, to a chorus of public support from Veracruz's other traders. What had transpired in the short span of time between the 1781 guild petition and the rejection of church burials and elaborate funerals in 1804?

Doctrines that stress the motivations of the heart often flourish in periods of rapid social change and appeal to new social groups seeking to justify their repudiation of traditional authorities. Veracruz merchants certainly fit this description. At the turn of the century, an increasing number of new merchants in the port city were plying their trade in the world market and vigorously challenging the traditional trade monopoly held by their Mexico City rivals. Veracruz's booming economy produced a critical mass of individuals whose new wealth placed them outside the old regime's social structure. But, as we have seen, it is good to avoid mechanistically associating the city's merchants with the new piety, as many of that class initially led the resistance to the new cemetery. The merchants' 1804 cemetery advocacy stemmed in part from the elites' uneasy relationship with both Veracruz's resident poor and the large numbers of migrants who fled crisis conditions in the Veracruz countryside to seek employment in the city's booming economy.[66]

THE MERCHANTS AND THE PLEBE: *SENSATO* RULE

The city's insalubrious conditions and inclement weather partially account for the dearth of permanent resident Spaniards and *criollos* (Spaniards born in the New World), who felt themselves to be poorly suited to tropical conditions. Travelers unanimously gasped in horror at the city's festering environs. As early as 1623, Thomas Gage noticed the "standing bogs" on the southwest side of the city, which exacerbated the already sticky air and the unhealthy climate that he blamed for the scant population. For Europeans, the port proved a veritable tomb during the frequent bouts of "black vomit." In 1763, visitor Father Francisco de Ajofrín noted that "European arrivals maintain their robustness and color for a mere six or eight months until the constant sweating slowly saps their vitality." The only relief from the heat came in the form of freezing northern winds (*nortes*) that fell without warning on the city, scattering sand and sending enormous waves crashing over the embankments.[67] Not surprisingly, those with the economic wherewithal to escape the city did so, leaving mulattoes and other *castas* (persons of mixed racial ancestry) as Veracruz's core population.

The 1791 Veracruz census demonstrates that the city's mulatto and black populations had deep roots in the community. More than half of each group were Veracruz natives.[68] Most white and mestizo males had been born outside the city, with the majority hailing from Spain. Furthermore, the city's residents of color outnumbered the whites. Thus, Veracruz's stable core population consisted of both male and female *castas*.[69]

Most of Veracruz's resident poor were neither independent craftsmen nor intimately connected to the city's minority elite population. Instead, they toiled on the docks in large work teams (roughly one hundred men), loading and unloading the ships, the life blood of the city. They often acted in concert to protect their interests. The merchants' guild scrambled to diffuse the subversive potential of stevedore captain José Cayetano Cordova's 1796 petition for guild status under maritime law, which would have allowed him to control the docks, to doom lucrative cargoes to rot at the workers' whim, and indirectly to set the price of each cart of merchandise moved to warehouses. Charged by the merchants' guild with investigating Cordova's petition, traders Tomás de Aguirre and José Ignacio de Uriarte declared that the stevedores were land workers and thus ineligible for consideration under maritime law. Furthermore, the experience of numerous port cities demonstrated that the graft and corruption of the dock workers' guild often paralyzed trade, thwarting merchants' interests.[70]

Receiving no surcease from the city council or the merchants' guild (*consulado*), workers and their often dubious representatives nevertheless continued to defend their interests. In 1804, work crew captain Francisco de Paula Garay noted a "state of abandon" on the docks. The dock workers, who unloaded the king's ships for a fraction of the fees paid by private vessels, often left their tasks to work for the highest bidder—or not at all. To remedy this situation, he proposed that his crew receive an exclusive monopoly on all loading and unloading in the port, and that the merchants' guild establish an official fee list for all merchandise.[71]

The merchants' response to Garay's petition, penned by Francisco García Puertas, reveals the ugly underside of the individualism that animated the *sensatos'* attack on corporate privileges and monopolies such as the one previously held by the Mexico City merchants. Echoing Council of Castile president Pedro Rodríquez, Puertas responded to the workers' request for a monopoly by declaring that "these types of privileges are odious." Thus, at the same time that the enlightened dismantled a rigidly hierarchical group-based society in the interest of freeing individual initiative, they simultaneously cut off avenues for the economically disadvantaged to act collectively, and even began to blame the poor for their condition. Puertas stated that "[d]espite the enormous quantity of money paid to stevedores, they are poor and dress shabbily, and when they fall sick they go door to door begging alms, or to the hospital if they are too weak—all of which can be blamed on their bad conduct as well as their unwillingness to establish a fund for the sick and debilitated."[72] City councilman Martín Sánchez Serrano shared Puertas's adherence to the tenets of *sensato* individualism, attacking workers' desire for a monopoly on the grounds that "nobody can impede a man from dedicating himself to the job that offers the best remuneration . . . especially not in Veracruz where . . . those with prudence and good conduct have moved up and into better positions."[73] The municipal authorities and the merchants' guild demonstrated their faith in this new litmus test of salvation by voting to choke off any collective advancement. Despite the merchants' formal disavowal of workers' influence over their decisions, the stevedores' demands could not be ignored, and by 1809 the *cabildo* had formally promulgated an official price list for the transportation of all goods entering or leaving the port.[74]

Thus, Veracruz's new merchants confronted a stable, culturally and economically influential resident population of *castas*, as well as a steady stream of rural refugees, without the infrastructure of charities, job-generating public works projects, and the police forces found in other cities such as the capital. As a matter of fact, only two public works had been completed by 1789, and the regular orders, not secular officials, dispensed charity to the small number of destitute.[75] This fact is critical to understanding the merchants' subsequent rejection of church burials and elaborate funerals because the *sensatos* sought to refashion the underclass into disciplined workers by transforming Veracruz in accordance with Enlightenment strictures, establishing and managing schools and charities, expanding the police force, installing streetlamps to facilitate surveillance, and wresting control of the hospitals from the regular orders. They would forge themselves into a self-conscious class that observed, edified, and physically cared for those they deemed their cultural inferiors. Imbued with the new individualistic theology, which both justified and inspired many Veracruzanos' economic ascension, the enlightened stressed the individual's responsibility for his economic plight. Thus the result of the new piety was the creation of a new moral-political ethos. The *sensatos* claimed their particular ethos to be universal because they believed that the status of enlightened was available to all who embraced the group's cultural attributes.[76] Furthermore, their self-confident moral authority derived from their assiduous adherence to the new religious sensibility and qualified them to refashion both the burial customs of elites and the undesirable mores of the poor.

In 1789, city councilman Antonio María Fernández lamented that vagrants abounded in the city, but rather than laud poverty's inherent blessedness and gently apply the balm of charity to heal the rifts between rich and poor, he tagged these immigrants "the lazy of both sexes" and advocated the construction of a poorhouse where the truly needy would be separated from pretenders. Furthermore, more schools under secular tutelage should be built to discourage layabouts' children from emulating their parents. Finally, he recommended that surveillance of the poor be stepped up through the establishment of neighborhood police (Alcaldes de Barrio) and the installation of numerous streetlamps.[77]

The late eighteenth century witnessed a boom in secular institutions designed to inculcate the poor with the enlightened's values, institutions overwhelmingly directed by the *sensatos* themselves. In 1787, backed by the donations of numerous merchants, Laso de la Vega and a small group of leading citizens organized themselves into the Sociedad de Amigos del País (Society of Friends of the Country) and founded a "patriotic school" patterned after those being formed by enlightened groups in Spain, Havana, Oaxaca, and Puebla. In a similar vein, the *sensatos* staffed the Junta de Policía, which initially oversaw the placement of cobblestones on the city's scraggly streets and later undertook other city improvement projects. The prominent Cossío House traders sponsored an indigents' home, which encouraged work and prohibited gambling and prostitution, and in 1801 influential residents spurred the city council's creation of a poorhouse (Casa de Misercordia), staffed by laypersons rather than by clergy and featuring large looms for spinning cotton.[78]

But nowhere was the *sensatos'* civic participation more apparent than in their systematic wresting of control of the city's hospitals from the religious orders, who, they felt, employed these institutions to shelter undeserving beggars rather than cure the sick. In 1791 a loosely organized group of *sensatos* ousted the Hipolite friars from the Hospital of Our Lady of Loreto, and the Ayuntamiento backed their takeover by refusing the friars entry, even after the Audiencia (High Court) approved their return. In 1798 the city council and the merchants' guild pooled their resources to open the Hospital of San Sebastián under lay rather than religious auspices, and in 1805 prominent residents and the municipal council petitioned Viceroy Iturrigaray to close the Hospital of San Juan de Montes Claros, whose central location they now deemed a public health risk.[79] Thus, although the secular authorities' support for religious festivals like that of San Sebastián barely wavered, and although elite leadership in the confraternities continued, the new civic improvement projects offered an alternative source of status. *Sensato* merchants could exercise (and indeed create) their new moral authority by observing, educating, and curing others rather than by strutting their status through the streets in religious processions.

The city itself became a testimony to the *sensatos'* new techniques of exercising power, a didactic space for everyone's internalization of enlightened values. Whereas in Mexico City, Viceroy Revillagigedo had employed state power to install street lanterns, in Veracruz enlightened residents pooled their resources to pay for illumination, and by 1802 the city boasted 226 lamps, a team of caretakers, and a city councilman who oversaw both maintenance and repairs. The *sensatos* further combated untidiness and disorder with stepped-up sanitary measures, such as garbage carts that ferried refuse out of the city to be unceremoniously dumped in the sea, and a 1797 order enjoining all residents to sweep in front of their houses on Wednesdays and Saturdays.[80] With these measures, the eyes of power zoomed in on the picayune details of daily life.

To enforce these more intrusive measures, to ensure that someone was observing the sundry unemployed residents who now eluded surveillance in elite households or shops, the Veracruz City Council established the Alcaldes de Barrio, the neighborhood police that had patrolled Mexico City streets since 1782. Designed to "prevent scandals, repress vices, extinguish laziness, and foment industry," the police force was manned by "honorable citizens" with the moral authority to provide an example to their charges. To facilitate rational surveillance, in 1797 the aldermen discussed dividing the city into four major police precincts, each divided into two minor wards.[81]

The creation of charities, lights, and police forces would ensure an urban environment and population more conducive to the port city's participation in the world market. Fired by an individualistic piety that stressed self-imposed discipline, and by that piety's subtle permutation into a moral justification for personal economic advancement or failure, the enlightened usurped the role of the religious as providers of charity and placed themselves in an unmediated, educative relationship with the city's underclass. Observing the indigents' efforts at the looms, donating money for the smart streetlamps that blazed late into the night, planning a new school with a more rational curriculum, or chastising the besotted as they spilled out of the taverns: enlightened Veracruz offered elites new sources of social identity—an identity based on self-control and the attendant moral authority to supervise others deemed less capable of controlling themselves.

Thus, although merchants dominated the ranks of the enlightened, we should avoid linking them too hastily to the new piety and its rejection of exterior social display. Veracruz's newly wealthy could have purchased prestigious church burial sites; they could even have sunk their fresh capital into elaborate, well-attended funerals. Instead, they loudly and publicly declared their support for the new cemetery and filled their wills with requests for humble funerals. In their relations with the city's combative underclass, the *sensatos* had learned to wield power by observation rather than immoderate display, and had rejected the community-based salvation represented by church burials. In its place they erected a more individualistic piety whose emphasis on the internalization of religious moral maxims gave them the justification to supervise others who had not taken the message to heart.

CONCLUSION

Veracruz's emotional sepulchral dramas, and the "true piety" that gripped the city's *sensatos*, suggest that the historiography of Mexican modernity may need reassessment. François-Xavier Guerra has defined social modernity as the predominance of a vision of society comprised of individuals. Guerra finds modernity's motor of diffusion in the new voluntary associations, which opened their membership to all individuals who could make a reasonable argument for admission regardless of their old-regime status, and thus provided the training ground for modern politics. Fermenting clandestinely during the reign of Bourbon enlightened despotism, these groups strutted into the open in Spain after the 1808 monarchical crisis. For America, 1808 also marked a critical turning point in the march to modernity, as pamphlets and periodicals promoting these new ideas arrived from Spain. Thus, the Enlightenment radiated outward from Spain and Europe; and indeed, Guerra asserts that except for a few isolated notions immigrating from France or North America, modern visions of community landed in Hispanic America in 1808.[82]

But the groundwork for the Mexican Liberals' vision of an all-inclusive nation of individuals was laid much earlier than 1808, and it came not from France, North America, or even Spain, but from parish and cathedral pulpits in places like Veracruz, Mexico City, and Puebla. The new piety acted as a solvent on the sclerotic and divinely sanctified social hierarchies of the old regime, splintering society into men who saw themselves as atomized individuals and who regarded their social position as due to hard work and self-control, an interiorization of morality. It was these same atomized individuals who peopled the texts penned by later nineteenth-century Mexican Liberals.[83]

In an 1837 work, Liberal José Luis Mora, the mastermind of the regime of licensed medical doctor Valentín Gómez Farías, applauded Mexico's advance to modernity: "If Independence had occurred forty years ago, a man born here would have shunned the title of 'Mexican' . . . for this man the title of judge or theologian or even of confraternity member would have been more valued . . . to discuss national interests with this man would have been equivalent to speaking to him in Hebrew; his only loyalty was to his small group and he would have sacrificed the rest of society to protect it."[84] It should come as no surprise that Mora saw the Bible as the basis of morality and founded a Mexican chapter of the London Bible Society, a group dedicated to distributing God's word to the general populace.[85]

Octavio Paz found Spain and her colonies lacking in a "modern moral consciousness." In Protestant countries and in France, with its influential Jansenist faction, the individualist impulse took hold among the populace before its manifestation as Liberalism; modernity was a philosophy before it was a political movement. By contrast, Latin America imported modernity, and rationalism was an acquired ideology. For Paz, the fundamental difference between Latin American democracy and its Anglo-Saxon version is attributable to the religious origins of the latter. The "true piety" of Veracruz's *sensatos* suggests that Mexico's Liberalism also had religious roots.[86]

SUGGESTED READINGS

Cooper, Donald B. *Epidemic Disease in Mexico City, 1761–1813: An Administrative, Social, and Medical Strategy.* Austin: University of Texas Press, 1965.

Fields, Sherry Lee. *Pestilence and Head Colds: Encountering Illness in Colonial Mexico.* New York: Columbia University Press, 2008.

Hernandez Saenz, Luz Maria. *Learning to Heal: the Medical Profession in Colonial Mexico, 1767–1831.* New York: Peter Lang, 1997.

Kellehear, Allan. *A Social History of Dying.* Cambridge University Press, 2007.

Larkin, Brian. *The Very Nature of God: Baroque Catholicism and Religious Reform in Bourbon Mexico.* Albuquerque: University of New Mexico Press, 2010.

McManners, John. *Death and the Enlightenment: Changing Attitudes to Death among Christians and Unbelievers in Eighteenth-Century France.* New York: Oxford University Press, 1981.

O'Hara, Matthew. *A Flock Divided: Race, Religion and Politics in Mexico, 1749–1857.* Duke University Press, 2010.

Reis, João José. "Death to the Cemetery: Funerary Reform and Rebellion in Salvador, Brazil, 1836." In *Riots in the Cities: Popular Politics and the Urban Poor in Latin America, 1765–1910,* edited by Silvia M. Arrom and Servando Ortoll, pp. 97–114. Wilmington, DE: SR Books, 1996.

Roach, Joseph. *Cities of the Dead: Circum-Atlantic Performance*. New York: Columbia University Press, 1986.

Sights

The Death of a Bureaucrat. 1966. Directed by Tomás Gutiérrez Alea (Facets Multimedia).

2

Church, Humboldt, and Darwin

The Tension and Harmony of Art and Science

Stephen Jay Gould

Since the first voyage of Columbus, Latin America—tropical paradise, home to a tremendous diversity of foliage, fauna, and human beings—has fascinated European intellectuals and travelers. Most came to conquer, to establish European control, to dominate the lands of the Western Hemisphere. Others, a small but important minority, made the Atlantic voyage not merely seeking the thrill of the exotic, although their writings attest to their awestruck state before many of the great natural wonders of the continent, but also greater intellectual truths. One such man was Alexander von Humboldt, whose investigations and subsequent writings about Latin America entranced and inspired still other adventurer intellectuals to venture forth to pursue aesthetic philosophies and formulate scientific treatises, always with Latin America as their muse. Stephen Jay Gould contemplates the attempt by Humboldt and his "students," landscape painter Frederic Edwin Church and Charles Darwin, to observe accurately and in detail the great diversity of nature in the Andean highlands. In the process, Gould ponders the relationship between representation of natural reality in Church's painting as a vision of harmony and Darwin's essential truth that the natural world was not governed by such moral imperatives.

The intense excitement and fascination elicited by Frederic Edwin Church's *Heart of the Andes*, when first exhibited in New York in 1859, may be attributed to that odd mixture of apparent opposites that has always characterized American showmanship—commercialism and excellence, hoopla and incisive analysis. The large canvas, more than ten by five feet, was set in a massive frame and displayed alone in a darkened room, with carefully controlled lighting and the walls draped in black.[1] Dried plants and other souvenirs that Church had collected in South America may have graced the room, complementing the subject of the painting. Visitors marveled at the magisterial composition, with its background of the high Andes, blanketed in snow, and a foreground of detail so intricate and microscopically correct that Church might have been proclaimed the Van Eyck of botany.

But public interest also veered from the sublime to the merely quantitative, as rumors circulated that the unprecedented sum of $20,000 had been paid for the painting (the actual figure of $10,000 was impressive enough for the time). This tension of reasons for interest in Church has never ceased. The catalogue produced by the Dallas Museum of Fine Arts upon the acquisition of *The Icebergs* contains, in order, as its first three pictures, a reproduction of the painting, a portrait of Church, and a photo of the auctioneer at Sotheby Parke Bernet gaveling the sale at $2.5 million as "the audience cheered at what is the highest figure ever registered at an art auction in the United States."[2]

A far more important tension, that between art and science, permeates our current concern with Church. This tension, however, is only retrospective, a product of divisions that have appeared in our society since Church painted his most famous canvases. Church did not doubt that his concern with scientific accuracy went hand in hand with his drive to depict beauty and meaning in its highest form. His faith in this fruitful union stemmed from the views of his intellectual mentor Alexander von Humboldt, a great scientist who had ranked landscape painting among the three highest expressions of our love of nature.

Church sent *Heart of the Andes* to Europe after its great American success of 1859. He wanted, above all, to have the painting shown to the ninety-year-old Humboldt who, sixty years before, had begun the great South American journey that would become the source of his renown. Church wrote to Bayard Taylor on 9 May 1859:

> The "Andes" will probably be on its way to Europe before your return to the City. . . . [The] principal motive in taking the picture to Berlin is to have the satisfaction of placing before Humboldt a transcript of the scenery which delighted his eyes sixty years ago—and which he had pronounced to be the finest in the world.[3]

But Humboldt died before the painting could be sent, and Church's act of homage never occurred. Later in 1859, as *Heart of the Andes* was enjoying another triumph of display in the British Isles, Charles Darwin's *On the Origin of Species* was published in London. These three events, linked by their combined occurrence in 1859—the first exhibition of *Heart of the Andes*, the death of Alexander von Humboldt, and the publication of *On the Origin of Species*—form the core of this essay. They represent, in my view, foci for understanding the central role of science in Church's career and for considering the larger issue of relationships between art and science.

As a professional scientist, I have no credentials for judging or interpreting Church's paintings. I can only say that I have been powerfully intrigued (stunned would not be too strong a word) by his major canvases. I first saw *Niagara* at the Corcoran Gallery of Art and marveled at the "odd" but exciting orientation at the lip of the great Horseshoe Falls. (In our parish of science, any describer should "naturally" choose the "fuller" and more "objective" view of the cascade head on from below.) Church's decision taught me something important about the power of human imagination in its fruitful union with accuracy.

I then developed a special interest in Church when his works stood out for me at the exhibition *A New World: Masterpieces of American Painting 1760–1910* at Boston's Museum of Fine Arts a few years later. I made a trip to New York to see *Heart of the Andes* at the Metropolitan as I was preparing this chapter. I marveled at the interplay between creation and destruction shown in *The Icebergs*, the fantastic geometry of erosion following the construction of these ice mountains. I thought that I saw the same themes even more complexly developed in *Cotopaxi*—the layered rocks of the foreground and the awesome symmetry of the volcano itself, contrasted with the destructive force of the eruption, the cloud of smoke that darkens the rising sun (which, as it moves up, shall emerge from the pall). I noted the unobtrusive signs of human life, drawn (I suppose) to emphasize the mastery of nature in comparative scales—the tower in Niagara, two figures by a roadside cross in *Heart of the Andes*, a single figure on the path in *Cotopaxi*, the shipwreck in *The Icebergs*. I smiled at the artist's signature, cut in bark on the highlighted tree in the foreground of *Heart of the Andes*—so faded into the scene in its organicism, yet so emphasized in its illumination.

But if I have no license to discourse on Church, at least I inhabit the world of Humboldt and Darwin, and I can perhaps clarify why Humboldt became such a powerful intellectual guru for Church and a whole generation of artists and scholars, and why Darwin pulled this vision of nature up from its roots, substituting another that could and should have been read as equally ennobling, but that plunged many votaries of the old order into permanent despair.

When Church began to paint his great canvases, Alexander von Humboldt was probably the world's most famous and influential intellectual. If his name has faded from such prominence today, this slippage only records a curiosity and basic unfairness of historical judgment. The history of ideas emphasizes innovation and downgrades popularization. The great teachers of any time have enormous influence over the lives and thoughts of entire generations, but their legacy fades as the hagiographic tradition distills thoughts judged as new and discards context. No one did more to change and enhance science in the first half of the nineteenth century than Alexander von Humboldt, the cardinal inspiration for men as diverse as Charles

Darwin, Alfred Russel Wallace, Louis Agassiz (whom Humboldt financed at a crucial time), and Frederic Edwin Church.

Humboldt (1769–1859) studied geology in his native Germany with another great teacher, A. G. Werner. Following Werner's interest in mining, Humboldt invented a new form of safety lamp and a device for rescuing trapped miners. Early in his career, Humboldt developed a deep friendship with Goethe, a more uncertain relationship with Schiller, and a passion to combine personal adventure with the precise measurements and observations necessary to develop a science of global physical geography. Consequently, recognizing that the greatest diversity of life and terrain would be found in mountainous and tropical regions, he embarked on a five-year journey to South America in 1799, accompanied by the French botanist Aimé Bonpland. During this greatest of scientific adventures, Humboldt collected 60,000 plant specimens, drew countless maps of great accuracy, wrote some of the most moving passages ever penned against the slave trade, proved the connection between the Orinoco and the Amazon, and established the altitude record (at least among westerners inclined to measure such things) by climbing to 19,000 feet (though not reaching the summit) on Chimborazo. On the way home in 1804, he visited the United States and had several long meetings with Thomas Jefferson. Back in Europe, he met and befriended Simon Bolívar, becoming a lifelong advisor to the great liberator.

The rest of Humboldt's professional life revolved around this voyage and the meticulous records and diaries that he had kept. Over twenty-five years, Humboldt published thirty-four volumes of his travel journal illustrated by 1,200 copper plates, but never finished the project. His large and beautiful maps were the envy of the cartographic world. Most important (for its influence on Church and Humboldt's other disciples), Humboldt conceived, in 1827–1828, a plan for a multivolumed popular work on, to put it succinctly, everything. The first two volumes of *Kosmos* appeared in 1845 and 1847, the last three in the 1850s. *Kosmos*, immediately translated into all major Western languages, may be the most important work of popular science ever published. It remains the greatest of all testaments to the essential humanism of science.

Humboldt's primary influence on Church can scarcely be doubted.[4] Church owned, read, and reread both Humboldt's travel narratives and *Kosmos* (or *Cosmos*, as translated into English). In an age when most painters aspired to a European grand tour to set the course of their work and inspiration, Church followed a reverse route, taking his cue from Humboldt. After his apprenticeship with Thomas Cole, Church first traveled, at Humboldt's direct inspiration, to the high tropics of South America in 1853 and 1857. In Quito, he sought out and occupied the house that Humboldt had inhabited nearly sixty years before. The great canvases of his most fruitful decade (1855–1865) are embodiments of Humboldt's aesthetic philosophy and convictions about the unity of art and science. Even subjects maximally distant from the tropics bear Humboldt's mark of influence. *The Icebergs* and Church's general fascination with polar regions closely parallel Humboldt's second major expedition, his Siberian sojourn of 1829. Church did not visit Europe until 1867, and this cradle of most Western painting did not provoke a new flood of great creativity.

We can best grasp Humboldt's vision (which so inspired Church) by examining the plan of *Cosmos*. On the first page of his preface, Humboldt states the grand aim of his entire work.[5]

> The principal impulse by which I was directed was the earnest endeavor to comprehend the phenomena of physical objects in their general connection, and to represent nature as one great whole, moved and animated by internal forces (1: vii).

"Nature," he adds later (1:24), "is a unity in diversity of phenomena; a harmony, blending together all created things, however dissimilar in form and attributes; one great whole animated by the breath of life." This twofold idea of natural unity forged by a harmony of internal laws and forces was no mere rhapsodizing on Humboldt's part; this vision represented his view of natural causation. It also embodied the guiding principles that animated Church and that Darwin would tear down with a theory of conflict and balance between internal and external (largely random) forces.

Volume 1 of *Cosmos* covers, on the grandest possible scale, the science that we would call physical geography today. Humboldt ranges from stars in the most distant galaxies to minor differences in soil and climate that govern the distribution of vegetation. (The book is fundamentally a geography, a treatise about the natural forms and places of things. Thus, Humboldt includes little conventional biology in his treatise and discusses organisms primarily in terms of their geographic distribution and appropriate fit to environments.)

But *Cosmos* takes seriously, and to the fullest possible extent, its own primary theme of unity. If volume 1 is a physical description of the universe, then volume 2—an astounding tour de force that reads with as much beauty and relevance today as in Church's era—treats the history and forms of human sensibility toward nature. (The last three volumes of *Cosmos*, published many years later, present case studies of the physical world; these volumes were never as popular as the first two.) Humboldt wrote of his overall design:

> I have considered Nature in a two-fold point of view. In the first place, I have endeavored to present her in the pure objectiveness of external phenomena; and secondly, as the reflection of the image impressed by the senses upon the inner man, that is, upon his ideas and feelings (3:5).

Humboldt begins volume 2 with a discussion of the three principal modes (in his view) for the expression of our love of nature—poetic description, landscape painting (need I say more for influence upon Church), and cultivation of exotic plants (Church made a large collection of dried and pressed tropical plants). The rest of the volume treats, with stunning erudition and encyclopedic footnotes, the history of human attitudes toward the natural world.

Humboldt embodied the ideals of the Enlightenment as well and as forcefully as any great intellectual—as Voltaire, as Goya, as Condorcet. If he lived so long, and past the hour of flourishing for his philosophy, he remained ever firm in his convictions, a beacon of hope in a disillusioned world. Humboldt conveyed the Enlightenment's faith that human history moved toward progress and harmony based on the increasing spread of intellect. People may differ in current accomplishments, but all races are equally subject to similar improvement. In the most famous nineteenth-century statement of equality made by a scientist, Humboldt wrote:

> While we maintain the unity of the human species, we at the same time repel the depressing assumption of superior and inferior races of men. There are nations more susceptible of cultivation, more highly civilized, more ennobled by mental cultivation than others, but none in themselves nobler than others. All are in like degree designed for freedom (1:358).

In expressing his liberal belief in progress, Humboldt contrasts his perception of unity with the standard views, based on division and separation, of such social conservatives as Edmund Burke. For Burke and other leaders of the reaction against liberalism, feeling and intellect are separate domains; the former, the chief mode of the masses, leads to danger and destruction. The masses must therefore be restrained and ruled by an elite capable of mastering the constrictive and empowering force of intellect.

Humboldt's vision, in direct contrast, is based on the union and positive interaction between feeling and analysis, sentiment and observation. Sentiment, properly channeled, is not a dangerous force of ignorance, but a prerequisite to any deep appreciation of nature:

> The vault of heaven, studded with nebulae and stars, and the rich vegetable mantle that covers the soil in the climate of palms, cannot surely fail to produce on the minds of these laborious observers of nature an impression more imposing and more worthy of the majesty of creation than on those who are unaccustomed to investigate the great mutual relations of phenomena. I cannot, therefore, agree with Burke when he says, "it is our ignorance of natural things that causes all our admiration, and chiefly excites our passions" (1:40).

Romantic nonsense might proclaim a superiority of untrammeled feeling over the dryness of accurate observation and measurement, but the

Enlightenment's faith in rationality located highest truth in the mutual reinforcement of feeling and intellect:

> It is almost with reluctance that I am about to speak of a sentiment, which appears to arise from narrow-minded views, or from a certain weak and morbid sentimentality—I allude to the fear entertained by some persons, that nature may by degrees lose a portion of the charm and magic of her power, as we learn more and more how to unveil her secrets, comprehend the mechanism of the movements of the heavenly bodies, and estimate numerically the intensity of natural forces. . . . Those who still cherish such erroneous views in the present age, and amid the progress of public opinion, and the advancement of all branches of knowledge, fail in duly appreciating the value of every enlargement of the sphere of intellect, and the importance of the detail of isolated facts in leading us on to general results (1:38–40).

Humboldt viewed the interaction of feeling and intellect as an upwardly spiraling system, moving progressively toward deep understanding. Feeling excites our interest and leads us to a passionate desire for scientific knowledge of details and causes. This knowledge, in turn, enhances our appreciation of natural beauty; nature in a unity; all forces push to the same goal; feeling and intellect are complementary sources of understanding; knowing the causes of things leads us to even greater awe and wonder.

> Thus do the spontaneous impressions of the untutored mind lead, like the laborious deductions of cultivated intellect, to the same intimate persuasion, that one sole and indissoluble chain binds together all nature. . . . Every imposing scene in nature depends so materially upon the mutual relation of the ideas and sentiments simultaneously excited in the mind of the observer (1:27).

Humboldt's theory of aesthetics is rooted in this idea of mutual reinforcement. A great painter must also be a scientist, or at least committed to the detailed and accurate observation, and to the knowledge of causes, that motivate a professional scientist. For the visual arts, landscape painting is the principal mode of expressing the unity of knowledge (as poetry serves the literary arts and cultivation of exotic plants the practical arts). A great landscape painter is the highest servant of both nature and the human mind.

Church accepted Humboldt's aesthetic theory as his own guide (and why not, for I think that no one has ever improved upon this primary statement of humanism). Church was identified and respected as the most scientific of painters (when such a designation implied admiration, not belittlement as it might today in some circles). His penchant for accuracy in observation and rendering, both for intricate botanical details in his foregrounds and geological forms in his backgrounds, was admired as a primary source of quality in his art and as a key to his success in awakening feelings of awe and sublimity in his viewers.

I do not, of course, say that Church attempted, or that Humboldt advocated, a slavish rendering of particular places with snapshot accuracy. Humboldt did stress the value of colored sketches from nature, even of photographs (though he felt, in the nascent years of this art, that photography could only capture the basic forms of a landscape, never the details). But Humboldt realized that any fine canvas must be an imaginative reconstruction, accurate in all its details of geology and vegetation, not a re-creation of a particular spot:

> A distinction must be made in landscape painting, as in every other branch of art, between the elements generated by the more limited field on contemplation and direct observation, and those which spring from the boundless depth and feeling and from the force of idealizing mental power (2:95).

None of Church's great tropical paintings are representations of particular places. He often constructed idealized vantage points so that he could encompass all life zones, from the vegetation of lush lowlands to the snow-clad Andean peaks, in a single composition. (For example, although Church's most famous painting of Cotopaxi includes no lowland plants, most of his other canvases of this great volcano feature palm trees and other luxuriant plants that actually grow nowhere in such proximity to the mountain.)[6] Moreover, though likely with no conscious intent, Church did not always depict his geological backgrounds accurately. Volcanologist Richard S. Fiske discovered that Church painted the symmetrical cone of Cotopaxi with steeper sides than the actual mountain possesses.[7] We may, however, view this "license" as a veering toward accuracy, for Humboldt himself had drawn Cotopaxi with even steeper slopes!

Humboldt's influence over Church extended to far more than general aesthetic philosophy and the value of science and accurate observation. One may easily identify landscape painting as the principal mode of glorifying nature in the visual arts, but which among the infinitude of earthly landscapes best captures the essence of wonder? Humboldt replied with the aesthetic conviction that still motivates such modern ecological movements as the battle to save the rain forests of the Amazon. Maximal diversity of life and landscape is the *summum bonum* of aesthetic joy and intellectual wonder. Maximal diversity is enhanced by two circumstances, which have their greatest confluence in the High Andes of South America. First, the vastly greater diversity of vegetation in tropical regions marks the torrid zone as immensely more varied than temperate areas inhabited by most Western peoples. Second, diversity is greatly enhanced by a range of altitudes, for the sequence of lowland to mountaintop in a single district may span the entire panoply of lowland environments from equator to pole, with an equatorial mountaintop acting as a surrogate for the Arctic. Thus, the higher the mountains, the more the range of diversity. The Himalayas might win our preference, but they lie too far north of the equator and do not include the zones of tropical lowland vegetation. The Andes of South America are the premiere spot on earth for landscape painting, for only here does the full luxuriance of the lowland jungle stand in the shadow of such a massive range of snow-clad peaks. Humboldt therefore went to South America, as did Darwin, Wallace, and Frederic Edwin Church, much to the benefit of art and history. Humboldt wrote:

> Are we not justified in hoping that landscape painting will flourish with a new and hitherto unknown brilliance when artists of merit shall more frequently pass the narrow limits of the Mediterranean, and when they shall be enabled, far in the interior of continents, in the humid mountain valleys of the tropical world, to seize, with the genuine freshness of a pure and youthful spirit, on the true image of the varied forms of nature (2:93)?

When Church was still a small boy, Humboldt's travel writings were setting the life course of a young English graduate who planned on becoming a country parson (not from any particular zeal for religion, but probably to maximize time for avocational interests in natural history). But Charles Darwin veered down a different course to become one of history's most important intellectuals—and Humboldt was his primary influence. Darwin read two books that focused his interests upon natural history in a more serious and professional way: J. F. W. Herschel's *Preliminary Discourse on the Study of Natural History* and Humboldt's *Personal Narrative of the South American Voyages* (1814–1829). As an old man, Darwin reminisced in his autobiography: "[These books] stirred up in me a burning zeal to add even the most humble contribution to the noble structure of Natural Science. No one or a dozen other books influenced me nearly so much as these two."

Moreover, directly inspired by Humboldt's views on the need for tropical travel, Darwin hatched a plot to visit the Canary Islands with some entomologist friends. Darwin involved his mentor, botanist J. S. Henslow, in the plan, and this step led, clearly if indirectly, to Darwin's invitation to sail on the *Beagle,* the beginning and sine qua non of his rendezvous with history. Mathematician George Peacock asked Henslow to recommend a keen young naturalist to Captain FitzRoy, and Henslow, impressed with Darwin's general zeal and desire for tropical travel, recommended his young protégé for the job. The *Beagle* spent five years circumnavigating the globe, but the trip was primarily a surveying voyage of South America, and Darwin spent the bulk of his time in and around Humboldt's favorite places. Can it be accidental that the twin discoverers of natural selection, Darwin and Alfred Russel Wallace, were both inspired by Humboldt, and both made their most extensive, youthful voyages to South America? On 28 April 1831, as Darwin made his preparations for the *Beagle,* he wrote to his sister Caroline:

> My head is running about the tropics: in the morning I go and gaze at Palm trees in the hot-house and come home and read Humboldt; my enthusiasm is so great that I can hardly sit still on my chair.[8]

Darwin's first view of the richness of tropical life led him to rhapsody, for the real objects were even better than Humboldt had described. In Brazil, Darwin wrote in his diary for 28 February 1832:

> Humboldt's glorious descriptions are and will for ever be unparalleled; but even he with his dark blue skies and the rare union of poetry with science which he so strongly displays when writing on tropical scenery, with all this falls far short of the truth. The delight one experiences in such times bewilders the mind; if the eye attempts to follow the flight of a gaudy butterfly, it is arrested by some strange tree or fruit; if watching an insect one forgets it in the stranger flower it is crawling over; if turning to admire the splendor of the scenery, the individual character of the foreground fixes the attention. The mind is a chaos of delight, out of which a world of future and more quiet pleasure will arise. I am at present fit only to read Humboldt; he like another sun illumines everything I behold.

And, more succinctly, in a letter to his mentor Henslow a few months later on 18 May: "I never experienced such intense delight. I formerly admired Humboldt, I now almost adore him."

Darwin did not only read Humboldt for the visceral wonder of it all; he evidently studied Humboldt's aesthetic theories with some care as well, as several entries in the *Beagle* diary testify. Consider this comment from Rio de Janeiro in 1832:

> During the day I was particularly stuck with a remark of Humboldt's who often alludes to "the thin vapor which without changing the transparency of the air, renders its tints more harmonious, softens its effects," etc. This is an appearance which I have never observed in the temperate zones. The atmosphere, seen through a short space of half or three-quarters of a mile, was perfectly lucid, but at a greater distance all colors were blended into a most beautiful haze.

Or this, from his summary comments upon returning in 1836:

> I am strongly induced to believe that, as in music, the person who understands every note, will, if he also has true taste, more thoroughly enjoy the whole; so he who examines each part of a fine view, may also thoroughly comprehend the full and combined effect. Hence a traveler should be a botanist, for in all views plants form the chief embellishment. Group masses of naked rocks, even in the wildest forms, for a time they may afford a sublime spectacle, but they will soon grow monotonous; paint them with bright and varied colors, they will become fantastick [*sic*]; clothe them with vegetation, and they must form at least a decent, if not a most beautiful picture.

Humboldt himself could not have written a better passage on the value of diversity and his favorite theme of aesthetic appreciation enhanced by detailed knowledge of individual parts—the union of artistic pleasure and scientific understanding.

So we reach the pivotal year of our drama, 1859. Humboldt lies dying in Berlin, while two powerful and influential men, half a world apart in geography and profession, reach the apex of a fame founded on Humboldt's inspiration: Frederic Edwin Church displays *Heart of the Andes*, and Charles Darwin publishes *On the Origin of Species*.

And we encounter a precious irony, an almost painfully poignant outcome. Humboldt himself, in the preface to volume 1 of *Cosmos*, had remarked on the paradox that great works of science condemn themselves to oblivion as they open floodgates to reforming knowledge, while classics of literature can never lose relevance:

> It has frequently been regarded as a subject of discouraging consideration, that while purely literary products of intellectual activity are rooted in the depths of feeling, and interwoven with the creative force of imagination, all works treating of empirical knowledge, and of the connection of natural phenomena and physical laws, are subject to the most marked modifications of form in the lapse of short periods of time. . . . Those scientific works which have, to use a common expression, become antiquated by the acquisition of new funds of knowledge, are thus continually being consigned to oblivion as unreadable (1:xi–xii).

In Darwin's hand, Humboldt's vision suffered this fate of superannuation in 1859. The exterminating angel was not the fact of evolution itself, for some versions of evolution as necessary progress, internally driven, fit quite well with Humboldt's notion of pervasive harmony. Darwin's particular theory, natural selection, and the radical philosophical context of its presentation drove Humboldt's pleasant image to oblivion.[9] Frederic Edwin Church, alas, was even more committed than Humboldt to the philosophic comfort of their shared vision, for Church (unlike Humboldt) had rooted a good portion of his Christian faith, for him a most important source of inspiration and equanimity, in a view of nature as essential harmony in unity.

Consider just three aspects of the new Darwinian world view. All confute central aspects of Humboldt's vision.

1. Nature is a scene of competition and struggle, not higher harmony. Order and good design arise by natural selection only as a side consequence of struggle, and Hobbes's "war of all against all" is the causal reality of most daily interactions in nature. The struggle is metaphorical and need not involve bloody battle (a plant, Darwin tells us, may be said to struggle against an inclement environment at the edge of

a desert). But more often than not, competition is overt, and some die that others may live. The struggle, moreover, is for the reproductive success of individual organisms, not directly in the service of any higher harmony. Darwin, in one of his most trenchant metaphors, seems to tear right through the faith of Humboldt and the canvases of Church in depicting apparent harmony as dangerously misleading:

> We behold the face of nature bright with gladness, we often see superabundance of food; we do not see, or we forget, that the birds which are idly singing round us mostly live on insects or seeds, and are thus constantly destroying life; or we forget how largely these songsters, or their eggs, or their nestlings, are destroyed by birds and beasts of prey.[10]

2. Evolutionary lineages have no intrinsic direction toward higher states or greater unification. Natural selection is only a process of local adaptation, as organisms change in response to alterations in their environment. The geological and climatological causes of environmental change have no inherent direction either. Evolution is opportunistic.
3. Evolutionary changes are not propelled by an internal and harmonious force. Evolution is a balance between the internal characteristics of organisms and the external vector of environmental change. Both the internal and external forces have strong random components, further obviating any notion of impulse toward union and harmony. The internal force of genetic mutation, ultimate source of evolutionary variation, is random with respect to the direction of natural selection. The external force of environmental change is capricious with respect to the progress and complexity of organisms.

Frederic Edwin Church was not the only humanist crushed by the new and apparently heartless view of nature. Few themes, in fact, are more common in late nineteenth- and early twentieth-century literature than the distress and ineffable sadness provoked by losing the comfort of a world lovingly constructed with intrinsic harmony among all its constituent parts. Thomas Hardy, in a striking poem entitled *Nature's Questioning,* lets the natural objects and organisms of Darwin's new world express their despair through stunned silence:

> When I look forth at dawning, pool,
> Field, flock, and lonely tree,
> All seem to gaze at me
> Like chastened children sitting silent in a school.
> Upon them stirs in lippings mere
> (As if once clear at call,
> But now scarce breathed at all)—
> "We wonder, ever wonder, why we find us here!"

I am no fan of psychobiography or psychohistory, and I will not indulge in speculative details about the impact of Darwin's revolution on Church's painting. But something must be said about the coincidences of 1859 and the last thirty years of Church's life. When I began this project, I was shocked to learn that Church had lived until 1900. His work and its meaning are so firmly fixed, in my eyes, to the world just before Darwin's watershed, that I had trouble imagining his corporeal self peering into our own century. (He reminds me of Rossini, living into Wagner's era, but with all his work done thirty years before in a different age of *bel canto*; or of Kerensky, deposed by Lenin, but then living for more than fifty years as an aged exile in New York.)

My impression is supported by Church's output. He continued to do some painting right into the 1890s, but his great landscapes were all behind him by the end of the 1860s. I know that several nonideological reasons may explain Church's withdrawal. For one, he became very wealthy from his painting (contrary to the stereotype of struggling artists) and spent much of his later life designing and furnishing his remarkable home at Olana (see James Anthony Ryan's essay).[11] For another (and one could hardly state a better reason), he had severe health problems with inflammatory rheumatism and eventually lost the use of his painting arm. Still, I wonder if the collapse of his vision of nature, wrought by Darwin's revolution, made it impossible ever to paint such landscapes again. If an uplifting harmony turns into a scene of bloody battle, is not the joke too bitter to bear?

Several scholars have commented that the large number of books about science that Church maintained in his library at Olana[12] prove his continuing concern for keeping up with the latest in scientific thought. But this claim cannot be supported, and the list implies rather the opposite. Yes, he owned many books about science, but as Sherlock Holmes recognized the absence of a bark as the most crucial bit of evidence (for the nonexistence of a dog), the key to Church's collection lies in the books he did not own. He maintained a good collection of Humboldt; he owned Wallace's books on geographic distribution of animals and tropical biology, Darwin's on the *Beagle* voyage and the *Expression of the Emotions in Man and Animals* (1873). He bought the major works by Christian evolutionists who continued to espouse the idea of necessary progress mediated by internal forces of vital matter—H. F. Osborn and N. S. Shaler. He did not have either of Darwin's evolutionary treatises, *On the Origin of Species* (1859) and *Descent of Man* (1871). More important, he apparently owned not a single work of a mechanistic or materialist bent—not a word of E. H. Haeckel and only a text on religion by T. H. Huxley, though their books were the most widely read of all late nineteenth-century popularizations of evolution. I think that Frederic Edwin Church probably did undergo a crisis of confidence akin to that suffered by the organisms of Hardy's poem—and that he could not bear to face the consequences of Darwin's world.

I cannot end on this somber note, not only because I try to maintain a general cheerfulness of temperament, but also because such a termination would not represent a proper end to my story. I want to finish by affirming something in Humboldt that I regard as more important than his falsified vision of natural harmony and, therefore, by upholding the continuing power and beauty of Church's great paintings. I also want to suggest that Hardy's sadness and Church's silence were not the best responses of humanists to Darwin's new world—the first reaction of shock and dismay perhaps, but not the considered conclusion of more reflection and understanding from both sides.

First of all, Humboldt was right in arguing, as quoted earlier, that great works of science supersede themselves by sowing seeds for further advances. This, Humboldt adds (directly following the last quotation) is an aspect of science's joy, not its distress:

> However discouraging such a prospect must be, no one who is animated by a genuine love of nature, and by a sense of the dignity attached to its study, can view with regret anything which promises future additions and a greater degree of perfection to general knowledge (1:xii).

Second, and of far more importance for this chapter, Humboldt was right again in emphasizing the interaction of art and science in any deep appreciation of nature. Therefore Church was absolutely right, as right and as relevant today as in his own time, in his fidelity to natural observation combined with the shaping genius of his imagination. Indeed, I would go further and argue that this vision may be even more important today than in the era of Humboldt and Church. For never before have we been surrounded with such confusion, never with such a drive to narrow specialization, never with such indifference to (or even disdain for) the striving for connection and integration that marks the humanist tradition. Artists dare not hold science in contempt, and scientists will work in a moral and aesthetic desert—a most dangerous place in our age of potentially instant destruction—without art. Yet integration is harder than ever, as jargons divide us and anti-intellectual movements sap our strength. Can we not still find inspiration in the integrative visions of Humboldt and Church?

I will not deny that such integration is more difficult in Darwin's world, a bleaker place, no doubt, than Humboldt's. But in another sense, the very bleakness of Darwin's world points to the right solution, one seen with crystal clarity by Darwin himself. Nature simply is what she is; nature does not exist for our delectation, our moral instruction, or our pleasure. Therefore, nature will not always (or even preferentially) match our hopes. Humboldt asked too much of nature, and pinned too much of his philosophy on a particular outcome. This is a dangerous tactic, for indifferent nature may not supply the answers that our souls seek.

Darwin grasped the philosophical bleakness with his characteristic courage. He argued that hope and morality cannot, and should not, be passively read in the construction of nature. These are human concepts, and must be shaped in human terms, not "discovered" in nature. We must formulate these answers for ourselves and then approach nature as a partner who can answer other kinds of questions for us—questions about the factual state of the universe, not about the meaning of human life. If we grant nature the independence of her domain, her answers unframed in human terms, then we can grasp her exquisite beauty in a freely given way, for we shall be liberated to approach nature without the need for finding inappropriate moral messages to assuage our hopes and fears. We can pay our proper respect to her independence and read her own ways as beauty or inspiration in our different terms. I give the last word to Darwin (diary entry of 16 January 1832), who could not run from the apparent truth of natural selection as a mechanism of change, but who never lost his sense of beauty or his childlike wonder. Darwin stood in the heart of the Andes as he wrote:

> It has been for me a glorious day, like giving to a blind man eyes, he is overwhelmed by what he sees and cannot justly comprehend it. Such are my feelings, and such may they remain.

SUGGESTED READINGS

Aguirre, Robert D. *Informal Empire. Mexico and Central America in Victorian Culture.* Minneapolis: University of Minnesota Press, 2005.

Beardsell, Peter R. *Europe and Latin America: Returning the Gaze.* New York: Manchester University Press, 2000.

Evans, Tripp R. *Romancing the Maya: Mexican Antiquity in the American Imagination, 1820–1915.* Austin: University of Texas Press, 2004.

Fishburn, Evelyn and Eduardo L. Ortiz, eds. *Science and the Creative Imagination in Latin America.* London: Institute for the Study of the Americas, 2005.

Helferich, Gerard. *Humboldt's Cosmos: Alexander von Humboldt and the Latin American Journey that Changed the Way We See the World.* New York: Gotham, 2004.

Manthorne, Katherine. *Tropical Renaissance: North American Artists Exploring Latin America, 1839–1879.* Washington, D.C.: Smithsonian Institution Press, 1989.

Navas Sanz de Santamaría, Pablo. *The Journey of Frederic Edwin Church through Colombia and Ecuador April-October 1853.* Villegas Editores, 2008.

Pike, Fredrick B. *The United States and Latin America: Myths and Stereotypes of Civilization and Nature.* Austin: University of Texas Press, 2009.

Poole, Deborah. "Landscape and the Imperial Subject: U.S. Images of the Andes, 1859–1930," in *Close Encounters of Empire: Writing the Cultural History of U.S.-Latin American Relations,* edited by Gilbert M. Joseph, Catherine C. LeGrand, and Ricardo D. Salvatore, 107–38. Durham: Duke University Press, 1998.

Siemens, Alfred H. *Between the Summit and the Sea: Central Veracruz in the Nineteenth Century*. Vancouver: University of British Columbia Press, 1990.

Sights

The American Travels of Alexander von Humboldt. 1999. Produced by Goethe Institut with the BBC. (2-part series) (FHS).
Art of the Fantastic (Organization of American States, Audiovisual Unit).
The Incas Remembered (World Video).
Fernando de Szyszlo (Organization of American States, Audiovisual Unit).
The Natural World of Latin America. Produced by Radiotelevision Espanola. (11-part series) (FHS).

3

Black Kings, Blackface Carnival, and Nineteenth-Century Origins of the Tango

John Charles Chasteen

Fiesta and music have always been instrumental in the fashioning of identity, whether at the individual, group (gender and ethnic), community, or national level in Latin America. The tango, both the music and the dance, has long been associated with Argentina and its national identity; its powerful rhythms have become the symbol of passion, sensuality, and erotic love. In its conventional appearance it is white, European, and therefore similar to the image of Argentina presented by elites in the late nineteenth century. Yet its origins rest with the black Argentine population, whose existence was ignored in the construction of a national identity. John Charles Chasteen traces how elites appropriated, refashioned, and redefined Carnival music and celebration, especially its original racial characteristics in Buenos Aires, until it became unrecognizable. He tracks tango from its black roots and charts its adoption by whites in twentieth-century working-class dance halls, Parisian salons, and finally white middle-class Argentine living rooms.

The essay invites comparison of Argentine Carnival and its characters with those elsewhere. Readers might consider celebrations of the holiday in its most famous form in Rio de Janeiro, Brazil, in Lisbon, Portugal, or even in Johannesburg, South Africa.[1] *The essay suggests the appearance and reappearance of various stock figures found in different expressions of popular culture. Among them was Juan Moreira, a* gaucho malo *stereotype. Eduardo Gutiérrez first created him in newspaper serials that were quickly reprinted as cheap books. Moreira just as quickly appeared in popular criollo literature, then in pantomime, circus, and, beginning in the 1880s, Carnival. Carnival featured many fashionable disguises, especially of gauchos and their counterparts, the* compadritos, *those rural migrants new to the city. The Argentine* compadrito *was the equivalent of the Mexican* pelado. *By the early years of the twentieth century, the Moreira and the* compadritos *had become stock characters in Carnival processions.*[2] *They danced to the tango with the black kings.*

The modern tango evokes visions of suave urbanity, of dissipated nightlife in formal evening dress, and especially of the slicked-down hair and gleaming smile of Carlos Gardel, international tango idol of the 1920s and 1930s.[3] In the tango, the culture of Buenos Aires seems fully to embody its vaunted Europeanness. And yet, *tango*—a word probably of African origin—once referred to the sort of dancing one did to drums. Originally it was the slaves of Buenos Aires who "attended tangos." But not so fast: Slaves in the South American city most famous for its European heritage? Here is something that has no place in conventional images of Buenos Aires or its famous dance, and yet a quarter of the population of the city was composed of enslaved Africans during the first half of the nineteenth century.[4] Indeed, despite its current European associations, the tango appears to have strong African as well as European antecedents.

Since the 1920s, when it became recognized as an unofficial national symbol in Argentina (and just across the wide estuary called the Río de la Plata, in Uruguay), the tango has been defined by three elements: a music of silences and expressive accentuations; a dance of sudden, dramatic turns and glides; and the biting lyrics of faithless love. Of these, the most distinctive element is the dance, with its turns and glides, its broad theatrical gestures, those close embraces and sultry attitudes. The music of the tango, punctuated with accordion riffs, seems, overall, languidly un-African, although there are moments of rhythmic dynamism—syncopated displacements of the accented beat—that probably do derive from remote African roots. Yet something important seems to be lacking. Where are the regular hip movements that create the rhythmic energy in most dances of African-American inspiration? This chapter examines their disappearance and accounts for the choreography that replaced them, a choreography characterized by exaggeration and attitude.

Here is the nub: exaggerated attitudes are what make the modern tango so recognizable and so notably easy to caricature. In fact, I will argue that the modern tango was created as a caricature, when whites mockingly imitated the dance of blacks. This idea is an old one—suggested as early as 1883—and it is mentioned in passing by all of the serious contemporary scholars who have discussed the origins of the dance.[5] Still, something makes one skeptical about it at first blush. It is hard to imagine just how this mocking imitation might have taken place, in what specific situations whites observed and caricatured black dancing, why they would have done so persistently enough to propagate a full-blown dance genre, and how such a caricature could have become a symbol of Argentine national pride. Nevertheless, the fact is inescapable. By the early twentieth century, the huge majority of the people dancing were white. Mockingly or not, they had taken over as the principal dancers of tangos as the white population of the city moved past the one million mark, boosted by massive immigration from Europe, and the black population dwindled to a few thousand. If the tango was originally a practice of black people, it could only have become a practice of white people through some process of learning by imitation.

If we want to trace the development of the tango, and if *tango* has meant many different things over the years, then we must be specific. For clarity's sake, I will assign year designations to various historical uses of the word *tango*. For example, the tango of 1800 was any sort of dancing that slaves did to drums. That is the place to begin. Our search will take us back to the time when enslaved people from Africa danced together as their principal form of group solidarity on the shores of the great muddy Río de la Plata. Very little evidence about the dancing of black people has survived from this period, so we will have to take advantage of whatever fragments exist. Some of the best ones come from Montevideo, Uruguay, the other major port city of the Río de la Plata.

BLACK KINGS

In the eighteenth century, when large numbers of African slaves arrived in the port cities of Buenos Aires and Montevideo, they organized themselves into groups called nations. These nations—Congos and Angolas, for example—gathered in vacant lots, along the riverbanks, or outside the city walls on Sundays and holidays.[6] There each nation selected a leader whom, much to the distress of the colonial authorities, they called a king; and they danced to distinctive "national" rhythms that identified the group. The black kings did not challenge Spanish rule, and they exercised authority only for specific, mostly ceremonial, purposes within their nation. The nations were defined by their African port of origin in the slave trade, so they did classify people approximately by their region of origin, but individuals of many different tribes and cultural traditions entered into each.[7] The rhythm and dance characteristic of each nation were thus, in some measure, an innovation fashioned out of the ethnic encounter among its members, people who found themselves thrown randomly together but who did feel some communality and who, needing each other, immediately created new signs of collective identity in a familiar African mode, one that often had sacred associations as well. The dances of the black nations remained important as long as people born in Africa figured largely in the black population. As for American-born blacks, they belonged to Catholic lay brotherhoods or mutual aid societies that also danced together. The number of such groups multiplied over time until it reached several dozen in the mid-nineteenth century.[8]

The aggregation of an American-born black population along the Río de la Plata brought another creative refashioning of black dance traditions on a larger scale—a dance form that the members of all of the black nations, brotherhoods, and societies could share. As early as 1789 a Buenos Aires official had observed that some of the dances of slaves were "no longer those of the people among who they had lived" in Africa.[9] Sometimes called tango or tambo, this new "generic" sort of black dancing eventually came to be designated *candombe*, a more specific name for the tango of 1800. Although profoundly significant in the lives of those who danced it, *candombe* was not sacred like the Brazilian *candomblé*, whose name it so much resembled. Rather, it was a social dance in a particularly full meaning of that term. By mid-nineteenth century, *candombe* had replaced the separate dances of nations as the chief dance performed by the followers of black kings in the Río de la Plata.

If the modern tango has African choreographic antecedents, they must have passed through *candombe*. What was this dance like? It is impossible to reconstruct *candombe* precisely. Early nineteenth-century descriptions convey no clear idea of the physical movements involved ("violent movements, ignoble postures, horrifying contortions," specified a typically unhelpful French observer in 1820[10]), and detailed choreographies taken from observation of twentieth-century dancing provide an unreliable guide to earlier centuries. All evidence indicates, at any rate, that *candombe* always involved a hip-driven style of body movement. This can be determined because of the inevitable association of such movement with the other, more easily described aspects of the dance, such as the occurrence of the *ombligada* (when two dancers slap their bellies together), and because a few reliable drawings indicate as much.[11] Later, some form of the Spanish word *quebrar* (break) became a conventional indicator of this movement that broke the straight line of the body at the waist to generate a sinuous, subtle, flowing motion, without bouncing knees or flailing limbs.

Black people sometimes danced secretly—at least insofar as that was possible, given that vigorous percussion was the sine qua non of their activity—but mostly they had spectators. As early as 1760, they were participating in the Corpus Christi procession in Montevideo, as we can tell from the deliberations of the *cabildo*, or city council. Interestingly, the dancers in question were organized through the initiative of a solid citizen, who offered one of his slaves as instructor for the group. A hitch occurred when soldiers scheduled to appear in the procession refused do so alongside black dancers, but the soldiers eventually relented, and the *cabildo* even subsidized the performance by supplying shoes (a contribution that the habitually barefoot dancers must have regarded with ambivalence).[12] Black dancers continued to participate in civic and religious festivals on both sides of the Río de la Plata throughout the colonial period, and that kind of public dancing was important enough to be exempted from the laws that (ineffectively) prohibited black dancing in all other circumstances.[13] The *cabildo*'s attitude is understandable. The participation of slaves and free blacks in civic and religious events signified their successful incorporation into colonial society just as the number of blacks in Buenos Aires and Montevideo rose beyond a quarter of each city's population.[14]

Given the importance of Catholicism in the ideology of colonial rule, the Feast of the Epiphany offered the perfect occasion for black dances that involved kings. In English, the Christmas story speaks of three wise men, but in Spanish they are called the three kings. Because Epiphany commemorates the veneration of Christ by kings who came from afar, the public parading of black kings during the holiday season could be understood—in view of the close association between church and state—as a ritual of submission to colonial authority. Thus, January (and especially the sixth day of the month, called in Spanish the Day of Kings) became a special time for *candombes*. Often the black dancers associated themselves with King Baltazar, who, according to tradition, was black. In Buenos Aires, by the late eighteenth century, the black Brotherhood of San Baltazar was raising money to commemorate Epiphany each year. In the late 1780s and 1790s, their dancing generated problems, petitions, and protests that became a matter of record.[15] Unfortunately, while these documents confirm the importance of black dancing in the period, they give little idea of exactly what went on. An 1827 traveler to Montevideo helps us a little more. On Epiphany of that year, after hearing mass, each black nation processed through the city streets and, arriving at the market square, put on a dance. The traveler, like almost all white observers, was impressed by how absorbed the dancers seemed and how much they enjoyed their dancing. "There," he noted, "more than six hundred blacks appeared to have reclaimed, in an instant, their nationality" and to have forgotten, at least temporarily, the privations and suffering of slavery.[16] This symbolic submission to the Christ Child performed by black kings and their nations drew crowds of white spectators for at least a century.

Black choreographic contributions to rituals of civic jubilation continued after Argentina and Uruguay became independent from Spain. At the height of the struggle for independence, in 1816, the black inhabitants of Montevideo staged a public dance in the main square as part of the patriot-held city's celebration of national independence (not fully consummated for twelve more years).[17] When Argentina's famous populist strongman of the nineteenth century, Juan Manuel de Rosas, took power in Buenos Aires, he gave black dancing a prominent place in public symbolism of his regime. As part of the patriotic May celebrations in 1836, Rosas sponsored a *candombe* in the main plaza that, according to his furious enemies, attracted many thousands of dancers and spectators.[18] "In the years of the Rosas tyranny," explained a newspaper a bit later, black people had a great influence. "They had associations in which they gave weekly or monthly dances, where they got drunk, slipped their traces, and occasionally killed somebody. They got so stuck up that, not content with any vulgar name for these orgies . . . they hit upon the name Academies, which sounded just fine to people so unfamiliar with the dictionary."[19] As a means of garnering their support, Rosas, accompanied by his family, often attended dances of the black nations of Buenos Aires. The dictator's daughter Manuelita even joined in, creating a scandal. A government newspaper had to defend her against the wagging tongues of the regime's enemies: "Manuelita de Rosas shows no reluctance to dance on certain occasions with the honest and hard-working mulattoes, pardos, and morenos."[20]

Black dancing survived the occasional prohibition, not only because it was politically astute of governments to allow it or because the dancers themselves enjoyed it, but also because white spectators liked it. When problems in the San Baltazar festivities led the public prosecutor of Buenos Aires to launch a campaign against black dancing in 1797, the fact that San Baltazar attracted white spectators (and the allegation that it perverted them) constituted part of his brief.[21] A famous description of early nineteenth-century *candombes* in Montevideo emphasized their function as spectacle for the Sunday outings of well-to-do families—the kids always asking for sweets sold by black "aunties" seated on the ground, trays of goodies on their laps. At the words "'We're off to see the Kings,'" wrote the nostalgic memorialist, "the children leapt for joy."[22] An 1862 newspaper calculated that six thousand spectators were on hand for the Epiphany dances in Montevideo that year. One could also visit the houses where the nations or mutual aid societies had their headquarters, doubling as dance halls with a man stationed at the door to take contributions from the spectators.[23]

The black kings of Montevideo and their followers continued to process through the streets, visit the shrine of San Baltazar in the cathedral, and then dance at their headquarters or in the street out front, invariably followed by curious white crowds. These old-style *candombes* continued until about 1875, but then the dancing processions of black kings finally died out. By that time the drums of Epiphany were a thing of the past in Buenos Aires, too.

BLACKFACE CARNIVAL

In the decades after 1850, the black population of Buenos Aires declined precipitously, from around 25 percent to less than 2 percent. The picture is similar, if not quite as drastic, in Montevideo. As the number of blacks fell and the number of whites soared, Afro-Argentines and Afro-Uruguayans became less assertive in their claims to public space, and the members of the younger generation often sought to blend in with white society. As part of this process of assimilation, they increasingly switched their street celebrations by a few weeks—from Epiphany to another holiday, the pre-Lenten Carnival, which usually falls in February. Carnival's important and little-known role in tango history merits a bit of background.

Today nothing is left of Carnival in Buenos Aires, and what remains in Montevideo is a pale reflection of years past. Yet Carnival was once a vibrant popular festival in Buenos Aires—vibrant and popular enough, in fact, to be prohibited by specific royal edict every year but one between 1784 and 1797, despite the best efforts of the government of Buenos Aires to sponsor masked balls so squeaky clean that the most puritanical could not object. In order to convince the Spanish king of the unimpeachable morality of dancing minuets and contradances at the city's masked ball, the city government carefully transcribed sworn testimony from a score of public officials and other important personages who attended. One pointed out, in defense of decency, that only Spaniards were admitted. Most agreed that the abundant illumination in the hall prevented any possible misbehavior. Men were required to remain standing when asking the seated women to dance, and guards outside segregated the dancers who stepped out into the dark to cool off, men to one side, women to the other.[24] All in vain: crown officials soon renewed the ban on Carnival.

After independence, in the 1810s, the street play characteristic of the festival was no longer banned altogether but instead was regulated, and its popular energies were politically harnessed. The detailed regulations published each year on the eve of Carnival stipulated that the costumed groups, called *comparsas*, had to register with the police. They also had to stick together and wear the number of their police registration. The regulations further stipulated that boisterous water fighting (the principal street activity associated with Carnival) could not begin before sunup or last beyond sundown. Passersby not involved in throwing water were to be granted safe conduct through the melee. In fact, however, the populist Rosas regime gave free rein to its partisans during street carnivals. Enemies of the regime who set foot in the streets might be drenched, dusted with flour or ashes, pelted with eggs, or physically assaulted, and they later remembered the drumming of *candombe* as the sinister soundtrack of the 1830s "Rosas Carnivals," their synonym for terror. The figure of the poncho-clad Rosas tussling at street carnival with the rowdy plebeian crowd dismayed the European-oriented, liberal adversaries of Rosas.[25] For several years, Carnival served the dictator's purpose as a bellows to fan the flames of populist protest against the liberal elite. Once Rosas had thoroughly purged his enemies, however, he banned the festival himself (in 1845).

After Rosas was overthrown in 1852, the ban was lifted and street carnival resumed in Buenos Aires, with the Europhile elite now setting the tone of the festivities. The city's theaters cleared away their ground-level seating and offered fancy costume balls for elite revelers. In the streets, water fighting became an adolescent battle of the sexes. Girls heaved water by the saucepanful from balconies, generally aiming at boys. Boys could return fire with hens' eggs—punctured, drained of yoke and white, filled with water, and the puncture plugged with wax—or even (though this was rather heavy ordinance to be aimed at a woman) with the huge eggs of the ostrich-like rhea of the southern grasslands. In 1855 a particularly drastic group of young men somehow laid their hands on a horse-drawn, hand-pumped fire engine and used its squirting hose to strafe the balconies.[26] While these antics dominated public space, Afro-Argentines danced carnival *candombes* in their clubhouses (structures called, among other things, tangos).

A new Carnival diversion began in the mid-1860s, when a *comparsa* of elite males began to parade through the streets with faces blackened as if for a U.S.-style minstrel show, calling themselves "Los Negros." This "Dramatico-Musical Society" included sons of the some of the richest and most powerful families in Buenos Aires. It made its social debut at a stylish private party in 1864, presented its musical act the next year at a public Carnival dance in the prestigious Teatro Colón, and took to the streets at Carnival the year after that. Los Negros established a permanent clubhouse and even printed their own occasional newspaper. In 1869 the paper announced that the membership stood at about fifty, twenty of them musicians.[27] They played both stringed and wind instruments and paraded in pseudomilitary uniforms with white pants and sky-blue jackets, kepis, and knee-length black boots. Their principal occupation was to march around in double file, stopping to play and sing popular airs of the day beneath the windows of young women of good family. Soon they had many imitators. By the 1870s the parading of a succession of uniformed musical groups, very often in blackface, had become a major event of Buenos Aires Carnival. Oblivious to the vulgar throng, the elite youth of Los Negros thought nothing of blocking the street and stopping the parade to serenade a strategic balcony.[28]

These confident young men represented the same elite families who had trembled at the Carnival drumming of Rosista blacks during the 1830s. Now they got a kind of revenge, dramatizing the love of docile, humble black men for their masters' untouchable daughters. Song after song takes up the same theme:

La comparsa de los negros,	The musical group Los Negros,
La más constante y leal,	Most trusty and most true,
A las amitas saluda,	Greets every sweet missy,
En el nuevo carnaval.	To give her this year's due.
Y a las niñas, como esclavos,	And each Negro offers, Missy,
Se ofrece para servir,	Slave in body and in soul,
Esclavos de cuerpo y alma,	To remain your faithful servant,
Y fieles hasta morir.[29]	Until his life is o'er.

And then the chorus: "Oh, white mistresses! For pity's sake hear our sad black voices . . . ." Alhough Carnival revelries can sometimes challenge or subvert the social order, their potential to rationalize and endorse it could hardly be more clearly expressed than in Los Negros's impersonation of blacks abjectly loving whites. Here, in ugly caricature, we confront that strange dimension of tango history: an extended tradition of mocking white impersonation of blacks.

When Buenos Aires whites impersonated blacks, they had two different sources of inspiration. On the one hand, they had real black people around them and had long been attracted to their music and dancing. On the other hand, most people are not very good at mimicking what they see and hear. Ask them to imitate a foreign accent, and you will get a very secondhand version of it. They will, in effect, try to reproduce imitations they have heard elsewhere, imitations that have been made memorable by selection and exaggeration. No doubt a few whites with particular skill and exposure to black speech, music, and dance did passable impersonations. For the most part, however, groups like Los Negros were not directly imitating Afro-Argentines at all. They were representing not black people but their idea of black people, molded and caricatured to serve their own emotional needs; drawing, too, on preexisting caricatures of blackness.

Impersonation of black music, dance, and speech had been happening in Spain since the sixteenth century. The great Golden Age playwright Lope de Vega has a play with a part scripted for dancers disguised as blacks. There was even a conventional mock-black dialect used by blackface actors in the Spanish-language theater. U.S. popular culture also had a clear influence. The elite of Buenos Aires was well aware of the minstrel show's popularity in the United States, and they had an opportunity to see the minstrel version of *Uncle Tom's Cabin* performed in Spanish adaptation as early as 1856. In fact, a series of theatrical tours visited Buenos Aires in the late 1860s, just as Los Negros began to transform street carnival there. In 1867 the city celebrated a Panamanian actor's impersonation of a black broom-seller, Negro Schicoba. And Louis Moreau Gottschalk, the Louisiana Creole pianist famous for his Afro-Cuban motifs, began an extended stay that same year. In 1868, theatergoers in Buenos Aires heard a U.S. minstrel performer render Stephen Foster songs in blackface to banjo accompaniment.[30] The next year the famous Christy Minstrels began a long tour of the area, inspiring one enthusiastic reviewer to write that "the blacks of Buenos Aires should learn to be blacks from the Christy Minstrels."[31] If *comparsas* like Los Negros were reacting against Rosista populism and drawing on Spanish theatrical traditions, they were also responding to a sense of international vogue.

Mocking representations of blackness were a dime a dozen in the mid-nineteenth century. Even real black people got in on this act. Real black people believed, understandably, that they could beat the phony ones at the game of representing blackness, and soon (by 1870) Buenos Aires blacks were mirroring white imitations of blacks—their uniforms, their serenades, even the mock-black dialect of the lyrics—all except for their obsessive theme of blacks loving white women. Because of strong traditions of black musicianship, the real black *comparsas* presented a formidable challenge to the white ones in blackface.

Not to be outdone, the blackface groups changed tactics and "went African," so to speak. Instead of military uniforms, they dressed as slaves or even as "savages" in imitation leopard skins and something like black tights, and they put on a full-scale satire of a *candombe*, including royalty and featuring percussion rather than the stringed instruments used by *comparsas* like Los Negros. Unlike the uniformed musical *comparsas*, these new groups more or less danced during their street performances. That is, they did a mocking imitation that was meant to represent—but was very far from really replicating—the elaborate choreography of early nineteenth-century *candombes*. Their repertoire as well grew less romantic and more satirical. The new groups were called *candomberos*, and there would be no Carnival without them for the rest of the century.[32]

But if the white *candomberos* thought they could triumph so easily, they were soon disappointed. By 1882, real black people were parading as *candomberos* too. Perhaps this is not surprising. Most interesting of all, the black *candomberos* made a point of not really dancing a *candombe* (which, though moribund, did still exist). Rather, in order to make plain that their *candombes* were not the authentic article—to signify that they were not experiencing blackness, so to speak, but performing it—the black *candomberos* wore blackface.[33]

Now, the complexion of many of the black *candomberos* was not very dark. Afro-Argentine males had always been overrepresented in the army, and so many died there that black women often had to find lighter-skinned partners. The black population of Buenos Aires was fading, partly through a decline in absolute numbers, partly due to the influx of European immigrants, and partly because some descendants of slaves were losing a black identity. Black *candomberos* reclaimed that identity in an ironic mode. In darkening their faces, black *candomberos* were quite explicitly imitating those who imitated them, and they must have done so with mocking intentions of their own. If the white *candomberos* wanted to make the blacks look silly, the black *candomberos* wanted to make the whites look pathetic. No doubt both succeeded. At any rate, by the end of the nineteenth century, the people of Buenos Aires—whites and blacks—had become quite accustomed to the notion of performing blackness, and the standard form of this performance was most assuredly a mocking imitation.

But is there a direct connection between Carnival blackface and the modern tango? Neither the musical *comparsas* of Los Negros's ilk nor the extravagant dramatizations of the *candomberos* involved couple dancing. Nor did their music have a characteristic tango rhythm. Their varied repertoire included waltzes, polkas, and other music performed in a straight, "white" style. They sang such music "out of character," apparently, then reverted to their performance of blackness for the songs that had mocking intentions made crystal clear by the lyrics in theatrical black dialect. But here is the link: When blackface Carnival groups moved back into character to present one of their familiar caricatures, it was invariably called a tango.

Any mocking musical impersonation of blackness was called a tango by about 1860. A leading author of Carnival blackface compositions was referring to this tango of 1860, as we can call it, when he wrote in his memoirs about transformations in Buenos Aires musical culture during the third quarter of the nineteenth century: "Tastes changed, and from romances and operatic arias, we went to . . . tangos! Black music had its great success at that time."[34]

Published lyrics from the period show that musical *comparsas* used the word *tango* only for the songs with lyrics in mock dialect, and this is the meaning specified by the entry under tango in a Madrid dictionary of the 1850s: "a song with black slang."[35] When the Spanish touring company presented its adaptation of *Uncle Tom's Cabin*, its blackface chorus sang "tangos." When Germán MacKay—the Panamanian blackface actor who presented El Negro Schicoba—sang his mock-dialect songs about liking to dance and making the girls blush, it was called a tango.[36] Apparently these tangos were derived musically from the Afro-Cuban *habanera*—a staple of Spanish touring companies in their performances throughout Spanish America by the 1850s.

Afro-Argentines, for their part, shaped these tangos in the performances of their Carnival *comparsas*. (Not all black Carnival paraders were *candomberos*, by any means. The city's black press deplored the *candomberos* and endorsed the more refined *comparsas*.) Compare the following *comparsa* lyrics printed by a newspaper of the black community of Buenos Aires in 1880:

Pedimos al que se digne	We ask those who lend an ear
Nuestro humilde eco escuchar	To the humble echo of our song,
Indulgencia, gratitud,	For indulgence, gratitude
Y constancia en el amar.[37]	And constancy in their love.

Such were the lyrics of a locally composed mazurka, almost certainly the work of an Afro-Argentine musician or poet, and their waltzes or polkas would sound similar. The words of a tango, on the other hand, went more like this:

Vamo a cantá, negrita,	Let's sing, my dark one,
Pur cierto,	Oh yeah,
Nuestro tango popular.[38]	Our tango from down home.

This, in fact, was the newspaper's theme tango. The next year, the black *comparsa* called Society of Humble Negroes presented a mazurka, a waltz, and a toast, all in standard Spanish, and two tangos, both in mock dialect.[39] The word *tango* now denoted, above all, an explicit representation of black identity.

THE "CUT-AND-BREAK" DANCE

A crude drawing of a stage tango performed as a couple dance was published in 1882. The man and woman face one another (as in *candombe*) and do not touch. This is the first evidence of the word *tango* used for a couple dance.[40] We have a more helpful (although insufferably snickering) description of the same dance from a Spanish traveler who visited the headquarters of Montevideo's Congo Nation in 1874: "A jet-hued gentleman rises ceremoniously and issues an invitation to some young lady the color of ripe blackberries, usually as correctly seated and as modestly dressed as any debutante recently presented to polite society." Taking his arm, the señorita looks back to see that the train of her gown is correctly stretched out behind her, and the two go to the center of the room, where they face each other a few yards apart. Hands on hips, the two then inch toward each other with undulating body motions and only small movements of the feet. These dancers—who were not imitating anybody—still called this dance *candombe*.[41] Far different from the street dances of half a century earlier, this was the living *candombe* that the blackface *candomberos* mocked (exaggerating some of the movements and missing others completely) while singing something droll in mock-black dialect. Done in mocking imitation, it became a tango.

The characteristic profile of modern tango choreography finally emerged from an encounter between *candombe* moves and the closed-couple choreography of the international ballroom repertoire. As *candombe* withered into a conventional courtship dance during the second half of the nineteenth century, Afro-Argentine and Afro-Uruguayan young people became interested in closed-couple dances (in which the dancers put their arms around one another), such as the polka, mazurka, and especially the *habanera*. Nevertheless, these young people could still do the *candombe* moves. For one thing, *candombe* remained a traditional first number at dances in the black community. For another, the hip-driven undulations of *candombe* easily merged with the closed-couple choreography of *habanera*, which appears to have been the most popular dance at black parties and in various other settings where black people danced in the 1880s.[42]

Because Cuban slaves (not liberated until 1886) consumed a lot of jerked beef from the Río de la Plata, a steady shipping trade linked Havana with Buenos Aires and Montevideo. According to myth, Cuban sailors taught *habanera* during their uproarious shore leaves in the red-light districts of the southern ports. While plausible, there is little evidence for this form of cultural diffusion (but no question about the influence, already mentioned, of touring musical theater).[43]

From whatever precise combination of influences, a flashy new style of closed-couple dancing, distinctive to the Río de la Plata and clearly recognizable as the choreographic antecedent of the contemporary tango, existed by 1890. Its most descriptive name was *baile de corte y quebrada*, or "cut-and-break" dance, referring to its sudden "cuts" (stops and turns) and "breaks" (swiveling movements). Another name was *milonga*. Then, by the first years of the twentieth century, the dance got its modern name. This was the tango of 1900.

Call it tango or *milonga*, cut-and-break dancing was not for everyone. The 1890 *Dictionary of Argentine Expressions* specified that *milonga* was "a dance found only among people of the lower orders."[44] Cut-and-break technique required that the dancing couple enter close bodily contact—something not allowed at middle-class gatherings, where standard decorum required that "light be visible" between the partners—and thus cut-and-break dancing developed in settings where middle-class proprieties could be flaunted with impunity. Gatherings of poor people in neighborhoods on the outskirts of Buenos Aires and Montevideo constituted one such situation, and this is why those neighborhoods and their inhabitants figure so largely in tango lore. "Around the edge of town," wrote a local observer of Buenos Aires in 1883, "the *milonga* has become so common that today it is obligatory at all third-rate dances graced by guitar, accordion, and kazoo."[45] In the center of both cities, large old houses subdivided into many tiny rooms—*conventillos*—sometimes housed hundreds of poor immigrants who were possible aspirants to this dance culture. There was little room to dance in a *conventillo*, but *conventillo* dwellers might flaunt their skills in cut-and-break dancing on street corners where organ grinders cranked out mazurkas, *habaneras*, or *milongas*.[46]

And, of course, close bodily contact was the order of the day in those most notorious sites of tango lore, the brothels that abounded in the port and market districts and around barracks in both Buenos Aires and Montevideo. Then there were the dance halls, called academies, where women were paid for each song danced, and finally the cafés—the Dovecote, the Mill, the Poor Devil, and so on—located physically in centers of active nightlife and functionally somewhere between brothels and dance halls. The brothels, cafés, and dance halls played an important role in tango history because they facilitated encounters between people of contrasting social class—especially between poor women and their better-off customers, but also between males of unequal status, from slumming aristocrats to small-time punks.[47]

Descriptions of cut-and-break dancing in any of these places usually present it as a way for a man to show off, a display of ability and attitude. The San Felipe Academy (dance hall) of Montevideo, located near the stretch of ground where black nations had assembled for *candombes* earlier in the century, became a famous venue for the *milonga*. We have a full description by someone who visited shortly before it closed in 1899. Dancing shook this tin-roofed structure of wood, lit by kerosene and adorned by streamers, until nearly dawn. It had no tables—only a raised stage for the band, benches around the walls for the women (who were hardly wallflowers, however), and wooden bleachers for male spectators. The women were poor, but the male crowd was mixed, including unequaled virtuosos (who were usually black) as well as knife-carrying toughs from poor neighborhoods and wide-eyed gentlemen from "decent" ones. Many of the fellows who went slumming at San Felipe were young, no doubt, and most seem to have felt themselves distinctly inadequate compared to their *milonga*-wise social inferiors. Our witness assures us that most men in attendance never danced at all but only watched, and tried a bit of "cutting and breaking" later, in front of a bedroom mirror.[48]

In the first years of the twentieth century, more and more middle-class men learned to tango. Gradually middle-class women learned too, especially when their husbands or brothers showed them a few steps they had picked up here and there in situations better left unspecified. But this was still nothing that any of them would do in "polite" company or at a "decent" house. The rapidly rising general interest in the infamous choreographic creation of the city's late-night misbehavers was expressed instead at public Carnival dances, when even middle-class people could flaunt propriety. "This seems to be the carnival of tangos and cheap dances," reported a Buenos Aires newspaper in 1903.[49] "One could say that the creole tango has been glorified in this year's carnival," according to the illustrated magazine *Caras y Caretas* the following year.[50] But the tango of 1900 was to be no passing fad. The dance of Buenos Aires brothels had been launched on the path to international celebrity.

Polite society of Buenos Aires resisted the tango until Parisians with a taste for the exotic embraced the dance on the eve of World War I and lent it their prestige. This stylized version of the dance finally won total acceptance in Buenos Aires upon its return home from Paris, and it also established a formal model still disseminated today in international ballroom dance competitions. The tango of 1900 had been bleached and ironed during its stay in Paris, its funkiness and hunched shoulders replaced by languid glides and pointed toes. It had become the "smooth" tango, the modern tango that comes to mind when we think of the dance today. During the 1920s and 1930s, it was finally embraced at all social levels back home in Argentina and Uruguay, too.

TRACES

What aspects of African dance tradition are clearly preserved in the modern tango? Few indeed. Some have suggested that the fluid striding of modern tango dancers across the floor recalls a promenade segment of *candombe* choreography. Others have proposed that African influences are responsible for the relative independence of movement between the dancers' upper and lower bodies. Still, casual observers of the modern tango find little to remind them of other dances created by slaves and their descendants throughout the Americas, dances that, while varied, nevertheless reveal clearly the dancers' family relationship and their African roots.

The tango is danced today in Argentina and Uruguay (though much less than half a century ago) and around the world, especially in Finland and Japan, but for the last century it has not been a dance of people of African descent. Contrary to the old racist notion, people of African descent do not have rhythm in their bones, but they often do have rhythm in their culture. Rhythmic complexity characterizes the music of the African diaspora, and dance holds a central place in the social life of the people who cultivate that music. As we have seen, the tango of 1800 was danced exclusively by black people, and it looked and sounded like African-American dances from all over the hemisphere, but the decline of the black population of the Río de la Plata after 1850 gradually removed polyrhythmic complexity from the performance of tangos. The smooth tango, back from Paris, seems to have lost polyrhythm altogether.

So, can it be said that the contemporary languid, gliding tango has African roots? Although appealing, the roots metaphor is misleading. Dance is a practice, not a vegetable. If we improve the question, asking what influence the dance practices of Río de la Plata blacks had on the evolution of the tango of 1900, the answer is, a very great influence. The blacks of the Río de la Plata stood out as musicians and dancers throughout the nineteenth century, attracting white spectators and becoming the object of routine imitation by whites. For about half a century before 1900, the word *tango* denoted not a step or a rhythm at all, but a mood, an attitude, an intention. To tango meant to dance black, whether in the spasmodic caperings of white *candomberos* or in the Afro-Argentine renderings of the standard ballroom repertoire performed tongue-in-cheek at a private dance. Cut-and-break choreography also had a heavy dose of posturing and attitude.

The subsequent international career of the dance has further effaced its African origins while accentuating the trace of caricature: those exaggerated gestures and attitudes that express a peculiar mixture of desire and hostility. Among twentieth-century dancers, the object of those contradictory impulses seems to be the dance partner, so that tango attitudes and gestures express a familiar tension in gender relations. Could this tension—perhaps the most distinctive dimension of the tango—result from a displacement of mixed feelings generated in nineteenth-century race relations?

SUGGESTED READINGS

Andrews, George Reid. *Afro-Argentines of Buenos Aires, 1800–1900*. Madison: University of Wisconsin Press, 1980.

Bergero, Adrana J., ed. *Intersecting Tango: Cultural Geographies of Buenos Aires, 1900–1930*. Pittsburgh: University of Pittsburgh Press, 2008.

Castro, Donald S. *The Argentine Tango as Social History, 1880–1955*. Lewiston, ME: E. Mellon Press, 1991.

Collier, Simon. *The Life, Music and Times of Carlos Gardel*. Pittsburgh: University of Pittsburgh Press, 1986.

Goldman, Gustavo. *Lucamba: Herencia Africana en el tango, 1870–1890*. Montevideo: Perro Andaluz Ediciones, 2008.

Guy, Donna J. *Sex and Danger in Buenos Aires: Prostitution, Family and Nation in Argentina*. Lincoln: University of Nebraska Press, 1991.

Lewis, Marvin A. *Afro-Argentine Discourse: Another Dimension of the Black Diaspora*. Columbia: University of Missouri Press, 1996.

Savigliano, Marta. *Tango and the Political Economy of Passion*. Boulder, CO: Westview Press, 1995.

Sights

Afroargentinos. 2003. Directed by Diego Ceballos and Jose Antonio Fortes.
El Día Que Me Quieras. 1986. Directed by John Reinhardt (Facets Multimedia).
Forever Tango: Live from the Teatro Coliseo Podesta, DPTV Media, 2008.
The Tango. 1998. Directed by Carlos Saura.
Tango: Baile Nuestro. 1988. Directed by Jorge Zanada (Facets Multimedia).
Tango Bar. 1935. Directed by John Reinhardt (Facets Multimedia).
El Tango en Broadway. 1994. Directed by Louis Gasnier (Facets Multimedia).

Sounds

Africa en América: Música de 19 países. Discos Corazón, 1992.
Piazolla, Astor. *Tango: Zero Hour*. Nonesuch Records.
Quinteto Pirincho. *Las Milongas mas Milongas*. EMI Europe Generic.

WEBSITE

http://www.todotango.com

4

"'Cartas y cartas, compadre. . . .': Love and Other Letters from Río Frío"

William E. French

No more artificial divide exists in discussions of nineteenth-century Latin America than the one created by historians and other scholars between literate and nonliterate peoples. In fact, those who could read read to those who could not, or told others about books and talked about newspapers and broadsheets. Those who could write incorporated, interpolated, and inserted oral traditions into their written accounts. Fiestas, such as Carnival, included individuals in costumes from fiction and nonfiction and other dramatizations by puppets, actors, and street-corner performers who had brought to life the written world. Moreover, those who could not write still sent informative messages, business updates, and passionate letters to lovers, associates, and family, many of whom could not read. Public scribes wrote epistles and, if necessary, read them as well. It is this relationship of a culture shared by those who could read and those who could not that William French explores at the intersection of literary and oral traditions brought together in the novel Bandits of the Río Frío *(1889–1891). This novel represents Mexico in the genre created by Italy's national romance classic, Alessandro Manzoni's* The Betrothed *(1827) and historical fiction initiated by Walter Scott's* Ivanhoe *(1819). Manuel Payno's work focuses on Mexican life, with its everyday traditions, stereotypical individuals, and political disruptions of the first half century after independence in 1821. It first appeared in serial form, and Bill French adopts the style for his essay, and in the standard cliff-hanger, leaves the reader eager to read his next installment.*

It would probably have come as little surprise to Manuel Payno, author of *Los bandidos de Río Frío*, a novel published in monthly installments in periodicals as it was written between 1889 and 1891, that artisans, mine workers, and other rural folk in Porfirian Mexico would be exchanging love letters.[1] Payno's inclusion of love letters in this novel, including those supposedly penned by plebeians, makes it an especially useful starting place for thinking about the relationship between writing and courtship, while allowing me, as well, to situate the writing of love letters within the broader reading and writing practices of the time, even novelistic and imaginary ones. Beginning here also helps to remind us that the novel, especially a sentimental novel like this one, and the letter, along with other forms of writing, could share many similarities, including the privileging of emotion, an emphasis on self-reflexivity and introspection, forms of narrative and emplotment, and the writing into being of a certain kind of subjectivity, both of self and other. Both the novel and the letter could be intertextual and dialogic, a conversation between a self and a presumed reader who is often even addressed directly and whose reaction is imagined or anticipated. I read *Los bandidos de Río Frío* through a particular lens—one shaped by years of engagement with actual love letters exchanged among common folk contemporaneous with this novel, letters that I located in judicial archives in Chihuahua, many of which were provided to judicial officials as proof of a written promise of marriage in cases dealing with certain practices that were criminalized in an attempt to uphold what the legal code described as the "good order of families." I am not arguing that the letters imagined into being in this novel reflected actual writing practices or that they served as a model for them.[2] I am hoping, though, that an engagement with elite daydreams about universal literacy will help illustrate not merely the centrality of writing as one's passport into the lettered city, but also the close relationship between literacy and orality as well as how, in place of one city and one literacy, the idea of many different neighborhoods, each with different "literacies," might better describe the geography of the lettered city.[3]

Los bandidos de Río Frío lends itself to many readings.[4] A potboiler that kept people on the edge of their seats waiting for more; an imaginative yarn based on true crimes and real events in the history of the republic; a foundational fiction whose characters knit Mexicans together both through their common speech, customs, and habits and in their movements across the range and breadth of the country; a meditation on the past and the future, through an insistent focus on inheritance, legacy, birthright, destiny and fate, both of the characters that tramp across its pages as well as the country they inhabit; and, it seems, the very embodiment of Angel Rama's argument concerning the incorporation of rural orality into the service of the lettered city, the novel is all that and perhaps more.[5] Implicated in, if not central to, all these readings is literacy, or literacies, manifested not only in Payno's preoccupation with charting the myriad ways that Mexicans of all classes in the nineteenth century participated in various reading and writing practices but also in his incorporation of the predominant genres of writing of the time, especially those associated with the newspaper, the legal system, and the letter, among others, into the novel itself.

As Payno's explicit concern is with forms of writing, the conventions and understandings associated with them, and the transformations they were undergoing, it is not by accident that the novel is littered with *letrados*. Three lawyers serve as main characters, moving the plot along by means of their activities while providing Payno with a pretext to include extensive discussions of the reading and writing practices associated with criminal investigations, other legal proceedings, the exchange of letters, political pronouncements, love notes, and the reporting of all such activities in a burgeoning press. The novel begins with a newspaper report of a cause célèbre, a criminal case concerning the sensational murder of a woman by her *novio* or intended, one that generated two thousand pages of legal testimony and supporting documents gathered into three large *expedientes*, and ends with a letter supposedly written to the author, belittling his writing ability while filling in the reader on the fates of the many characters in an imagined future that has supposedly taken place since the end of the events covered in the novel itself. In between, one lawyer, Bedolla, who becomes a criminal judge responsible for protecting "the honor of families" and presiding over the kinds of crimes against the good order of families I mentioned in the introductory paragraph, gains and loses political influence on the basis of his own incompetence in handling the criminal case that begins the novel while another, Lamparilla, searches for the legal documents that will prove that his client, Moctezuma III, is the legal heir to extensive properties and haciendas, a patrimony that has been denied to him. A third, Olañeta, uncovers the errors or helps resolve the work of the previous two, protecting the various protagonists at the same time; it is Olañeta, as well, who finally brings the entire criminal conspiracy from which the novel takes its title to an end, a task he accomplishes while simultaneously engaged in an inner struggle, that often takes place in his library, between his romantic feelings, or what he refers to as fleeting sentiments, on the one hand, and his learning, the timeless wisdom gleaned through hours of engagement with the yellowed parchment of his books, on the other. All the while, an increasingly sensationalist press trumpets these and other events in newspaper articles and anonymous broadsides to a growing public that its very activity of publishing is helping to bring into being.

The presence of such a public, or publics, in the novel, recognizing themselves in the newspapers and becoming aware of and judging the actions of similarly positioned readers, now fellow constituents at the court of public opinion and members of an expanding public sphere, makes apparent that *letrados* were not the only ones engaging with the written word. In fact, Payno takes great care to spell out the reading and writing abilities of almost every character, regardless of whether they are lawyers, members of the aristocracy, or the humblest of his characters. Whereas characters of higher social standing are often portrayed ensconced in their libraries, adept at manipulating the forms and formulas of literate society, those from the popular classes are almost always shown as in the process of learning to read and write (if they don't already know how to do so), incipient or potential, if not already fully, residents of the lettered city.

As a result, scenes of reading and writing, especially associated with the teaching of literacy, abound in the novel. A poor boy, finding himself a servant in Olañeta's home after being abandoned in a garbage dump, rescued, and then subsequently running away from the lathe turner to whom he had been apprenticed, is seen diligently applying himself to "reading and writing Spanish grammar in the library"[6] under the kindly lawyer's supervision, the continuation of an education that began with informal lessons in reading and math in the marketplace and during his stint in the poorhouse. (Readers themselves are ushered off to the library to read about the history of this institution![7]) Two rural *curanderas* responsible for his abduction, and more often than not likely to be cast at the time as the epitome of rural, feminine ignorance and superstition, perfect foils to urban, male medical knowledge, instead exchange curative roots and herbs with a schoolteacher at a nearby municipal school for women in return for lessons from a spelling book, a transaction that takes place on the street corner where they sell their wares. Another woman, the cook in the house of one of the main criminal masterminds in the latter part of the novel, seals the legal fate of this character by including as part of the recipes she writes into her recipe book the detailed evidence that she has incriminating him. As for Moctezuma III, heir to the patrimony of his ancestors and resident on a rural ranch far from the city, Payno states, "Of course he knew how to read, and he wrote in a stubby but completely legible hand."[8]

Comfortably situated within the genre of the foundational fiction, that novel of nineteenth-century Latin America that crafted the nation discursively by bringing together love of country and romantic love in mutually reinforcing allegory, *Los bandidos* clearly links literacy with national imagining.[9] Here, all characters are literally reading on the same page of the novel of the nation; likewise, they experience the passage of the time as national time, that is, simultaneously, something achieved not only by means of the form of the novel itself but also through its intertextuality, that is, the inclusion of letters and newspaper articles (even the original manuscript of the Enabling Act of the Republic hanging in a gold frame is featured, should Payno's point about writing the nation into existence be missed).[10] At critical junctures in the novel, however, the bricks and mortar of the lettered city—those legal documents, wills, marriage banns, deeds, newspapers, and letters plastered into its pages—are revealed as little more than a crumbling façade through which can be seen the way things really work. The character

Bedolla, for example, law degree in hand and serving in the esteemed position of criminal judge, regards the documents generated by the criminal justice system, the declarations, the testimonies, the evidence, as so much blather (*mucha paja*). Having gained the ear of the President of the Republic, he owes his influence to his sycophancy rather than to his wisdom or education, which he has completed, as Payno puts it, "without managing either to read with punctuation or to write even a single line without misspellings."[11] It is likewise this same Bedolla ("who didn't write and who, as a matter of fact, had never been able to piece two sentences together"[12]), who came to control the supposedly independent capitaline press. As for Lamparilla, one of the other lawyers, all the legal deeds and certified documents in the world are not sufficient to recover Moctezuma III's lost patrimony—it is only through making use of important personal connections in the judicial system along with applying brute force, the seizure of these lands by means of force of arms, that this is accomplished.

Just as the forms of the lettered city are not always sufficient for the task at hand, the written word itself is often found wanting and gives way to orality or the spoken word in various places in the novel. Even as the servant Juan puts his new knowledge of literacy to use by reading about himself in the newspaper delivered to the home where he works, the lawyer who is teaching him to read learns the truth about Juan's past when he overhears a conversation taking place in the kitchen, allowing him to chart a different destiny for the boy (although, simultaneously, clearly linking orality with the feminine and spaces such as the kitchen, and reading with the masculine, especially in such venues as the library).[13] Similarly, although the main criminal mastermind, a man known as Relumbrón (the glittering one or Flash), is assured of criminal prosecution because of evidence written on recipe cards, it is only by means of eavesdropping on the conversation between this figure and his father that the cook has managed to gather such detailed information in the first place.[14] Referring to yet another character, a member of the aristocracy, the lawyer Oñate describes him as a person whose word is as good as a written contract.

More than simply a convenient device for moving the plot along or resolving actions, the centrality of orality at various points in the story serves rather to highlight the profound engagement between the written and spoken word that takes place in the novel more generally. It is not by chance that the novel is often described as being "chatty" in tone—in fact, it is as much a conversation with the reader in written form as it is a novel, a point the author, as well as his critics, makes. At many places in the text, the reader ("patient and curious") is interpellated and directly addressed (as she is in this chapter), at certain times to be asked for forgiveness, at others to be assured of the truthfulness of the tale, and, at still others, to have the novel's purpose explained to them.[15] Moreover, along with national customs and national types, typical Mexican popular expressions and manners of speaking are incorporated into the text, allowing readers at the time to see in written form what they might hear in the streets in their everyday activities. In this regard, the novel itself is similar not only to many of the fictitious letters included in it but also to written correspondence more generally. The novel, written in monthly installments and published in the press, as well as marriage banns, wills, and letters could be (and were) read out loud, often to those whose levels of literacy precluded a solitary reading. In fact, the properties of the novel that resonated with listeners have proven particularly enduring, as *Los bandidos* was still being read to children in Mexico a century after its writing.[16]

Payno's focus on customs, costumes, and the quotidian, especially forms of speech, and the conversational tone adopted in the novel itself seem as much designed to critique the conventions of the lettered city as they do to capture orality in its service; at the very least, Payno, with his writing choices, brings into question, perhaps even breaks down, the sharp distinction usually posited to exist between these two realms. A number of hybrid forms of text are presented, in which, much as in the novel itself, the spoken and the written, literate and popular, are interfused. Near the beginning of the novel, for example, the written portion of an ex-votive image (itself an example of a genre that represents the coming together of written and pictorial forms), usually composed to give thanks for divine intervention, instead mocks the inability of a highly trained doctor from Mexico City's prestigious medical academy to cure a rural patient, a woman who had been pregnant for eleven months.[17] As we have already mentioned, a humble cook writes out recipes that result in Relumbrón's just desserts. Barbers and other tradesmen know of crimes because of the newspapers they have read or the broadsheets they have heard hawked in the streets. The use of double-entry accounting is mocked when it is used by elite passengers to tally up the supposed benefits of having been robbed rather than their losses ("the numbers don't lie" states one of the book's robbery victims, or perhaps better, "beneficiaries," according to the new method of reckoning).[18] At the heart of the book, rather than separating the *letrados* from the unlettered and isolating the threats to civilization in the barbarous wilderness inhabited by the illiterate in Río Frío, is Payno's vision that, perhaps, Río Frío is not so very far from the capital, that supposedly respected and well-off residents in Mexico City, at the center of the lettered city, can be corrupted by money and the developmentalist version of progress (as implied by the name of the criminal mastermind, Relumbrón, or "Flash"). Although it might be argued that this is only accomplished by making all Mexicans potentially residents of the lettered city, it is a lettered city in which the new neighbors are loud, boisterous, and unruly.

One of the forms of writing in the novel that Payno identifies as increasingly characterized by the intermingling of the written and spoken word is the letter, especially that associated with love. While in the novel, letters of all kinds, formal and informal, genuine and forged, are central to carrying out business, both of the aboveboard and Río Frío variety, as well as to arranging everything from matters of state to those of family, it is the love letter, penned by men and women, from the most aristocratic to the most humble, that makes possible relationships that transcend social barriers, even if only with difficulties. Here, Payno's point seems to be that the heart cannot be controlled, that love, when it strikes, is blind to barriers of social class, status, and age. It is through love letters, for example, that the son of a hacienda overseer and the daughter of the most wealthy and conservative aristocratic family can aspire to, and finally succeed in forging, a life together. Another main character from the popular classes, Cecilia, receives love letters, read into the text of the novel by one of Cecilia's suitors, the lawyer Lamparilla, from men located on various rungs of the social ladder, ranging from a humble butcher to a small-store owner/black marketeer, the district's political chief, and, finally, the wealthy son of one of the region's largest hacienda owners.

If all lovers, like all countrymen, were joined by their common ability to dominate the written word, if not their hearts, the meanings and understandings associated with both the writing of love letters and their exchange could vary. For those with only the most tenuous grasp of the written word, letters, according to Payno, rather than serving as an integral aspect of courtship, usually followed it. Addressed to the head of the woman's household instead of exchanged between the courting couple, such letters pleaded for forgiveness for an act already past, the unauthorized abduction of the woman from her household, or a *rapto,* rather than planned for a future one, that of formal marriage. Forgoing in this manner the written trappings of official family formation (the banns, the certificates), an omission that Payno characterizes as laziness and that results in the formation of a couple in every sense except the formal one, an engagement with writing is, nevertheless, maintained.[19] For most other courting couples in the novel, love letters themselves are essential, either to develop the courtship itself or to overcome the distance and circumstances that make it impossible for the couple to communicate in any other manner. In this courting correspondence, as in other cases of letter writing found in the novel, the written word generally, and letters, specifically, are assumed to reveal the fundamental characteristics or qualities of those writing them. Commenting on the letters he is exchanging with the Marquis of Sauz holding him to his previous promise to marry the aristocrat's daughter, the suitor—highly honorable, yet presently impoverished—remarks that each letter corresponded to the true character or nature of the person writing it. While the aristocrat's letter revealed his harsh and snobbish character, the suitor's frank and likable disposition was immediately apparent simply by reading his response.[20]

In a similar manner, the love letters written to Cecilia, mentioned above, offer direct access to the inner character, qualities, and even the social standing of those composing them. That from the butcher, written on business stationery from the "Dwarf's Bacon Shop, of the great city of Chalco," seems to conjure, out of the form and content of his missive, the very letter writer himself. The fat and twisted letters scrawled on the yellow-tinged stationery smelling of butchered hogs; the misspelled words; the rendering into written form of an essentially spoken Spanish ("pamí" instead of "para mí," "quentra" instead of "que entra," "mitá" in place of "mitad"); the sexual innuendo and double entendre; and the concern with demonstrating economic resources sufficient to undertake marriage along with his embarrassment at approaching the subject directly, in face-to-face conversation, not only rehearse the butcher's character but offer a visual, aural, and even olfactory portrait of its writer and perhaps of stereotypes of the artisan world at the same time.[21] So, too, does Payno manage to capture, not only with this letter, but also in the discussion of Cecilia's entire correspondence, the fundamental situatedness, one within the other, of the written and the oral. As Cecilia explains, she keeps the love letters in order to have them as proof or evidence should some busybody want to talk about her; as such, and apart from their content, they are physical tokens to be deployed in an oral public sphere in which respectability and reputation are asserted and contested through such means as gossip. She also gives her word, and keeps it, that she will marry Lamparilla, the lawyer courting her, only once he has triumphed in his legal quest to obtain formal written title to the lands claimed by Moctezuma III. Along with many of the characters in the novel, Cecilia not only negotiates in matters of the heart but over the very manner in which, orally or in writing, such transactions are to take place.

While the love letters from those suitors higher up the social ladder may be less colloquial than that of the butcher, they are no less revealing. The letter from the local political prefect, for example, on glossy paper newly imported from Paris expressly for the purpose of the writing of love letters, came emblazoned with a little Cupid furiously shooting his arrows at a fat heart and looking more like a street urchin than the symbol of love; its prose exposed him to be similarly badly formed—a hypocrite as well as a bully, the prefect reveals himself in the letter as a man accustomed to getting his way by means of the arbitrary exercise of authority while simultaneously terrified by the powerful hold a woman had over him.[22] By contrast, that written by the storeowner was steeped in the gendered values of middle-class respectability, its concern with frankness in manners of speech, its preoccupation with reputation and honor, both his own and those of the object of his affection, and its attention to propriety. It has little to say about love, envisioning their marriage instead as a business partnership in which the pooling of resources would lead to ever more lucrative dealings, both in the store and in his sideline business of running contraband alcohol. Framed in terms of rational self-interest rather than as an appeal to emotion, the bargain as set out in this letter nevertheless included the expectation that Cecilia would act as the mother of his seven children, a circumstance that, in her opinion, promised no end of argument and domestic discord, even if highlighting women's roles as mothers, both of the family and the nation, in his middle-class discourse.[23]

If the letters from the butcher, prefect, and storeowner give expression to characteristics, preoccupations, and values commonly associated with these figures, turning them almost into "types" or stereotypes that are meant to represent classes or social strata in the same manner as other characters in the novel represent regions, so too does that from the son of a powerful hacienda owner portray the values associated with his social position, enabling Payno to explore the highly charged zone where the discourse of equality and chance in matters of the heart runs headlong into the fixedness and inequality of position when it comes to family and social standing, the single most dominant tension that structures the novel. In contrast to the previous relationships, this one, at least initially, seems to be one of equals, that is, if equality is conceptualized in terms of their mutually felt desire rather than in their social standing. Cecilia clearly articulates her physical attraction to don Pioquinto, drawn, she states, to his youth, his body, to the promised pleasures of the flesh, in much the same terms as he expresses his longing for her in the opening lines of his letter, prefiguring, in his hopes for a glimpse of her body through the curtains as she bathes, the culmination of their desires. Unable to conceive of a concomitant social equality to match that of their desire, don Pioquinto spends the rest of the love letter outlining his elaborate scheme to bring the two lovers together while maintaining intact social hierarchy and inequality. To avoid the scandal that would follow from the marriage of such social unequals yet nevertheless satiate his desires, he proposes that Cecilia come to the hacienda he will be in charge of administrating in the position of cook, offering her the (relatively) lavish wage of six pesos a month plus five and a half *reales* as a weekly ration, a sum that, in addition to the excess she could skim in the purchasing of supplies, would allow her, in his calculation, to put aside some twenty-five or thirty pesos a month without his father being able to complain in the least. Despite don Pioquinto's attempt to shroud with a cloak of morality the dubious arrangement, by offering a vision at the end of his letter of the couple kneeling together at a private mass in the hacienda chapel, as if happily ever after, he can accomplish only the form and not the substance of holy matrimony—the implication that Cecilia will be his mistress, not his wife, is impossible to miss.[24]

Cecilia's response is also worthy of consideration, turning on its head, as it does, the supposedly unassailable social hierarchy assumed by don Pioquinto (and by, perhaps, readers as well). Whereas, in response to the previous propositions, Cecilia resolves matters verbally, either by sending a message through one of her female servants or by means of a conversation, in person, with the suitor, a perfectly acceptable option offered explicitly by these earlier correspondents (who, interestingly, all acknowledge her ability to respond in writing but respect that she may not choose to do so), in this case, a formal written response is forthcoming. In both form, the use of writing, as well as in its content, the letter is an insistent assertion of equality and, simultaneously, a challenge to the social and gender hierarchy through the skillful use of analogy. If you are hungry, she tells don Pioquintito (addressing him now in the diminutive), I can give you a job carrying fruit in the market for a salary of eight pesos a month and a *real* daily for your ration. Moreover, mocking him as well as the manner he proposes for her to make additional income, she offers to pay so that he can eat every day at *agachados*, booths where vendors heat up the scraps of food and leftovers purchased from the kitchens of the rich, a variation of the very arrangement he was suggesting she accept.[25] In this brief letter, she asserts that she is his equal in every way—as an owner, a patron who can provide employment and food, a person who commands, and a writer. It is as if the social blindness that is meant to characterize love both contributes to it and is structured by another assumption—that all are equal in their ability to write love letters. Equality, or at least the ability to disregard social barriers in love, draws sustenance from as it is premised upon love letters as an exchange between equals; it makes of love letters a potentially radical venue for the leveling of hierarchies of social class and of gender.

The positioning here of Cecilia as don Pioquinto's equal, achieved by means of demonstrating her ability to manipulate the written word, contrasts strikingly with the role she has been assigned in much of the rest of the novel, that of the verbal pole in an oral/literate binary comprised by her relationship with Lamparilla, one of the many lawyers in the novel. While Lamparilla lives in the world of contracts, deeds, wills, statements in judicial procedures, and political pronouncements, that composed of "letters and more letters," the phrase uttered about him that we have borrowed to frame this chapter, Cecilia is grounded in the local, the particular, the popular, the everyday, the subsoil from which that which is uniquely Mexican has been nurtured and grown. A voluptuous fruit vendor, she is the very embodiment of the bounty of the land, preparing its most savory, and specifically national, dishes, rooted in local tastes, ingredients, and means of preparation and described in local parlance and manners of speech that all, *letrados* included, can partake, enjoy, and praise. Their constitution as a couple presents Payno with almost endless opportunity to mediate or negotiate across this local/*letrado* divide, with orality becoming a shorthand for the particularly and specifically Mexican and Cecilia its most important spokesperson. When Lamparilla proposes, for example, Cecilia gives her word that she will marry him only once he has successfully recovered Moctezuma's patrimony, a promise made orally that she honors. When Lamparilla waxes poetic about the "sublime," the apogee in a geography of sentiment brought into being by means of the spectacle of nature, Cecilia counters that the poor were born to work and, unlike *licenciados*, did not have the head to think of such things. When he writes verses to attempt to woo her, she reads them through the lens of her own experience, transposing his references to literature and history to the register of daily life, to local figures she knows, to the particular and specific, before expressing her hope that the words he has written might eventually be made into a song and accompanied by guitar (a prospect that he relishes rather than rejects).[26]

Payno makes a complicated argument that resists being reduced to a conflict between the oral and the literate, even though that binary is indeed employed at numerous points in the novel. Much of it has to do with his assumption that it is place itself that generates unique qualities, characteristics, traits, and types.[27] In his discussion of Relumbrón's gang, who act almost like surrogate Rurales in imposing their own brand of order, disorder really, to better carry out their illegal activities, Payno identifies these men as being from the pueblo of Tepetlaxtoc, the history of which he also sets out. A pueblo of the ancient Mexicans, Tepetlaxtoc had been converted during the colonial period into a Christian community, dependent on the friars more than on any civil authority; during this era, Payno rhapsodizes, nowhere was more "tranquil, more ordered, more moral and pacific than the pueblo of Tepetlaxtoc." Although the arrival of a hacienda and a *pulque* tavern initially ushered in "an age of fashion" and improvement, a change to less benevolent ownership led to the advent of a different clientele at the *pulqueria*, and an uneasy relationship between it and hacienda workers and town residents. Such was the pool from which Relumbrón formed the ranks of his band, one about which Payno, perhaps surprisingly, is more complimentary than critical. Describing the men from Tepetlaxtoc as a "true aristocracy" of the "race of men" who were neither Spaniards nor Indians but "true Mexicans," he characterizes them as fearless, excellent horsemen, profoundly religious, and ready for any eventuality. Far from being like the petty thieves found in the hovels of Mexico City, sporting nicknames and associating with women who called themselves names like the "Bedbug" and the "Tick," these instead were valiant and upright men who, when desiring women, grabbed healthy country girls *"a lo hombre,"* that is, like men, lifting them up behind them on the saddle and galloping away, at times in a hail of bullets. Such a band of men, Payno concludes, revealing in addition to his own prejudices about race, masculinity, and religiosity the fantasy, perhaps shared by many in positions of authority, that such raw material could be melded into a more amenable finished product, lacked only an organization and those in charge who could command and sustain them until they could earn their livelihood honorably.[28]

The same was true for women, who, having been raised, for generations, in relative isolation in different parts of the country, came not only to take on unique characteristics as regional "types," according to Payno, but also brought into being, through the alchemy of metonymy, the very region from which they came. The chapter discussing the yearly trade fair at San Juan de los Lagos is particularly revealing in this regard.[29] After enumerating the products for which various regions are known—prized mules from Tamaulipas, sheep with thick white wool from New Mexico, sweet potato candies from Querétaro—Payno turns his attention to the traits, qualities, and characteristics, as well as to regional markers like clothing, distinguishing the women who had dared to make the trip. Here, a woman of the northern frontier, skin white as alabaster with abundant black hair, dressed in a tight-fitting blue suit that reached to her collar, came face to face with, among others, a stout *china poblana*, bedecked in double or triple petticoats with *rebozo* on her shoulders and her arms bare, the first, composed and cool, and the latter, more lively and full of zest, two of many regional types on display for any traveler to the fair. So avowedly were they the essence of a particular place as well as its most compelling representation, they seemed, according to Payno, to be from different and distant countries, as removed from each other as was Paris from Berlin, yet fashioning, through the bringing together of these unique parts, the single whole of the Mexican nation.

If Payno often employs orality as the predominant means for expressing the local customs, characteristics, and types that come together to form what is uniquely Mexican, it is in no way meant to deny the concomitant local command of literacy. As we have seen, although Cecilia continually returns to ground all explanations and understandings in various forms of orality and the spoken word, not only in her relationship with Lamparilla but by apologizing continually for her inability to spell correctly or for not understanding literary or other references or for not understanding what she is signing when she becomes involved in a judicial procedure, she is more than capable of asserting her own equality, as a writer and as a person, in her written correspondence with don Pioquintito. Despite the fact that all characters in the novel, from the humblest *curandera* to recruits for the army to the daughter of an aristocrat, are portrayed as learning to read and write, if they do not already do so, and thus are cast as potential if not currently already residents of the lettered city, its forms and formulas are presented as far from an unalloyed good for Payno. In fact, the novel can be read as a profound critique of the lettered city, its incompetent lawyers, its inaccurate and sensationalist, even compromised press, its forgeries, its titles and deeds that are useless unless backed by force, its flawed bookkeeping, its yellowing and dusty parchment, its fake library that serves as a false front for hidden treasure, the sugarcane crop dying while its supposedly enlightened administrator sits in yet another library reading the latest methods for growing cane while ignoring local knowledge, its triumph of form over substance. Despite the fact that the destiny of every character in the novel is mediated through some kind of written form—the love letter, the discovered note that reveals true identity, titles and deeds, judicial decisions and evidence, recipe books, the newspaper story—such technologies can also be employed by the criminal enterprise of Relumbrón linking Río Frío to the heart of the Republic, in this instance, in the form of written notes made by one of his accomplices and submitted to Relumbrón, in which were specified potential victims of robbery, their habits, and any items of worth, information that then circulated through the network of thieves facilitating its work.[30]

Rather than that pitting the oral against the literate, the main tension that structures relationships, especially those of couples, is that of morals and manners, encapsulated in the hopes expressed by many in the novel that every couple be comprised of those sharing an equality of education.[31] While hearts might fail to heed social barriers, to think that love would herald their complete disappearance altogether was unrealistic, even, in the words of Oñate, the judge responsible for imposing the rule of law, utopic.[32] Yet, whereas inequalities derived from birth, race, and fate might prove difficult enough to overcome, those based on manners and morals simply could not be. Much like his argument concerning the centrality of place to the formation of qualities, characteristics, and traits, *educación* was the product of one's surroundings, amenable to change only if caught early enough. In the case of Casilda, the old lawyer's love interest, the power of example provided both by the nunnery where she worked as well as by Amparo, the morally upright young woman in whose household she served, had raised her *educación* to the point where it became possible to even consider, if not act on, his desire to make a life together. When it came to Lamparilla and Cecilia, whom we have already discussed in some detail, while all other inequalities proved surmountable, leading, initially, to a happy life together, those of *educación* soon drove them apart. For Cecilia, it was simply that she tried to take them up too late in life. Unable to learn fine manners and social etiquette either from school or in the presence of a suitable family, she continued with her local manners and ways of speaking, leading Lamparilla not only to drink, gambling, and jealous outrage, but to pining for what might have been, for a more suitable match (for someone with his pretensions) with a woman from the aristocracy.[33] Finally, and as if to underline the centrality of place to manners and morals, Juan's wife Lucecilla, although of humble origin in Mexico, became adept at speaking French, as well as at playing the piano, painting landscapes, and writing correctly in Spanish and French, as well as in fine manners generally, courtesy of her three-year stay at the Convent of the Sacred Heart of Jesus while accompanying Juan while he studied in Paris.

Resituating difference into the realm of manners and morals, Payno continues nevertheless to hold in tension the oral and the literate, the local and the national, tacking between these poles depending on the task at hand, at times to praise the local as the essence of the truly Mexican, at others to argue for its improvement; at times to ridicule prejudices that disdained local knowledge and ways of doing things, at others to advocate bringing over the latest breeds of cattle and sheep from Europe; at times to mock double-entry accounting and privilege local bookkeeping premised upon experience and local needs, at others to privilege phrenology, European science, and mesmerism. Increasingly enmeshed in the forms of writing that characterized life at the end of the nineteenth century, for better or worse, and situated in an imagined future where all are reading on the same page of the novel of the nation, the novel's characters, nevertheless, continue to give expression to customs, characteristics, and the local in oral form. In doing so, Payno expresses neither a longing for the past nor a yearning for the modern, but brings the two, simultaneously, into being, placing his characters resolutely at home (or not at home) in both, oscillating between these poles that increasingly structured people's lives, holding out the promise of a future nation premised upon the combination of long-standing ties to place with their newly acquired common literacy. However, while all might equally be producers as well as the products of the texts of their times, an equality the consequences of which are imagined most radically in the exchange of love letters, differences in manners and morals not only reestablish hierarchies of gender and social position but justify the role of a select few in guiding the entire process.

Having, in the penultimate chapter of *Los bandidos*, resolved the various plots that structure the novel as well as relieved readers of their suspense by revealing the fates of those characters and, especially, those courting couples to whom they had become attached, Payno, in the book's final chapter, situates himself in the novel's present, as the actual author who had just finished writing the novel, while simultaneously reiterating how many of its events and personalities had been premised upon an actual episode in Mexico's history, the operation of a criminal ring by a certain Colonel Yáñez, a high-ranking figure during the time of Santa Ana.[34] In this chapter, Payno, describing himself as the lone guest in an isolated hotel overlooking a beach in Normandy, France, ponders the lives of the fishermen and their families that he has been watching from his room as he has written the book, noting how profoundly they had been shaped by this place and the sea. So it was in Mexico, where place had yielded its harvest not only of Mexican foods, like the fruit Cecilia sold in the market, and savory dishes but also of local types, the *china poblana*, the woman from Chihuahua, the men from Tepetlaxtoc, the *tapatías*, whose customs, habits, and manners of speech marked them as regionally specific but nevertheless as resolutely Mexican. Whereas it was sight, his view from the room, that enabled him to draw such conclusions concerning Normandy's present, it was memory that served as Payno's window on Mexico's past.

In the midst of this scene before him that encapsulated in the present the same process that the historical scenes he had just finished recounting accomplished in Mexico's past, a (fictitious) letter arrives from a dear friend of the author in Mexico. Whereas other texts produced in Mexico and circulating in Europe remarked upon in the novel serve only to confirm European prejudices and underwrite calls for intervention by portraying Mexicans as backward, barbaric, and in need of being saved from themselves, this letter points to the future rather than the past. Overturning some of the conclusions presented by the author himself in the penultimate chapter, the letter updates the author (and, of course, you the reader) on the fate of some of his characters and their relationships, revelations, the author warns, that readers can choose to "swallow" or not. Despite the humor and playfulness captured by the idea that a friend of the author could know the fate of the characters being written about, an idea that seems to collapse history and fiction (in that some of the characters may have been historical figures and others inventions of the author), this intervention from Mexico more importantly establishes a trajectory into the future, an ongoing future brought into being by this past in which the characters continue to go about their lives. While Payno is adamant that the novel is meant as a legacy, presenting Mexico's customs and practices to present and future generations, its project, like the lives of its characters, is ongoing, as much forward-looking as it is nostalgic—documenting that which is particularly Mexican, even if changing or disappearing, becomes the raw material for the creation of a national literature which, if generated out of Mexico's past, will write the future nation into existence.

Presented as the final chapter, this letter, along with the author's reminiscences and the establishment of the actual historical setting from which many of the events and personalities of the novel are derived, serves to make apparent the author's own voice and the constructedness of his text, highlighting the need of the reader to beware not only of the conclusions the author presents but of the forms used to present them. Locating himself, as we have just established, in an isolated hotel overlooking a beach in Normandy, pondering the lives of the fishermen and their families as he writes, Payno highlights his own authorial presence as he destabilizes it, the historical nature of the material as he fictionalizes it, the finality in the relationships of the fictional/historical characters that have been resolved in the penultimate chapter as contingent, up for grabs, one point of view among others that may be contradicted in a letter, newspaper story, or in some other form, along with the grounding of his "chatty" prose in the world of the oral. Collapsing genres, authorial authority, even time, serves in no way to diminish the impact of the work—in fact, it may do precisely the opposite. Combining all these forms serves to write into being a broad audience that can read (or hear) itself as "Mexican" while simultaneously receiving an education as to the forms of sentiment, feeling, and self that might be appropriate to inhabit such a category of belonging.

As I have read *Los bandidos* through a lens shaped by an ongoing and long-term engagement with everyday writing, especially love letters, writing that has been structured by as it has helped compose one of the main institutions of the lettered city, the judicial system, perhaps it is only fair that I conclude by reflecting on how this novel might be useful in helping to inform a reading of such documents. Although the fictitious love letters included in the novel are much more useful as a means for Payno to stereotype and poke fun at the preconceptions and prejudices of the various classes composing them (artisans, local political authorities, storekeepers, and elites) than they are as a means of exploring the construction of subjectivity or of self-reflexivity, the link between writing and matters of the heart, even among the humblest of characters in the novel, resonates with contemporary understandings and popular practices. This is not to argue that most people living in the mining and agricultural communities of late nineteenth- and early twentieth-century Chihuahua were reading on the same page of the novel of the nation or in many of its other texts as are the incipient readers and writers of *Los bandidos*. They were not. Nevertheless, many were accomplishing the exchange of love letters through the help of intermediaries, a possibility also suggested in the novel, something they saw as important to do. Whereas even lawyers in the novel might visit those skilled in the writing of love letters or consult their Galván or other etiquette books to produce more satisfying exemplars of this genre, humble Chihuahuans might use *amanuenses* or conceive of letter writing and reading as a group endeavor or both. One of the literacies that must be attended to in historical research, that associated with courtship in this case, then, might need to be conceptualized as much more indirect and collaborative than many of the other forms that might be present.

Moreover, love letters, just as they serve for Cecilia in the novel as physical tokens that might be deployed to ward off gossip and uphold reputation, are likewise, for many appearing in the judicial record, essential symbols of a courting relationship, regardless of or in addition to the actual words expressed in them. In this sense, the novel helps us understand that love letters may be performative, that is, that they may bring into being the very thing that they discuss. Unlike in the case of Cecilia in the novel, ending a courtship resulted in their return and, often, their destruction rather than their preservation. Moreover, Cecilia's behavior in the novel is especially suggestive because it demonstrates how Payno sees love letters as incredibly powerful in the leveling of inequalities of gender and class. At this point in time, I can only hope that readers, much like those in a previous century waited for the next installment of a novel to be published, have been sufficiently tantalized to the point of being inspired to see how these insights have been worked out in my forthcoming monograph on love letters.

SUGGESTED READINGS

French, William E. "'Te amo muncho:' The Love Letters of Pedro And Enriqueta," in Jeffrey M. Pilcher (ed.), *The Human Tradition in Mexico* (Wilmington, DE: Scholarly Resources, 2003), pp. 123–35.

Glantz, Margo. "Los Bandidos de Río Frío de Manuel Payno: La utopía del robo," *Estudios* 15: 29 (enero-junio 2007): 73–93.

Historia mexicana 173, vol. XLIV num. 1 (julio-septiembre 1994). Special issue on *Los bandidos del río frio* with essays by Paul Vanderwood, Barbara Tenenbaum, Margo Glantz, and Josefina Vazquez.

Manzoni, Alessandro. *The Betrothed.* Trans. by Bruce Penman. London: Penguin Books, 1972.

Pérez Montfort, Ricardo. *Avatares del nacionalismo cultural: Cinco Ensayos.* México: CIESAS, 2000.

Rama, Angel. *The Lettered City.* Trans. by John Charles Chasteen. Durham: Duke University Press, 1996.

Sights

Los Bandidos De Río Frío, Columbia Pictures, Filmadora Argel. 1956. Rogelio A. González, director. Starring singer Luis Aguilar.

Los bandidos del río frío. Television series. IMDbPro 1976. Antulio Jiménez Pons, director.

5

Peddling the Pampas

Argentina at the Paris Universal Exposition of 1889

Ingrid E. Fey

World trade fairs and international exhibitions (the most prestigious taking place in Europe) were quite the rage during the late nineteenth and early twentieth centuries. Such events gave each participating nation the opportunity to engage in self-promotion through the display of specific material culture. In the case of Latin America, the political elites quickly saw the significance of fabricating an image of their nation that would be acceptable to the all-important European audience. Latin American leaders of the era sought to encourage European immigration to their nations, to increase trade relations, and, especially, to demonstrate the extent to which their countries had achieved modernity. Thus, socioeconomic policy goals formed part of the discussion during the planning of each nation's pavilion and the consideration of which specific attributes of the nation would be highlighted. National identity was categorized, sanitized, and labeled for an international audience. Architecture, lighting, musical accompaniment, and ritual all were essential to the image of modernity projected at these exhibitions. Conspicuous display and consumption became the accouterments of progress. Ingrid Fey examines the planning, cost, criticisms, and final outcome of Argentina's participation in the Paris Universal Exposition of 1889. She analyzes the rationale for the inclusion of certain artifacts of Argentine culture while other aspects were kept out of view.

In 1916, J. M. Hammerton, an Englishman purporting to "make a try at the truth" about Argentina, published an account of his travels in that country entitled *The Argentine through English Eyes*. Hammerton found much to admire in the Argentine capital, Buenos Aires, which over the course of the past thirty years had experienced dramatic economic growth and rapid urban expansion and beautification. It was in this context that Hammerton considered the building on the Plaza San Martín then housing the National

Museum of Fine Arts so thoroughly disappointing. Not mincing words, he complained, "[The Art Gallery] is a gim crack affair of iron frame, wood, and gaudy tile. Although it looks quite attractive in a photograph, the shoddy workmanship, the great chunks of colored glass used as items of decorative scheme, and the general air of temporariness inseparable from the purpose for which it was originally designed, leave one with the impression that the Argentines set a very low value on their art treasures." The sooner the decrepit palace of the arts was tossed on the "scrap-heap," the better.[1] Such a harsh appraisal of the building housing Argentina's national art collection makes it difficult to imagine the great hopes and dreams that its creators had attached to the structure when it was first built in Paris, in 1889, to serve as Argentina's pavilion at the Paris Universal Exposition. Making use of the most modern in materials and design, Argentine exposition planners erected their palace at the foot of the Eiffel Tower to dazzle the world with Argentina's modernity and cosmopolitanism. Once the pavilion had served its purpose on the Champs de Mars, it was taken down and transported to Argentina, where, reconstructed, it served as a museum until its demolition in 1933.

Like other Latin American elites in the late nineteenth century, Argentine elites in the 1880s had a clear notion of an international exposition's power to project positive images of the nation before an international audience. And like other Latin American elites, Argentines believed that the projection of such images constituted an essential part of the modernizing process by encouraging European investment in and emigration to their nation. With such thoughts in mind, Argentina had been involved in a number of these events and had even hosted its own international expositions throughout the second half of the nineteenth century.[2]

Yet for Argentine elites, the Universal Exposition of 1889 stood apart from other expositions for two major reasons. First, as a celebration of the centennial of France's republican revolution, the exposition enabled the Argentine republic to prove its allegiance to the values of that revolution, which functioned in the minds of many governing elites in Latin America as a measure of political modernity and civilization.[3] Second, the exposition coincided with a massive push by the Argentine government to stimulate European—preferably French—immigration, to promote the exportation of frozen and refrigerated meat to European markets, and to secure diverse, constant streams of foreign capital with which to fund projects connected to the expansion of Argentina's economy. From the pavilion's inception, then, Argentine exposition planners envisioned the structure's elaborate architecture, lavish decorations, and myriad exhibits of Argentine products as important mechanisms for making the nation known to European immigrants and investors. Once lured to Argentina, these European contributions to Argentina's economic growth were to propel the country into the ranks of the world's most modern nations. In 1889, the pavilion that British traveler Hammerton so roundly criticized in 1916 served both as a reflection of the elites' desires for the future modernization of Argentina and as an important strategy for making their dreams reality.

Nearly all expositions of the nineteenth and early twentieth century represented efforts by national and regional ruling elites to put their notions of progress into tangible form. Elites crafted expositions to instruct and inspire visitors to learn about and conform to their plans for social, political, and economic modernization. The Argentine pavilion erected in 1889 at the foot of the Eiffel Tower was no different.[4] The rather eclectic, exotic structure that emerged from the elites' planning aimed to entice foreigners with Argentina's uniqueness and bountiful wealth. It also sought to impress foreign visitors that Argentina had all of the necessary features of modern, "civilized" nations and lacked those aspects associated with "barbarity," namely a tropical climate inhabited by a large indigenous, black, or mixed-blood population. In a nutshell, the pavilion was intended to express the entire continuum of Argentine progress by demonstrating the elites' views of the nation's seemingly brief and distant past, its auspicious present, and its boundless, euphoric future.

The Argentine pavilion conveyed an image of Argentina as a land of both an abundance and a dearth of wealth, population, and progress. This bifocal depiction of Argentina evoked the long-held and tenacious belief—most commonly associated with Argentine statesman Domingo Faustino Sarmiento's 1845 work *Facundo*—that there were actually two Argentinas.[5] One Argentina, embracing chiefly the coastal cities, was in step with cosmopolitan trends and was eager to modernize, using European and North American civilizations as its guides. The other Argentina—the interior, and the source of much of the wealth needed for such modernization—was relatively empty, awaiting the influx of capital, European farmers and technology, and such other "civilizing" forces from the cities as fashion, education, and railroads. Yet, unlike Sarmiento's irreconcilably dualistic vision of Argentina, the pavilion reflected the productive partnership that had emerged between the two Argentinas in which the countryside fueled the expansion of modern cities while the modern cities applied their expertise to the rational and scientific exploitation of the countryside. The pavilion thus mirrored the "provincial cosmopolitanism" or "cosmopolitan nationalism" that characterized the national identity of Argentina's elites during this period, through its uneasy juxtaposition of Argentine tradition and cosmopolitan modernity.[6]

In 1889, Argentine exhibition worker Gabriel Carrasco proclaimed that "making ourselves known, therein lies the secret to realizing the prosperity of our country!" Carrasco's opinion was not unique. Since Argentina's independence in 1810, a broad cross-section of the elite had firmly believed that publicity was all that was necessary to draw the foreign capital and labor that appeared to be the keys to Argentine modernity. By the second half of the nineteenth century, expositions figured as an important part of this process of self-promotion within an international theater of display and competition. Nevertheless, Argentina's presence at the Universal Exposition of 1889 was unprecedented in the number of products shown and in the lavishness of its pavilion.

In large part, the ostentation of Argentina's presence at the 1889 exposition stemmed from the amazing economic growth that had taken place in Argentina during the 1880s. Between 1880 and 1890 the country's population swelled from 2.4 million to 3.4 million, including a net inflow of 850,000 immigrants, primarily from Spain and Italy. Foreign investment grew by almost 800 million gold pesos, shipping through Argentine ports quintupled, and export earnings increased from 58 to 165 million gold pesos.[7] Along with its rapid population growth and unprecedented economic prosperity, Buenos Aires came to possess all of the amenities to be found in the great cities of Europe and the United States; its street design and urban architecture reflected the wealth, opulence, and francophile tendencies of the city's upper classes. Despite Argentina's apparent capacity for endless expansion, this glittering and astounding economic growth rested on rather shaky foundations. By 1890, a year of both a massive economic crisis and an aborted coup attempt that succeeded in forcing president Juárez Celman to step down, Argentina's boom was beginning to bust.

In 1887, when president Juárez Celman requested the sum of 200,000 pesos for the collection, transfer, and installation of items for the Universal Exposition of 1889, the economic and political crises of 1890 were still in their infancy. Faith ran high in the opportunities presented by the exposition for Argentina's continued economic miracle. In his letter to congress, Juárez Celman pronounced, "Expositions are an efficient means for making known Argentina's industrial and commercial forces and they constitute opportunities that we must take advantage of for displaying before the peoples of Europe not only the variety and abundance of our products, but also the vast extension of our territories and their capacity for supporting, in conditions of well-being, a population mass against which the actual number of our inhabitants will appear insignificant."[8]

In support of the president's request, one congressional deputy argued that even though Argentine industry was not very advanced, the promotion of the country's natural resources would further the cause of industrialization, which for him signified the foundation of wealth in Argentina.[9] While traveling in Europe, general, former president, and ardent promoter of Argentine "progress" Julio Roca seconded these opinions. He sent a stream of letters to the exposition commission then being formed in Buenos Aires urging that the government spare no expense to represent the nation in a grand style. Roca stressed that the exposition provided the nation with a chance to create "a practical display of what [Argentina had been] advertising in all places." In his view, it was "indispensable to be triumphant, in these moments when we are object of a favorable reaction, [when] Europe begins to pay attention to us and prepares a great immigration of men and capital." To this end, Roca urged that the pavilion be made with elegance and sobriety, leaving aside all that was frivolous and not to European tastes.[10] Strike while the iron is hot, Roca advised, and make a good show of it. To meet this challenge, Argentines on both sides of the Atlantic engaged themselves in the many preparations involved in such an important and massive undertaking.

In October 1886, president Juárez Celman appointed an exhibition commission headed by the vice president of the senate, Antonio Cambaceres (1833–1888), to plan Argentina's participation in the fair. The commission's first responsibility was to prepare a report detailing its plan for participation in the exhibition. The commission was then to gather two of every specimen chosen to be sent to the Universal Exposition, with one going to a permanent exhibit of Argentine progress.[11] Among the commission's other members were Julio Victorica and Francisco Latzina, directors of the departments of agriculture and statistics, respectively; the presidents of the Sociedad Rural, the Club Industrial, the Sociedad Científica, and the Instituto Geográfico; and the editor of one of Buenos Aires's two major dailies, *La Prensa*.[12] The exposition commission thus brought together the most important representatives of industry, commerce, science, agriculture, and culture. Antonio Cambaceres was himself a businessman and politician with extensive experience organizing industrial expositions and promoting various business enterprises and public works programs. He had also been instrumental in president Juárez Celman's rise to power and that of vice president Carlos Pellegrini. Before Cambaceres's untimely death in 1888 (after which he was replaced by Eduardo Olivera, who had similar experiences as an active member of the Sociedad Rural), the commission had set into motion the preparations needed to orchestrate Argentina's participation in the Universal Exposition in Paris.

A web of contacts resulted from this planning that stretched across the country and undertook to funnel information and goods to the central exposition commission, located in Buenos Aires. Agents working on behalf of the central exposition commission helped to establish provincial commissions directed by government officials and comprised of the provinces' most important men. These commissions then collected materials for the exposition and arranged for their arrival in Buenos Aires in time for transferal to Paris. In connection with these procurement activities, a major agricultural and livestock census was undertaken in late 1888 at the behest of the central exposition commission. Just as exposition planners intended to do with the actual products put on display, the census organizers aspired to "make known for the first time, in a systematic enumeration, the species, riches, and topographical distribution of agricultural cultivation and the rearing of animals" to be found in Argentina.[13] The result was a volume filled with tables, maps, and charts detailing the known and potential human and agricultural resources to be found in Argentina's prime growing regions. These books were later distributed throughout Europe in honor of the exposition.

While these activities were taking place in Argentina, many Argentines living or traveling in Europe played their part in preparations for the exposition. General Roca and others forwarded European exposition publications to assist the central exposition commission in Buenos Aires with its planning. Roca also orchestrated the hiring of an advisor, an Argentine then on the staff of a French exposition publication, *Moniteur de l'Exposition*. This man, Enrique Cabiran, went on to play an integral role in the preparations for the pavilion, using his knowledge of European expositions to enhance the effectiveness of his nation's image production. Roca then pressed for the establishment of an ad hoc exposition commission that would undertake the numerous preparations that had to take place in Paris. In October 1887 the government authorized the creation of this ad hoc exposition commission in the French capital, which later became formalized as the official Argentine representative body at the exposition. Eugenio Cambaceres, an Argentine novelist then living in France and the brother of Antonio Cambaceres, headed up the Parisian commission.[14] Cambaceres was the ideal figure to represent Argentina in the French capital, for he was a cultured man of letters, son of a French immigrant to Argentina, and a member of one of the largest landowning families in Argentina.[15] Ironically, his last novel, *En la sangre* (1885), attributed Argentina's ills to the massive infusion of marginal elements from the rural areas of Europe. In his view, reckless governmental policies favoring unlimited immigration threatened the resilience of Argentina's New World genes.[16] However, his critical stance on immigration seems to have focused primarily on Italian immigrants, an attitude quite common among the Argentine elite at the time.[17]

Argentines refused from the start to consider sharing a general pavilion for all Latin American nations, so Cambaceres's primary responsibilities in Paris were to secure a spot for the Argentine pavilion on the Champs de Mars and to hire the architects, artists, and contractors necessary for its construction. The ad hoc commission was also to help organize the exhibition once the display items from Argentina arrived in Paris. After winning a spot of 1,600 square meters next to the Eiffel Tower, Cambaceres held a contest among French architects for the pavilion's design. The terms of the contest were that the exhibition space had to equal 3,000 square meters and have a second floor, and the structure had to be of iron and readily collapsible for transport back to Buenos Aires. Finally, the cost could not exceed 300,000 francs, including expenditures for painting, adornments, and works of art.

On April 19, 1888, the jury met in Paris's town hall, the Hôtel de Ville, to choose a winning plan from the twenty-seven submitted. Hoping to ensure European acceptance of their pavilion, the jury consisted of both the ad hoc committee and several French exposition officials, among them Monsieur Alphand, the general director of works for the exposition, to whom Cambaceres ceded his presidency of the jury. After deliberations, the jury chose the French architect Albert Ballu to direct construction of the Argentine pavilion.[18] The commission then ordered the execution of works of carpentry, ornamentation, window glass, electric wiring, bronze, artistic fabrics, sculpture, and painting from various other French craftsmen. It also held a competition among top French furniture makers to see which one could create the loveliest display cases from various Argentine woods.[19]

From the outset, Argentine exposition planners, in the perceived absence of a national architectural style and sufficiently talented architects and artisans, made use of the best French craftsmen that money could buy to assist in the fabrication of an acceptable image for a European audience. In this way, Argentina's French-made pavilion very clearly paralleled the aims of the Argentine elite: through the exploitation of their nation's natural wealth, they would purchase the trappings of modernity in Europe and transport them whole back to Argentina. In another sense, the pavilion reflected a form of collaboration between Argentine wealth and European know-how that could result in an impressive and rapid "modernization" of Argentina's image.

A GRAND OPENING

France officially inaugurated the Universal Exposition on May 6, 1889. Argentines, like the rest of the world, had eagerly anticipated the event's opening for months. Major newspapers in Buenos Aires regularly ran articles detailing preparations for the event, the construction of the Eiffel Tower, and the history of expositions in Europe. Even so, to be in Paris for the exposition was an awe-inspiring experience. As one Argentine described it, "The Exposition is an ocean, in which the imagination becomes bewildered and feelings become weary, given over as they are to a sustained contemplation in which every object calls attention, demanding serious study, in order to even vaguely appreciate and remember it."[20]

Argentina's exposition commission officially inaugurated the pavilion on May 25, Argentina's independence day.[21] Planners intended the inauguration to have the air of a national party; however, the festivities also revealed the intent of Argentine exposition planners to link their nation's fortunes to those of France.[22] The inauguration revolved around the visit of President Carnot and other French functionaries. With last-minute preparations complete and the Argentine soldiers dressed in their uniforms and standing in place, President Carnot arrived at the Argentine pavilion at two in the afternoon, accompanied by General Brugère and Colonel Lichtenstein. These men were met by Ricardo Lezica, the interim exhibition commissioner, vice president of Argentina Carlos Pellegrini, and the French exhibition officials Spuller, Tirard, and Berger.[23] As Carnot made his way into the crowded pavilion, a band broke out into the boisterous rhythms of the *Marseillaise,* the French national anthem, and a celebration of the battles of the French Revolution. Following the group's inspection of the second-floor exhibits, the band played a version of the Argentine national anthem that the French composer Edmund Guion had newly orchestrated. A second rendition of the *Marseillaise* followed.[24] The French president and his functionaries then ceremoniously wrote their signatures on the first page of an album, which read, "Today, the 25th of May, 1889, glorious anniversary of the Argentine Republic, Monsieur Carnot has honored us with his visit to the exposition of the Argentine Republic." Afterward both sides toasted the triumphs, prosperity, and well-being of the Argentine and French republics. Organizers next distributed bouquets of blue-and-white flowers and blue-and-white sachets laced with the "Scent of the Argentine Pavilion" to the many Argentine women in attendance.[25] Once the French functionaries retired from the event, Pellegrini pronounced the Argentine pavilion inaugurated.[26]

Through this elaborate spectacle Argentines infused their entrance into the Universal Exposition with an unmistakable deference for France and its republican heritage. Having President Carnot's signature in their pavilion album proved that expositions were a primary means of making oneself known, that in fact Argentina had made itself known, at least to the president of France. The two nations' toasting each another implied a certain equality in relations between France and Argentina and symbolized a relationship that was integral to Argentine elites' visions of their nation's future. At least here, in the shadow of the Eiffel Tower, Argentines could for a brief afternoon feel themselves a viable competitor in the "struggle of the century." Standing witness to these ritualistic activities as eager supporters were hundreds of Argentines who were either living in Paris or visiting the Paris exposition.[27]

TEMPLE OF THE *RASTAQUOUÈRE*

The Argentine pavilion stood alongside the base of the Eiffel Tower, in between the pavilions of Mexico and Suez and separated by a narrow passageway from the pavilion of Brazil. As the centerpiece of Argentina's participation in the Universal Exposition, the pavilion revealed most clearly the image that Argentine planners hoped to project to the world and the links with Europe that they aspired to develop. One of the key aims of the Argentine exposition planners was to turn out an exhibit that would outshine other Latin American nations. Realizing that Argentina's industry could not possibly compete with that of Europe or North America, the planners made sure the pavilion would surpass those of other Latin American countries then supplying raw materials to the markets of industrialized nations.[28] Despite General Roca's admonishment to create a sober and tasteful pavilion, the Argentine pavilion was actually fairly ostentatious and showy. In fact, for some, the pavilion bordered on garishness and merely confirmed Parisians' view of Argentines as *rastaquouères*, a term Parisians used throughout the period to describe Argentines who traveled to Europe and spent huge sums of money to imitate European customs and fashions, usually incorrectly.[29] However, viewed in another light, such gaudiness merely reaffirmed the wealth to be made "down Argentine way."

Just as the *rastaquouère* purportedly flaunted his wealth before a foreign audience, so Argentines viewed the expenditure of enormous sums on the pavilion as an important element of their overall exposition presence, distinguishing them from their continental neighbors. As construction began on the pavilion, the Argentine exposition commissioner in Paris justified spending increasingly substantial sums by stating that, given Argentina's rapid growth and unprecedented visibility in Europe, it was only natural to spend more than other nations. More important, Cambaceres argued that increasing sums were needed if the pavilion was to compete with Mexico's, located next door.[30] In the end, costs for the Argentine pavilion far surpassed initial budget projections, with the government claiming to have spent more money than all of the other Latin American nations combined.[31] Although that statement is an exaggeration, at 3,500,000 francs Argentina did spend on its pavilion a million francs more than Mexico (2,500,000 francs) and almost three times more than the United States (1,147,500 francs).[32] By publicizing the immense cost of the pavilion and creating a structure that would spark European curiosity from considerable distance, Argentines clearly expressed their view that "the [Río de la Plata was] the American region that marched in the vanguard of civilization and South American advances."[33]

Related to Argentina's attempt to demonstrate its supremacy among Latin American nations was the essentially European nature of the pavilion. By emphasizing their country's proximity to European civilization and its ability to purchase that civilization, Argentines could simultaneously impress Europeans and other Latin Americans, who, like the Argentines, were often eager to transplant the latest European features to their homelands.

By choosing a French architect to create their nation's pavilion and French artists to adorn it, the exhibition commission publicized Argentina's receptivity to and admiration for European ingenuity. The pavilion seemed to radiate the welcome that planners wanted to convey to enterprising Europeans with skills vital to the modernization of Argentina. As one exhibition publication deceptively proclaimed, "The Argentine is hospitable and polite to strangers. The well-educated European is heartily welcomed into the family circles."[34]

Significantly, the pavilion did not rely on antiquated European styles but sought to capture in form and function the most modern architectural, artistic, and mechanical inventions. An iron skeleton supported the entire structure and was designed to allow for the pavilion's easy disassembly and transport to Argentina. This form of construction placed the pavilion in the ranks of the Eiffel Tower and the Gallery of Machines, both of which relied on revolutionary uses of iron for their structures, and demonstrated a firm commitment to material progress.[35] The domes on top of the pavilion, the use of banners on the pavilion's spires, and the elaborate portal marking the entrance displayed a remarkable similarity to the Central Dome of the French exhibition. One Franco-Argentine publication explicitly compared the two structures: "The Argentine pavilion, like the Central Dome, proves that modern architecture is not limited to the monochromatic and straight Eiffel Tower, and thus victoriously refutes old-fashioned contemplators of past architectural formulas."[36] Through their embrace of modern, cosmopolitan architectural fashions, Argentines revealed their tendency to modernize in a manner that would place them in the ranks of Western European powers.

While no doubt impressive during the day, it was at night that the Argentine pavilion shone in all its glory. The exterior walls of the pavilion were decorated with stained-glass windows, bricks, ironworks, tiles, glazed earthenware, and a multitude of glass stones. Each night bright electric lights would shine forth from the pavilion, creating a dazzling display that imparted to the building a "fairy-like aspect."[37] A French writer described the pavilion this way: "At the hour of illumination, the pavilion burns and glows like a flash of lightening from a pair of Bengal lights. It appears incrusted with diamonds and precious stones. A detachment of twenty soldiers, swarthy in appearance, is in charge of guarding this part of the exposition. It is obvious that the Republic of Buenos Aires [sic] has done things on a grand scale and has spared no expense."[38]

Despite the occasional remarks that the pavilion was a bit too extravagant, a nice example of *rastacuerismo*, Argentines were successful in impressing their European audience at least with the pavilion's external appearance.[39] For French visitors, the spectacle of the Argentine pavilion may have conjured up visions of a modern-day El Dorado, reinforcing the image of the Americas as a land of bountiful riches waiting for European discovery.[40] But this El Dorado was not the land of innocent natives that it once was. Now Americans were in control of the very force that seemed poised to transform Europe: electricity. In the use of electric spotlights, the Argentines hoped again to compete favorably with the Eiffel Tower that loomed overhead and that inspired Carlos Pellegrini to write, "[The exposition] is marvelous . . . above all the nocturnal illumination of the great fountain and the Eiffel Tower."[41] Moreover, through its use of dazzling light display, the Argentine pavilion could play an important role in the creation of the *cité féerique* on the Champs de Mars.[42] As a palace of dreams—a fairy palace—the Argentine pavilion might be able to enchant Europeans in a way that would prove beneficial for both them and Argentina. The Moorish flavor of the external architecture only accentuated this legendary aspect and evoked for one writer the *Thousand and One Nights*.[43]

The entrance to the Argentine pavilion was one of the most striking of the Latin American pavilions at the Parisian exposition. It conveyed an immediate inventory of Argentina's resources and the nation's receptivity to European immigration and investment. Connecting the hypermodern, Europeanized exterior of the pavilion to the pavilion's interior, which was dominated by the display of primary goods, the entrance symbolized the means by which one Argentina would come to dominate the "other" less developed and "barbarous" Argentina. The entrance's focal point was a gold statue above the doorway portraying a young woman resting on the back of a well-fed bull. Other gold figures clustered around the pair's feet, representing various aspects of work. A stained-glass window rose up behind these statues, prominently displaying the Argentine coat of arms and those of the various provinces. Mosaics on either side of the gold sculpture depicted animal husbandry and agriculture, the two main sources of Argentine wealth. Animal husbandry was symbolized by a gaucho—the Argentine cowboy—seated on the ground next to a white horse, some sheep, and a dog. Agriculture was figured as a farmer dedicated to his labors.[44] This use of symbols succinctly surveyed the major components of Argentina's economy: minerals and capital (gold), livestock production (sheep, cattle), agriculture (farmer), and labor (youth, farmer, gaucho). Absent from the portrait were grinding poverty and backbreaking work: a cloud of rural repose seemed to envelop all of the entrance's elements. In contrast to the sooty streets, crowded living conditions, and dismal factories of Europe, the image of Argentina conveyed by the entrance was that of a rural oasis with all of the best accouterments of modern civilization.

The display immediately visible to visitors entering the pavilion reinforced the message conveyed by the statues at the entrance and graphically depicted the dual nature of Argentine society. A monumental female figure representing a stable, fertile, and magnanimous Argentine Republic welcomed visitors with an outstretched hand. A huge map of Argentina made of plaster and an exhibit of frozen meat stood directly behind this statue, luring visitors beyond the entrance. The map stood to the right of the statue and displayed Argentina's principal cities, rivers, mountains, and other spots of interest. Moreover, it showed in vivid form the size of Argentina and the uninhabited spaces between population centers that were waiting to be filled by eager European immigrants. For a Spanish immigrant to Argentina, the significance of these empty spaces was clear: "Contemplating the map, the observer realizes much more clearly that in such a vast zone there is capacity for an entire world and that what is lacking here, namely land, in Argentina abounds; and what abounds here, namely men, is lacking there."[45]

The Sansinena Company's exhibit of frozen Argentine meat stood to the left of the map, in a small structure resembling one of those ghoulish crypts in the Recoleta Cemetery of Buenos Aires. There were always a few sides of defrosted beef or mutton under glass for perusal, and these were among the most popular items on display. Occasionally free samples of cooked meat were also distributed.[46] The primacy accorded to this exhibit reflected the Argentine government's desire to get a viable frozen meat export industry off the ground by convincing Europeans that Argentine meats could compete with those of European butchers.[47] Such a display may have also worked to encourage immigration by advertising to the French populace the abundance and availability of high-quality food in Argentina. The first impression that Europeans received of Argentina was thus one of simultaneous abundance and absence: abundant land and food and scarce competition with other humans for those riches.

Rising above the frozen meat and map was a stained-glass window depicting Argentina and France meeting in an allegorical setting. Significantly, exhibition planners chose to have this scene minted into a medal in honor of Argentina's participation in the Universal Exposition.[48] The scene depicted two classical female figures meeting—a meeting of sister republics. The French Republican figure sat on a throne, holding a scepter topped with the *coq gaulois*, the symbol of French nationality. Behind her rose the Eiffel Tower, ultimate symbol of the French Republican government. To her right stood the Argentine Republic, approaching France somewhat deferentially. Argentina held a shield on which two hands clasping were engraved; carefully cultivated fields, flocks of sheep or other livestock, and sheaths of wheat surrounded her. Here the competitive aspect of world fairs gave way to a symbolic representation of one nation's respect for the superiority of another. Also implied, however, were the mutually beneficial ties that could blossom between the two republics. France represented for Argentina a fountain of technology and liberal political thought. On the other hand, Argentina could provide France with the bounty of its soil in a rewarding exchange. Emphasis on the republican nature of the two nations was also important. By stressing the republican nature of Argentina, the pavilion strived to convince Europeans that Argentina was ruled by law and governed democratically—it was no longer home to *caudillos* and the barbarism that had obsessed Domingo Faustino Sarmiento earlier in the century. In the accompanying literature as well as in the pavilion, exhibition planners emphasized somewhat disingenuously that in Argentina, "the aristocracy of wealth does not exist, but the aristocracy of intellect is generally recognized."[49] The casting of this scene into commemorative medals, which were then distributed to the exposition commission members and other important French officials, suggests that it succinctly conveyed the essence of the exposition's meaning for Argentina's exhibit planners.[50]

Looming over the pavilion's foyer was the central dome, with its four smaller cupolas. Paintings adorning these structures conveyed in kaleidoscopic form the essential components of Argentine wealth and liberal historiography through images carefully chosen by Argentines themselves.[51] Each of the four cupolas held four images representing diverse fields of economic and cultural endeavors. All of these images—and others scattered throughout the pavilion—were executed by the most admired and important French painters and sculptors of the day. Tony Robert-Fleury, for example, contributed paintings of a grape harvest and of men on horseback tossing a fishing net into a river.[52] Jules Lefèbvre provided images of architecture and sculpture.[53] Works by Fernand Cormon, Albert Besnard, and Henri Gervex depicted scenes of industry, commerce, railroads, electricity, and commerce.[54] Bronze sculptures representing agriculture, commerce, industry, art, and science floated at the four corners of the central dome.[55] Although the French creators of these artworks had relied on sources sent from an Argentine museum for their models, the completed works were nevertheless "purified" and exoticized for foreign consumption.[56] One particularly candid exposition worker criticized the idealized images that graced the walls of the pavilion. To his dismay, the desire to hire famous European artists had outweighed the need for what he termed "accuracy" and "natural beauty" in the visual representations of his homeland. He reported that, with their dress and lily white complexions, Argentine women shearing sheep appeared more like Orientalist concoctions than like true Creole women. Making matters worse, the paintings showed the wool being caught in baskets ("Who uses baskets to catch wool!" he exclaimed). Even more ridiculous in his mind was a gaucho—the epitome of the pampas nomad—shown leaning out of a window, a symbol of sedentary life. At last the engineer queried, "Are these images of national customs? No, they are most definitely a form of French advertising." In his mind, Argentina should have done as Mexico had done, which was to utilize the talents of national artists and architects to demonstrate pride in the nation's talent.[57] Rare in their candor and nationalistic tone, this exhibition worker's comments never made their way into public discourse, which throughout the exposition tended to laud the pavilion's decoration and displays.

The entrance to the Argentine pavilion enveloped visitors in idealized images of the nation's wealth; it bombarded them with symbols and tangible and edible proof of Argentina's bounty even before visitors moved into the galleries that displayed the articles sent from Argentina. If visitors left after seeing just the entrance and the foyer, they would have had a clear notion of what Argentina had to offer immigrants and investors. However, the goal of the entrance was to lure visitors into the pavilion's interior.

UPSTAIRS, DOWNSTAIRS

The exterior and the interior of the Argentine pavilion replicated the productive relationship that had evolved between modern, "civilized" Argentina and rural, "barbaric" Argentina. As described in the previous section, the external structure attempted in appearance to compete with and pay homage to an increasingly modern France. By contrast, the general focus of the pavilion's interior was to display the raw materials and agricultural products whose export made such modernity possible. Industrial display, much to the chagrin of Argentines themselves, was poor in comparison. Thus, the two Argentinas, one modern and European, the other rural and backward but potentially rich, complemented each other in the structure of the pavilion itself. The dynamic partnership between these two Argentinas continued within the pavilion.

Beyond the main entrance, the Argentine pavilion's interior consisted of the central dome, below which a dramatic staircase of wood and metal transported visitors to the second level. Galleries extended to the right and left of the dome on each level. The ground floor presented much of the agricultural and forest wealth of the nation. To the right of the map and meat displays were the products of agricultural wealth: barley, grape pomace, rice, black and white oats, millet, beans of every kind, peas, coffee, aniseed, and a wide variety of corn and wheat flours. These items were displayed in flat vials above which hung their annual production figures. In addition to these goods were linseed, hemp, castor, and olive oil, preserves, cheeses, crackers, candy, wine, and some liqueurs. Sugars from Tucumán and Salta rounded out the eastern wing. To the left of the meat display was an impressive display of Argentine woods, dyes, and medicinal herbs. The display of woods garnered more prizes than any other section of the Argentine exhibition.[58]

An ornate staircase transported visitors literally and figuratively upward toward the more "civilized" Argentina that dominated the second floor. Displays of Argentine industry and education predominated on the second level. This floor thus contrasted with the first floor in displaying the trappings of modernity to be found in Argentina. The second floor exhibited a variety of consumer items manufactured in Argentina: shoes, hats, cloth, linen, furniture, beds, wardrobes, musical instruments, and glassware. Other such items included stockings, ceramic goods, perfumes, brushes, combs, buttons, preserved ostrich feathers, matches, trunks, and many saddlery items. The author of one guidebook described the scene this way: "Here, skins covered with their fur, there, rawhides or leather prepared for shoe-making and saddlery. All the cases which contained the different articles were elegantly made and attracted visitors who were astonished to see amongst these products several specimens rivaling those of the Parisian manufacturers."[59]

In addition to these consumer products were displays designed to convey more clearly the modern, "progressive" aspects of Argentine civilization. An immense second-floor exhibit of Argentine publications included novels, books of poetry, textbooks, treatises on various topics, and almost 350 journals, revues, and newspapers. Alcorta noted in his report that many visitors were surprised by the vast number of newspapers that they saw displayed on a wall. There were also numerous collections of photographs, statistical charts, and graphs. Education received some attention with a showing of schoolbooks and works by young Argentine authors. The University of Córdoba's exhibit of Argentina's minerals, reptiles, and fish, also on the second floor, revealed the potential wealth to be found in Argentina through the application of modern mining techniques and the advanced technical knowledge of Argentina's scientists.[60]

The second floor of the exhibition portrayed the second Argentina, the nation that viewed positivist modernization and technological prowess as the keys to Argentina's entry into the modern world. Alcorta recounted with pride the exclamations of European visitors when they toured the exhibition: "[Argentines] have things like those here! There are tramways, there are plazas, and there are gardens like ours!" He felt confident that although Argentine industry was not as well represented as that of other nations, the Argentine pavilion had nevertheless proved to the world that Argentina was able to provide for itself a wide variety of goods, "giving . . . an idea of the state of civilization, that [Europeans] do not attribute to us."[61]

Beyond the actual types of items on display, Argentines demonstrated their modernity in the ways that diverse items were categorized and organized. Through the scientific classification of goods of all kinds, Argentines emphasized the completeness of their adoption of the ideals of the European Enlightenment, the primary cultural orientation of the exposition's French planners. This orientation involved a need to categorize and typologize and to glorify education and social progress. In addition, the Argentine exhibit conveyed a willingness to participate in the "ethos of materialism" and the "celebration of the marketable commodity."[62] For Argentine elites, the Enlightenment penchant for inventory and classification of the material world became the touchstone for the dominance of civilized Argentina over its barbarous half. Moreover, the victory of Argentine civilization appeared to Argentine elites as the key to their nation's future position as a world power.[63] These messages were not lost on the French. As one French journalist remarked,

> In its gigantic palace, the Argentine Republic exhibits a thousand specimens of wheat, five hundred of corn, its frozen meats, wools, skins, and leathers.
>
> This accumulation of materials explains and justifies the high expectations of the young Republic. Enlightened by the secular experience of Europe, employing from the start the most scientific procedures and the most perfected machines, opening its arms wide to emigrants, making a call to capital from the whole world, she inspires confidence that the Argentine Republic has overcome the most difficult period of the life of nations.
>
> If [Argentina] can cede some of its audacity to prudence and *sang-froid*, there is no doubt that the future that awaits her will surpass the level of its vast ambitions.[64]

Although clearly Eurocentric, this response to the Argentine pavilion revealed that the Argentine exposition planners had succeeded in conveying an image that inspired European confidence in its modernity, and curiosity in the potential wealth to be found in its natural and agricultural resources. Nevertheless, there remained some skepticism regarding the Argentine character, viewed as almost too confident and boastful—ever the *rastaquouère*.

THE ONLY GOOD INDIAN

European racial theorists of the late nineteenth century tended to view mestizos, blacks, and indigenous peoples as inherently inferior to whites and, as a result, subject to racial degeneration, crime, and violence. Latin American elites understood the damage that such theories could do to the progressive images they were fabricating for the exposition; therefore, they sought to counteract them in numerous ways. In the case of Argentina, exhibition planners simply chose to stress the absence of "uncivilized" groups in its pavilion's displays.

On a daily basis, the most visible Argentines at the pavilion were twenty soldiers brought to stand guard ceremoniously at the building's entrance. To the chagrin of Carlos Pellegrini, these soldiers were primarily *chinos*, or half-breeds. He wrote to his brother in Argentina that "[the exhibition planners] have sacrificed aesthetics for truth, because this is the true figure of our soldier."[65] Although authorities in Argentina displayed a certain reluctance to send a group of soldiers to France—partly owing to their racial qualities, it seems—José Paz, the Argentine minister to France, urged them to go forward. He argued that in their uniforms, which were almost identical to those of the French army, the soldiers' "Argentine" (read mestizo) origin would pass unnoticed. The soldiers' adoption of European garb and military regimentation would, Paz hoped, obscure their racial inferiority because such dress and behavior was not what Europeans expected to see in mixed-race peoples, to whom they attributed lawlessness and dishonesty. More important, he asserted, given the present state of European nationalist rivalries, the soldier was the symbol of progress and civilization. He wrote, "[I]t is my belief that, at present, it is by way of a soldier that one best impresses upon the multitudes a favorable judgment of the civilization of a country that is far away, more than by many other forms of industry and of the advertising of ideas to which many societies often resort."[66]

No trace of Argentina's "uncivilized" indigenous population, past or present, existed in the pavilion's displays. When a French woman asked a pavilion employee to see photographs of savages, she was politely told that there were none in Argentina; all had moved to the cities and were now educated, valued citizens. As proof, the woman was introduced to an Argentine employee in the pavilion who claimed to be a direct descendant of the most powerful Indian cacique in all of Argentina. According to the journalist who reported this meeting, the woman left satisfied, having met an Indian who was perfectly dressed and who spoke with more intelligence and formality than a government official.[67] This absence had been very much by design; when various provincial exposition commissions offered to send "curiosities" related to the Indians in their regions, their offers were politely refused. In the view of the exposition planners, such goods did little to demonstrate the productivity of the land and would only confirm erroneous opinions of the state of Argentine culture.[68]

The Universal Exposition of 1889 closed its doors in the fall of that year. By that time Argentina was standing on the precipice of a major financial and political crisis. This crisis eventually resulted in the resignation of president Juárez Celman in August 1890 and the settlement of a major financial overhaul designed to appease (and rescue) Argentina's European investors, especially the British banking house Baring Brothers. The year 1891 was the first time that there was actually a net outflow of immigrants from Argentina.[69] Because of these factors and others, it is difficult to register quantitatively the immediate results of the Argentine exhibition presence. Nevertheless, it is possible to trace Argentine opinions with regard to the nation's participation in the fair. Overall, Argentine elites felt satisfied that they had shown Europe their nation's potential wealth; on the other hand, there continued to be skepticism within the Argentine elite as to the veracity of the exhibition image—with good reason.

Surprisingly, exposition workers who reported on the pavilion provided quite realistic criticism and praise of the pavilion's success. Enrique Nelson's letter to exposition commissioner Eduardo Olivera in Buenos Aires at the end of the summer of 1889 was, for example, quite candid. His letter opened with praise for Argentina's ability "to call attention to itself, to attract with irresistable force a world eager for new horizons." He went on to assure Olivera that after some of the early excesses and tasteless features of the pavilion had been removed or changed, the French public found the pavilion to be both *"superbe"* and *"fastueux"* (superb, splendid). Confidentially, Nelson admitted that the pavilion had many shortcomings, the worst of which had been hidden from public view. He informed Olivera that the pavilion had been erected "amidst the most colossal disorder and disorganization" that he had ever seen. Moreover, the pavilion's shoddy construction was such that it was one of the most fragile pavilions at the fair, making it the least apt to be disassembled and moved with any success. In Nelson's mind, the pavilion would have been much better had it been planned and constructed by people with more "refined tastes." Ultimately, he believed, "the Argentine pavilion [did not] reflect the sacrifices made for it, nor did it merit the commentary that it had stirred up."[70]

Santiago Alcorta presented a much more positive image of Argentina's exposition presence in his official report on the event. He believed that the Argentine pavilion had greatly expanded the knowledge of Argentina among people from many different nations. As proof, he cited an alleged conversation between famed British statesman William Gladstone and Argentine exhibition commission vice president Rafael Igarzabal at a Parisian banquet. During this exchange Gladstone had reportedly crooned, "You represent, sir, a country of wonders; your evolution in progress and wealth constitutes one of the phenomena of the present epoch." In its attempts to astound Europeans with Argentine progress, Alcorta clearly felt confident with the pavilion's success. In turn, he asserted that Argentina's self-presentation would give "incalculable results" further down the road.[71] The exact nature of these results remained inarticulated, but given the context of the exhibition's planning, capital, immigrants, and modernization would likely be at the top of his list.

Alcorta also noted some general lessons he had learned in the process of this exposition that would help Argentina in future expositions. Among these lessons, Alcorta stressed the importance of staffing the pavilion with people who could speak the language of the nation in which the exhibition was being held. He explained that this factor was vital when jurors visited, because a good guide could improve the chances of earning a medal. Alcorta also recommended that only goods worthy of being shown be sent for display; it was a waste of the government's money to do otherwise. For example, no items with labels imitating European brand names—such as perfume, wine, or liquor—should be sent; it would only force the members of the commission hastily to change the labels. Finally, he noted that since the majority of visitors to the pavilion were simply curious sightseers, elaborate and lengthy publications were not necessary. Less scientific and more popular treatises on the nation would have had a greater impact. When deemed important, special deluxe editions of these works could go to the jury members.[72]

Debates in the Argentine congress concerning funding for later exhibitions revealed that other elites shared Alcorta's generally positive views of Argentina's presence at the 1889 exposition. When contemplating the allocation of 100,000 pesos for the Chicago World's Columbian Exposition, slated for 1893, one deputy declared that Argentina's financial situation—then abysmal—made participation too extravagant. He felt that a poor showing in Chicago would be worse than no showing at all. In response, another deputy reminded him of the achievements of the Parisian appearance: "You will recall, Mr. President, that the Argentine Republic presented itself in the Paris exposition of 1889 in conditions that demonstrated before the world all of the wealth of the nation; and you should also recall the structure that the pavilion of the Argentine Republic was, which among the South American pavilions, called the attention of men of commerce, men of industry from all parts of the world. . . . A million, or maybe a million two hundred gold pesos were spent to demonstrate to the world the riches, the treasures that in industry, commerce, and mining the Argentine Republic possesses."[73]

In the opinion of this deputy, the 1889 pavilion and all the expenditures associated with it had achieved their foremost goal, which had been to "make Argentina known." In his view, participation in other world fairs was essential, even in times of economic hardship, to maintain (or repair) Argentina's image as a cache of bountiful riches awaiting European ingenuity. Moreover, Argentina needed to present a progressively better image at these fairs, in order to give tangible proof of its wealth and development.

Interestingly, the allocation of funds for a smaller Argentine showing at the Chicago exposition received support as a counterweight to the extravagance of the 1889 exposition. Most vocal in this sentiment was deputy Lucio V. Mansilla, who ridiculed the lavishness of the Paris pavilion and the Argentine tourists who flocked to the occasion. To the snickers of his audience he exclaimed, "In this exposition of Paris, more was spent on the palace of the exposition than on making the Republic's products known. And who knows! If looking for the origins of the multiple causes has brought us to this crisis, isn't it feasible to find them in some way in the Paris exposition? How many thousands of Argentines went to Paris, for no better reason than the exposition! How many millions of pesos did these Argentines take with them!"

While Mansilla wrongly asserted that all sorts of Argentine artistic objects filled the pavilion—he used the term *mamarrachos* (monstrosities)—his overall point was that Argentina should send to Chicago simply what it best knew how to make, abandoning the costly pretense of progress that it had fabricated for Paris. Nevertheless, he supported the plan for Argentina's participation in the Chicago event, asserting that such attendance would help further relations between the United States and Argentina.[74]

The fate of the 1889 Argentine pavilion revealed to some degree the transparency of Argentine "order and progress" displayed before European investors and immigrants. To the delight of Argentine elites, the pavilion had won a perfect score of 25 from the exhibition jury, ahead of Mexico (which received 22 points) and Brazil (20 points), thus upstaging their main Latin American rivals' exhibition constructions.[75] The onset of economic difficulties foiled plans to use the pavilion in Buenos Aires for an international exhibition to be held in 1890. The enormous cost of transporting the structure back to Buenos Aires pressed Argentines to try to sell off the pavilion in Europe; when a good price could not be secured, it languished in France until arrangements could be made for its shipment back to Buenos Aires. In February of 1890 the intendent of Buenos Aires received funds from the federal government to hire the ship *Ushuaia* to transport the pavilion back to Argentina. A storm at sea led to the loss of several important crates of material; more things were lost to exposure as the structure sat in Palermo, awaiting reconstruction. These materials would eventually be replaced by reproductions imported from Europe. Finally, in September 1892 a deal was made for the pavilion's reconstruction on the Plaza San Martín. A British contractor won the bid to reconstruct the pavilion in return for rents from the building. After much delay and negligence, "this building . . . that had been reproduced in all the magazines" found its home in Buenos Aires.[76] It went on to house sporadic exhibitions of Argentine industrial products and, later, the Museum of Fine Arts. The Argentine pavilion remained on the Plaza San Martín until 1933, when it was demolished to make room for the new Parque Retiro.[77]

J. M. Hammerton's harsh criticism of the Argentine pavilion as it appeared in 1916 revealed quite clearly the power that a nation's architecture had to bolster or undermine foreigners' faith in that nation's level of modernity. The elite creators of Argentina's showing at the Universal Exposition of 1889 understood this phenomenon and planned accordingly. For them, the creation of an image of Argentina as young, fertile, racially pure, and exotic, yet thoroughly civilized, was more than a publicity stunt. It was simultaneously a reflection of elite desires for the future and an important strategy for making such visions reality. The pavilion's architecture, ornamentation, and displays thus evolved in response to what elites viewed with disdain in their homelands, how they imagined their nation evolving toward a brighter, "whiter," more civilized future, and what characteristics they felt would best attract European immigrants and capital. The pavilion, with its idealized, purified juxtaposition of Argentina's natural bounty and the modern progress that such bounty had produced, reflected nearly perfectly the beliefs and aspirations of Argentina's elite—a glittering, cosmopolitan testament to the fortunes to be made from the wealth of Argentine soil.

SUGGESTED READINGS

Abels, Margaret Hutton. "Painting at the Brazil Centennial Exposition." *Art and Archaeology* 16 (summer 1923): 105–14.

Beezley, William H., ed., Special Issue of *Studies in Latin American Popular Culture* 38 (2010) on Latin America at the World's Fairs.

Chasteen, John Charles, and Sara Castro Klaren, eds. *Beyond Imagined Communities: Reading and Writing the Nation in 19th-Century Latin America.* Baltimore: Johns Hopkins University Press, 2003.

Kaminsky, Amy. *Argentina: Stories for a Nation.* Minneapolis: University of Minnesota Press, 2008.

Levine, Daniel H., ed. *Constructing Culture and Power in Latin America.* Ann Arbor: University of Michigan Press, 1993.

Masotta, Carlos, ed. *Indians in Argentinean Photographic Postcards of the 20th Century.* Buenos Aires: La Marca, 2007.

Rydell, Robert. *All the World's a Fair: Visions of Empire. International Expositions 1876–1916.* Chicago: University of Chicago Press, 1984.

Shumway, Nicolas. *The Invention of Argentina.* Berkeley: University of California Press, 1991.

Tenorio-Trillo, Mauricio. *Mexico at the World's Fairs: Crafting a Modern Nation.* Berkeley: University of California Press, 1996.

Yeager, Gene. "Porifiran Commercial Propaganda: Mexico in the World Industrial Expositions." *The Americas* 34 (October 1977): 230–43.

Sights

Argentina y sus Imágenes. 2003. Horizons Collection.
Don Segundo Sombra. 1989. Directed by Manuel Antín (Facets Multimedia).
Doña Bárbara. 1943. Directed by Fernando de Fuentes (Facets Multimedia).
Martín Fierro. 1968. Directed by Leopoldo Nilsson (Facets Multimedia).

Sounds

Songs of the Gauchos (FHS).

6

Death and Disorder in Mexico City

The State Funeral of Manuel Romero Rubio

Matthew D. Esposito

Government rituals such as funerals, parades, and commemorations of monuments or national holidays provided exceptional opportunities for political leaders to present the official interpretation of cultural trends and historical events to the general public, especially in the heavily populated cities. Official rituals served political and didactic ends. Leaders could invent new traditions and eliminate old ones as they attempted to forge legitimacy for their rule by linking their political accomplishments to those of previous heroes. State funerals in particular lent themselves quite well to such didactic purposes while also creating new heroes for the admiration of the masses. In the late nineteenth century, these funerals could also serve as showcases of modernity. In between the eulogies and the patriotic panegyrics, funeral processions highlighted the material progress of the newly refurbished Latin American capitals. Such rituals also became display cases for urban social relations between rulers and those they governed. Matthew Esposito analyzes the significance of the official funeral of Manuel Romero Rubio, father-in-law and right-hand man of the quintessential Liberal dictator, Porfirio Díaz of Mexico, and links the funereal spectacle to questions not only of legitimacy but also of order and progress.

State funerals were one of the most significant and frequently performed political rituals of the regime of Porfirio Díaz (1876–1911). Their importance can be measured by their number. Over the course of the regime, political leaders organized, financed, and performed more than one hundred national burials. On ten occasions they ordered the exhumation of the remains of national heroes and had them reburied in spectacular state ceremonies.[1] Civic funerals served as a vehicle for promoting political legitimacy and state formation through the public commemoration of the cult of heroes.[2]

During the Porfirian years, the state sponsored various civil festivals. Official memorial services honoring the nation's war dead took place on every national holiday, and days of public mourning were declared on the anniversaries of the deaths of Vicente Guerrero (February 14), Benito Juárez (July 18), Miguel Hidalgo (July 30), Cuauhtémoc (August 21), the Niños Héroes (Boy Heroes, September 8), and José María Morelos (December 22). State funerals marked the official enshrinement of leaders in the growing pantheon of national heroes. Díaz's inauguration of the Rotonda de los Hombres Ilustres, in 1877, and the famous marble mausoleum of Juárez, in 1880, demonstrated his concern with promoting the cult of heroes to legitimize his government.[3]

The Porfirian state honored distinguished public leaders through elegant funeral ceremonies. Enormous crowds of up to 150,000 citizens, or one-third of Mexico City's population, attended these great public spectacles.[4] The bureaucratization of the event guaranteed a significant official presence. The government designed the funerals to draw all patriotic citizens and to make both visual and acoustical appeals to curious spectators. These state funerals were costly theatrical performances that showcased the capital city and projected a modern image to foreign observers, not least of whom were prospective business investors. Moreover, state funerals served the state's pedagogical aims: public buildings, streets, and cemeteries became classrooms for informal instruction. In each state funeral program, the public lying-in-state, procession, and burial were surrounded by visual emblems intended to inculcate civic and moral values in illiterate citizens. Fallen leaders were promoted as archetypical patriots to be venerated by the masses. Spectacle and public oratory were used as didactic tools in an incessant moralizing campaign. Funeral orations, sometimes attended by thousands, taught lessons of the past, reinventing the historical memory of the popular classes. In small and large ways, state funerals crystallized national identity.[5]

The state funeral of Manuel Romero Rubio in October 1895 demonstrates the typical Porfirian ceremony and reveals a good deal about its function. This funeral was the most extravagant, highly attended, and disorderly national burial of the era. Indeed, the government spared no expense in making it the national drama of 1895, coincidentally a week before the Catholic Church's coronation of the Virgin of Guadalupe on October 12, 1895.[6] Thousands of visitors, including Mexicans from the outlying states and ecclesiastics from all over the world, poured into Mexico City for the ceremonial crowning of the Virgin. Many were in town in time to witness Romero Rubio's burial. In addition, 1895 was the first year in which Mexico operated under a balanced budget, and the state funeral was organized to present to the world a modern, prosperous image.[7] Despite the state's intentions, the performance fell short of expectations and cast into relief the tensions between the ruling and popular classes. Romero Rubio's burial provides more than a snapshot of fin-de-siècle political culture in 1895; it also serves as a lens through which to examine social relations between the ruling elite and popular classes, the sources of Porfirian legitimacy, and the process by which Díaz perpetuated himself in office for more than three decades.

Romero Rubio was among the nation's foremost statesmen at the time of his death. Born in 1828 to a wealthy criollo family in Mexico City, Manuel was only two years older than Porfirio Díaz. As a young man, he pursued a career in law and, like many of his Liberal brethren, forged his reputation in the crucible of the Revolution of Ayutla that permanently forced Santa Anna out of the country in 1854. Like Benito Juárez, Romero Rubio called for reducing church influence and establishing a Liberal government. He participated in the War of the Reform (1858–1861) and, although he possessed no military training, became an officer, with eventual promotion to brigadier general. The arrival of the French in 1862 again took Romero Rubio into the field, where he fought against Maximilian's forces until he was captured by the enemy and allowed to go into exile in Europe. The restoration of the Republic returned him to congress. His home became the meeting place for delegates, who worked out conflicts and details before the official vote. In 1874 he helped procure passage of the constitutional amendments calling for a bicameral legislature and guaranteeing civil marriage, lay cemeteries, and separation of church and state. Later, president Sebastián Lerdo de Tejada appointed Romero Rubio foreign relations minister. His service lasted less than three months before Díaz's revolution of Tuxtepec forced the president and his minister into exile. After returning to Mexico, Romero Rubio was both beneficiary and benefactor of the Díaz policy of conciliation and quickly returned to congress.

In that same year, 1880, Porfirio married Romero Rubio's oldest daughter, Carmen, ironically Sebastián Lerdo de Tejada's goddaughter.[8] The marriage helped consolidate a political alliance between competing Liberal factions; together, Romero Rubio and Díaz plotted to bring Díaz back to power in 1884. A social leader, Romero Rubio tutored a generation of powerful bankers, lawyers, and intellectuals, known as the *científicos*, who followed the doctrines of Auguste Comte and Herbert Spencer. José Y. Limantour recalled that several prominent young men met regularly at Don Manuel's law office to discuss Mexico's future.[9] Romero Rubio also seems to have been a silent partner in the state-subsidized newspaper, *El Partido Liberal*, the official voice of *Porfirismo* that was edited by Justo Sierra.[10] On December 1, 1884, Díaz appointed his father-in-law minister of the interior. They celebrated that evening together with other cabinet members, enjoying music performances at the Romero Rubio residence.[11]

The paternalistic Romero Rubio brought a new element into the Porfirian government, and his influence was felt over the next decade through the appointment of his circle of friends and relatives to important government posts. Various *científicos* entered public office under the protection of Romero Rubio,[12] who exhibited a preference for working behind the scenes as an administrator, legislator, organizer, and above all a conciliator. He developed a knack for administrative efficiency while serving as secretary of both the Supreme Court and the Federal District government.[13]

Although Díaz generally juggled the offices of the ministers, Romero Rubio had remained minister of the interior for more than a decade. In this capacity he administered the penal system, instituted the sanitary regulations of the Federal District and national territories, and, in Mexico City, regularly inaugurated and visited schools, hospitals, prisons, and asylums. Although he believed that charity was best left to private benefactors, he started a registry of all charitable institutions in Mexico City, contributed to several, and served as honorary president of some working-class associations and mutualist societies. Through three censuses that he ordered, in 1889, 1890, and 1895, his name reached into every home of the republic.[14]

Romero Rubio died suddenly and unexpectedly of a brain hemorrhage on Thursday morning, October 3, 1895. As a result, civil government temporarily shifted from the National Palace to the Romero Rubio residence on Calle de San Andres, and, after Generals Felipe Berriorzabal and Mariano Escobedo arrived, the house also took on the appearance of military headquarters. Díaz quickly formed a junta to make funeral preparations. Sentries at the entrance of the home regulated traffic and maintained order.

Messengers rushed in and out of the house with instructions and telegrams. Cannons, fired every half hour at the Citadel, added to the solemnity. Prominent citizens arrived to console the family; one journalist counted thirty horse-drawn carriages in the street by noon. Every high government official paid his respects. Crowds representing all social classes soon gathered in the street outside the home.[15]

Normal business and social activity halted as state functionaries scrambled to prepare the funeral. Díaz requested foreign relations minister Ignacio Mariscal to notify government offices and send official announcements to the members of the diplomatic corps. Subsecretary Manuel Aspiroz named an honor guard for the lying-in-state.[16] Romero Rubio's personal secretary, Rosendo Piñeda, notified the state government by telegram.[17] In the chamber of deputies, Guillermo Prieto delivered a powerful speech, imploring patriotic deputies to approve a national burial. Congress resolved that the national government would assume all funeral costs, then adjourned for three days. An official period of mourning was announced. The senators and deputies ordered their chambers decked in black bunting for nine days and national flags flown at half-mast for three days. Members named committees to console the family, ask permission for the body to be transferred to the congressional building, and prepare public security.[18]

The city council canceled its sessions, illuminated the balconies of the municipal palace for three days, and named a commission to express its sympathy to the president and his family. Councilmen asked residents of San Andrés and adjacent streets to use mourning colors to decorate the facades of their homes. Ayuntamiento president Sebastián Camacho composed a message to Díaz, reminding him of the public demonstration that the city council had held for Romero Rubio less than a month earlier, during which the councilmen had thanked him for his friendship and contributions to the city. Romero Rubio had replied with the affectionate expression, "General Díaz is my family."[19] Schools suspended classes. The Chamber of Commerce obliged business leaders to close their shops. The normally ubiquitous musical groups in public squares and parks were nowhere to be seen, and these places and the promenades were deserted. The Arbeu Theater, Principal Theater, and Orrin's Circus canceled all performances. The German, Spanish, French, and National casinos and the Jockey Club dressed their buildings in mourning and closed their doors. Doña Carmen canceled plans to distribute gifts to the poor in the Alameda.[20]

As numerous priests arrived at the Romero Rubio residence to offer condolences, the Liberal, anticlerical newspaper *El Siglo XIX* accused the "hateful clergy" of trying to "gain entrance to the house."[21] Romero Rubio's anticlericalism was well known, but this did not dissuade Father Abad Plancarte at the Colegiata de Nuestra Señora de Guadalupe from offering a prayer for him and leading the congregation in an "Our Father" and two "Hail Marys." He prayed for Señora Castello de Rubio, Manuel's wife, and asked parishioners to comfort the oldest daughter, the "caring and pious" wife of the president. Parishioners knelt and prayed for the family. The flag at the Colegiata was flown at half-mast. The tolling of church bells competed with cannon salvos.[22] Such behavior reflected to some extent Díaz's reconciliation policy.

Mexico's most distinguished artist, Jesus Contreras, was chosen for the traditional task of forming the death mask, a deeply rooted tradition that originated in Europe. Artists in the nineteenth century used plaster of Paris (*yeso*) to create a lasting mold of the deceased's face for posterity. Sculptors used the masks as models to reproduce an accurate visage on busts, statues, and sepulchral monuments. Contreras had achieved his national reputation for his bas-reliefs on the Cuauhtémoc monument, the equestrian statue of Ignacio Zaragoza in Puebla, and the statues of Ramón Corona in Guadalajara, Juárez in Chihuahua City, and González Ortega in Zacateacas. He also served as the director (Díaz was the honorary president) of the Fundación Artística Mexicana, the company the federal government contracted to produce all the statues along the Paseo de la Reforma. The

Porfirian government sent Contreras to Europe, where he studied sculpture in preparation for his work on the Mexican Palace at the Paris Universal Exposition of 1889. In the palace, his sculptures of the ancient indigenous leaders Cuauhtémoc, Cuitlahuac, Cacama, Netzahualcoytl, Itzcoatl, and the king of Tacuba were displayed. His marble sculpture *Desepoir y Magre Tout* won first prize at the Paris exposition and brought him international prestige. He also served as a city councilman in the Federal District. If there was an "official sculptor" of the Porfiriato, it was almost certainly Contreras, as he made dozens of death masks of prominent Mexicans, including Romero Rubio.[23]

The official junta transferred the body to the national legislature. Shortly before 4 P.M., Díaz dispatched dozens of messengers to distribute both official and private mortuary announcements throughout Mexico City. These black-bordered cards, called *esquelas*, were always hand-delivered. The official cards, destined for government employees, requested their presence at the funeral ceremony in the chamber of deputies the following day. The private set, printed on imitation vintage paper and bearing a black cross (perhaps at the request of Manuel's pious wife), asked guests to attend the burial at the French Cemetery.[24]

The president considered burying Romero Rubio in the Rotonda de los Hombres Ilustres but acquiesced to family requests to bury him in the family vault. The Romero Rubios had just lost a daughter, María, to illness and had spent 40,000 pesos on a gothic-style marble mausoleum in the prestigious French Cemetery. The family, Porfirio and Manuel included, had visited the new tomb in August to place flowers and a golden cage containing a white turtledove on the grave of María.[25]

Congressmen and councilmen arrived at the Romero Rubio residence to escort the casket to the congressional building, but a severe thunderstorm delayed them for almost two hours. A cortege of eight hundred dignitaries eventually processed the casket to the chamber. Behind President Díaz, a long train of mourners bearing wreaths and umbrellas marched solemnly to the sound of the national anthem. The rain-soaked route was decorated with black bunting and crepe paper. Overhead a series of arc lights fitted with tricolor lamps especially for the occasion illuminated the marchers. One journalist remarked that the lights emitted an "eerie green glow" that gave a "weird effect to the slow moving procession."[26]

Arriving at the chamber of deputies, mourners found an improvised chapel ablaze with light. The chapel had been decorated by a congressional committee. Wide mourning curtains cascaded from the second-floor theater box railings and banisters. Clusters of tricolored flags sat in the aisles. Decorators covered the inappropriately colored crimson curtain that fell from the ceiling to the speaking platform with an enormous tricolor flag and placed before it the elegant black-and-silver coffin. The city council had sent twenty floral wreaths to cover the coffin. Teams of deputies and senators rotated as honorary bodyguard for the duration of the night.[27]

The early-morning public viewing of the body as it lay in state proved chaotic. Friday morning was miserably wet. Crowds from all classes began to gather at 6 A.M. After two hours of waiting the public grew restless, and when officials finally opened the building an impatient crowd rushed for the door, causing a brief period of total chaos. Sixty forceful policemen reestablished some semblance of order, but for hours people continued to push and shove, and "invade all of the theater boxes and aisles of the chamber."[28]

The legislative chamber had been transformed overnight. The decorating committee had surrounded the casket with a garden of plants, flowers, and floral wreaths and had completely carpeted the auditorium floor with flowers and potted pines throughout the room. Floral fragrances were overwhelmed by the odor of burning sulfur in the two dozen flowerpots used to represent eternal flames. Decorators also ran black crepe throughout the hall. The chandelier burned 220 white and green bulbs that cast brilliant light on the entire scene. Through a square piece of glass inset into the upper third of the coffin the bust of the fallen hero was visible.[29]

The central events of the state funeral—an official ceremony in the chamber of deputies held for the governing class and a procession through the streets for the general public—were scheduled for Friday afternoon. The two events, while connected as part of a coherent agenda, had distinct intentions and meanings. The funeral ceremony, an exclusive event, gathered national representatives together to reemphasize their collective worth after death claimed one of their prominent members. The public procession, which involved all citizens, represented a manifestation of state power. Both private affair and public display compensated for the momentary weakening of the social hierarchy brought about by the loss of Romero Rubio.

The seating arrangement at the chamber attested to its exclusivity and presented a tableau of political authority. In the center of the row closest to the casket sat President Díaz. Cabinet members and the presidents of both congressional houses flanked him. Opposite Díaz, veteran congressmen, the Federal District governor, and Supreme Court justices filled two rows. Behind them the entire chamber of deputies occupied seats as if in session. Prominent men of society, journalists, and diplomats representing the United States, Europe, and Latin America shared the box seats surrounding the floor. The funeral ceremony assembled more powerful men than even Díaz's state-of-the-union message of the previous April. The public galleries were virtually empty. As if to guard against the type of popular disorder that had marred the funeral of the independence heroes in July, the 21st Battalion guarded the portico of the congressional building during the ceremony.[30]

Authorities from each branch of government eulogized Romero Rubio. President of congress Alfredo Chavero spoke for the national legislature, Ignacio Mariscal for the executive branch, and supreme court justice Félix Romero for the judiciary. In each eulogy, orators expounded on the personal traits of the deceased and emphasized Romero Rubio's exploits during the Reform War and the French Intervention, linking him with the most recognizable heroes of the Republic. Chavero gave a history lesson that traced Romero Rubio's triumphant marches with Generals Jesús González Ortega and Ignacio Zaragoza and reminded listeners of Romero Rubio's struggle with the church, stating that his true deities were "the Fatherland and Liberty." Foreign relations minister Mariscal praised Romero Rubio's work for the cause of progress and pointed to his role in inspiring the heroic career of General Santos Degollado. As in most Porfirian-era funeral orations, the final orator rounded out the eulogy with a didactic message. Magistrate Romero said that Romero Rubio's life and death served as lessons to the generation attending "this touching ceremony." He implored everyone to approach the casket, learn from Romero Rubio's example of political firmness and republican energy, and close ranks with President Díaz to preserve unity, peace, and the greatness of the Republic.[31]

These speeches, as well as the obituaries published in Liberal newspapers, praised Romero Rubio as a hero worthy of national and international glory. The respected congressman and nationalist poet Guillermo Prieto recounted Romero Rubio's crucial role in reorganizing Republican forces and finances in Tamaulipas during the French invasion. "With the authority of his patriotism Romero established Harmony, inspired confidence in commerce, left command of the plaza to General Pavón, gave 20,000 pesos to Vargas so that he could unite with forces situated in Querétaro, sent resources to Juárez and utilized the forces of Gómez and Cuesta with singular good judgment and patriotism." For services rendered, Prieto wrote, the state of Tamaulipas declared Romero Rubio an illustrious citizen, or *benemérito*.[32]

Just as the government asked every high official to attend the ceremony in the chamber of deputies, it required policemen, soldiers, and military cadets to provide security and contribute to the upcoming public spectacle, the funeral procession. Anticipating that a large crowd of spectators would line the long route from Factor Street to the French Cemetery in the suburb of La Piedad, planners mobilized every symbol of Porfirian authority to maintain order. Cadets from the Military College at Chapultepec filed from the congressional building's portico, where the casket would emerge, down the stairs to the end of the street. The *rurales*, Díaz's rural constabulary, assumed command at the corner of Vergara and San Francisco Streets. Mounted gendarmes spaced themselves to Independence Street, where the regular gendarmes stood watch. Several artillery corps guarded the penultimate leg along the bumpy road to La Piedad. Four hundred students of the Industrial School for Orphans, known as Romero Rubio's Tecpan boys, reverently formed an aisle from the cemetery's entrance to the Romero Rubio chapel. They wore black ribbons on their left arms and carried bouquets of flowers to deposit at the tomb. A detachment of mounted *rurales* accompanied the hearse from start to finish. An awesome display of state authority guarded the border between the elites of the procession and the popular classes on the sidewalk. The martial air was announced acoustically as cannon at the Ciudadela fired three salvos every half hour until Romero Rubio was interred.[33]

Perhaps the show of force was necessary, since newspapers estimated that between 100,000 and 250,000 citizens lined the streets to witness the procession. Although there is no way to verify attendance figures, newspapers uniformly spoke of the "awesome attendance," "the jumbled masses," "multitudinous throng," "immense crowd," and "wave of human flesh" that made it impossible to move along sidewalks or in the streets. Some four hundred government employees, two hundred army officers, one hundred bankers and businessmen, three hundred congressmen, two platoons of *rurales*, and numerous veteran soldiers marched in the procession. Observers counted over a thousand mourners in the procession, excluding the military units and the civil servants that followed the procession and the security forces that lined the route of march.[34] Everyday life in Mexico City had halted, freeing up bureaucrats, students, businessmen, and factory workers, judging from the number of working-class associations flying their banners in the procession. The railroad brought citizens from neighboring states.[35] Tens of thousands occupied plazas, alleys, balconies, and rooftops. The road to La Piedad, which linked the downtown area with the French Cemetery, was lined with countless campesinos. One newspaper asserted "without hyperbole" that three-fourths of the city's inhabitants attended.[36]

In certain aspects the funeral resembled a civic festival, including the departure from normal time. The solemn spectacle of the enormous procession contrasted starkly with everyday living. The appearance of six huge, spirited black horses slowly pulling an elegant black hearse through lines established by uniformed men inspired awe among a people accustomed to dodging smaller carriages drawn recklessly by undernourished horses. On this day, the only horses that appeared were those fit beasts mounted by the corps of *rurales* and gendarmes, and the horses, draped with black robes, that pulled the hearse. Adding to the impression of the horses' natural beauty and strength were the six groomsmen who walked beside the hearse, each holding a horse's bridle. Atop the hearse appeared six golden angels. Two horse-drawn drays carrying five hundred funeral wreaths and resembling parade floats followed. Some of the wreaths were so large they required eight men to carry and load them on the platform cars. The one from Guanajuato's governor Luis González Obregón was made of silver.

Newspaper reporters claimed that no person had ever received a larger number of funeral wreaths or been attended by more mourners from all classes of society.[37]

The procession following the hearse provided a linear representation of Porfirian political and social structure. In this ceremony, Díaz performed the role of mournful president rather than son-in-law, riding at the head of the procession rather than with his family. His car was followed by the elite of Porfirian politics: cabinet members, congressmen, and foreign ambassadors. Behind them appeared the heart of the procession: two coaches for the Romero Rubio family and friends. The bureaucratic body was represented next, by delegations of the Supreme Court, the Military Supreme Court, and representatives of the various ministries. Military commanders and city government officials rounded out the official section. Families that the Romero Rubios invited to attend, a privileged upper class that had helped perpetuate the authoritarian regime, formed the next section. Delegations of workers' guilds and mutual societies and an entire division of soldiers brought up the rear. The organizers had taken the precaution of providing an ambulance equipped with six stretchers at the end of the line. The majority of the city's urban working class and poor were allowed to participate only as spectators from positions on the sidewalk. The state encouraged observers but set limits on the extent of popular involvement. Disenfranchised members of society were relegated to the sidewalks and alleys, their positions reflecting the distance between rich and poor.[38]

If order represented one theme of this pageant, progress was the second. The organizers planned the route to travel through the wealthiest urban streets in Mexico City and tour the city of palaces. Leaving the government district of Factor and Vergara Streets, the cortege passed before the resplendent colonial buildings along San Francisco, San Juan de Letrán, and Independence Streets. Mourners moved through the shadows of the imposing facades of the Casa de Azulejos (the Jockey Club), the American Club, the Mexican Company of London, the Exposition Company, and the Escandón mansion.

The processional route was decorated in mourning black, but also in the national colors, demonstrating the government's intention to make this a day of public mourning as well as patriotism. All along the route decorators placed green shades over every lamppost, drawing attention to the great progress the government had made in replacing gas-powered public lamps with electric lighting. City workers also strung special green lightbulbs across intersections. The beautiful black carriages that belonged to the elite were parked along the streets.

The funeral marchers boarded forty-seven streetcars at Independence Street and advanced rapidly toward the cemetery, until an engine of progress halted the procession: an unexpected passenger train of the Valley

Railroad passed by. Passengers crowded windows and platforms to witness the spectacle.[39]

The crossing passenger train broke the procession in half and was only one of the unforeseen problems that disrupted the funeral. Inclement weather on October 3 delayed the transfer of Romero Rubio's body to the congressional building. In the chamber of deputies, a candle or sulfur-burning pot ignited one of the curtains draped over the coffin platform just as pallbearers were placing the casket. Two congressmen burned their hands extinguishing it. During the official ceremony, "an African heat" in the auditorium, intensified by the burning lamps, had forced suffering officials outside for fresh air.[40]

The sheer mass of humanity that turned out for the event created a number of problems. The forty-seven special streetcars made available for the members of the procession proved inadequate. With the last of the cars filled, those bringing up the rear boarded improvised carriages to travel to the cemetery. The foremost problem to beset the funeral procession, however, was the disorderly crowd, whose numbers and enthusiasm exceeded all estimates. Soon after the casket emerged from the congressional building the "thinly placed" Chapultepec cadets failed to restrain the crowd from surging into the mourners. In the streets, hundreds of people grabbed a place in the procession, paying respect to Romero Rubio or, in some instances, mocking the elite. Rurales drove disorderly citizens back onto the sidewalks, and policemen "used clubs freely" to contain a throng that congested every street.

Nevertheless, the police found it difficult to maintain much order. The crowd itself badly squeezed some individuals as it surged forward to see the procession. Others scaled carriages parked along the route to glimpse the procession. Hats and umbrellas fell victim to the stampede. The crowd slowed up streetcars on several Federal District lines. Thieves had a field day. Archbishop of Oaxaca Eulogio Gillow, one of the president's closest friends, lost a watch costing U.S. $800 to a pickpocket, who sacrilegiously finagled it off his wrist.[41]

The solemn quality of the state funeral frequently degenerated into sporadic spurts of crowd-induced chaos. The crowd's response demonstrated the persistence of popular or folk liberalism, a legacy of Juárez. People had a sense of what was fair, a certain notion of the moral economy of their festive and participatory rights. Just as the people believed they had dignity as individuals, constitutionally established as citizens of Mexico and demonstrated through their personal honor, they also had the right to participate in civic celebrations such as public funerals.[42]

The modern, progressive state funeral degenerated as the procession entered the bucolic area on the approach to La Piedad. Campesinos appeared everywhere, peering from rooftops and tree branches. Here the poor played unrehearsed roles, and the state's manifestations of power and modernity lost their potency. A microcosm of the era, the funeral procession acted as a lightning rod for the conflict between the elites and lower classes. When the cortege arrived at the French Cemetery, chaos again ensued as the police lost control at the cemetery entrance and citizens poured through the gates. Guardians at the gate finally reasserted authority and forced the crowd into a nearby ditch. Nevertheless, one of the scheduled speakers could not make it to the podium because he was trapped behind the compact wall of people outside.[43]

The funeral cortege arrived at the cemetery and passed through the saluting Tecpan students to the sound of muffled drums and mournful cornets. Pallbearers set the casket under an ornate catafalque erected next to the Romero Rubio chapel, and Juan de Dios Peza, the official bard of the Porfirian regime, recited poety before the crowd. The casket was consigned to the vault with the assistance of a single priest, whose presence scarcely compensated for the absence of church influence throughout the civic ceremony. Cannon and rifle salvos followed the interment. The procession had begun an hour late, at 3:30 in the afternoon, and the burial was completed by 5:30, but, in keeping with tradition, mourners returned along the same route to the point of origin by 7 P.M. The funeral march, burial, and return had lasted three and one-half hours.[44]

Despite obstacles, the funeral ceremony of Romero Rubio was, in the final analysis, a magnificent manifestation of a nation in mourning and therefore a success for the Porfirian government. The funeral did not come off as planned; as state theater the project gasped and sputtered, but the enthusiasm of the crowd, not the effectiveness of state management, offered a barometer of Porfirian success. Public emotion was successfully tapped. That the forces of order failed to contain the masses was not seen as a dissolution of order but as a model for popular participation. The working-class crowd insisted that it be allowed to participate and, despite the government's forces, it did. The funeral drew more popular participation than the government had planned. Romero Rubio was supposed to be carried off to the cemetery in the company of a limited number of government officials; instead, he was swept there by the country.

Public discussion of Romero Rubio and his career continued across the nation in the following weeks. Within days of the funeral, sensational rumors spread that Romero Rubio, a Mason and an anticleric, had embraced Catholicism and reconciled with God just before he died. Conservative Catholics had routinely denounced Romero Rubio for persecuting the Catholic press, subordinating the legislative to the executive branch of government, and even depreciating silver coinage. Gossip over his alleged last-minute conversion and deathbed confession reached fever pitch in the national press, as Liberal newspapers waged war on the assertions of the conservative ones. Like Juárez, Romero Rubio was a *puro*, an advocate of a strong liberal and secular state devoid of church influence in politics, society, and educational affairs. His widely known anticlericalism was a defining characteristic of his political reputation. Now the Catholic press attacked him. "Mr. Romero Rubio," *La Tribuna* charged with ridicule, "one of the most active promoters of the . . . 'Laws of the Reform,' . . . at the hour that he felt death call him, calls to a nearby priest [and] . . . reconciles with the Catholic Church." *Diario del Hogar*'s José Rivera responded coldly, berating the article as "profoundly slanderous" for depicting Romero Rubio as a Nero- or Diocletian-like persecutor of Catholics. He also replied that the priest who administered the last rights on behalf of the family encountered a Romero Rubio almost lifeless from the brain hemorrhage that had rendered him comatose and then killed him. It seems the Liberal press sought out Rosendo Piñeda, Romero Rubio's personal secretary and "political protege," who was with him at the time of his death. Piñeda explained in a letter published in Liberal newspapers that Romero Rubio was irretrievably unconscious when the family priest Prebitero Violante arrived, and that he died shortly thereafter.[45]

The collective memory of Manuel Romero Rubio survived at least as long as the Porfirian state, as public officials throughout the republic commemorated him in various ways. Telegrams and letters expressing the deepest sympathies to Díaz and praising the fallen statesman poured into the National Palace from throughout the republic.[46] Chihuahuans held a literary event in Romero Rubio's honor. Abstaining from the Coronation of the Virgin ceremony, the editors of *El Partido Liberal* deposited a copy of their newspaper wrapped in black crepe, along with a bundle of flowers, at his tomb on October 12.[47] The family, including President Díaz, visited the tomb on All Souls' Day, November 1. On the Day of the Dead, November 2, 1895, the monument that called the most attention to itself was the sepulchre of Don Manuel Romero Rubio. Four hundred uniformed students of the Industrial School for Orphans had covered his tomb with wreaths and flowers picked from the school grounds. The eleven-year-olds delivered speeches, recited poetry, and otherwise posthumously thanked Romero Rubio for his support of the school. The following day employees of the interior ministry joined delegates from the state of Michoacan in a tribute to Romero Rubio, celebrating the one-month anniversary of his death. Special streetcars were provided to transport them from the Plaza de la Constitución to the Panteón Frances. Meanwhile, in San Luis Potosí, Governor Carlos Diez Gutiérrez decorated the forum of the Teatro de la Paz with pyramids, one of which was crowned with a portrait of Romero Rubio, and held a ceremony in his honor. Finally, a hundred lawyers from the capital district bar association processed to his tomb on November 4.[48]

A chapter in Mexican history closed in 1895, but a new one was being written about Romero Rubio. A year after his death, Sebastián Camacho and Alfredo Chavero led another procession to the French Cemetery in Romero Rubio's honor. Senator Apolinar Castillo's commemorative speech praised Don Manuel, renewed memories of his life, and placed him in the continuum of Liberal heroes. "Nations justly revere all their great men," he said; "[W]e see in Hidalgo the creative force which brought forth Morelos and Guerrero . . . in Juárez the creative force of Miguel and Sebastián Lerdo de Tejada, of Ocampo and Zaragoza, and in Porfirio Díaz . . . the many able men who have worked and are still working with him for the aggrandizement and peace of the Republic. . . . Life is mnemonic, gentlemen, the present is bound to the past by memory . . . [departed] great men continue to be useful to humanity. . . . [49]

The glorification of Romero Rubio continued in October 1896 at the National Theater, when his closest compatriots placed him on a pedestal. On the stage a bust of Don Manuel was erected, accompanied by a weeping allegorical figure of the Patria. In the theater's foyer, large blocks of ice with flowers frozen inside were arranged in a hollow cube; the lights inside shone brilliantly through. An orchestra performed classical compositions along with a short piece composed in remembrance of Romero Rubio. Congressman José María Gamboa's speech pursued the same themes of Liberal continuity, adding that the present generation would transmit its admiration of Romero Rubio to the next. Joaquín Casasus renewed memories of the magnificent funeral of the previous year during which public officials, war veterans, youths, businessmen, great men and common men alike formed the cortege. His speech sounded brief praise—"We come today to celebrate the apotheosis of one of the most noble and August personalities of our contemporary history"—but resounded with exaltation of the regime: "Peace has to rest on three solid foundations: material improvements, popular education, and order."[50]

Manuel Romero Rubio passed away quietly on October 3, 1895, surrounded by his closest family and friends. Within a single workday Díaz had prepared a sumptuous state funeral ceremony, the performance of which deviated from intentions. Porfirian mythologizers used state funerals to reconstitute the social order, improve Mexico's international image, and coalesce civic ideology. The ceremonies also reflected the state's attempt to rewrite national history from the standpoint of its great men. Porfirians bolstered the image of their late companions in arms and determined the positions they would hold in the growing cult of heroes. During the heyday of the regime, the state funerals succeeded in maintaining an illusion of strength and modernity, despite minor setbacks. Frequent, lavish, and orthodox, the ceremonies reminded citizens of the relationship between their heroes and Porfirio Díaz, the powerful leader who buried them all.

SUGGESTED READINGS

Ben-Amos, Avner. "The Sacred Center of Power: Paris and Republican State Funerals." *Journal of Interdisciplinary History* 22, no. 1 (summer 1991): 27–48.

Earle, Rebecca. "Sobre Héroes y Tumbas: National Symbols in Nineteenth-Century Spanish America." *Hispanic American Historical Review* 85, no. 3 (August 2005): 375–416.

Frank, Patrick. *Posada's Broadsheets: Mexican Popular Imagery, 1890–1910*. Albuquerque: University of New Mexico Press, 1998.

Johns, Michael. *The City of Mexico in the Age of Diaz*. Austin: University of Texas Press, 1997.

Johnson, Lyman. *Death, Dismemberment and Memory: Body Politics in Latin America*. Albuquerque: University of New Mexico Press, 2004.

Lehning, James R. "Gossiping about Gambetta: Contested Memories in the Early Third Republic." *French Historical Studies* 18, no. 1 (spring 1993): 237–54.

Leonard, Irving. *Baroque Times in Old Mexico*. Ann Arbor: University of Michigan Press, 1959.

Lomnitz-Adler, Claudio. *Death and the Idea of Mexico*. Brooklyn, NY: Zone Books, 2005.

Posada, José Guadalupe. *Posada's Popular Mexican Prints*. New York: Dover Publications, 1972.

Ramos, Frances. "Succession and Death: Royal Ceremonials in Colonial Puebla." *The Americas* 2003 Vol. 60, No. 2: 185–215.

Reis, Joao Jose. *Death Is a Festival: Funeral Rites and Rebellion in 19th-Century Brazil*. Chapel Hill: University of North Carolina Press, 2003.

Schwartz, Stuart B., ed. *A Governor and His Image in Baroque Brazil: The Funeral Eulogy of Afonso Furtado de Castro do Rio de Mendonça*, edited by Juan Lopes Sierra, translated by Ruth E. Jones. Minneapolis: James Ford Bell Library of the University of Minnesota, 1979.

Strocchia, Sharon. *Death and Ritual in Renaissance Florence*. Baltimore: Johns Hopkins University Press, 1992.

Sights

Como Agua para Chocolate. 1992. Directed by Alfonso Arau (Facets Multimedia).
Day of the Dead (Facets Multimedia).
Evita: The Woman behind the Myth (Facets Multimedia).
Guantanamera. 1994. Directed by Tomás Gutiérrez Alea (Facets Multimedia).
Kordavision. 2005. Directed by Hector Cruz Sandoval.
Macario. 1958. Directed by Roberto Gavaldán (Facets Multimedia).
Mystery of Eva Perón. 2008. Directed by Tulio Demicheli.
Santa Anna. Su Alteza Serenísma. 2001. Directed by Felipe Cazals.

7

Images of Indians in the Construction of Ecuadorian Identity at the End of the Nineteenth Century

Blanca Muratorio

Central to government legitimacy was the need to define national identity in relation to the larger global community. During the late nineteenth century, Latin American elites had a number of opportunities to present their nations to the world, especially European audiences, through international expositions and fairs. The Latin American elites, conscious of the multiethnic nature of their societies and of European fascination with the Latin American "other," could not neglect the indigenous or black presence as a defining characteristic of Latin American culture. Nevertheless, the ethnic other, whether black or native, was redesigned as part of a prized mestizo culture more acceptable to the elites' vision of the nation. This was an autonomous definition, an exercise in what we can call semiotic control that left no room for natives' or blacks' interpretations of their own past or their contributions to the nation's future. Their identity was manufactured and linked to contemporary concepts of modernity. In this essay, Blanca Muratorio analyzes the Ecuadorian elites' fabrication of Indian-ness during the observances of the fourth centenary of the discovery of America, in 1892.

The quincentenary of the discovery of America, in 1992, generated heated controversy regarding its meaning and symbols, a controversy that the modern media turned into a worldwide spectacle. On the one hand, the anniversary produced an overwhelming number of academic books, glossy articles in even glossier magazines, conferences and museum exhibits of all types, a world exposition in Seville, and endless homages to Columbus, the main hero (or villain) of the enterprise, including the inauguration of a monumental and controversial lighthouse in the Dominican Republic where his alleged remains have finally come to rest. On the other hand, the celebrations of 1992 provoked the condemnation and protests of indigenous peoples of

North and South America, also expressed in conferences, gatherings, meetings, and alternative rituals, most of which were organized with the active support of intellectuals and nongovernmental organizations. Both types of occurrences took place in an international context in which the European Economic Community was being consolidated on one side of the Atlantic while the political power of the indigenous organizations on the other side of the ocean was gaining strength.

In Ecuador, 1992 was marked by a successful march of Amazonian Indians from the province of Pastaza to the center of government in Quito. They demanded their land titles, their cultural autonomy, and recognition as distinct nationalities. This march was preceded and made politically possible by a national Indian movement that, in 1990, had managed to paralyze the highland region of the country for several days. Banners, T-shirts, and slogans emblazoned with "500 years of resistance" were gloriously displayed and chanted on both occasions. For the first time in history, the Indians made the front pages of the country's main newspapers for almost two weeks.

The polemic over the quincentenary also rekindled an older debate over the nature of cultural and national identity that, unlike previous such debates, was multivocal and multiethnic. Newspaper articles with titles like "Indigenism vs. Hispanicism," "Latin America or Hispanic America?" and "Our Roots" discussed issues of cultural identity in relation to pressing international problems such as Andean economic integration, the question of ethnicity, and internal individual and national identity.[1] One of these articles carried a photograph showing Durán Ballén, the newly elected president of the republic, standing next to the statue of Sebastián de Benalcázar, founder of the city of Quito. The caption declared that the president was the direct descendant of this Spanish conqueror and an unnamed indigenous woman. On the same page was another picture of an Ecuadorian, a graduate in economics from Yale University and a high executive for the United Fruit Company in Honduras, dressed in the inevitable poncho and Indian hat, who claimed to be the direct descendant of Atahuallpa and therefore the current king of the Tahuantinsuyo.

The search by European or *criollo* elites for indigenous legitimation of their domination began much earlier, when the Spanish conquerors used Inca leaders in their power rituals.[2] It was also evident during the Independence period, when Simón Bolivar and José Antonio Sucre were crowned as heroes by aristocratic Quiteña ladies dressed as Sun Virgins. It continued throughout the nineteenth century and into the present. As Hans-Joachim König has argued, the problems of identity and legitimation represent the most fundamental challenges in the process of formation of the nation-state.[3] In part, these are the issues underlying the statements of the president of Ecuador when, through the authority of his self-representation, he again raised the ghost of "inclusive *mestizaje*" as the key to national identity, and when, in his inaugural speech to Congress on August 10, 1992, he warned against what he called "the dangerous fostering of distinct nationalities that seek to destroy national unity, the one and only common identity in need of consolidation."[4]

The collapse of the hierarchical order of identities, according to Jonathan Friedman the result of the disintegration of Western hegemony, is also manifest in Ecuador at the national level.[5] For Native Americans have rejected the dominant identification by white and mestizo society and have tried to open up social and political spaces that would allow them a more autonomous definition of identity. The reaction of the present group in power seems to be to search for its roots in an individual and collective mestizo identity. Unlike the civilized and modern European selfhood, constructed primarily by distancing itself from and in opposition to a primitive and savage Other, the Andean white and mestizo population has always, by definition, been forced to incorporate that savage or primitive native alter ego into its own self-identification. The particular "Indians" evoked, internalized, or rejected in the individual and collective representations of identity adopted by whites and mestizos took diverse forms in different historical periods, even though, as Thomas Abercrombie has argued, the general shape of the colonial discourse seems to remain the same.[6] This chapter analyzes this process as it unfolded during a critical period of changing hegemonies in the history of Ecuador.

Ecuador's participation in the observances surrounding the fourth centenary of the discovery of America, in 1892, occurred during the period in Ecuadorian history known as Progresismo (1884–1895), in which the society underwent a social, economic, and political transformation that finally consolidated radical Liberalism and spelled the demise of a Conservative, Church-dominated hegemony.

During this period, the intellectual and political debate involved many of the images and concepts of "Indian-ness," "*mestizaje*," "nation," and "Ecuatorian-ness" that would again be in the foreground in 1992. In the Progresismo period the debate was a monologue of the white and mestizo elites, from which the voice of the Indian as a historical actor was conspicuously absent. During the nineteenth century, Native Americans used other cultural and political forms to express their interpretations of and protests about their own reality.[7] Here we are concerned with the image makers, their ideologies, and their culture. The conquest, and the exploitation of the Indians that continued during the Republican period, gave the white and mestizo (here sometimes also referred to as *criollo*) image makers a monopoly on what Terry Goldie calls "semiotic control,"[8] or, more specifically, the power to imagine and represent the Indians outside of their own symbolic world.

During the period of Progresismo, the *criollo* elite had access to several international stages on which to display their ideology and legitimize their power. Among them were the Historical American Exposition in Madrid, in 1892, the World's Columbian Exposition in Chicago, in 1893 (both in celebration of the 400th anniversary of the discovery of America), and the controversial 1889 Paris Universal Exposition, organized to commemorate the centenary of the French Revolution. The analysis of these three exhibitions, primarily through the eyes and voices of the Ecuadorian participants, attempts to link histories of power with anthropologies of culture through the study of cultural conceptions of ethnicity and nationalism in relation to the history of the creation of the Ecuadorian nation-state.[9]

THE "GRAND TOUR" OF THE INDIANS TO PARIS, MADRID, AND CHICAGO

In 1891, Spain invited American and European countries to Madrid to commemorate the fourth centenary of the discovery of America. The center of the celebration was the Historical American Exposition, intended to illustrate the state of civilization of the New World in the pre-Columbian, Columbian, and post-Columbian periods. In addition, at the request of the royal commission in charge of the celebrations, the American countries were encouraged to reproduce in the Parque de Madrid some "primitive dwellings or monuments" and to send (live) "indians to inhabit them."[10] In March 1891, president Antonio Flores Jijón created the Ecuadorian Organizing Committee (Junta Directiva) to promote the celebration of the fourth centenary, both in Madrid and in Chicago. The preparations made by Ecuador to participate in these events and the country's subsequent presence at the expositions generated an abundant documentation, including requests for funds from congress, articles in newspapers, catalogues of the expositions, and a book especially written for the Chicago exposition. The explicit as well as the veiled images of Ecuadorian Indians in these documents and at the three world exhibitions reflected the iconography of "Indians" then dominant in literature and in the visual arts. Furthermore, these images were incorporated as important elements in the political rhetoric of an emerging nationalist ideology. Those class groups that were in a position to control the power of the state wrote the texts and selected and imposed the cultural traditions.

In the latter half of the nineteenth century, the new coastal bourgeoisie, blessed by an increasingly profitable cacao boom, had gained partial control of the state through three presidents (José María Plácido Caamaño [1884–1888], Antonio Flores Jijón [1888–1892], and Luis Cordero [1892–1895]). The coastal bourgeoisie looked to the outside world to gain legitimacy for Ecuador as a "civilized" society, to accumulate its own symbolic capital, and to construct its own cultural hegemony in an era when commercial success and cultural progress were perceived to be closely intertwined. The tradition this Ecuadorian elite invented for the country was intended to convey that message and was manufactured primarily for external, not internal, consumption. The three exhibitions provided an irresistible ritual stage to display publicly an incipient feeling of a new national self, to enact what Eric Hobsbawm would characterize as its "rite of passage" as a new nation, and to consolidate the nation's position as a viable actor in the international market.[11]

Beginning with the Crystal Palace, in 1851, international exhibitions had become transnational stages for celebrating global competition for commodities, the successes of imperialism, and the emergence of modernism as a cultural form.[12] By organizing and classifying the world as an exhibition, world fairs created and reified difference, turning cultures into objects that could be displayed in glass cases in an evolutionary order that reflected Western cultural hegemony. By the end of the nineteenth century these dominant ideas had established a close relationship between technological progress, evolutionism, and scientific racism.[13] The world fairs thus became coherent symbolic universes in which those ideas were embodied in the treatment of architectural space, the display of objects, the organization of events, and the ritual display of subordinate Others. Furthermore, these displays of hegemonic power were legitimated by a scientific discourse provided by the most prestigious anthropologists of the time, working in powerful academic institutions in North America and in Europe.

The coastal Ecuadorian elite that contributed to the organization and textual justification of the three international exhibitions had social and economic access to the ideologies and practices of that globalizing modernism. The elite sought Ecuador's participation in the new "imagined ecumenity" created by the market, even though Ecuador was struggling politically to achieve the "imagined community" that allows for the constitution of the nation-state.[14]

THE NARRATIVE IMAGES AND THEIR DISPLAY

In the document requesting funds from congress for the Madrid exhibit, the author, Pallares Arteta, provided two vivid and contrasting images of Ecuadorian Indians: the "savages," of whom the "Jíbaros" and the "Záparos" from the Amazon region were given as examples, and the highland Indians from Otavalo. Pallares Arteta gave "compelling" reasons why the first group of indigenous people should not be housed in the "primitive dwellings" at the Parque de Madrid and why, in his opinion, the Otavalo Indians were the most suitable group for that exhibit.

According to Pallares Arteta, the "savages" would never be convinced of the need for and advantages of the trip. Even if they made the journey, they would almost certainly cause "serious inconveniences" for the person in charge, insofar as their "dullness" and "stubbornness" prevented them from following any instructions. Furthermore, they did not speak Spanish or Quechua. He claimed that "they [were] good for nothing," "lack[ed] the most elementary notions of civility, morality or decency," and were "too fond of alcohol" (a potential embarrassment to the Ecuadorian government if they were caught inebriated by the Spanish police). On a final note, Pallares Arteta added that they would not be able to perform their job of "keeping the dwellings neat and tidy." By contrast, although the Otavalo Indians were not "pure," according to Pallares, they still preserved and were "outstanding" for their "correct features," "above average height," and "vigorous forms." In addition, they were "intelligent, hard working, sober, of good manners, and accustomed to neatness, order and cleanliness." Finally, the Otavaleños could offer special attractions such as their "San Juan dances," their "ball game" (similar to the "most popular Spanish Jai-Alai"), and their totora boats, on which they could sail the lakes of Madrid Park. Not only would these exotic talents attract and entertain the public, but the small fee that would be charged for this entertainment could, Pallares noted, help pay for the expense of transporting and housing the Indians themselves.[15]

The section of the *General Catalogue* of the exhibit pertaining to Ecuador has a long introduction presenting the "official" history of the country from its pre-Columbian past to the present, and an itemized list of the 1,327 items exhibited. The great majority of these items were pre-Columbian artifacts consigned to the all-inclusive category of "Incásicos" (Inca-era items); the exceptions were a shrunken head and a life-size figure of a Jíbaro Indian, which were set up as the centerpiece of the Ecuadorian pavilion.[16]

In the introduction to the *General Catalogue*'s Ecuador exhibit, the anonymous author incorporated an existing mythic history that established close kinship ties between the Caras, allegedly the first civilizers of Ecuador, and Atahuallpa, the last Inca emperor.[17] The Incas themselves were presented in this conjectural history as possessing "great noble character." In addition, the text stated that the Inca religion, "although erroneous," was not considered "bloodthirsty," because "the sacrifices performed by the Quiteños and the Peruvians corresponded to the gentleness of their beliefs." In sum, the image of the Incas was that of "a very advanced civilization."[18] Carbo, the author of *El Ecuador en Chicago*, a book written in relation to the World's Columbian Exposition, went even further and naturalized the Incas' most famous leader as "the Ecuadorean Huayna-Capac."[19]

The only other powerful image of Ecuador presented in the introduction was a contemporary set piece describing not life in the highlands but life on the coast, where one could find "several banks enjoying solid credit," a "vertiginous commercial life," and a place where "all the people [were] well off due to the abundance of well remunerated work available." Finally, the introduction highlighted Guayaquil, the main port of the republic, which exported more than half a million quintals of cacao annually, in addition to rubber and coffee. All of these products won prestigious prizes at the Paris and Chicago expositions.[20]

It is evident from these documents that the organizers of the exhibit—mainly Antonio Flores and Pallares Arteta—carefully orchestrated an economic representation of the country to promote the already dominant interests of a specific class, the coastal merchant and land-owning bourgeoisie. In this depiction the Indian was conveniently left out. The image makers were aware of the deplorable situation of both the landless *montuvio* (mestizo) workers on the cacao plantations and the highland Indians concentrated in the haciendas. However, their wretched reality was artfully inverted and hidden under the general image of a prosperous and well-remunerated coastal population, the product of the cacao boom. Iconographic silences are often more eloquent than explicit representations in revealing the ideology and practices of the dominant *criollos* vis-à-vis Native Americans.

THE ARISTOCRATIC PAST

When the image makers turned to cultural progress, the other term in the nineteenth-century equation of economic success with advanced civilization, they engaged in a very selective use of the images of Indians current at the time, emphasizing the past and the future rather than the present. The past was brought to life in the images of the Incas and the mythical Caras. Their history could not be denied (since their artifacts were obviously being excavated), but it could be touched up and reinvented to demonstrate historical continuity and to legitimize the origins of all Ecuadorians. Ecuadorians were not to be considered second-class Europeans but the descendants of a noble and aristocratic race. Thus, an important pillar in the social construction of national identity was neither liberal democracy nor the Enlightenment, but an aristocratic racism that traced the ancestry of Ecuadorians to a real or mythical native aristocracy.[21] No mestizo, then or now, has ever traced his or her ancestry to a poor Indian peasant or to a "savage" from the Amazonian tropical forest.

This aristocratic image of the Incas also catered to a European public that, by mid-nineteenth century, had already seen representations comparing the Incas with the great civilizations of Egypt and Rome or with the Sun King Louis XIV. Perhaps with these existing comparisons in mind, the image makers placed the importance of the archaeological pieces excavated in Ecuador on a par with the Egyptian tomb excavations (particularly mummies). Hugh Honour points out that whereas at the great international exhibitions of the mid-nineteenth century, the Latin American nations were "represented almost exclusively by natural products," an exception was made regarding the Incas and the Aztecs.[22] The comparisons with classical civilizations and the singling out of indigenous peoples rather than products reflected the European public's fascination with the exotic and the primitive, cultivating that attitude of modernism that David Harvey calls "the spatialization of alterity."[23]

The tradition invented by the image makers appropriated not only the cultural glories of pre-Columbian civilizations but also their historical past, so as to incorporate it as a myth of origin and as an integral part of the collective self. This selected past represented the particular *criollo* ideology that Minguet calls "archaeological patriotism."[24] This ideology "implies the valorization and exaltation of the old Mexican and Andean civilizations as well as the appropriation of their corresponding pasts and the identification with the history that produced them."[25] The coastal commercial bourgeoisie was also searching for a place in the global market created by modernism. The symbol that best expressed this ideological ambiguity of the Ecuadorian elite was the "Inca palace," built by a famous French architect as the Ecuadorian pavilion at the 1889 Paris exhibition and located at the foot of the then recently built Eiffel Tower, the quintessential symbol of modernity and progress at the end of the nineteenth century.

In contrast to the historical Incas, the image of the Indians from Otavalo was designed to represent the future. For the elite image makers, the Otavaleños symbolized what all Native Americans could become if the process of civilizing them was allowed to take its "natural" course.[26] In Pallares Arteta's report, the description of the Otavaleños' behavior and generally "clean" attitude as hard workers and respectful of order can be regarded as a good example of the effectiveness of liberal ideology and laissez-faire economics. This belief was reinforced by the fact that all of the Otavaleño skills were considered marketable—a particularly relevant consideration, because European audiences lived in an era that saw the birth of the modern entertainment industry and advertising.[27] Thomas Cook had already expanded his tours to include all of the major world fairs and had begun advertising the images of non-Western Others in posters and tourist guides.[28] Moreover, the relation between ethnological exhibitions and circus performances at the world fairs favored the acceptance of the current racial and evolutionist theories by the mass of the visiting public.[29]

The hard and oppressive reality lived by the majority of the Otavalo Indians, a reality that was excluded from the idealized image presented for external consumption, has been thoroughly examined by social scientists[30] and can also be seen in some of the photographs that, until recently, had been hidden in the privacy of hacienda homes. The few images of natives that appeared in *El Ecuador en Chicago*, the first "illustrated tourist guide" written by an Ecuadorian journalist (and published in New York for the 1893 Chicago exposition), were idealized studio photographs of posed Indians, or those in which Indians were shown as already domesticated and civilized under the tutelage of the missionaries. At the turn of the century, the Ecuadorian elites were not yet ready to promote the exoticism of Native Americans as a tourist commodity.

A PRESENT WITHOUT A PAST OR A FUTURE

Examining the narrative in conjunction with the ethnographic artifacts exhibited, the image that emerges of "the savages" (the noncivilized natives) appears at first sight to be transparent but in fact is riddled with ambiguities. At least three different images existed: the savage as nature, as "infidel," and as "Jíbaro." First, in the "Informe" of 1892, the Jívaros and Záparos were presented merely as examples of all savages. Their image was constructed in the semiotic field that considered the savages part of nature. They were regarded as equal to animals in the sense that they lacked any "sensible language," seemed compelled by nature to be "stubborn" and "dirty," and were deprived of any notion of social, civilized life: "their essence [was] privation."[31] This image of the savage conformed to the ideology that Robert Berkhofer refers to as "scientific racism," in which social progress, racial hierarchization, and Darwinian biology converged. According to Berkhofer, the result of this convergence was a savage that not only had "darker skin" and "bad manners" but "inferior organic equipment as well."[32] In many of the European travelers' illustrations, the savages are graphically depicted as one with nature, as literally part of a tree, or hanging from it like monkeys.

The second image of the savage was that of the "infidel" who was granted the possibility of being incorporated into the scheme of evolutionary progress. In contrast to the first image of savages as part of nature, the second representation of them as pagans and infidels returned them to history, but a history whose pace was only in the power of the self to advance. The corresponding images were produced by missionaries in the form of postcards used to sell the work of the missions abroad. Their main iconic objective was to document the steps allegedly already taken by the indigenous converts toward their total integration into white culture and society. Unlike present-day tourist postcards, in which a deliberate attempt is made to construct difference and exoticism, especially with the new "noble ecosavage," the missionary postcards wanted to package familiar commodities: savagery and exoticism conquered; domesticity achieved; likeness, not difference.[33]

Finally, the third image of the savage as "Jíbaro" emerged primarily out of the ethnographic exhibit in the Madrid historical exposition, which was dominated by a full-size figure of a Jívaro Indian and by a *tsantsa*, the shrunken head for which these Indians became famous in Europe. By selecting the Jívaro to represent physically (but not personally) the image of the savage, the image makers were responding both to their own ambiguous love-hate relationship with this Amazonian group and to the demands of their European audience. Anne-Christine Taylor has argued that the image of the Jívaro in the Ecuadorian mind, from colonial times to the present, has oscillated between two poles. On the negative side, the Jívaros were considered the quintessential savages, defying all the canons of European civilization. On the positive side, they were regarded as the "indomitable nation" and as a model of macho warrior individualism and love of freedom to be emulated by the new Ecuadorian nation.[34] This multifaceted image of the "Jíbaros," the invented Jívaro, perfectly fit the intentions of the image makers at the Madrid exhibit: to impress a cultivated European public and to heighten the Ecuadorian elites' newly acquired sense of national identity and pride.

THE VISUAL AND NARRATIVE LANDSCAPE OF INDIAN-NESS AND NATIONALISM

To better understand the meaning of the images presented at the Madrid exposition and the two world fairs, it is necessary to situate them in the larger context of the discourse on Indian-ness and nationalism shared by the Ecuadorian cultural elites at the close of the nineteenth century. On the one hand, the aesthetic and scientific interest in Ecuador shown by famous European travelers of the time contributed to a more positive evaluation of local customs, languages, and landscapes by the local elite. On the other hand, the powerful image manipulators, who shared the social world and the semiotic codes of painters and writers, took those images for granted as part of the then-hegemonic visual landscape.

The representations of Native Americans that dominated that visual landscape were primarily produced by four Costumbrista painters, Rafael Salas, Agustín Guerrero, Rafael Troya, and Joaquín Pinto, whose more profitable clients were Europeans. It was then fashionable for travelers to write and illustrate detailed accounts of their experiences in books or journal articles, which were then published in Europe; these illustrated travel diaries were extremely popular with a nineteenth-century public obsessed with a precise and tangible realism.[35] When they were not accompanied by their own artists, the travelers often searched for illustrators among the locals. They also commissioned paintings to take back with them to Europe, especially to France and Italy, where "ethnographic and costumbrista publications were much in fashion."[36] Most foreigners wanted to take back images of the "exotic" and "typical" indigenous populations, and the Costumbrista painters seem to have obliged. The scientists, like vulcanologists Stübel and Reiss, were more interested in landscapes, and the natives then became attached to nature as an appendage.[37] Toward the end of the nineteenth century, Joaquín Pinto became the undisputed fashionable artist; among his clients were the minister of France, who bought twenty-three of his watercolors; other important diplomats; and the Frenchman F. Cousin, who commissioned an entire collection of one hundred watercolors of "costumbrismo indígena."[38]

Costumbrismo in painting has been characterized as a reaction against the scholasticism and somber religious iconography of colonial art. In addition, it was influenced by Spanish literary romanticism and developed out of the liberal individualism born in the new Republican period and reflected in the innumerable portraits of the independence heroes.[39] Viewed in conjunction with other developments at the time in music and literature, *costumbrismo* also reflected the newly acquired feelings of "deep nationalism," which made the artists "turn their eyes" toward a constructed pre-Columbian "indigenous heritage" and the discovery of their own landscape.[40]

Costumbrista painting was the result of a romantic search for the national self through the representation of ethnic diversity and local customs. It tried to satisfy, and was strongly influenced by, the literary realism of the last two decades of the nineteenth century, and particularly by photography. From this point of view, it adopted the gaze of the European Other to represent its own indigenous reality. The latter was then turned into a folkloric idealization, easy to sell in a European market that also consumed equally constructed images of the Orient and of Africa. Costumbrista paintings coexisted with the *cartes de visite*, the photographs in postcard form representing native types from all over the world that became popular tourist and collectors' items and were exhibited at all the world fairs of the period.

The natives behind the costumes were represented as types—as José María Vargas says, "for the functions they performed for society."[41] The power of the image was conveyed by the frame in which the Indians were constrained rather than by the human identity of those occupying the roles. The consistency of the painters' concentration on the superficial and picturesque details of costumes idealized ethnic types and made real Indians invisible. Thus, the watercolors of the period reveal a highly stratified and rigid social world in which indigenous peoples played a role strictly demarcated by the hegemonic sign makers. The lonely figures are totally decontextualized, deprived even of their own natural surroundings because they have been incorporated into an urban landscape. The achieved portraiture was thus a milestone on the one-way road to acculturation and miscegenation. The natives were also frozen in time. Exercising what Johannes Fabian calls "chronopolitics," the image makers deprived them of their own cultural time.[42]

EXHIBITION NATIONALISM AND THE INTERNAL OTHER

In the world fairs of the nineteenth century, political iconographies celebrated ideologies of nationalism and imperialism with the conspicuous display of internal and external Others. All the organizers of the three exhibits discussed here considered Ecuador's participation to be a patriotic act, because it concerned the good name and future well-being of the nation. The nationalist symbols displayed at the fairs for the external consumption of other nations reflected an iconographic consensus that consistently excluded real Native Americans since, allegedly, they were citizens of the republic and as such were already invisibly absorbed into the corporate self. Internally in the country, the semiotic struggles between an ultraconservative Catholic Church and the moderate Progresismo leaders revealed the subtle contradictions of this myth of assimilation. An iconographic battle over the statue of Ecuador's independence hero will serve as an example.

SUCRE, THE INDIAN, AND THE LION

The journalist and politician Juan León Mera was the most prominent intellectual of the ultramontane, clerical trend within the conservative movement. He declared his work to be inspired by a pre-Columbian past populated by Virgins of the Sun and by heroic and villainous Incas and Shyris, in this way claiming a type of nationalism that Eric Hobsbawm calls "literary and folkloric."[43] One of Mera's least-known literary pieces concerned a debate that originated in the 1880s over a statue of José Antonio Sucre, one of the fathers of independence. According to Mera, the maquette for the statue, to be erected in the Sucre theater, represented "the Hero in the attitude of liberating and protecting a young Indian woman who symbolized the Motherland." The hero had his right foot on top of a lion representing the defeated Spanish empire. A furious Spanish ambassador protested against this representation of Spain, and the municipality agreed to remove the lion, replacing it with a neutral piece of stone. Several years after the event, Mera's indignation was provoked by the fact that the "antipatriotic, humiliating, and shameful mutilation" had turned the statue into an erotic representation of a "vulgar and ridiculous Sucre [as] a very embroidered and decorated soldier embracing a bashful and intimidated Indian woman." Once the symbols disappear[ed], Mera argued, there [was] no history.[44]

Despite the obviously white facial features of the Indian woman, what seemed to embarrass Mera was not the abstract disappearance of history but the mere intimation of crossbreeding between a *criollo*, hero of the Motherland, and an Indian woman stripped of her symbolic clothing. This representation of the Indian as a passive feminine presence or, according to Mera, "a bashful and intimidated Indian woman" was a common trope in nineteenth-century iconography of the Indian in the Americas and Europe. Among the Ecuadorian image makers, the romantic and even eroticized image of the warrior Jívaro was, of course, always masculine. By contrast, indigenous women were never represented erotically but rather were sentimentalized as innocent receptors of Christian morality and civilization. The same was also true of North American nineteenth-century sculptures of Indian women, although in North America *mestizaje* never created an identity problem for the dominant group.

The symbolic mantle of *patria* that worried Mera so much in Sucre's statue was useful to hide the feminine sexuality of the Indian, always the most problematic aspect of self-recognition in mestizo identity. The prolonged debate over this statue was really about the cultural and ethnic identity of that mestizo middle class of intellectuals to which Mera himself belonged. He was torn between a "Hispanicism" to which he claimed to be "irresistably attracted" because of "blood, language, and love for heroism and glory" and his need to assert what he called "americanism," if and when it was not seen as "contaminated" by incorporation of real Indians. Mera and others like him fell, then, into the same contradiction that Gerald Sider considers central to the colonial encounter between Europeans and Indians: that between "the [Europeans'] impossibility and the necessity of creating the other as the other—the different, the alien—and incorporating the other within a single social and cultural system of domination."[45] It was the negation of this contradiction, or the inability to resolve it, that compelled the intellectuals and powerful image makers of the nineteenth century, and of contemporary Ecuador, to invent a hegemonic national identity that incorporated unnamed or mythical Indians, preferably ones belonging to an aristocracy or to the male sex.

CONCLUSION

Adopting a historical perspective, this discussion has focused attention on the self as the main speaker in the dialogue between dominated Indian-ness and dominant nation-state. As the dominant image maker at the turn of the nineteenth century, the coastal bourgeoisie used the Indians as semiotic pawns for its own interests and to legitimize its own economic achievements.[46] In the process, it also started to construct a new image of Ecuador as a corporate self. In this dominant representation, the image of *mestizaje* emerged as a master fiction constructed in a historical dialectical process of exclusion and inclusion of the Other.[47] As pseudo-Europeans, the *criollos* pretended to hide the dialogue of domination by turning it into a monologue of the self who had finally assimilated the Other, or was in the process of doing so. It is possible to say, borrowing a concept from Mason, that this was the quintessential egocentric strategy of structuring alterity.[48] In the process the real Indian was obliterated from consciousness, to be selectively assimilated as the historical and, if possible, the archaeological exotic Other. This strategy also created the illusion that the indigenous Other, as forged by the dominator, could be brought into the imagined community through the doorway of invented natural ties.

Times have changed, and the Ecuadorian indigenous peoples are increasingly becoming their own image makers in the national and international arena. The new *criollos* are fighting back by reinventing their own and the nation's cultural and ethnic identity. In addition to the president of the republic making *mestizaje* fashionable again, the Ecuadorian pavilion at Seville Expo 1992 adopted the diplomatic and for a long time chic attitude among the upper middle classes: the aestheticization of the Indian, the Indian that can be owned in archaeological private collections or displayed in institutional museums. The pavilion showed, "with dramatic illumination," the giants of the *bahía* pre-Columbian culture from the coast, which were described as "shamanistic idols from 2000 years ago." The "exotics in costume" whom all the visitors wanted to photograph were only mannequins of the famous Corpus Christi dancers from the highlands.[49] As Foster has argued, the myth of the Other as the exotic is perpetuated by its appropriation as an objet d'art, a commodity, a focus of wonder and contemplation.[50] This postmodern appropriation of the archaeological Indian as an objet d'art is significantly different from the "archaeological patriotism" characteristic of the *criollo* elite at the close of the nineteenth century. Today, real Indians, unlike the mythical ones, have assumed their political roles as historical agents, claiming for themselves the reevaluation or invention of their past to redefine their present, questioning the historical and iconographic monopoly of the *criollos* that archaeological patriotism assumed as given.

The folkloric Indian at the Seville exposition was turned into a tourist attraction and an ambassador of an allegedly unified nation that in fact is being forced to redefine the imagined community by its contemporary, and real, indigenous citizens. One of them, a courageous young woman from Otavalo and a museum professional with a degree from Leeds, was the only indigenous person in a position of relative authority at the Ecuadorian pavilion and at Expo as a whole (with the exception of a Cree Royal Canadian Mounted Police officer at the Canadian pavilion). Defying the ideological call of the Confederation of Indigenous Nationalities of Ecuador to boycott Expo, she insisted on participating as a professional curator and guide. Reviewing her experience at Expo, she said, "I'm glad I came to remind a European public not more enlightened than Columbus that we Indians are still alive."

SUGGESTED READINGS

Becker, Marc. *Indians and Leftists in the Making of Ecuador's Modern Indigenous Movements*. Durham: Duke University Press, 2008.

Colloredo-Mansfield, Rudolf Josef. *The Native Leisure Class: Consumption and Cultural Creativity in the Andes*. Chicago: University of Chicago Press, 1999.

Gerlach, Allen. *Indians, Oil, and Politics: A Recent History of Ecuador*. Wilmington, DE: Scholarly Resources, 2003.

Hill, Jonathan David, ed. *Rethinking History and Myth: Indigenous South American Perspectives on the Past*. Urbana: University of Illinois Press, 1988.

Jara, Rene, and Nicholas Spadaccini, eds. *Amerindian Images and the Legacy of Columbus*. Minneapolis: University of Minnesota Press, 1995.

Pallares, Amalia. *From Peasant Struggles to Indian Resistance: the Ecuadorian Andes in the late Twentieth Century*. Norman: University of Oklahoma Press, 2002.

Selverston-Scher, Melina. *Ethnopolitics in Ecuador: Indigenous Rights and the Strengthening of Democracy*. Coral Gables, FL: North-South Center Press at the University of Miami, 2001.

Urban, Greg, and Joel Sherzer, eds. *Nation-States and Indians in Latin America*. Austin: University of Texas Press, 1991.

Van Cott, Donna Lee, ed. *Indigenous Peoples and Democracy in Latin America*. New York: St. Martin's Press, 1994.

Whitten, Norman E., Jr. *Cultural Transformation and Ethnicity in Modern Ecuador*. Urbana: University of Illinois Press, 1981.

Sights

Arctic to Amazonia. Indigenous Perspectives on Development and Survival of the Planet. Directed by Robbie Leppzer.

Birth and Belief in the Andes of Ecuador. 1995 (UCMEC).
Columbus Didn't Discover Us. 1992. Directed by Robbie Leppzer.
Crude. 2010. Directed by Joe Berlinger.
Ecuador: Divided over Oil. 2004 (FHS).
Río Negro. 1990. Directed by Athualpa Lichy (Facets Multimedia).
Taypi Kala: Six Visions of Tiwanaku. 1994. Produced by Jeffrey D. Himpele (UCMEC).
Transnational Fiesta. 1993 (UCMEC).
Weaving the Future. 1997. Directed by Mark Freeman.

8

Many Chefs in the National Kitchen

Cookbooks and Identity in Nineteenth-Century Mexico

Jeffrey M. Pilcher

What a propitious subject Jeff Pilcher identified—household expressions of national culture! Festive meals celebrate family occasions, holy days, and civic holidays. Special dishes represent these celebrations, family identity, and the occupational and ethnic groups in society. Meals serve as ephemeral artistic expressions of popular history and powerful social symbols. Examples abound. The pit cooking of traditional meats and vegetables in the Peruvian highlands, called Pachamanca, *was a ceremony honoring the earth goddess Pachamama.*[1] *Patricia Quintana wrote a cookbook that followed Mexico's civic and religious calendar and offered family recipes for each holiday.*[2] Chiles en nogada *became the special food for Mexican Independence Day because the dish contains the three colors of the national flag. Popular history recounts that cooks in Puebla, Mexico, created it to honor a visit by one of the first presidents on Independence Day.*[3] *Other Mexican regions and families have their own Independence Day specialty, such as* tamales de espiga *(corn pollen) in San Pancho, Morelia.*[4] *In Peru, bread represented independence and also, when the loaf combined a variety of flours from corn, sweet potato, and other potato tubers, the unity of its different peoples.*[5] *Many foods, especially sweets, have religious associations, such as the rich Peruvian colonial soup called* sopa teóloga, *the Mexican Lenten tamales known as* tamales de vigilia, *and* turrón de Doña Pepa—*almond sweets associated with the image of Christ of the Miracles, in Lima.*[6] *As Jeffrey Pilcher shows, food expresses the popular culture and history of the nation.*

Laura Esquivel's best-selling novel, *Like Water for Chocolate,* uncovered an affinity between two usually distinct genres, the romance and the cookbook. The story relates the forbidden love between Tita, who is bound by custom to remain single and care for her widowed mother, and Pedro, who marries Tita's older sister to be near his beloved. Their passion is expressed—through the magical realism of Latin American literature—in the dishes she feeds him, the *mole poblano* (turkey with chile sauce) she sensuously grinds on the *metate* (grinding stone), and the quail in rose petal sauce that literally burns down the house. The manuscript cookbook in which Tita records these culinary secrets thus becomes part of the novel, inspiring the historian to ask, if a modern author can write recipes into a narrative, what narratives did women of the past write into their recipes?[7] The kitchen tales of nineteenth-century Mexico went far beyond the domestic world of food and love to imagine national communities, although the communities imagined in the published works of male professional chefs differed sharply from those imagined in the manuscript collections of female household cooks.

Attempts by Mexican patriots to forge a national cuisine reflected the deep historical connections between food and identity. Native Americans considered themselves to be "the people of corn" and even placed themselves in a cosmological food chain by offering human sacrifices to maize gods. Europeans, meanwhile, took communion through the medium of wheat—according to Catholic doctrine, the only grain acceptable for the Holy Eucharist. After the conquest, Spanish priests attempted to teach Native Americans to eat wheat as part of their evangelical message. They succeeded on ceremonial occasions—witness the elaborate breads prepared for the Day of the Dead—but maize remained the everyday staple. Over time, corn tortillas became associated with poor Indians and mestizos, while wheat bread was reserved for elite Spaniards and *criollos*.

Following independence, liberal governments sought to abolish the distinctions between Europeans and Native Americans in order to forge a common Mexican nation. Nevertheless, while *criollos* invoked the ancient splendor of the Aztec empire to justify separation from the Spanish empire, they rejected living Indians as culturally backward and unfit for participation in civic life. Native Americans could gain citizenship in the new nation only by sacrificing their traditional lifestyles and adopting the trappings of European culture. Intellectuals sought to inculcate liberal values in the masses through broadly conceived educational campaigns. With varying degrees of success, they used secular education, religious icons, and patriotic festivals to instill a feeling of common purpose. They invented a national cuisine as well, but divisions of race, class, region, and gender frustrated nineteenth-century attempts to serve *la patria* (the fatherland) at the dinner table.

MANY MEXICOS, MANY CUISINES

Deciding what constituted the authentic national cuisine was of ongoing concern during the nineteenth century. *El cocinero mexicano* (The Mexican Chef), published in 1831, a decade after independence, set the tone for the national cuisine. The anonymous author adopted a sharply patriotic tone, praising "truly national" spicy dishes and denouncing the delicate European palates unaccustomed to chile peppers.[8] A later edition of the work admitted that foreign dishes appeared in the text, but only after they had been "Mexicanized"—adapted to Mexican tastes.[9] A few years after *The Mexican Chef* appeared, the *Nuevo y sencillo arte de cocina* (New and Simple Art of Cooking) advertised recipes specifically "accommodated to the Mexican palate," which supposedly had no use for "European stimulants."[10] Nevertheless, Narciso Bassols began his two-volume *La cocinera poblana* (The Puebla Cook) with the pessimistic claim that cookbooks contained an abundance of useless foreign recipes.[11] Vicenta Torres de Rubio reiterated this attack on irrelevant cookbooks, observing that Mexicans neither seasoned nor condimented their food according to European practices.[12] A group of women from Guadalajara declared that most cookbook authors copied recipes without concern either for quality or utility.[13]

Authors employed a number of devices to define the national cuisine. Chefs cooked everything from stuffed onions to barbecued meat *a la mexicana,* dedicated dishes to national heroes (Moctezuma's dessert, Donato Guerra's cod), and even decorated "monstrous pastries, like those of the middle ages" with portraits of prominent public figures.[14] They explored the national taste for foods such as "patriotic" frijoles, and an 1886 banquet attended by the minister of government and foreign dignitaries featured *mole poblano,* identified as the "national dish." Writers also celebrated the recognition of their food in foreign countries. In 1898 a newspaper proudly announced that New York's finest restaurants served *mole* and other Mexican dishes.[15]

The audience for this national cuisine was largely confined to the literate middle and upper classes. Over the course of the nineteenth century, about fifteen separate cookbooks were published in Mexico. Multiple editions of these works brought the total number up to nearly forty, with perhaps a few thousand copies printed of each edition, for a total of as many as a hundred thousand cookbooks. Several of these works listed dual publication in Mexico City and abroad, principally Paris, which must have delighted Mexican patriots desiring foreign approval of their national cuisine. About four or five volumes, both new works and reprints of old ones, appeared each decade from 1831 until 1890, and at least eight cookbooks were published in the final decade of the century. Additional recipes printed in domestic manuals, calendars, and newspapers ensured that cooking instructors reached a broad audience, at least among the privileged classes.[16]

The authors of this national cuisine came primarily from the liberal intelligentsia. The anonymous author of *The Mexican Chef* employed many themes of the Enlightenment and denounced Spanish conservatism. His publisher, Mariano Galván Rivera, was a political moderate who produced a series of famous almanacs as well as women's calendars, travel guides, and textbooks. Although later jailed for supporting the French intervention, Galván had employed liberal ideologue José María Luis Mora in the 1830s to manage his journals. Leading liberal newspaper editors, including Vicente García Torres and Ireneo Paz, also entered the cookbook trade. Vicenta Torres de Rubio, the first woman to publish a cookbook, moved in liberal circles and even included menus from political banquets in her work. Manuel Murguía dedicated a cooking manual to Mexican señoritas in 1856, two years after he printed the first edition of the Mexican national anthem. One of the goals of these writers was to create a sense of national identity through shared cultural values. They observed that Mexicans not only spoke the same language and shared the same history, they also ate the same chiles and frijoles.[17]

While emphasizing national unity, cookbook authors also recognized regional diversity. Common references appeared to the *moles* of Puebla and Oaxaca, the black beans and seafoods of Veracruz, and the grilled meats of Guadalajara and Monterrey. Yet, compared with modern works, nineteenth-century cookbooks included within the national cuisine only a handful of regional traditions, essentially those from areas with heavy Hispanic settlements. The virtual monopoly of *criollo* kitchens becomes apparent in the comparative treatment of *mole*. Puebla's chief rival in producing this dish, the southern state of Oaxaca, is known today as "the land of seven *moles*." But nineteenth-century cookbooks ignored the more indigenous versions of Oaxacan *mole* such as *verde*, a green stew perfumed with the incomparable anise-like fragrance of *hoja santa*. They focused instead on *negro*, a spicy black sauce similar to Puebla's fabled dish. An 1834 volume explained that the *moles* of Puebla and Oaxaca "owe their particular good taste to the types of chiles employed; the first making use of a sweet chile called the *mulato*, and the second from a Oaxacan chile called the *chilohatle*."[18]

By defining even chile peppers in *criollo* terms, the nineteenth-century national cuisine ignored a gastronomic geography dating back to pre-Columbian times. Native culinary traditions centered on civilizations such as the Nahua, Maya, Zapotecs, Mixtecs, and Totonacs—ethnic groups that rarely corresponded to Mexican political boundaries. The Huasteca, for example, split between the states of San Luís Potosí and northern Veracruz, seldom appeared on national maps. This heavily forested region contained only a small Hispanic population of rancheros with little political prominence. Nevertheless, large numbers of native communities thrived in the area and developed an enormously sophisticated cuisine. Modern ethnographers have counted forty-two distinct varieties of tamales, including the fabled meter-long *zacahuil*. Other regional dishes, such as the Pacific Coast hominy stew *pozole*, likewise received little notice because of their indigenous associations.[19]

Published cookbooks had little room for the corn cuisine of the streets. One book, supposedly "accommodated to the Mexican palate," contained not a single recipe for tamales, enchiladas, or quesadillas.[20] Another manual defined tortillas for the benefit of foreign readers, explaining that they appeared on even the most affluent tables in remote provincial cities. The recipes assured Europeans that sophisticated continental cuisine prevailed, at least in Mexico City.[21] And when corn confections did appear, their marginal status was emphasized by their placement in sections designated *almuerzos ligeros* (light brunches).[22] Of course, a lack of written recipes does not prove that elites never ate popular foods. The Indian servants who did the cooking hardly needed instructions for making enchiladas, and virtually all were illiterate anyway. Nevertheless, cookbooks often contained positive censures against the derogation of serving Indian foods. One volume explained that the wealthy had virtually no use for the popular corn drink *atole*.[23] The *Diccionario de cocina* (Dictionary of Cooking), published in 1845, pointedly questioned the morals of any family that ate tamales, the food of the "lower orders."[24]

Even as cooking manuals concentrated on European traditions, clashes between elite and popular conceptions of the national cuisine became obvious, particularly in the streets of Mexico City. Late-eighteenth-century economic growth attracted thousands of rural immigrants, which the city strained to accommodate in hastily built tenement houses. These newcomers brought with them the traditional maize cuisine of the countryside, setting up braziers on any convenient street corner. Curbside *enchiladeras* became ubiquitous, causing officials to complain that virtually every street and plaza in Mexico City had its own resident cook.[25]

Foreign travelers remarked on the enormous variety of foods available from vendors in the capital. Women wandered the streets with baskets of corn confections such as tamales and quesadillas, while men carried improvised ovens with pastries and *barbacoa*. Fiestas provided the primary focus for popular cuisine, as they had since the days of Moctezuma. In the week before Christmas, people exchanged food and drinks in *posadas*, festive reenactments of the holy family's search for shelter in Bethlehem. All Souls' Day or the Day of the Dead was another popular holiday during which adults offered ritual foods to departed relatives while children devoured candy skeletons. The most spectacular celebration of the year came during Holy Week, when great crowds converged on the capital from distant villages and ranches. Throngs of people danced through the streets, guzzling fruit drinks and devouring ice cream, in a movable feast of popular cuisine.[26]

In the early years of the Republic, Mexicans of all classes participated in these festivals, but the process of modernization brought increasing attempts to restrict lower-class foods. Authorities launched ongoing campaigns against the traffic hazard of street vendors. Sanitary regulations also restricted the sale of vegetables and mushrooms by small-time merchants, at times going to the extreme of banning *chiles rellenos* (stuffed chiles), but these proclamations were invariably repealed because of popular outcry.[27] By 1900 Mexican elites had come to view popular cuisine not only as unfashionable, but also as a positive menace to society. Using language from the newly developed science of nutrition, Francisco Bulnes attributed Indian backwardness to the supposed inadequacy of maize-based diets. Julio Guerrero went further, stating that criminal behavior resulted from the "abominable" foods eaten by the lower classes.[28]

Even sympathetic authors expressed a marked ambivalence about the acceptability of the national cuisine. An 1897 editorial in *El Imparcial* entitled "The influence of mole" and signed pseudonymously by Guajolote (Turkey) wavered between nostalgic love and bourgeois scorn. "Baptisms, confirmations, birthdays, weddings, even last rites and funerals, to merit the name, have to be accompanied by the national dish, be it green like hope, yellow like rancor, black like jealousy, or red like homicide, but in abundance, in a broad *cazuela*, thick, pungent, with metallic reflections, speckled with sesame seeds, a magical surface." Guajolote attributed both the genius and the defects of the national character to the influence of chile peppers, then concluded with a warning. "Doctors counsel parsimonious use, even if it be *en nogada*, of this other enemy of the heart, that combined with *pulque* and tortillas, serves as fuel for the untiring machine of the proletarians and even of some who are not."[29]

Reform efforts therefore emphasized public cooking classes as a means of weaning the lower classes from corn and chile peppers. Not coincidentally, police inspectors led the recruiting campaign, an indication of the perceived importance of diet in maintaining social order. The classes, used to attract students to vocational schools, emphasized European models, such as modest French family cooking. Teachers inveighed against the "disgraceful habit" of eating spicy foods and advised their students to give up popular Mexican dishes in favor of English cooking—a drastic measure indeed.[30] Cookbook author Jacinto Anduiza summed up the belief that culinary techniques would contribute to the process of education that would level society, in other words, eradicate popular practices seen as immoral by Europhile elites.[31]

EUROPEAN FASHIONS, *CRIOLLO* TASTES

Fanny Calderón de la Barca, the Scottish wife of Spain's first minister to independent Mexico, wrote scornfully of the elite's clumsy attempts to imitate European cuisine. She described one of her first meals after arriving in port as "the worst of Spanish, Vera-Cruzified." Parisian chefs employed in the capital's wealthiest homes produced no better results; she thought one dish resembled mining slag. Mexican culinary skills, whether in carving meat, seasoning stews, or dressing tables, invariably fell short of her exacting standards. Yet eventually she stopped drawing comparisons with Europe, accepted Mexican cooking on its own merits, and, on her departure in 1842, wrote that "Veracruz cookery, which two years ago I thought detestable, now appears to me delicious."[32] Fanny's experience revealed that even the most dedicated followers of European fashion imparted a uniquely Mexican flavor to their cooking. The elite's deep aversion to the lower classes nevertheless kept them from accepting native foods as part of the national cuisine.

Like the upper crust from New York to St. Petersburg, wealthy Mexicans cultivated a taste for French haute cuisine prepared by male chefs. France had begun to assert a culinary hegemony over Europe at the dawn of the eighteenth century, when the Sun King Louis XIV's absolutist policies had shorn nobles of their political power. With few social functions beyond dueling and the salons, bored aristocrats turned for diversion to such pastimes as music, painting, and cooking. This aristocracy of the spoon, which actually included many members of the middle classes, rejected the heavily spiced foods of the Middle Ages and adopted the Enlightenment ideal that cooks should reveal rather than distort the true nature of foods. In the first decades of the nineteenth century, chef Antonin Carême perfected the laborious and expensive techniques of classical French cuisine. Beginning with *fonds*, deeply flavored broths, he performed a complex alchemy by concentrating and reducing, adding and extracting, garnishing and gilding, to return in the end to a simple and unified whole. Although Carême worked for only the wealthiest of aristocrats, other chefs such as Jules Gouffé extended *la grande cuisine* to a bourgeois audience, a process that culminated under Auguste Escoffier in the *fin de siècle* Age of Great Hotels.[33]

French culinary influence in Mexico cannot be dated with precision. Many writers date the arrival of continental cuisine to the French intervention, 1862–1867, but this is too late by at least a decade. Even a century earlier, manuscript cookbooks displayed an affinity for French names but not for the new techniques.[34] The first published works of the early republic demonstrated greater command of this exacting art. Gallic styles seem to have gradually displaced colonial dishes of Iberian descent over the course of the nineteenth century, even as Spain itself declined in political and cultural influence. Indeed, the disastrous war with the United States that terminated Spain's empire in America coincided with the 1898 opening by Escoffier and César Ritz of the Carlton, Europe's most fashionable hotel.[35]

Continental influences came to permeate nineteenth-century Mexican cooking literature. Kitchen manuals and the women's pages of newspapers contained recipes for Parisian soup, hollandaise sauce, eggs in aspic, truffled pheasant, chicken cardinal, *vol-au-vent à la financiere*, and *bifstec à la Chateaubriand*.[36] For women unwilling to spend hours preparing such dishes and unable to employ a chef to do it for them, specialty shops sold gourmet pâté and pastry. Wine merchants imported hams, cheese, olive oil, and salted fish, in addition to barrels of Bordeaux wine and Jerez sherry.[37] Mexicans could also enjoy the pleasures of Parisian dining vicariously through translations of French writings. Jean Anthelme Brillat-Savarin's *Physiology of Taste*, one of the masterpieces of culinary literature, appeared in its first Mexican edition in 1852, a few decades after its publication in French. In 1893 a Mexican press issued a special edition of the celebrated cookbook by Jules Gouffé, former chef of the Paris Jockey Club.[38]

Aspiring gourmets indulged their appetites for continental cuisine in Mexico City restaurants and social clubs. In the 1850s, the Tívoli of San Cosme began offering fine dining in an idyllic setting. Tuxedo-clad waiters moved smoothly through the tree-lined courtyard with platters of *noix de veau diplomate* and *becassines à la cavaliere*. The magnificent Chapultepec Castle, illuminated in the distance by moonlight, lent a romantic air unsurpassed even by the view of the Notre Dame Cathedral from La Tour d'Argent. In 1870 another Tívoli opened in Tlalpan, catering to Mexico City's wealthy people who fled the urban hustle, particularly during the riotous celebrations of Holy Week.[39] By the end of the century, talented chefs such as Paul Laville and V. Barattes could sell their talents to the highest bidders from a number of exclusive restaurants and social clubs. Mexico's greatest coup in international dining came in 1891, when Don Ignacio de la Torre y Mier persuaded the celebrated Parisian chef Sylvain Daumont to come to Mexico City. The Frenchman caused such a sensation that within a year he left the Mexican millionaire to open his own restaurant.[40]

Banquet menus testify to the cosmopolitan tastes of the country's leaders. An anonymous mid-nineteenth-century painting hanging in the National Museum of History at Chapultepec Castle and portraying a feast for a General León of Oaxaca shows the symmetrical place settings, the multiple dishes, and the innumerable wine bottles of classical continental cuisine. A dinner for five hundred held in the National Theater to celebrate President Porfirio Díaz's birthday in 1891 featured French food, wines, and cognac. Only men were seated for this banquet; their wives had to view the proceedings from the theater's box seats, an indication of their exclusion from full citizenship in this patriarchal nation. Meanwhile, provincial elites paid lavish sums to rent French chefs for important events such as a 1903 Monterrey banquet for Governor Bernardo Reyes. The quest for imported civility reached its pinnacle in 1910 during the centennial celebration of independence in a series of banquets honoring President Díaz, cabinet members, and foreign dignitaries. Not a single Mexican dish appeared at any of the score of dinners dedicated to this patriotic occasion. Sylvain Daumont served most of the food, and G. H. Mumm provided all of the champagne.

Even the Mexican colony in New York commemorated the centennial with French food.[41]

Notwithstanding this desire to appear cosmopolitan, Mexicans demanded a uniquely national flavor in their haute cuisine. Foreigners such as Fanny Calderón de la Barca often made scathing comments about their inability to execute properly European culinary techniques. Critical Mexicans likewise recognized that continental dishes underwent a process of creolization. Antonio García Cubas lampooned the pretentious Tívoli restaurant, wondering who had granted diplomatic credentials to a piece of veal and predicting that anyone who ate the horseman's snipe would receive spurs to the stomach. He noted that many dishes parading as French bore little resemblance to Parisian preparations.[42] These differences, while appearing outlandish to contemporaries, provide modern readers with valuable clues to the nature of Mexico's national cuisine.

Chile peppers constituted the greatest shock to foreign palates. Mexican *adobos*, for example, differed from the marinades used to preserve meat in Europe principally because they included chiles. The eighteenth-century French culinary revolution had banished such sharply spiced foods common to medieval and early modern Europe. The Enlightenment ideal of flavors—"exquisite but not strong"—left Mexican cuisine as a self-conscious anachronism.[43] Some obsequious cooking experts conceded this point and joined Europeans in denouncing spicy foods. More nationalistic authors bitterly refuted the European opinion of peppers as poisonous and condemned the continental "war against stimulants, principally chiles."[44]

Another characteristic of Mexican elite cuisine was the profusion of meat. A quick glance at any nineteenth-century cookbook reveals an enormous variety of seasonings and dressings for meat.[45] Nor was this creativity limited to cookbooks; women prepared these diverse recipes on a daily basis. One foreign traveler observed that wealthy families ate the same meats prepared in different styles several times a week.[46] Fanny Calderón de la Barca described plates filled with meat, fish, and fowl served indiscriminately at every meal. She recorded that the wealthy ate meat for virtually every meal and in astonishing quantities, more than in any other country in the world.[47] Visitors from Europe and the United States almost invariably criticized Mexican meat dishes as overcooked. An Englishman, lamenting the lack of juicy roast beef, blamed local butchers for cutting meat in a "slovenly and injudicious manner."[48] In fact, tradesmen carved beef to suit their customers' preference for well-done steaks. Mexicans abhorred the dripping, rare fillets served in Europe and cut their meat into thin strips, pounding and marinating to tenderize them. Such techniques often constituted the "Mexicanization" of European dishes: a recipe for *bifstec à la Chateaubriand* appears to foreigners like fajitas with French fries.[49]

Mexican elite men used cuisine as a symbol of the progressive Western society they hoped to create. But one must beware their public representations of national character made in cooking manuals and stylish restaurants because they may have had little relevance for the majority of the people, particularly for women within the domestic sphere. To understand actual culinary practices, it is necessary to peer into the smoke-filled confines of nineteenth-century kitchens where women were preparing the future of Mexico's national cuisine.

COOKBOOKS AND NATIONAL IDENTITY

Benedict Anderson has persuasively argued that modern nations were forged not through the development of tribal customs in the distant past, but rather in the eighteenth century as a product of the Enlightenment. The standardization of vernacular languages through the spread of print and literature allowed people from different ethnic groups to imagine "national" communities that had not previously existed. Nineteenth-century Mexican elites certainly used instructional literature to attempt to mold a patriarchal nation based on Western European models. Cooking manuals contributed to this identity by assigning women to a domestic role within the nation and spelling out acceptable cultural (eating) practices. But standards of domestic morality and national identity created by male authors did not necessarily reach a complaisant female audience. Indeed, community cookbooks produced in turn-of-the-century Mexico imagined an alternative vision of the nation and of the female place within it.[50]

Nineteenth-century Mexican standards of domesticity established an inherently unequal relationship, placing a woman under the authority of her husband. She could legitimately leave him only if he beat her excessively, and the law defined adultery as a crime for females but not for males. The culinary arts provided a natural medium for inculcating these gender roles because the kitchen was a primary focus of domesticity. Even women with servants spent a large part of each day making sure their family was well fed.[51] Professional cookbook authors explicitly supported the subservient role of women in the domestic world. In the introduction to one family manual, María Antonia Gutiérrez cautioned that a woman must "maintain a pleasant and agreeable home so that her husband would not abandon her."[52] Jacinto Anduiza elaborated this theme in an 1893 cookbook that attributed many of the worst domestic calamities to failures in the kitchen. He warned that men dissatisfied with their wives' cooking would seek their pleasures in taverns and bordellos.[53] Many upper- and middle-class women accepted—at least in public forums such as newspaper letter columns—the image of matrimony as a burden requiring constant work and self-abnegation on their part to ensure their family's happiness and honor. Nevertheless, manuscript works and community cookbooks contained other possible constructions of the domestic sphere.

Even to begin expressing themselves, Mexican women had to break a longstanding male monopoly on the cultural capital of literacy. Jean Franco has shown that during the colonial period, clergymen exercised editorial control over female authors such as the poet Sor Juana Inés de la Cruz, and after independence liberal intellectuals took over the task of instructing women in their duties of citizenship.[54] By the end of the nineteenth century, works by female authors had begun to expand through educational campaigns. One measure of this literacy was the growing popularity of manuscript cookbooks, which had impressed foreign visitors as early as 1880. Fanny Gooch observed that affluent Mexican ladies took great pride in their handwritten volumes, although she noted that a hired cook often followed her own recipes and ignored her mistress's instructions.[55] Simone Beck, the famous French cooking teacher, recalled that her mother had likewise filled notebooks full of recipes even though a hired cook did the actual work.[56] In the 1890s these manuscripts developed into community cookbooks as women came together to publish their recipes. Indeed, cookbooks may actually have helped spread writing skills by providing women with a medium for expressing themselves, a poetry familiar from their hours in the kitchen.

These nonprofessional books testify first to the sociability of Mexican women, for housewives carried on a brisk market in recipes as well as gossip. María Luísa Soto de Cossío, a rancher's wife in Hidalgo, included in her personal cookbook dishes from her grandmother, Aunt Gabriela, and a neighbor Virginia. She also copied out recipes from the published *Recetas prácticas*, a volume she may have borrowed from a friend.[57] Manuscript cookbooks even served as albums for recording family traditions, with dishes handed down from mothers and grandmothers. The fact that the older women were often illiterate added further to the value of their daughters' books. The exchange of cooking tips also reached beyond the extended family to become the focus for Catholic charities, which were one of the few legitimate female activities outside the home. A group of matrons in Guadalajara prepared a recipe manual to support the local orphanage, and several community cookbooks from Mexico City were dedicated to works such as cathedrals for Saint Rafael and Saint Vincent DePaul.[58]

In 1896, Vicenta Torres extended this community of cooks throughout the Republic in her *Cocina michoacana*, a serialized guide to the cuisine of Michoacán. Printed in the provincial town of Zamora and sold by subscription, it began with local recipes submitted by women within the state. Nevertheless, she soon expanded her audience to reach cooks from all over the country. A woman from Celaya sent her recipe for "Heroic Nopales," from

Guadalajara came a green chile lamb stew, a Mexico City matron offered her favorite meat glaze, and a reader in the border town of Nuevo Laredo even sent her "Hens from the Gastronomic Frontier." By printing recipes from throughout Mexico, Torres provided the first genuine forum for a national cuisine. Contributors exchanged recipes with middle-class counterparts they had never met and began to experiment with regional dishes, combining them in new ways that transcended local traditions. Thus, women began to imagine their own national community in the familiar terms of the kitchen rather than as an alien political entity formulated by men and served up to women in didactic literature.[59]

Torres and her collaborators conceived of their work as a community cookbook, first for the state of Michoacán and later for the entire nation, in which they shared in the common oral culture of the kitchen despite the distances separating them. Confident that readers were familiar with the basic techniques of cooking, they provided correspondingly vague instructions. One woman wrote simply to fry pork chops in "sufficient quantities of pork fat" until well done and to serve with "hot sauce to taste." A contributor to another community cookbook listed among the ingredients for *mole poblano*: "of all spices, a little bit." A recipe for stuffed chiles read, "having roasted and cleaned [chiles], fill with cooked zucchini squash, onion, oregano, etc." It went without saying that cooks would adjust their seasonings to taste, for recipes served merely as written keys to a much fuller language of the kitchen.[60]

Certainly cooks adapted the recipes they found in cookbooks to fit their personal tastes. María Luísa did not simply copy verbatim the dishes presented in the *Recetas prácticas*; she simplified procedures, removed extraneous ingredients, and on one occasion found it necessary to change "stirring frequently" to "stirring continuously," a lesson perhaps learned at the expense of a ruined dinner.[61] Moreover, they read selectively, passing over impractical dishes such as Manuel Murguía's absurd recipe for stuffed *frijoles*, which involved cooking beans—"but not too soft"—slicing them in half, inserting a bit of cheese, dipping them in egg batter, and frying them in oil.[62] Male chefs, for whom cooking provided a degree of status, may have delighted in such outlandish preparations, but housewives tended to view cooking as an everyday chore and therefore stressed practicality.

Women also used cuisine as a means of defining a uniquely religious version of the national identity. Torres and her correspondents, while not afraid to experiment with the techniques of foreign haute cuisine, emphasized national dishes that often held religious significance. Most prominent were the colonial *moles*, "those essentially American dishes," which they considered indispensable for festivals such as the Day of the Dead. Another culinary tradition with patriotic affiliations developed around the Virgin of

Guadalupe. Having first appeared to an Indian in 1531, the saint gained a universal appeal in Mexico that was recognized even by such anticlerical liberals as Ignacio M. Altamirano. In 1895, church officials acknowledged the Virgin's power as a national symbol by formally crowning her the patron saint of Mexico. Vicenta Torres paid homage a year later by inserting in her cookbook a recipe for *gorditas* (small corn griddlecakes) from the Villa de Guadalupe Hidalgo, the location of the Virgin's shrine.[63]

The Virgin's incorporation into the national cuisine illustrated not only the religious character of female patriotism but also the peculiar selection process that transformed local dishes into national symbols. Residents of Guadalupe Hidalgo made a living by selling the plump, sweet, silver-dollar-size corn griddlecakes to visiting pilgrims. But among their own families they celebrated December 12, the Virgin's day, by eating barbecued goat with *salsa borracha* (drunken sauce). Nevertheless, the *plaza gorditas* ultimately gained recognition as the food of the Virgin, so that by 1926 a newspaper ran a cartoon showing a man refusing to accompany his plump wife (in Spanish, also a *gordita*) on a trip to the Virgin's shrine with the excuse: "Why take a *gordita* to *la villa*?"[64]

As in the case of *gorditas*, this exchange of recipes even began to cross established class and ethnic lines, perhaps because women worried less than men about the social stigma attached to Indian dishes. Unlike the usual practice of segregating enchiladas into the ghetto of "light brunches," the *Recetas prácticas* integrated these foods among other recipes for meats and vegetables. Another cookbook prepared by a charitable women's organization in Mexico City gave more recipes for enchiladas than for any other type of food.[65] Vicenta Torres made a virtue of including recipes of explicitly Indian origin, assuring readers that these "secrets of the indigenous classes" would be appropriate at any party. Along with tamales, she included *gordita cordials*, *pozole de Quiroga*, and *carnero al pastor* (Shepherd's mutton), but out of deference to her elite audience, she carefully set them apart with the label *"indigenista."*[66]

But care must be taken in interpreting this acceptance of native food as an indication that ties of gender were breaking down lines of class. Even middle-class women, after all, could generally count on a household servant to do the difficult work of grinding corn and chiles. Moreover, these same women shared with elites an admiration for French haute cuisine. Yet they also embraced a genuinely Mexican national cuisine based on colonial *moles* and even pre-Columbian *tamales* that were rejected by Eurocentric male elites. Being excluded from power themselves, perhaps women simply had less motivation to maintain the distinctiveness of *criollo* culture. After all, they based their image of the nation on the Virgin of Guadalupe, a symbol shared with the Indian masses, rather than on the trappings of Western industrial society idealized by elite men.

A MESTIZO CUISINE

Mexican leaders of the nineteenth century hoped to build a modern, patriarchal nation based on Western European models. Cookbooks offered a valuable means of indoctrinating women into this new order by emphasizing European dishes and disparaging Indian foods. In this way, intellectuals hoped to cleanse Mexico of the vestiges of its pre-Columbian past. Corn became a symbol of the disorderly and unsanitary elements of society, such as street people and backward villagers. Women were considered especially vulnerable to the immoral influences of the streets, hence the need to keep them locked away in the kitchen. Reformers focused particularly on lower-class women in an attempt to improve family diets and morality and thereby transform the proletariat into imitations of the bourgeoisie.

The dictatorship of Porfirio Díaz and its ideal of imported progress collapsed with the Revolution of 1910. From this social upheaval emerged a new group of leaders who sought to reformulate the sense of national identity and create an ideology with broad appeal to the Indian and mestizo masses. The revolutionaries launched a cultural campaign to legitimize themselves as representatives of the mestizo "cosmic race." They glorified the pre-Columbian past in murals, museums, and movies and decried the deposed dictator as a toady to foreigners. The culinary expression of this new ideology was stated succinctly by a leading nutritionist, Rafael Ramos Espinosa. He formulated the simple equation that people who ate only corn were Indians, those who ate only wheat were Spaniards, while Mexicans were those people fortunate enough to eat both grains.[67]

Mestizo cuisine was not identified as a national standard until the 1940s, but the roots of its recognition lay in the late nineteenth century. Cookbooks written after World War II, which offered Indian foods as a symbol of the Mexican nation, grew out of the community works produced at the turn of the century. The social gatherings of women sharing family recipes developed into organized cooking classes, and successful teachers in turn provided recipes to women's magazines and published cookbooks of their own. Their ties to oral culture nevertheless remained close, as can be seen from the hospitable author who invited readers to her Mexico City home for further instructions.[68] The most prominent teacher, Josefina Velázquez de León, traveled throughout the Republic, holding cooking classes and collecting regional recipes. She published more than 150 cookbooks exalting tamales and enchiladas as culinary manifestations of Mexican nationalism. Her audience came from the rapidly growing middle class, the wives of businessmen and professionals who shared a vision of the mestizo nation. Although stark inequalities remained between rural and urban diets, maize had finally regained its place at the Mexican banquet table.[69]

Laura Esquivel's novel provides an apt metaphor for the transformation of Mexican cuisine and society. Her heroine, Tita, declines a respectable marriage to an American doctor so that she can continue an illicit affair with her Mexican lover. In the same way, Mexicans have begun to give up the slavish imitation of foreign models and show pride in their Indian heritage. Foreign influences certainly persist, with American fast food displacing French haute cuisine as a modern status symbol. Nevertheless, the Indian dishes scorned by nineteenth-century elites have been enshrined as the national cuisine. *Pozole*, formerly a "secret of the indigenous classes," now serves as the symbol of Guadalajara's cooking. And tamales, once the food of the lower orders, have become the heart of the country's haute cuisine. Tita learned "the secrets of love and life as revealed by the kitchen"; modern Mexican women have followed that same path to define their national identity.

SUGGESTED READINGS

Appadurai, Arjun. "How to Make a National Cuisine: Cookbooks in Contemporary India," *Society for Comparative Study of Society and History* (1988): 3–24.

Coe, Sophie D. America's First Cuisines. Austin: University of Texas Press, 1994.

——. *The True History of Chocolate*. New York: Thames and Hudson, 2000.

Ledogar, Robert J. *Hungry for Profits: U.S. Food and Drug Multinationals in Latin America*. New York: IDOC, 1975.

Long, Janet. *Food Culture in Mexico*. Westport. CT: Greenwood Press, 2005.

Otero, Gerardo, ed. *Food for the Few: Neo-Liberal Globalism and Biotechnology in Latin America*. Austin: University of Texas Press, 2008.

Pilcher, Jeffrey. *¡Que vivan los tamales! Food and the Making of Mexican Identity*. Albuquerque: University of New Mexico Press, 1998

——. *The Sausage Rebellion: Public Health, Private Enterprise in Mexico City, 1890–1917*. Albuquerque: University of New Mexico Press, 2006.

Rubin, Lawrence C. *Food for Thought: Essays on Eating and Culture*. Jefferson, NC: McFarland, 2008.

Scholliers, Peter, ed. *Food, Drink and Identity: Cooking, Eating and Drinking in Europe since the Middle Ages*. New York: Berg, 2001.

Super, John C., and Thomas C. Wright, eds. *Food, Politics, and Society in Latin America*. Lincoln: University of Nebraska Press, 1985.

Wilk, Richard R. *Home Cooking in the Global Village: Caribbean Food from Bucaneers to Ecotourists*. New York: Berg, 2006.

Sights

Como Agua para Chocolate. 1992. Directed by Alfonso Arau (Facets Multimedia).

Food, Inc. 2009. Directed by Robert Kenner.

Like Water for Chocolate. 1993. Directed by Alfonso Arau.

Politics of Food. 1998 (PBS).

Hamburgers: Jungle Burgers. 1985 (Icarus).
Hungry for Profit. 2000. Directed by Robert Richter.
Land Without Bread. 1932. Directed by Luis Buñuel (Facets Multimedia).

Sounds

Anthology of Mexican Sones. Discos Corazón, 1992.
"Danzones del porfiriato y la revolución." Testimonial/RCA/BMG, 1994.
Mariachi Reyes del Aseradero: Songs from Jalisco. Discos Corazón, 1992.
La Negra Graciana: Sones Jarochos with the Trio Silva. Discos Corazón, 1992.

9

The New Order

Diversions and Modernization in Turn-of-the-Century Lima

Fanni Muñoz Cabrejo

Nineteenth-century Latin American policy makers recognized the importance of entertainments and public diversions to the creation of cultural modernism in their nations. Like the colonial "social engineers" of the Bourbon period, the new Latin American elites sought to inculcate values they considered more compatible with the ideology of the time, namely, positivism and a fascination with European culture. The new pastimes, generally promoted in the capital cities and often linked to issues of hygiene and public safety, were devised to control the passions of the lower orders and encourage rational and ostensibly modern behavior. Although the new entertainments did not always succeed in modifying the behavior of the general public, they did have a permanent impact on the urban landscape. Fanni Muñoz Cabrejo discusses the efforts of nineteenth-century Limeños to effect the cultural modernization of their city.

Beginning in the mid-nineteenth century, Peru's new elite, its numbers augmented by new Liberal professionals and influenced by European theories of economic development and social reform, sought the creation of a new national culture to guarantee Peru's membership in the "concert of European, white, and civilized nations."[1] In clear opposition to the traditional Hispanic colonial mentality, the elite reformers adopted a rational, materialistic, and utilitarian vision that rested on the new medical description of the human body, inspired the creation of a new penitentiary system, and encouraged the political participation of the general population.[2] The reformers regarded their social campaign as an integral part of the modernization process, whose objective was nothing less than the creation of a new culture.[3] Because the modernizers attributed to different diversions the capacity to promote or obstruct progressive changes in society, they attempted to transform public amusements so as to transmit the values, tastes, and customs of a new, modern Peruvian society.

In the second half of the nineteenth century, modern ideas found expression in the urban landscape. Lima, the capital, underwent a dramatic transformation from a colonial town to a modern city. In 1840 Lima had a population of 53,000, with blacks, *criollos*, mestizos, and whites composing a diverse culture. Walls constructed in 1685 still separated the urban center from surrounding Indian farming villages (called *chacras*), orchards, and rural dwellings. The architecture had a religious character: churches, monasteries, hospitals, and parish houses predominated. Owing to the absence of sewers, the city was awash in stenches.[4]

Lima began to change in the 1850s as urban planners enlarged its space, modified its sanitation system, constructed civic buildings, and designed new building ornamentation as expressions of the national community. As the size of the city tripled,[5] planners introduced a new street pattern, opened up new avenues, and paved old ones, and, in 1870, brought down the city walls. Public health concerns led to more open spaces, modern sewers, and water systems. The construction of new public buildings and the ornamentation of older structures added to the appearance of a new, modern capital.[6] Nevertheless, Lima remained a city with an overwhelming number of poor residents. The 1908 census reported that the city had 172,927 inhabitants. Of these people, 77 percent lived in poor conditions and 10 percent in what was regarded as adequate shelter. The remaining 13 percent enjoyed good living arrangements.[7]

The city at this time had six districts, or wards. In the first and second wards, located in the historic center of the city, aristocrats and commoners shared the same neighborhoods. The wealthy lived in colonial mansions. Since the end of the eighteenth century, commoners had lived in rented rooms in buildings called *callejones*—former colonial buildings that had been converted into rooming houses for fifty to two hundred persons. The name *callejón* referred to a passageway between two rows of rooms in the adobe building. At the entrance and in the center were fountains that provided water for drinking and washing clothes, toilets, and waste disposals for the entire building. People of all ethnic backgrounds lived in the *callejones*. During the first decade of the twentieth century, oligarchic families fled these neighborhoods for new housing developments.

Each of the city's wards had a distinct economic, social, and cultural character. The first, second, and fourth wards (the latter boasting a new residential neighborhood) served as the center from which the reformers initiated their campaign for a new culture. These neighborhoods were home, as one contemporary author reported, to "those privileged classes that sought the foreign ideal."[8] Part of the second and all of the third and fifth wards consisted of plebian neighborhoods. The oldest of these neighborhoods,

Rimac, in the fifth ward, had a primarily black population. In the other districts lived the city's mestizo, indigenous, and Chinese residents.[9] These wards were the most densely populated. As contemporary observers noted, "From Capon to Siete Geringas the change is visible in the buildings. Commerce becomes retail in nature. There are no theaters and circuses, with spectacles being reduced to cockfights. Puppet shows are sometimes seen in the streets or in the bare yards. Gone also are the acrobatic shows."[10]

The new urban patterns coincided with new municipal authority in Lima. In 1853, municipal reforms gave expanded authority to local Lima officials. The city councilmen extended civil control over public spectacles and festivities. They explained their action as an enterprise for "the development and progress of the arts." The new municipal charter also removed church jurisdiction over celebrations and public activities, assigning it to city officials (the Alcaldes), who could approve (with a permit) or deny requests for celebrations. In making decisions, these officials declared their intention of guaranteeing the "good customs and the moral and religious values" of the general population.[11] In this way the modernizing elite also tried to impose new values that were rational, scientific, and positivist, without dismissing the religious principles in which they had been educated.

Given the primitive living conditions of the majority of the population and the slow pace of development of the city, the elites considered the formation of a middle-class culture and lifestyle of imminent concern in the modernization of Peru. Although most of the elites imaged the ideal citizen of the new city as racially white and culturally *criollo*, their campaign took on a homogenizing character. Blacks, Chinese, and Indians—the majority of Lima's population—were included in the civilizing project. The modernization campaign expected these people to abandon their traditional customs and participate in the middle-class lifestyle.

The elites' denunciation of Lima's traditional lifestyle applied to popular forms of entertainment, many of them reflecting the colonial legacy of festivals and diversions. Travelers who visited Lima between 1810 and 1920 characterized Limeños as given to pleasure and gluttony, to "easy and dissolute customs."[12] After independence, numerous religious celebrations still were at the heart of the festive life of republican Lima. The centers of social life—the plaza, churches, and streets—also played host to civic festivals, theater entertainments, cockfights, gambling, carnival activities, and parades. Each ward gave special character to these celebrations. Moreover, *tertulias* (social gatherings) became common in the homes of the middle and upper classes, with counterparts in the festivals held in the *callejones*. Cafés appeared at the end of the seventeenth century and served as places for middle- and upper-class men to play billiards; the plebian classes sought out their own cafés to enjoy singing and playing table games, especially dominos.[13] In 1841 the French vice consul A. De Botmiliau gave an account of the festive atmosphere of the city. He said that no difference existed between the Peru of the republicans and the Peru of the viceroys. He continued, "Does there not exist today the same desire for spectacles, pomp, and other pleasures of the eye?" And—most upsetting to reformers—he added, "It is pointless to search for intellectual and other signs of the moral transformation that the country announces."[14]

Peruvian elites believed that diversions—sport and recreation—had an educational function that could be used in creating modernity. In this opinion they resembled the Peruvians of the eighteenth century, imbued with Enlightenment ambitions, who attempted to eradicate amusements they considered vulgar or licentious.[15] Foreign travelers and social commentators recorded the elites' inclination toward leisure. According to these observers, all the social classes, without distinction by ethnic or economic categories, judged honest work to be inferior to amusement. Francisco García Calderón added that among Peruvians, "the will is light, inconsistent, weak, and erratic."[16]

Other commentators in the eighteenth century blamed blacks for having a pernicious influence on society, charging them with excessive sensuality and idleness. Blacks had come to Peru as slaves during the colonial period and made up a substantial proportion of the population of Lima at the end of the nineteenth century. The attack on black culture came as the city declined as a commercial center, followed by the invasion of vagrants known as "urban plebes" beginning in the middle of eighteenth century. Although mestizos and Indians formed part of this group, blacks stood out and soon were labeled thieves, bandits, and dishonest street vendors.[17]

Just as they had a century before, elite reformers condemned Carnival and other fiestas, card games, and popular theater, arguing that these activities promoted disorder, gambling, and inferior aesthetic values. The newspaper *El Amigo del Pueblo* described Carnival as "a savage and immoral festival, a diversion where social considerations were not respected and women were immodest. Carnival days equal wantonness and insolence. . . . Mobs of black men and women with torn costumes and painted faces came out in droves."[18]

The reformers also attacked bullfights and cockfights as barbarous diversions that retarded social progress. These popular and bloody entertainments, according to the reforming elites, did nothing to develop rational thought but rather promoted the irrational passions of the common classes. It was not a coincidence, these commentators continued, that in England, the most modern civilization, these forms of entertainment had been eradicated.[19] Señores Yáñez and Ganoza, members of Lima's commission to prohibit blood sports, issued a statement after witnessing these spectacles. Bullfights and cockfights, they said, "impart a cruel and cold feeling, and instead of providing something useful to the masses, it excites them to see the destruction of useful animals." In response, on October 28, 1892, city councilmen prohibited the exhibition and fighting of animals.[20]

Certain vices cut across all social classes, and everyone came under fire. In 1857, Manual Atanasio Fuentes conducted a statistical survey of the city. Reporting an alarming number of vagabonds and petty criminals, he determined that the dominant vices of these individuals were drunkenness and gambling. Moreover, he found that these same activities were common throughout Lima; the first was "widespread among the lower classes, while the second affect[ed] almost all of the social classes"[21]—every neighborhood in Lima had its gambling houses. Robert Proctor, an English visitor to Lima in 1824, had observed that games of chance everywhere were "played with great excess" and that "some of the most prestigious families soon find themselves poor due to their devotion to gambling."[22] Fuentes concluded that gambling weakened national customs and destroyed the individual's intellectual potential. Newspaper editors, echoing the Fuentes report, referred to gambling as "a cancer that demoralized the country" and called for prohibition.[23]

Even when the government prohibited gaming houses in 1877, the practice proved difficult to eradicate. Gambling continued nearly unabated until the first decade of the twentieth century. Colonel Domingo J. Parra, Minister of Government and Police, appealed to Congress in 1900 for help in eliminating gambling centers. He repeated the opinion of reformers that, because of widespread gambling, "moral elements and civil respect are becoming backward [as are] the citizen's political and civil rights, because he prefers to look in these caverns of degradation instead of using his skills and strength in honest work."[24]

Disregarding critics, the elite reformers concluded that the attitudes and activities of the lower classes represented the obstacle to progress and the formation of a new bourgeoisie. They considered the social values and customs of the majority of the Indian, black, and Chinese populations to be socially stagnant owing to their barbaric customs, idleness, and bad hygienic habits.[25]

The Chinese were especially singled out for contributing to retrograde development. Chinese workers destined for the coastal plantations had begun arriving in 1849. Between that year and 1874, approximately 100,000 Chinese arrived in Peru. Reformers charged them with retrograde behavior because of their use of opium, their theater, which offered plays judged to be obscene (called "*sicalipticas*"), and their teahouses, which were presumed to be fronts for brothels.[26] The reformers added that it was not just the Chinese who frequented the brothels but men from throughout society. After 1859, numerous campaigns were directed against Chinese-owned gambling dens throughout the Huaquilla area. Newspaper editors railed against the popular Chinese game called "*sol de salir*" and other games of chance.[27] The attacks on traditional leisure activities almost always reflected the racial views of the modernizing elite.[28]

By 1890 the prospects for introducing a new cultural model had improved because the nation had achieved social order and economic prosperity and the national government had consolidated its authority through modern institutions. After 1895 the economy flourished through the export of cotton, textiles, and minerals and by attracting foreign investment, especially British. Moreover, the campaigns against gambling, vice, and traditional recreations coincided with the promotion of modern sports. The enthusiasm for "Sports" (the term itself defined the activity at the turn of the century) came to signify not only the modernizing elites' emulation of European society, but also their program for using modern sports to form the ideal bourgeois man: autonomous, virile, healthy, slender, and clean (because sports became linked to personal hygiene).[29]

The first modern sports, such as horse racing, rowing, sailing, cycling, tennis, and soccer, were promoted by the elites, especially foreigners. Between 1873 and 1903, members of the foreign community formed the first sports clubs. The English established the first one, the Salon de Comercio, in 1845. In 1865 the name was changed to the Lima Cricket and Lawn Tennis Club, and in 1900 it was changed again, to the Lima Cricket and Football Club. Other early sporting organizations included the Regatta Club (1875), the Cycling Club of Lima (1896), and the Shooting Club (using blanks; 1890).[30] Residents of Lima from all social classes soon took up these recreational activities. Bicycling and soccer acquired general popularity—bicycling perhaps because it was not necessary to own a bicycle; agents rented bicycles to eager cyclists. In 1897, Lima had seven such rental agencies.[31]

Soccer also acquired a popular following. The Englishman Antonio Garland organized the sport shortly after arriving in Peru; the players were students who had studied in England. The game's popularity spread rapidly as Peruvians quickly took it up. The first contest between Peruvians and Englishmen was played on June 24, 1894. The Lima Cricket and Lawn Tennis Club began organizing regular matches between Anglo and Peruvian squads on the grounds of Santa Sofia. Local students also began playing pickup games on the same pitch. The next year, during the Independence celebrations, the first international contest matched a visiting English team against a Peruvian side. This was also the first match to attract an audience of fans.[32]

Around 1896, reformers began to argue for extending the new sports ethos to the entire population. The government of Nicolás de Pierola emphasized the importance of a modern physical education program that would build "an organic and morally strong generation."[33] The president's call led to a congressional proposal for the construction of gymnasiums and other recreational facilities. As in Europe, the gymnasiums proved to be popular with the public universities because they did not require expensive equipment.[34] Recognition of the value of physical exercises for boy students was extended to girls as well in the Regulation for Primary Instruction issued by the government of Augusto B. Leguía in 1908.

Toward the end of the nineteenth century, the governing elites intensified their efforts to promote diversions as a way to inculcate new values. This campaign reflected a widespread opinion that the lower classes possessed retrograde behavior. Luis Antonio Eguiguren expressed the elites' view as he described the ordinary men of Lima: "[They] participate in cock fights with the same passion that pervaded the Coliseum, enjoy themselves in cinemas, occupy *rocambor* tables and wrap themselves in politics, but not without burning part of their gunpowder in a salute to God. Peru does not need this type of man."

Eguiguren had definite ideas about the habits of the new Peruvian that the nation would need to achieve modernization. He called for "a practical man of action and of just spirit. This is the strong and healthy man, keeper of truth, partisan of good, respectful of the law. In this man, wisdom should unite, with a certain eye, a virile will endowed with a powerful initiative capable of resisting the trials of life and overcoming any difficulty." He declared that models of this man existed in North America, and that Peruvians should look to such examplars as "Roosevelt, hunter of beasts, and Rockefeller, a financier who monopolizes all business."[35]

Using amusements to reform national values required regulating the theater. The Castilla government revised the laws governing the theater that had existed since the colonial era, in the Regulation of Public Theaters of 1849. This law was intended to regulate theatrical productions in such a way as to educate the spectators in what could be called the bourgeois aesthetic. The law gave opera precedence over the traditional Spanish-style comedies, in effect giving priority to the "conventional dictates of the European bourgeois" over "popular and spontaneous forms [of entertainment] of the colonial era."[36]

Castilla's government put its intentions into practice by sponsoring performances and by controlling the major theater. The government contracted with European companies to visit Lima. The regime brought Italian opera, French comedy, and French ballet companies to Peru. In 1852 the government assumed control of Lima's major performance hall, El Teatro Principal. Later, in 1872, responsibility for the theater passed into the hands of the city administrators.[37]

The Peruvian elite expressed only moderate anticlericalism. They continued to expect the precepts of the Roman Catholic religion to guide the ethical behavior of everyday life. Trying to maintain this balance of Catholic and modernist values in the theater, in 1873 the city officials created the position of inspector of public performances (*inspector de espectáculos*); this functionary censored the theater until 1898, when authorities issued new regulations governing theaters and spectacles. The inspector denounced any public performances that offended Catholicism, the official religion of the state. The law governing the theater specifically instructed the censor to ensure that "the mysteries and religious ceremonies, the images of God and the saints, and the remaining sacred objects not be profaned through reproduction and exposition." Moreover, the regulation advised that "[p]lays that excuse incest, adultery, violence, assassination, suicide, and other crimes will be censured" and "dramas that incite passions will not be allowed."[38]

The ordinances governing entertainment that were enacted between 1849 and 1919 reveal the reach of the modernizing campaign to form a modern culture. These regulations outlined the expected behavior of the public, the actors, and businessmen. The rules also established censorship to ensure the formation of approved values. The goal of both regulations and censorship was to develop respect for work, the spirit of action and volunteerism, and a bourgeois sensibility characterized by prudent manners, a refined aesthetic appreciation, and control of passions. These values reflected the European education and experience of members of the Peruvian elites, especially those who had studied in English and German schools.

The new ordinances regulated the location and nature of entertainment. City licenses specified schedule times, days, number of performances, prices, and advertising. The regulations stated the need for security measures and hygienic conditions in spaces reserved for public diversions. Enforcement relied on inspectors. For example, they reported unkempt conditions in the city's three theaters. Owners had done little to modify the ancient, badly constructed buildings, improve the unsanitary conditions, or provide for the safety and comfort of audiences. The new regulations demanded that these facilities comply with sound architectural and construction designs.[39]

As the reformers modernized the city, they designated areas for public entertainment. During the colonial era and in the early days of the republic, most public diversions (with the exception of bullfights, theaters, and cockfights)—that is, the spectacles, games, and dramatizations—occurred in the main plaza, the church, and the markets.[40] As new diversions appeared, they required new locations, such as exhibition salons, concert halls, cinemas, and bicycle courses. In Lima in 1886, twelve public spaces were allocated for entertainment. These spaces included the Plaza de Toros, finished in 1768, the cockfighting arena, begun in 1762, the new Alameda, the Garden of the Exposition Palace, the Hippodrome for bicycle racing, and four theaters. The number of public spaces allocated for diversions had increased to 187 by 1929. The new locations featured seventy-one theaters and cinemas, eighty-seven soccer clubs, and twenty-five billiard halls and music salons.[41]

City ordinances prohibited use of the streets and the main plaza for public performances other than religious processions, civic fiestas, and military drills. City officials specifically banned puppet shows, musicians playing small portable pianos or organs, and public spectacles regarded as disorderly or that might contribute to an atmosphere conducive to bad behavior among the townspeople. Public meetings in the streets or the plaza were explicitly prohibited.[42] The new allocation of public spaces for diversions permitted closer control over individual behavior. In these spaces, diversions were clearly delineated and regulated.

One feature underscoring the difference between older and newer diversions was the hour during which they took place. Nighttime activities began to occur in the middle of the eighteenth century but were suspended in 1753 because of governmental fears that darkness aided disorderly activities. Nighttime diversions returned to Lima around the middle of the nineteenth century, in part as a result of the installation of gas lighting in 1853 and electric lights in 1902. The lights permitted new uses of space and freedom of movement. Nocturnal diversions resulted in extraordinary license fees. The Chinese theater, for example, had to pay fifty *soles* for a license because its performances extended beyond midnight, the usual closing time for public entertainments.[43] Because the closing time was frequently breached, the town council felt obliged to solicit from the national government revocation of the ordinance mandating the curfew. The council argued that the law ran counter to the idea of progress and the principles of liberalism that governed a modern nation.

The council sent one of its members, Pedro Revoredo, to argue for a series of reforms before the central government. Revoredo insisted that the 1863 regulations governing theaters reflected the sensible manners and colonial ideas of the time but expressed "anomalous dispositions, absurdities, and contradictions against the principles of civilization and liberalism that are the glorious guidelines of the age [1890] that we travel through; the presence of censorship constitutes an offense against the liberties of thought and industry that the entire world proclaims."[44]

This request to expand the hours for theater performances generated a discussion of the character of Lima's public. Opponents of the change alleged that European customs could not be extended to Lima's population because the manners of the latter, unfortunately, were "somewhat lax." Members of the federal government's commission on public diversions (*comisión de espectáculos*) agreed and, noting that the audiences included many minors, domestics, and factory workers, expressed the fear that these workers and young people would develop undisciplined habits by attending late-night theatrical performances. Moreover, the commissioners felt it was imprudent to attempt to imitate the practices of the great capitals of the world, because in London, Paris, and Madrid the principles of order and the habits of hard work were more ingrained in the general populace. Moreover, the commissioners added, rigid closing times, usually 12 midnight, governed performances in these cities. If theater performances continued after midnight, the owners paid very high prices for the licenses. Following these arguments, the government increased its management of nocturnal hours. These regulations continued into the 1920s and 1930s.

The campaign to improve the behavior associated with theatrical activities resulted in a directive that theater actors and owners behave in a professional manner. Moreover, commissioners urged the public to dress and behave properly inside the theater. The municipal police code had a section dedicated to recreation and entertainment, public order, and morality; it stipulated that those attending diversions should "guard their behavior, making sure their words or actions do not offend decency, order, calm, or the enjoyment of the rest of the public, under penalty of being expelled." Disorders occasionally broke out in theaters that required the police to restore order.

The city's behavioral standards met with opposition from audiences, actors, and owners. Evidence of this opposition exists in the fines imposed by the city government on theater owners. An 1891 address by Manuel Aurelio Fuentes, inspector of public diversions, demonstrates the efforts of the government to impose order in the theaters. Fuentes complained of the difficulty of imposing rational measures regarding public behavior on a population accustomed to disregarding the law. Even commonsense regulations met opposition—such as that mounted by the owners of the Politeama theater, who refused to implement a fire prevention program.[45]

SOME FINAL REFLECTIONS

The modernizing campaign of the Peruvian government and the Lima administration included using entertainment as an important method to promote a new moral, bourgeois culture. At the same time, technological innovations and material transformations led to an increase in the number of public spaces and private areas available for diversions. Not only was there a corresponding selectivity to the forms of entertainment allocated to the rich and poor sectors, there also existed spaces where members of both groups mixed. Although such mixing was not always harmonious, Lima's poor tried to increase and democratize these sites.

Traditional entertainments still took place, especially in the neighborhoods where city inhabitants could escape political control. It was difficult to change the customs of the population, both inspectors and visitors noted. As Pedro Dávalos y Lissón observed on his return to Lima in 1906, the behavior of the public in the theater was "grotesque . . . upon leaving the theater, men bathed the sidewalks with their urine. All this was the result of a lack of modesty rules."[46]

The reformers had to confront both traditional social patterns and diverse popular forms of entertainment classified as "vulgar, barbaric, and licentious." The civilizing project undertaken by the elites tried to impose limits on the freedom of the body. Their new order called for a bourgeois definition of the body in which caution, modesty, and modernization would dominate. For these reformers, the formation of a rational mentality and the inculcation of a work ethic formed part of the ideal "civilization."

SUGGESTED READINGS

Arbena, Joseph L. *Sport and Society in Latin America: Diffusion, Dependency, and the Rise of Mass Culture.* Westport, CT: Greenwood Press, 1988.

Beezley, William H. *Judas at the Jockey Club and Other Episodes of Porfirian Mexico.* Lincoln: University of Nebraska Press, 1987; 2nd ed., 2004.

Beezley, William H., Cheryl English Martin, and William E. French, eds. *Rituals of Rule, Rituals of Resistence: Public Celebrations and Popular Culture in Mexico.* Wilmington, DE: SR Books, 1994.

Higgins, James. *Lima: A Cultural History.* New York: Oxford University Press, 2005.

Hunefeldt, Christine. *Liberalism in the Bedroom: Quarreling Spouses in Nineteenth-Century Lima.* University Park, PA: Pennsylvania State University Press, 2000.

Lobo, Susan. *A House of My Own: Social Organization in the Squatter Settlements of Lima, Peru.* Tucson: University of Arizona Press, 1982.

Meade, Teresa. *"Civilizing" Rio: Reform and Resistance in a Brazilian City, 1889–1930.* State College: Penn State University Press, 1997.

Needell, Jeffrey. *A Tropical Belle Epoque: The Elite Culture of Turn-of-the-Century Rio de Janeiro.* New York: Cambridge University Press, 1987.

Osorio, Alejandra B. *Inventing Lima: Baroque Modernity in Peru's South Sea Metropolis.* New York: Palgrave Macmillan, 2008.

Overmyer Velasquez, Mark. *Visions of the Emerald City: Modernity, Tradition and the Formation of Porfirian Oaxaca, Mexico.* Durham: Duke University Press, 2006.

Robert, Karen. "The Argentine Babel: Space, Politics, and Culture in the Growth of Buenos Aires, 1851–1890." Ph.D. dissertation, University of Michigan, 1994.

Viqueira Albán, Juan Pedro. *Propriety and Permissiveness in Bourbon Mexico,* translated by Sonya Lipsett-Rivera and Sergio Rivera Ayala. Wilmington, DE: SR Books, 1999.

Sights

Alias la Gringa. 1991. Directed by Alberto Durant (Facets Multimedia).
Martin Chambi and the Heirs of the Incas. 1986 (Cinema Guild).
Metal and Melancholy. 1994. Directed by Heddy Honigmann (Icarus Films).
Oblivion/Olvido. 2007. Directed by Heddy Honigmann (Icarus Films).
Popular video of Peru (International Media Resource Exchange).

10

From the Ruins of the Ancien Régime

Mexico's Monument to the Revolution

Thomas L. Benjamin

Monuments have been used to create a sense of community, legitimate political regimes, and elevate individuals and causes to heroic stature. As mnemonics (or perhaps as granite or marble synecdoches), these monuments broadcast cultural lessons, especially instruction in national history, personal deportment, and community values. As Mexico's leaders attempted to build a new nation, unify a fractured society, and extend economic and political justice to Mexicans, they had to explain the meaning of revolution. Thomas Benjamin explores this search for symbols to create the myth of the revolution and the monuments to express the value of this experience. His chapter suggests comparison with the new monuments and hallowed locations described by Mona Ozouf in her examination of French Revolutionary monuments and festivals. Following Benjamin's example, one could raise questions about the monuments of other Latin American revolutionary movements and regimes.

Commemorative monuments have as their most obvious purpose the evocation and celebration of the past in the present. Their purpose is to make us remember, but to remember (and forget) in a particular manner. Often monuments are intended to reinforce a sense of local or national, ethnic or class identity, an identity linked to the actions, ideas, values, and virtues of the persons or events commemorated. In this sense they are exhortations to imitate our worthy predecessors: they remind us how to behave and what to believe. They are also intended to create a sense of generational and national solidarity. Finally, regimes erect monuments to emphasize their real or alleged continuity with a great epoch or leader and thereby to obtain the sanction and legitimation of some revered past.[1]

Certain monuments are designed to create a setting for ritual performances, for commemorative celebrations and ceremonies. The creation of an artificial space sets the stage for a concentration of political suggestions: of connotations, of emotions, and of authority. Some monuments become identified with recurrent calendrical celebrations. The monument, the setting, the performance, and the particular day combine to evoke symbolic reassurance that the state, the regime, or the leader is faithful to some sacred origin.[2]

The past is often contested terrain in politics, and official culture seeks control of the high ground. Commemorative monuments and civic celebrations shape, institutionalize, and disseminate particular versions of the past while excluding, suppressing, and devaluing other versions or traditions. When successful, they form part of a more comprehensive ideology or discourse that employs myths and symbols to promote loyalty and patriotism (read: conformity and obedience) to regime, state, and nation.[3]

Mexico's Monument to the Revolution can be "read" for such intents and meanings. As a product of Mexico's postrevolutionary official culture, the monument represents and portrays the mythic or invented revolution that emerged in revolutionary discourse after 1911 and became official and authorized by the 1930s. Many elements of this mythic revolution had emerged quite early in revolutionary discourse, during the violent decade of 1910–1920, without much dissent. Revolutionary politicians, intellectuals, and journalists generally reified and defined "the Revolution" as popular, democratic, and nationalist, a genuine social revolution, a continuation of the revolutions of independence and the Reform, and unambiguously victorious in the struggle against "the reaction." During the 1920s the idea of a continuing and permanent revolution, a revolution converted into government and advanced through reform, was added to the interpretation. The last and certainly most important concept in the definition, the singularity of the revolution and the essential unity of the various struggles, movements, and contentious factions, was constructed during the 1920s. It was during the 1930s that all of the elements of the official history of the Mexican Revolution were put together for the first time and sanctioned as Mexico's national, dominant social memory.[4]

The Monument to the Revolution embodied the most important elements of the mythic revolution in its origins, construction, form, and sculpture. This text of stone constitutes, in effect, the first official history of the Mexican Revolution. It sought to legitimate the postrevolutionary political elite by emphasizing, first, the popular and unified nature of the revolution; second, the identification of the revolution with the Republic and its central defining struggles for independence and definition; and third, the continuity between the new political system and the revolution.

THE ABSENCE OF SYMBOLIC VIOLENCE

In ancient Egypt and post-Soviet Russia the smashing of statues marked the beginning of a new age. Dramatic political upheavals are often accompanied by icon smashing, symbolic violence against the monuments erected by the defeated old regime.[5] The defeat and discrediting of the regime of Porfirio Díaz in 1911, however, was not accompanied by any outburst of iconoclasm. This absence of symbolic violence is particularly interesting and significant since the Porfiriato, the age of Díaz from 1876 to 1911, was the first great age of commemorative monument building in modern Mexican history.

The triumph of liberalism over its domestic and foreign enemies by 1867, and the stability and prosperity of the later Díaz years, permitted an unambiguous and unopposed celebration of Mexico's liberal past. In 1885 Ignacio Manuel Altamirano complained that "we have a very small number of national monuments, whether due to internal wars, or whether the best materials have priority or because the press and the artists themselves were not zealous enough in promoting the construction of public monuments to our heroes, and lastly, perhaps due to apathy, which is the very essence of our nature."[6] Altamirano listed only five monuments, all of them celebrating the heroes of independence. Thereafter, notes Carlos Monsivais, came "the invasion of statues."[7]

By the time of the Porfiriato, argues Charles Hale, liberalism had become a unifying political myth. Porfirians viewed the struggle for independence during the 1810s and the struggles for reform and republican government during the 1850s and 1860s as two stages of an ongoing political-social process. The Díaz regime embraced and encouraged this unifying political myth in order to reconcile the partisans of all liberal factions and to present itself as the worthy successor to the glorious liberal tradition.[8] In 1877 the government decreed that three *glorietas* on the Paseo de la Reforma would be reserved for monuments to Cuauhtémoc, the heroes of independence, and the heroes of the Reform. The Cuauhtémoc monument was unveiled in 1887, and in 1910, during the centennial celebrations, the Column of Independence was inaugurated by Díaz. Between 1889 and 1899, thirty-four statues of mostly Independence- and Reform-era heroes were erected along the Paseo de la Reforma in Mexico City. Each state was invited to immortalize two of its native sons. On the centennial of the birth of Benito Juárez, in 1906, construction began on the Hemiciclo (semicircle) de Benito Juárez, located in the Alameda Central on Avenida Juárez.[9] Through commemorative monuments and civic celebrations, independence, the Reform, and the Díaz regime were symbolically superimposed.

The Porfirian regime did not erect monuments—self-conscious monuments—to itself. Its monuments were not commemorative but utilitarian: railroads, bridges, and particularly grand public buildings that announced the power, progress, and style of Porfirian Mexico and the Díaz regime. The Italian architect Adamo Boari drew up plans for a monument-statue glorifying Porfirio Díaz, but the regime fell before it was constructed. Because the revolutionaries of 1910 and after saw themselves as the rightful heirs of Mexico's liberal tradition (and the Díaz regime as a deviation), they embraced the same pantheon of national heroes glorified by the Díaz regime. Revolutionaries had no need to smash the statues of the old regime. Rather, through annual commemorations, they made them their own. Independence, the Reform, and the Revolution became the new historical trinity of Mexican history, the three stages of an ongoing struggle creating a politically, socially, and economically independent nation.

A BABEL OF COMMEMORATIONS

There was no "invasion of statues" in the two decades after 1911. Civil war, factionalism, governmental instability, and competition for scarce pesos no doubt accounted for this inattention. As in Porfirian times, state and national governments proclaimed that their social improvements and public works—schools, sports parks, *ejidos*, and irrigation works—were the real monuments to the revolution. There was as well, perhaps, a reluctance based on a supposed revolutionary mentality. As one journalist noted, when revolutionaries begin to raise statues, they have lost interest in action: "they enter the [era of] drowsy boastfulness and bourgeois epilogues." An editorial in *El Universal* in 1923 suggested it was premature to erect a monument to the revolution. Such an attempt, it was noted, would only produce "a monument to our vanity."[10]

During the 1910s and 1920s, national governments remained pretty much unengaged in commemorating the revolution in ceremony or stone. Likewise, no official and authorized history of the Mexican Revolution appeared in print before the 1930s. This aversion of Mexico's official culture to activity commemorating the revolution, however, did not mean that no such activity occurred in Mexico during this time. The vacuum was filled by partisan, factional interests that claimed that the revolution prior to the 1930s was shaped more by the unregulated, multivocal expressions of vernacular culture. The revolutionary past was contested, as commemorative activities demonstrated.[11]

During the 1910s and 1920s, commemorative activity became the responsibility by default of revolutionary factions and smaller groups of partisans. In December 1911, followers of Aquiles Serdán proposed the erection of a monument "in order to honor the immortality of the eminent proto martyr of the reconquest of our political liberties and[,] obeying the impulses of our hearts[,] gratitude."[12] The same group organized the first annual commemoration of the assassination of Francisco Madero and Pino Suárez on February 22, 1914 (and many years later they formed the Bloque de Precursores de la Revolución en los Años de 1909, 1910, y 1913 to promote the commemoration of Serdán, Madero, and Carranza).[13] Later in the decade, Maderistas (followers of Madero) organized as the Comité Pro-Madero organized the November 20 and February 22 commemorations, while Carrancistas (followers of Venustiano Carranza), through their control of the government, commemorated the anniversary of the signing of Carranza's Plan of Guadelupe (March 26) and virtually ignored November 20. After Carranza's downfall in 1920, the new Obregonista faction (followers of Alvaro Obregón) in power ignored March 26 and made November 20 a day of national celebration. The Agrupación Pro-Madero, as it was now known, however, continued to organize the festivities for November 20 during the 1920s, while some former Carrancistas commemorated March 26. Beginning in 1923, the Asociación de Constituyentes de Querétaro began to commemorate the signing of the Constitution of 1917.[14]

During the 1920s, additional partisan cults of martyrs commemorated the assassinations and deaths of Emiliano Zapata, Ricardo Flores Magón, Felipe Carrillo Puerto, and finally Alvaro Obregón, and constructed worthy tombs and monuments. The Zapatistas erected Zapata's tomb and statue in Cuautla, which served as the setting for annual commemorations of the "Apostle of Agrarianism." Local and state governments got into the act by sponsoring or cosponsoring ceremonies, busts, and statues of local heroes of national stature, while labor and agrarian organizations and political parties did the same for their class-oriented heroes. In 1927 the Liga Nacional Campesina proposed a monument to Zapata, not one with all of the "vulgarity of bourgeois art," as in Porfirian times, but a monument "very Mexican and very evocative of the peasantry at the same time"—a pyramid.[15] This proposed monument, like many others, was never built, but in subsequent decades Zapata statues and monuments proliferated throughout the country.

The greatest single monument to an individual revolutionary was that dedicated to Alvaro Obregón. Unlike the partisan-sponsored commemorative celebrations and statues of the 1910s and 1920s, the Obregón monument was constructed by order of the national government of President Abelardo L. Rodríguez. In this case the followers of Obregón, many of whom occupied some of the most important posts in government, managed to elevate their vernacular symbolic interest to official status.[16]

During the 1910s and 1920s, Mexico's vernacular revolutionary culture created a babel of commemorative ceremonies, statues, and tombs sponsored by competing cults of martyred revolutionaries. Each cult celebrated its partisan revolution, thus effectively denying, in word and deed, the singularity of the revolution. A similar situation existed with regard to the writing of history. In the 1930s, revolutionary official culture asserted itself; this led to the first official and authorized history of the revolution and the construction of a monument to the revolution itself. This development did not bring an end to the commemorative activities of the cults or the writing of factional, partisan history, although such vernacular creations no longer had pride of place. The vernacular babel was superseded by the mythic pretensions of official culture.

A MONUMENT TO THE MYTHIC REVOLUTION

The assassination of the "Caudillo of the Revolution," Alvaro Obregón, in 1928, the Escobar rebellion, and the subsequent presidential election of 1929 highlighted the divisive lack of unity among those who called themselves revolutionaries. The possibility of civil war between revolutionary factions, as in 1914–1915, was real. In 1929 outgoing president Plutarco Elías Calles and others in his ruling group attempted to unify all revolutionaries into one national revolutionary party. To reinforce the idea of unity, Calles emphasized the concept of "the revolutionary family," which suggested the common origins and principles of all revolutionaries and their essential unity in the past and present.[17] In the aftermath of this crisis, the ruling group sought to reconcile the historical factionalism of the revolution, to heal the divisive wounds of memory, by constructing a history of the revolution acceptable to all factions and a monument to symbolize revolutionary unity and continuity. The official culture of postrevolutionary Mexico made the first concerted efforts to establish a national, inclusive social memory of the revolution.[18]

Beginning in 1929 and 1930, the ruling group and its associated intellectuals and journalists began to invent a singular, unified, and coherent Mexican Revolution. The rival revolutionary factions and traditions were amalgamated. Their genuine differences were downplayed and their shared goals and particular contributions to the one revolution, *"la Revolución,"* were emphasized.[19] The idea of an essential singularity to *la Revolución* was the last and indispensable element of the invention of the "mythic" revolution. It was the element of coherence binding all of the other concepts and, in a practical political sense, binding most revolutionaries, past and present, to one discourse legitimizing the new state, its institutions, and its leaders.

In 1930 the official newspaper of the National Revolutionary Party editorialized that it was time to stop writing partisan, factional history and building statues to the *caudillos* of revolutionary factions. One day, continued the editorial, a monument to the revolution would be erected. "That would not be in order to satisfy [some] faction, but rather to consecrate the great event of our racial, cultural, and economic integration, a necessary fact of our civilization. In that moment, there will not exist agrarianism, not Zapatism, nor Carrancism, nor Callesism."[20] In 1932, the governor of Querétaro proposed a national competition among artists to design a monument to the revolution to be erected in his state, a monument that would crystallize in a definitive form the goals and ideals of *la Revolución*. Governor Saturnino Osorinio called on "all the old revolutionaries in order that forgetting grudges setting aside all the feelings of hate and personal differences, they would heed the voice of the Revolution and extend their hearts that all beat for the same desire."[21] This monument was never built, but the idea clearly was gathering force.

In 1932, workmen began to demolish the iron frame structure of the never completed and long-abandoned Palacio Legislativo Federal, located in the Plaza de la República in Mexico City. Designed by the French architects Emile Benard and Maxime Roisin, the Beaux-Arts revival Palacio Legislativo was projected to be "the most important building that Porfirianism thought to erect."[22] Construction began in 1903 and was interrupted in 1912; for the next twenty years photographs of Mexico City documented this symbolic ruin of the old regime.

Carlos Obregón Santacilia, an architect trained at the Academy of San Carlos in the later years of the revolution and one of the favorite architects of the Sonoran governments of the 1920s, intervened to save and transform the iron frame of the Palacio Legislativo.[23] Obregón Santacilia suggested to Alberto J. Pani, minister of hacienda and official patron of a number of the architect's public buildings, that the Palacio Legislativo be converted into a monument to the revolution. Pani's first reaction was negative. The following day, however, perhaps after consulting with the *Jefe Máximo de la Revolución*, former President Calles, Pani asked Obregón Santacilia to design a monument.[24] On January 15, 1933, Calles and Pani presented a formal initiative to president Abelardo L. Rodríguez for the construction of a monument to the revolution. Eight days later the president approved the request and established the Great Commission to the Patronage of the Monument to the Revolution, to be chaired by Calles, and gave the metallic structure of the Palacio Legislativo to the commission.[25]

Architect Obregón Santacilia proposed to save only the central part of the structure, which supported the dome, to create a massive tetra pylon. The four piers of the iron skeleton were encased in concrete and sheathed in Mexican volcanic rock (*piedra chiluca*), producing four great arches, each more than eighteen meters wide and twenty-six meters high. Obregón Santacilia preserved the original design, which placed a hemispheric dome on top of an elliptical dome. This double dome prevented the tall arches from diminishing the monumental effect of the exterior hemispherical roof, which now reached a height of sixty-five meters. The base of the plaza itself was gradually raised several meters and inclined upward toward the monument, enhancing the monumentality of the plaza and the monument itself. Below the raised floor of the monument, rooms were constructed whose function was to be determined later.[26] The style of the monument was "modern regionalism"—a fusion of Mexican themes and materials with art deco lines.[27]

In early 1933 an open competition was held for the design of four sculpture groups, to be placed one on each corner at the base of the double dome on the monument. The winner, Oliverio Martínez, known for his monument to Emiliano Zapata in Cuautla, placed three figures in each group. The large size, clarity, and simplicity of these figures, and their distinctiveness in relief, made them visible and understandable to observers near and far. Their absence of clothing gave them a timeless quality. Martínez's figures are strong, proud, unbowed peasants and proletarians, soldiers and citizens, men and women, and unmistakably Mexican—Indian and mestizo.[28]

Obregón Santacilia, Calles, and Pani proposed, designed, and constructed a monument with a message, a text interpreting modern Mexican history in stone. The mythic revolution it proclaimed and symbolized was victorious and popular, a continuation of earlier liberal struggles and permanent. Most important, the revolution as represented by the monument was singular and unified.

The mythic revolution as it was interpreted in the 1930s was unambiguously victorious, a victory of "the people" against "the reaction." In their formal proposal Calles and Pani referred to the monument as "a Triumphal Arch."[29] The very origin of the monument symbolized the triumph of *la Revolucíon* over the Porfirian regime. As Obregón Santacilia noted later, "Out of the ruins of the ancien régime, from the very building designed to perpetuate it, arose the Monument to the Social Revolution that defeated it."[30] Monumentality has long symbolized conquest and triumph. The Monument to the Revolution, both massive and tall, was designed to be, as Calles and Pani wrote, "the greatest in the Capital of the Republic," one possessing "features of beauty and a magnitude of extraordinary commemorative force."[31] The sculpture groups and the absence of images or names of great *caudillos* proclaimed the popular character of the revolution. "It will glorify, in the abstract, the secular work of the people."[32]

This monument to the people was to be paid for by the people through a national subscription. Newspapers often reported the small but onerous contributions of distant pueblos and poor *ejidos*. The construction of the monument would also be of a popular, revolutionary character. The stone for the monument was provided by the workers of the Sindicato Revolucionario de Obreros Canteros de la República Mexicana, reportedly the first union officially recognized by the new revolutionary government in 1911.[33]

The mythic revolution extended far into the past and continued into the present and future. Calles and Pani argued, consistent with revolutionary discourse extending back to the 1910s, that the "great Mexican Revolution" ("the struggle of the people for the conquest of their rights") developed in three stages. The first stage, "political emancipation," was the struggle for national independence in the 1810s; the second stage, "spiritual emancipacion," was the Reform and the struggle against the French Intervention of the 1850s and 1860s; and the third stage, "economic emancipation," was the struggle of the people, beginning in 1910, against the privileged and for popular government and a more equal division of wealth. This continuity of struggle would be portrayed by Martínez's four allegorical sculpture groups. The group on the southeast corner symbolized national independence, the one on the northeast corner symbolized the redemption of the peasant, and the last group, located on the northwest corner, symbolized the redemption of the worker.[34] Insofar as the Sonoran revolutionary governments, and Calles himself in particular, emphasized the idea of permanent revolution, Calles and Pani proposed that the monument (like *la Revolución* itself) "should prolong its commemorative action, also into an undefined future." The monument should be inscribed with the words "To the Revolution of yesterday, of today, of tomorrow, of always."[35] This inscription was never executed.

Finally, the mythic revolution portrayed by the monument was singular, unified, and impersonal. This message was related through obvious omissions. The "fundamental characteristic" of the monument, noted Calles and Pani in their proposal, is that "it will not be erected to the glory of specific heroes, martyrs, or caudillos."[36] The monument, a reaction against twenty years of personalism and factionalism in Mexican social memory, would ignore the revolutionary factions and their chiefs altogether and glorify only *la Revolución*.[37]

Construction of the monument proceeded in fits and starts, interrupted by long delays during periods of inadequate funding. Although it was intended that the monument would be financed by voluntary contributions from the public, most funding came from the National Revolutionary Party, the government of the Federal District, various departments of the national government, and state governments. Three thousand workers eventually were employed on the project. Obregón Santacilia later reported that during construction he filled the 30,000-square-meter plaza three times with stone for the monument. Construction of the monument was completed in 1938 during the presidency of Lázaro Cárdenas. There was no specific inauguration of the monument; the first ceremony held under the dome and in the plaza occurred on November 20 ("Revolution Day"), 1938. Thereafter part of the November 20 festivities each year has taken place at the monument.[38]

THE TOMB OF THE REVOLUTION

A public monument is a continuing presence in a community, but is it an active presence?[39] In 1960 the monument's architect, Carlos Obregón Santacilia, declared proudly that the monument had become "the indispensable stage for the most emotional acts of the nation, to where the greatest number of citizens are drawn to [because] already they feel that it is always theirs."[40] This is clearly the image projected by Balmori's 1940 woodcut showing President Cárdenas addressing a mass audience; the people with their banners and even the towering popular, populist president are dwarfed by the revolution as symbolized by the monument.[41] The commemorative and didactic function of the monument, it would appear, served the purpose designed by its creators.

Appearances can be deceiving. The Monument to the Revolution never became the center stage of revolutionary commemorations in Mexico City. The annual November 20 celebrations involve speeches at the monument early in the day, but the parade and the festivities culminate in the Zócalo, the sacred center of the Republic. It is there that the president addresses the assembled multitude and, by radio and television, the nation. The monument could not compete with the evocative power of the Zócalo, but its mythic image was enhanced after its construction by an afterthought.

In the late 1930s, perhaps at the suggestion of congress, Obregón Santacilia designed a Panteón de los Hombres Ilustres to be located in front of the monument, a cemetery for the leaders of the revolution.[42] The Panteón was never realized, but by an order of congress, a copper urn containing the ashes of Venustiano Carranza was deposited in a crypt in one of the four piers in January 1942, on the twenty-fifth anniversary of the signing of the constitution in 1917.[43] Over the next three decades the ashes and remains of Francisco Madero (1960), Francisco Villa (1965), Lázaro Cárdenas (1970), and finally Plutarco Elías Calles were transferred to the different piers of the monument. The government has attempted to obtain the remains of Emiliano Zapata for the monument but the family has resisted the transfer. Busts of Cárdenas and Calles adorn their respective crypts.[44]

The placement of the ashes and remains of the five revolutionary leaders modified and enhanced the meaning of the monument. Originally designed to glorify "in the abstract, the secular work of the people," the monument became increasingly identified with the great *caudillos* of the revolution. The deposition of the ashes and remains of leaders who were, in life, rivals, in some cases bitter enemies, breathed life into the concept of the singular and unified mythic revolution much more than the cold, abstract design did. While partisan organizations, the separate civic associations of Carranza, Madero, Villa, and Calles, still maintain "the sincere veneration of our great patricians," the orations from the beginning have emphasized revolutionary unity and the need to respect and love "our institutions."[45]

These prestigious tombs transformed the monument into a sacred monument of the nation.[46] More so than any other feature, the crypts turned the monument into an active presence in the symbolic life (and commemorative calendar) of Mexico. On the anniversaries of the assassinations and deaths of the five leaders the state organizes commemorative ceremonies at the monument, which is decorated for the occasion with huge Mexican flags, banners, and portraits. The ceremonies involve orations, the laying of wreaths, musical performances, and military honor guards. "Year after year," noted José González Bustamante in 1951 at a ceremony honoring Carranza, "we come to this Monument which the Mexican people have consecrated as the sanctuary of the Revolution in order to remember the great leaders who rest below these stones."[47]

By the 1960s, the monument had come to symbolize different revolutions, even different Mexicos, for different observers. For those who spoke on behalf of the state, it remained "the grandiose Monument to the Revolution, stone symbol of the Mexican calling for the causes of Democracy, Liberty, and Justice."[48] Critics of the political system that honored *la Revolución*, on the other hand, came to view it as the "emblem of the consolidation of political power in Mexico by means of the Institutional Revolutionary Party."[49] For one commentator, the monument signified not the perpetuation of the revolution but its disfigurement and death: "We can state that the Monument to the Revolution, given its frame by Porfirio Díaz and redecorated by the stupidity of the merchants of the Revolution, and before which is sacrificed the effectiveness of suffrage, officiating the priests of the decadence of a libertarian revolution converted into a single party, is nothing more than a Tomb of the Revolution."[50]

For the cartoonist Rocha, years later the plutocracy has taken the places of honor on the monument while the ordinary Mexicans once honored in the sculpture groups are now on the street selling fruit to survive.

Nevertheless, the mythic image of the monument persists. This persistence is revealed less by the ceremonies staged by the state and official party than by dissident groups, organizations, and parties, which sometimes use the monument and the plaza for demonstrations of protest against the regime. At these times the monument becomes a reproach aimed at the regime, a symbol not of revolutionary continuity but of discontinuity. When in 1975 the dissident labor movement, led by the Tendencia Democrática of SUTERM, chose the monument as the backdrop for its protest demonstration, the symbol was turned against the regime. "Live up to the democratic and revolutionary ideals of the Revolution." This was the new meaning of the monument.[51]

SUGGESTED READINGS

Hass, Kristin Ann. *Carried to the Wall: American Memory and the Vietnam Veterans Memorial.* Berkeley: University of California Press, 1998.

Newman, Simon Peter. *Parades and the Politics of the Street: Festive Culture in the Early American Republic.* Philadelphia: University of Pennsylvania Press, 1997.

Ozouf, Mona. *Festivals and the French Revolution*, translated by Alan Sheridan. Cambridge: Harvard University Press, 1988.

Tenenbaum, Barbara A. "Streetwise History: The Paseo de la Reforma and the Porfirian State, 1880–1910." In *Rituals of Rule, Rituals of Resistance: Public Celebrations and Popular Culture in Mexico*, edited by William H. Beezley, Cheryl English Martin, and William E. French, 127–50. Wilmington, DE: SR Books, 1994.

Sights

Barrios of Solitude. 1998. Directed by Patricio Guzmán (Filmaker's Library).

El Bulto. 1991. Directed by Gabriel Retes.

The Last Zapatista. 1996. Directed by Susan Lloyd (UCMEC).

Memorias de un Mexicano. Salvador Toscano (Madeira Cinema).

Sounds

The Mexican Revolution: Corridos about the Heroes and Events, 1910–1920 and Beyond! Arhoolie Productions, 1996.

20 Exitos de Agustín Lara. RCA/BMG, 1991.

Toña La Negra; La Sensación Jarocha. Discos Peerless, 1991.

11

Racial Parity and National Humor

Carmen Miranda's Samba Performances, 1930–1939

Darién J. Davis

Technological advances in the twentieth century made the commodification of popular cultural traditions possible. In the case of Brazil, the popularization of samba (the music, the dance, and its connection to the great spectacle, Carnival) became inseparable from Brazilian identity. To the elites, such popular music forms were clearly associated with the lower classes and with people of color—those whom just a few decades earlier they had labeled uncivilized and premodern. The commodification of popular forms such as the samba allowed the creation of a national culture that presumably overcame racism. In the case of samba, a musical form central to the idea of Afro-Brazilianness was filtered through and mediated by representatives of the white middle class, performers who appropriated the music of poor people of color. The music and the lyrics remained linked to blacks, the original composers, but these artists were only tangentially recognized by white society. Darién Davis describes the emergence of Carmen Miranda as official negotiator between the samba tradition of poor blacks and mulattoes and white elite and middle-class consumers as the populist Vargas regime sought to create a national culture.

Brazil is not and never has been a racial democracy. Yet students of Brazilian history and culture cannot but marvel at the many cultural creations forged as a result of the melding (unequal, to be sure) of the three major civilizations on which Brazilian culture is based: the Luso-Portuguese, the African, and the Tupi-Guaraní. Late-nineteenth-century images of slaves and masters gave way to twentieth-century national representations that downplayed racial conflict and promoted an idealization that defended the status quo.[1] Still inadequately examined are the ideological and hegemonic roots of the racial democracy that emerged as a nationalist ideology in the

1930s, when racial "exceptionalism" was still acutely visible in popular and high culture.

The 1930 Vargas revolution institutionalized a nationalism that placed *brasilidade* (Brazilianness) above racial, ethnic, and class identifications. At the same time, musical and artistic expressions of the popular classes that bore strong black influences caught the attention of the major radio stations in São Paulo and Rio de Janeiro, which were bent on marketing "national culture" to a growing urban people. Discrimination, prejudice, and fear of the largely black and mulatto popular classes ensured that black music would not be disseminated in its original form.[2] Moreover, within the dominant culture's major means of communication, black music and musicians would receive national attention largely through white interpreters and sponsors or, to borrow an image from Franz Fanon, through the utilization of white masks.[3]

Into this context stepped Carmen Miranda, not yet in platform shoes or with the tutti-frutti hat that would become her Hollywood trademark in the 1940s. Her ascent to the center of Brazilian popular culture, particularly from 1929 to 1939, provides us with a perfect opportunity to examine the relationship between racial representation and Brazilian popular music. The nationalist rhetoric of Getúlio Vargas's government (1930–1945) attempted to nationalize "the popular." To do so, the administration required an image, a face, that could be applauded by the upper, middle, and popular classes. Less than fifty years after the abolition of slavery (in 1888), that face would naturally be one of a white person: Carmen Miranda, born in Portugal but raised in Brazil. In addition, as a national performer, Miranda showcased popular black musical rhythms with lyrics that spoke of poverty, the importance of music to daily life, race, and patriotism. More important, Miranda's personal charisma and charm, combined with her ability to inject humor, satire, criticism, and laughter into her musical creations, drew fans from both the popular sectors and the growing middle class in a nonconfrontational manner.

Long before Carmen Miranda set foot on American soil, in 1939, she had already learned how to navigate the complex music industry of radio and live performances. Showcasing some of the most creative aspects of popular music to a quickly expanding national audience, she soon became a household name. Humor, satire, and exaggeration of black and other popular rhythms were central to Carmen's musical repertoire. Through her unique character and delivery, she was able to utilize the creations of the mostly black popular classes, identifying with them because of her humble beginnings. She was also able to exploit the technology of the urban elite and the state because she was white. This double, almost entrepreneurial, exploitation allowed her to play a crucial role in bringing Brazilians of all ethnicities together through music.

The problems besetting a historical analysis of racial prejudice in a society that rhetorically celebrates the absence of such racism are exacerbated in underdeveloped societies such as Brazil's, where millions of citizens have little or no access to the means of communication. The increasing number of radio stations and newspapers in the 1920s increased contact between regions while promoting knowledge about national events within Brazil. By the 1930s, radio had become the principal instrument of mass communication for a population that was largely illiterate.[4] The absence of members of the popular classes, particularly black and mulatto professionals, in the communication industries is a further indication of institutionalized racism.

Not coincidentally, the nationalization of black culture occurred at a time when Rio de Janeiro's Carnival, the Brazilian celebration that represents the inversion of identity par excellence, underwent significant transformation and emerged as a federal production with nationalist criteria for participation. But Carnival was already a deeply divided activity, celebrated both in the *favelas* and in the grand salons behind closed doors. Creating an official Carnival and promoting an official *música popular brasileira* (Brazilian popular music) offended the taste of many members of the elite, who maintained considerable influence over industries. Thus, Vargas's nationalism would rely on what Michael L. Conniff has called the "populist-authoritarian counterpoint," an ideology that, in its more progressive phase, appealed to the masses but that ultimately depended on a strong moralistic bourgeois pattern of organization.[5]

MUSIC, HUMOR, AND THE NATIONALIST CLIMATE OF THE 1930S

Music and politics have been closely intertwined for centuries. Music has been employed to celebrate and promote, as in the case of national anthems, but also to denounce, as the New Song Movement of the 1960s and 1970s demonstrated.[6] Some musicians have willingly lent their services to political causes with which they identify, others are content to find a forum for self-expression. Humor has played a crucial role in musical performance, particularly in popular music that attempts to appeal to a mass audience. Composers and interpreters have relied on caricature and exaggeration to engage their audiences, sometimes resorting to parody, sarcasm, and irony to generate what Freud called "comic pleasure."[7]

Culturally determined, comic pleasure depends on the relationship of the performer to the audience as well as on such external factors as the political climate. Although Freud insisted that audiences enjoy comedy most when personal feelings are not involved, much humor results from ridicule.[8]

Within the nationalist (and often censured) climate of Brazil in the 1930s, political ridicule of the Vargas regime was almost nonexistent. Nonetheless, musicians found all manner of ways to laugh about the national character even as they celebrated nationhood. Lyrics and musical scores provided the framework for performances, but successful execution depended on the personal style and voice of singers such as Carmen Miranda.

Although Miranda adamantly proclaimed herself apolitical, she enthusiastically promoted Brazilian popular music through a personal campaign that thrust her into the limelight, drawing praise from her nationalist-minded fans and criticism from others who believed she was a fraud. Indeed, her relationship with the Vargas regime was not incidental. Often called the "Smiling Dictator," a rubric bestowed on her by the journalist Cesar Ladeira, Miranda's position as representative and promoter of Brazilian popular music throughout South America received the support of Getúlio Vargas, the more important dictator of the time and someone she knew personally. Miranda's rise to national attention and ascent as the "Queen of Popular Music" in some respects paralleled Vargas's own emergence as a populist politician and "Father of the Poor."

The Vargas nationalist campaign promoted economic and cultural integration and a sense of a national family. This would be the basis of a new Brazil that he as *paterfamilias* would direct. Carmen Miranda soon became the matriarch of popular music and a crucial element in Vargas's vision of the new Brazil. Thus, with the support of many other artists and intellectuals, Vargas began a national integration policy that sought to forge a greater sense of national identity among the all-too-independent states of Brazil. Reforms included the creation of a federal bureaucracy, denying states the right to negotiate treaties, banning all foreign languages, and controlling immigration. Vargas also created a state media system and, through the Department of Press and Propaganda (DIP), maintained a sense of national order within which celebration of *brasilidade* could occur.

To promote national culture, Vargas sought out local talent he could rely on to represent Brazil and its national interests in various cultural forums, both at home and abroad. Recognizing the powerful force that music played in the lives of millions of Brazilians, Vargas established several national forums for the promotion of Brazilian popular music. He created the Brazilian Popular Music Day, supported the DIP's efforts in the weekly national music program *A Hora do Brazil,* and mandated under local *carioca* authorities that patriotic themes be a requirement for participation in Rio's Carnival, an event that was quickly becoming a national celebration despite its *carioca* venue. Satire and parody were encouraged, particularly around themes that criticized what the regime saw as unpatriotic.

Carmen Miranda, the talented yet sequacious "Remarkable Little Girl," fighting for national notoriety and a chance to interpret Brazilian popular music, became a natural Vargas ally. Like many Brazilian artists and musicians, she was influenced by the growing nationalism that urged Brazilians to promote their national culture. But Carmen Miranda was not Brazilian in the formal sense. She was born in Portugal and maintained a Portuguese passport for most of her life.[9] Yet she became the embodiment of Brazilian popular music and an ambassador of black popular rhythms and forms such as the *batucada* and the samba both within and outside of her adopted country. Miranda's personal commitment to Brazilian popular music at a time when many of the middle and upper classes shunned the would-be genre is well documented, and her emphatic declaration, "I never sing if I'm not absolutely identified with the spirit of the music and the lyrics," indicated that she was more politically compromised than she publicly admitted.[10]

Vargas, who had been Miranda's neighbor when they both lived in Catete, had appeared with her during the Day of Brazilian Popular Music in 1939. The local press, which was largely censured, particularly after the creation of the Estado Novo (New State) in 1937, had already baptized Miranda the "Queen of Samba" after she won a series of popular music competitions. The DIP, responsible for the Vargas regime's propaganda and censorship, played a significant role in promoting her performances abroad, and in 1939 it became Miranda's sponsor in the United States.[11]

Miranda's commitment to *brasilidade* was never ideological. She harbored a personal commitment based on her desire to prove her own Braziliianness and to be recognized not as a Portuguese immigrant but as a native Brazilian. She gravitated to musical forms and rhythms that were part of her life experience, the forms and rhythms of the black and mulatto musicians who surrounded her, and the songs and music that pervaded the lower and lower-middle classes of Rio de Janeiro. After her travels throughout Brazil she appropriated the role of the *Bahiana*, one of the most recognized national types and the only female icon that rivaled the male prototypes such as the *malandro* (dandy), the *gaúcho* (cowboy), and the *jagunço* (gunman). Clearly conscious of the power dynamics inherent in her appropriation of the *Bahiana* role, she never sang or performed her music in a straightforward manner. She injected sensuality, wit, playfulness, humor, and satire into the captivating songs written for her.

In the 1930s, song festivals or modest concerts were the major forums for displaying popular music to the growing middle classes, although more and more records were beginning to propagate the talents of popular greats such as Mario Reis, Francisco "Chico" Alves, and Carmen Miranda. Of course, public performances abounded in *favelas* and in public spaces such as Praça Onze. Yet few of the *favelados* received national recognition, although the musical productions associated with Rio's Carnival quickly gained national fame. Indeed, only a handful of performers, including

Miranda, Francisco Alves, Stefana de Macedo, and Gastão Formenti, dominated the radio stations and the attention of the press. The most popular interpreters of samba emerged from song festivals or concerts such as Noite Brasileira, Tarde da Alma Brasileira, and Tarde do Folklore Brasileiro. All were organized in the major theaters in Rio.[12] As early as 1933, Carmen Miranda was certainly at the top of the list. Only a few performers, those well received at the festivals, went on to perform for the radio stations.

First discovered in 1929, when Josué de Barros took her to a Radio Sociedade song festival at the age of twenty, Carmen Miranda was destined to become the major female radio star, rivaling RCA's Chico Alves. Within a year Miranda became so successful that she was the first singer to receive a contract from a radio station, Radio Mayrick Viega, and she performed with unprecedented regularity for other radio stations. In 1934, listeners elected her the "Rainha do Broadcasting Carioca" (Queen of Carioca Broadcasting) in a competition held by the newspaper *A Hora.* Only a year earlier she had traveled to Argentina as the "Ambassador do Samba," after winning another national competition, the Concurso Nação-Untisal.[13]

Miranda showcased the writing talents of almost every major composer of the 1930s. Her performance, a perfect reflection of an age of national optimism, joviality, and pride in Brazil, brought her praise from many quarters. Through her raw talent and vivacious will, she won the hearts of the middle and popular classes that Vargas had so diligently courted. However, because of her use of the popular idiom and the attention she received, she was to meet with widespread criticism from the elite accustomed to promoting European and Euro-Brazilian culture. As José Ramos Tinhorão reports in his *História social da música popular brasileira,* while the elite and upper-middle class still looked to Europe, the culture of the urban masses was about to explode nationally, and Miranda would play a significant role.[14] With reason, she was known as the "Remarkable Little Girl," practically an upstart, who had taken black music and was promoting it as Brazilian.

RACE AND HUMOR IN MIRANDA'S PERFORMANCE

Despite the overwhelming importance of Africans and their descendants, prior to the 1930s, Brazilian nationhood was largely a white construction. In the 1920s modernist writers began to change that perception, and by the 1930s blacks were celebrated, although rhetorically, as a crucial link in the construction of "Brazilian race." Writers such as Gilberto Freyre constructed what they deemed a viable and stable myth in a time of national turbulence, an activity that struck Emilia Viotti da Costa as a "Proustian search for a lost past."[15]

Whereas sexuality played a crucial role in Freyre's construction and rendition of nationhood and blackness,[16] Miranda's evocation of Brazilian sexuality, and of black mulatto sensuality in particular, was balanced with humor. That blacks and mulattoes appeared in Miranda's songs is no surprise. This was popular music, after all. More compelling was the voice that Miranda, a white woman, assumed as a performer and recording artist. It was a voice that chronicled life among blacks, mulattoes, and the popular classes. This was partly due to the fact that many of Miranda's writers were black or mulatto (for example, Assis Valente, Synval Silva, Pixinguinha, Dorival Caymmi). At the same time, she had no compunction about assuming the *favelada*'s or the mulatta's poetic voice or becoming the storyteller or the satirist of the popular classes.

Carmen succeeded in becoming a "Brazilian singer" largely through the use of humor and folklore and by presenting stereotypical images familiar to a national audience of blacks and mulattoes. On a few occasions she lent her satirical style to social criticism in a manner atypical of her time. Her passion for the popular vernacular often led people to call her vulgar. That "vulgarity," however, allowed her to break racial taboos and defy gender roles that sought to confine women. By singing comedic and satirical samba tunes rather than ballads (*canções*) or folksongs (*folk-lore*), Carmen presented the popular language, rhythm, and aesthetic qualities of a music with mostly African influences. Although much of the black culture content emerged in picturesque form, she clearly encouraged the celebration of popular culture songs such as "Disso e que eu gosto" (That's what I like).[17]

The celebration of popular music by a nationally known artist, coupled with official state support, helped expand the audience for samba. Miranda's role can be likened to that of a crossover artist who succeeds in acquiring a wider audience for her music when she becomes more mainstream. But Miranda was no crossover. She was a bridge between the national and the popular. Part of the success of her performance lay in its subversive, satirical quality. On the one hand, many of the songs that she recorded explicitly called for a recognition of the legitimacy of popular music and thus represented an implicit criticism of bourgeois cultural values. She never begged audiences to value popular music but rather demanded it in humorous ways, or more accurately aggressively claimed authority very often associated with humor.[18] On the other hand, her role as an agent in "gentrifying" popular music is undeniable. She served as a middle-class vehicle between the mostly black and mulatto *favelados* and the nation. In an unconventional publication based on personal interviews and conversations with Carmen Miranda, Dulce Damasceno de Brito, a journalist and friend of Miranda's, displayed her own (middle-class?) prejudice toward popular music when she wrote, "Her special style gave popular music something that it lacked: class."[19]

Miranda's early domination of the recording industry with such classics as "Se o samba e moda" (1930), "Taí o para você gostar de mim" (1930), and "Moleque indigesto" (1933) guaranteed her a place in early Brazilian films such as *Voz do Carnaval* (1933), *Alô, Alô Brasil* (1935), and *Alô, Alô Carnaval* (1936). Although the incipient patriotism that her songs promoted marked her as a product of the Vargas era, her representation of the voices of blacks and mulattoes linked her to the cultural populism of the modernists. She was so popular that composing giants such as Pixinguinha[20] and others of the Velha Guarda wrote compositions for her, as did young and coming artists such as the Bahian Dorival Caymmi, who provided her with much of the inspiration for the *Bahiana* image that she later took to Broadway and Hollywood.[21]

Her hymns to the Brazilian nation and Brazilian culture include such playful renditions as "Minha terra tem palmeiras," written by João Barro and Albert Ribeiro. Her rendition of Amado Regis's samba "O samba e o tango" juxtaposed the rhythms of the Brazilian samba with those of the Argentine tango.[22] Despite the explicit message of national pride, both songs defy the solemnity associated with die-hard nationalists who presented Brazil in ultraidealistic imagery. "O samba e o tango" is essentially a playful nationalist battle between Brazil and Argentina in which Brazil prevails, while "Minha terra tem palmeiras," a *marcha*, presents Brazil as a land of rum, rhythm, fruit, blondes, and chocolate *morenas*, where one can "cut loose." The satire is found not only in explicit references in the lyrics but also in Carmen's own playful performance style and in the samba and *marcha* rhythms, which sometimes lend themselves to celebratory humor, mockery, or surprise.

"Eu gosto da minha terra" (I like my country), by R. Montenegro, which Carmen recorded with the Victor Orchestra in August 1930, lauds Brazilian civilization and the Brazilian "race" that resulted in so many beauties and pleasures:

> Of this so beautiful Brazil
> I am a daughter, I live happily.
> I am proud of the race
> Of pure people of my country.
> Look at my gaze
> (For) it says that I am Brazilian,
> And my samba reveals
> That I am a child of this country.
> I am Brazilian, I have a magical charm.
> I like samba,
> I was born for this.
> The foxtrot does not compare
> With our samba; that is a rare jewel.

> I know how to say better than anyone
> All the beauty that the samba has.
> I am Brazilian, I live happily.
> I like the things of my country.
> I like my country and I always want to live here
> To see the very beautiful Southern Cross
> From the skies of the land where I was born.
> Abroad, out of tune,
> Samba loses its value.
> Yes! I'll remain in my land.[23]

"Eu gosto da minha terra" is compelling because of its unequivocal faith in Brazil. The ultrapatriotic message given a playful execution became a Miranda trademark evident in other songs, such as "Terra morena," which proclaims that "God is Brazilian," and "Nova descoberta," which describes Cabral's love affair with Brazil.[24] Such exaggerations made Brazilians feel good about their nation and was a vital part of Carmen's humor that endeared her to her public.

In the first stanza of "I Like My Country," a somewhat trivial title (instead of "I Love My Country") that keeps solemnity to a minimum, the singer hails the Brazilian landscapes and applauds, in the tradition of racial democracy, a sense of a cosmic Brazilian race to which she belongs. The second stanza reinforces an appreciation for popular culture, such as the samba, and a rejection of foreign influences, much as did the nationalist-minded *antropófagos* of the modernists of the 1920s.[25] Finally, she rejects exile or going abroad, to remain in her national home. Sung by a woman born in Portugal who maintained her Portuguese passport, this song is an affirmation of Miranda's own sense of *brasilidade*—an issue Miranda would grapple with all her life.

According to Damasceno de Brito, Miranda considered herself Brazilian. "I was born in Portugal. But I consider myself Brazilian. I am more carioca, a sambista from the favela, more carnivalesca than a singer of fados."[26] That Carmen considered herself "carnivalesque" underscores her vision of herself within the satirical Brazilian musical genre. Nonetheless, Brazilians were saddened when they found out that she was born in Portugal and not in Brazil, an issue that would later provide critics with reason to disown her.[27] On the other hand, the fact that she was Portuguese and chose to celebrate her Brazilian identity was manipulated to promote Brazil's encompassing sense of racial democracy. Indeed, Vargas's anti-immigrant tactics, which increased during World War II, all but forced immigrants with strong foreign identities to embrace Brazil. Thus, Carmen's evocation of a Brazilian race connected her once again with Gilberto Freyre and other theorists of racial democracy while downplaying her foreign birth.[28]

The adaptation of the Portuguese to the tropics, a crucial element of Brazilian racial democracy that endowed the Portuguese with a propensity to mix peacefully with other cultures, was emphasized in Paulo Barbosa and Vicente Paiva's 1935 hit, "Salada portuguesa" (Portuguese salad):

> My green path
> Once came from Portugal.
> Come, my people, let's celebrate Carnival.
> Manuel joins the parade, and so does Maria.
> During the three days of merriment
> Pierre and Colombina, Father John and black Mina too.
> Grandfather already told me:
> In Brazil there is happiness.
> Carnival has existed
> Since the days of Cabral.[29]

This simple carnival tune acknowledges a Brazilian greatness independent of the Portuguese, without mentioning the indigenous populations. It was a Portuguese mariner, Cabral, the first Portuguese to land in Brazil, in 1500, who according to this song first perceived the "Brazilian joy" in this somewhat anachronistic melody. According to Edigar de Alencar, the song was accepted as a carnival entry precisely because it gave Brazilians the opportunity to present themselves in more favorable terms than the Portuguese, yet it also allowed immigrant families such as Carmen's to affirm a Brazilian-Portuguese connection.[30]

Nonconfrontational, frivolous musical compositions proliferated in the 1930s, owing in part to the DIP's censorship machine and in part to the general tendency toward national celebration. However, many musicians insisted on social commentary and criticisim within this broader frame of national pride. Carmen Miranda was among them. Her status as the "Ambassador of Brazilian Popular Music" afforded her an opportunity to comment on social relations and to address the nation didactically. Her "carnivalesque" aesthetic elicited laughter but challenged authority (within limits).

"Sahe da toca Brasil," a poignant example of her social critique style, managed to be nonconfrontational while stressing the need for Brazilians, particularly white Brazilians, to change their attitude toward blacks. At the same time, the song also seems to criticize the *favela* dwellers for being complacent. Miranda and her musicians and writers wrapped their poignant lyrics in a rumba tune, in a manner that might seem contradictory. The song begins with a solemn pulsating instrumental before becoming a dance tune rumba that implores its listeners to "Sahe da toca Brazil. Teu lugar não é aí" (Get up from your burrows, Brazil. That's no place for you), implying a greater place to be conquered. The song chronicles the ascent of national music from the slave quarters to the salons, imploring all Brazilians to understand the significance of that change:

> Brazil, which used to be a slave quarter
> Danced in the macumba, striking its feet on the ground.
> It is good not to ever forget that
> The dance is now in the ballroom.
> Brazil, leave the favela [the past]!
> The skyscraper is what matters [modernity].
> It's too sad that many good people
> Loving you so much, do not understand you.
> Brazil of the two avenues
> of Copacabana Beach and of the asphalt,
> To your people bright and strong
> No one ever has sung to very loudly.[31]

Stanza two laments that many people do not understand that it is time to change, while stanza three claims that no other country has "sung to" or celebrated "a tua gente branca e forte." The double meaning of "branca e forte"—bright and strong, white and strong—provided a surreptitious venue for social criticism with sarcasm, a venue often employed by Carmen.

Race relations became more explicitly the subject of Miranda's 1939 recording of "Preto e branco" (Black and white). Technically a dialogue-like duet with Almirante (A; Carmen is C), "Preto e branco" offers a humorous look at race relations in Brazil while at the same time criticizing Brazil's aversion to blackness:

> C: They say that those whites of today are angry at all blacks.
>
> A: What is good is black: Black is the Diamond [Brazilian soccer player], and coffee . . .
>
> C: Black is the gaze of Mary, the wife of St. Joseph . . .
>
> A: Black is the ink we write with that gives value to the paper . . .
>
> C: Black is carbon that makes fire and passes through the chimney . . .
>
> A: To give work to men . . .
>
> C: And black was St. Benedict, in whom whites have so much faith . . .
>
> A: And the mouth of the night is black, like a black man from Guinea.
>
> C: The snow is sometimes more black than any black woman you'll see.
>
> Black is the hair of the virgin . . .
>
> A: And the beard of St. Miguel . . .
>
> C: The feathers of the goose are black.

A: Love pains are also.

C: Only whites don't want to be black.

A: The mulattoes don't want to either.

But black's consolation, let anyone say it,

Is that God made him white.

C: Where was that?

A: On the soles of his feet.

C: Very good![32]

Audiences hearing the sardonic humor of "Preto e branco," which might have caused them unease at the outset, got a catharsis with the last verse, which diffuses any tension: God also made blacks white, but in a particularly unnoticeable and humorous place.

Humor, particularly caricature, often has as its victims those who are laughed at by the comic performer or observer, and Brazilian racial humor often came at the expense of blacks. While Carmen unconditionally renounced racism and her racial satire often carried humorous social commentary, her songs often reinforced stereotypes prevalent in the 1930s. "O nego no samba," for example, recorded by Carmen Miranda with the Victor Brasileira Orquestra in December 1929 and released in May 1930, underscores the natural ability of blacks to dance and the whites' difficulty in acquiring these "Brazilian talents":

Black samba
Sways the hip.
Black samba
Has parati [a type of rum].
Black samba, oh, oh,
Always on the beat.
Black samba, my sweetheart,
Makes me crazy.
In samba, whites break into pieces.
In samba, a good black has a swell time.
In samba, whites don't have a chance, my good friend
For samba—blacks are born to do it.[33]

This samba affords the singer an omniscient vision that she enjoys and celebrates with her listeners, all the while reinforcing the exoticism and the voyeuristic nature of white-black cultural interactions.

In the 1935 release of the *marcha* "Mulatinho bamba" (Smart little mulatto), Miranda reinforced similar qualities of the mulatto, only now with more sensual undertones and an emphasis on his physical beauty:

Mulatinho bamba,
Oh mulatto, my little mulatto bamba,
How you distinguish yourself when you samba.
In the circle he's a revelation,
When he stamps his feet
My heart begins to beat,
And he knows how to perform a step
Dancing with elegance
To the rhythm.
He doesn't walk around armed with a knife
Nor with a kerchief on his chest
Nor a straw hat.
A fine mulatto, he is well-dressed.
He has gestures and attitudes
Of a congressman.
Because of this dear mulatto
I remain at the window
All day,
When he walks by on the sidewalk
He seems like a Clark Gable
In chains.[34]

Here it is important to pay attention to the poetic voice, which is that of a (probably) black or mulatta woman from the popular classes. Despite the rhetoric of racial democracy, the unwritten social norms considered interracial romance or marriage a taboo. Blacks were better off with blacks, mulattoes with mulattoes, and whites with whites. Nonetheless, in this song Carmen Miranda, the white performer, once again assumes the role of a voyeur who is seduced by the beauty and elegance of a mulatto. Moreover, the third stanza offers a positive image of a mulatto, who implicitly denounces the *malandro* by refusing to carry a knife. Such positive appraisals were fully in step with the Vargas regime, notorious for its condemnation of antisocial behavior among the popular classes.

The narrative voice in the 1934 "A voltar do samba" (Coming back from the samba) further indicates the necessity of white performers appropriating the voice of mulattoes or mulattas in order to sing their story.

Returning home from the samba
Oh, God, I feel so tired
After returning from the batucada
That I participated in at Praça Onze.
I won a bronze harlequin.
My sandal heel broke
And I lost my mulatto there on the pavement.
I'm not interested in knowing. . . .
Someone came to tell me

That he found you grieving
With tears in your eyes, crying.
Cry, mulatto, my pleasure comes from seeing you suffer
So that you know how much I loved you
And how I suffered to forget you.
You were my friend
And I don't know why
I met you in the circle dancing
With a tambourine in your hand, keeping the beat.
Now, mulatto, for you I will not do anything disrespectful
I'm going for revenge and. . . . [35]

Carmen's appropriation of the voice of a *favelada*, most likely a mulatta, is itself satire. Only in this populist dynamic could she lecture her audience without bringing ridicule on herself.

Miranda's rendition of the problems of the poor and the working classes was not altogether inappropriate. Her father was a barber, and she herself worked in a hat shop before being discovered. It is likely that she did not see her performance and recordings of popular music as appropriation but considered them part of her own experience. Moreover, her presentations of black terms, images, and rhythms were not always within a racially hegemonic context. Miranda inserted herself within a broader context as an intepreter of the popular aesthetic. Her speaking as a *favelada* aids her in expressing the view from the *morro*.

"Recenseamento," recorded in 1939, has a reference to a 1940 census describing the poverty in the *morro*, yet it emphasizes the role of music and celebration in making life worthwhile, a matter of national pride:

I obey everything that is law
Afterward I became quiet and sad.
My brown-skinned boy is Brazilian, he's a rifleman,
He's one of those who go out with a flag on his battalion.
Our house is nothing great
But we live in poverty without owing one cent.
We have a tambourine, a cuíca, and a tamborim,
A reco-reco and a small guitar and a big one too.[36]

Others, such as "O imperador do samba,[37] "Gente bamba,"[38] and "Deixe esse povo falar,"[39] underscore the importance of respect for popular music and the importance of music to the national soul. "O imperador do samba," for example, begins by asking the audience for silence, respect, and order because the emperor and the empress are about to enter. The double meaning is clear: Carnival is fantasy, but an emperor is an emperor and deserves respect. At the same time, the solemn mood of this samba gives it a seriousness that calls for respect. This theme is repeated in a more upbeat manner in songs such as "Minha embaixada chegou," recorded in 1939.[40] Roberto da Matta has written extensively on Carnival's role in subverting the social order.[41] Unfortunately, within a wider social context, the benefactors of the humor and satire germane to Brazilian Carnival are the upper and middle classes, who are mostly white.

Not all of the compositions of this period that make reference to blacks or mulattoes are altogether stereotypical. "A preta do Acarajé," first recorded as a duet with Dorival Caymmi and Miranda (1939), presents elements of the Bahian folklore in nonstereotypical terms. It describes a scene at ten o'clock on the streets of Salvador while also emphasizing the hard work that blacks often endured to produce something pleasurable for consumption: "Todo mundo gosta de acarajé" (Everyone likes *acarajé*) but "ninguem quer saber o trabalho que dá" (No one wants to know how much work it takes).[42] Nonetheless, taken as a whole, images of blacks, even in popular music, remained relatively static during World War II. Interestingly, it is this image of the *Bahiana*, the most folkloric black female icon in Brazil, that Miranda adopted in 1939 and was to catapult her to stardom in the United States.

Neither Brazil nor the United States was ready for images of the black popular masses to grace important national media such as radio and film. Indeed, Orson Welles's film of Carnival celebrations in Rio that depicted black youth dancing and celebrating was never released because, according to Welles, the Hollywood studio executives never even listened to the music, believing that "he [was] just shooting a lot of jigaboos jumping up and down."[43] Thus, the artificial black *Bahiana* with a white face who was dressed like an overgrown fruit remained the image of Brazil. Miranda was not deceiving herself, however. She was quite aware that her act was all in fun. Despite modern multicultural sensibilities, which might criticize her ignorance or nonchalance about the repercussions of her actions, her musical career was responsible for showcasing the talents of many composers and musicians who might not have had other venues.

When Carmen Miranda left for the United States, in 1939, her farewell song was "Adeus batucada," written by Sinval Silva, a composer and also her chauffeur.[44] The *batucada*, as Mario de Andrade reports, "was a popular synonym for the samba in the 1920s and 1930s."[45] That an ode to samba became a metaphor for her farewell to Brazil was not coincidental. After Miranda left Brazil, her musical performance changed dramatically. Although she left as an ambassador of Brazil, she ended up playing and singing more rumbas, congas, and other Spanish-speaking hybrid styles than Brazilian forms. She may have honored the samba, as the lyrics say, but it was mostly in private.

Her journey north occurred precisely at the moment when she had made the appropriation of a black musical icon complete. Her musical partnership with Caymmi had allowed her to discover and tailor the *Bahiana* to her own frutti taste until her death in 1955. Indeed, Carmen's personal style and charisma and her sense of humor were often considered as outrageous as her outfits, partly because she was a white woman with money who put on black costumes and promoted black music.[46] No wonder some in the Brazilian elite resented her. Remarkably, it was the popular classes that continued to support her throughout the 1940s and early 1950s.

Despite her stereotypical representations, Miranda had showcased images and styles from the popular classes. She exploited humor to preach to both black and white Brazilians about race and nationhood in a nonconfrontational manner precisely at a time when the myth of racial democracy was most powerful. The Brazilian system certainly allowed her to rise on the coattails of black and mulatto entertainers and composers, and Vargas's nationalist-minded regime assured her of contracts and an audience. Yet she also served as a conduit through which many lesser-known musicians could present their talents. Brazilian white racial hegemony, like hegemony elsewhere, provided a set of rules that defined the perimeters of human opportunity, and Vargas's focus on nation to the exclusion of race further marginalized many emerging black voices. Performers and artists implicated in the system must certainly be examined on an individual basis. Carmen Miranda, the musician, performer, entertainer, and satirist with a host of competing motivations, certainly deserves more attention.

SUGGESTED READINGS

Conniff, Michael. *Urban Politics in Brazil: The Rise of Populism, 1925–1945*. Pittsburgh: University of Pittsburgh Press, 1981.

Davis, Darien, ed. *Beyond Slavery: The Multilayered Legacy of Africans in Latin America and the Caribbean*. Lanham, MD: Rowman and Littlefield, 2007.

Fitch, Melissa. "Carmen, Kitsch, Camp and My Quest for Coordinated Dinnerware," *Chasqui: Revista de literatura latinoamericana* 40.2 (2011).

Gil Montero, Martha. *The Brazilian Bombshell: The Biography of Carmen Miranda*. New York: Donald I. Fine, 1989.

Guillermoprieto, Alma. *Samba*. New York: Vintage Books, 1990.

Haberly, David T. *Three Sad Races: Racial Identity and National Consciousness in Brazilian Literature*. New York: Cambridge University Press, 1983.

Hanchard, Michael, ed. *Racial Politics in Contemporary Brazil*. Durham: Duke University Press, 1999.

McCann, Brian. *Hello, Hello Brazil: Popular Music in the Making of Brazil*. Durham: Duke University Press, 2004.

Sansone, Livio. *Blackness without Ethnicity: Constructing Race in Brazil*. New York: Palgrave MacMillan, 2003.

Schneider, Ronald M. *Brazil: Culture and Politics in a New Industrial Powerhouse*. Boulder, CO: Westview Press, 1996.

Schreiner, Claus. *Música popular brasileira: A History of Popular Music and the People of Brazil*. New York: Marion Boyars, 1993.

Shaw, Lisa. *History of the Brazilian Samba*. New York: Ashgate, 1999.
Vianna, Hermano. *Mystery of Samba: Popular Music and National Identity in Brazil*. Chapel Hill: University of North Carolina Press, 1999.
Williams, Daryle. *Culture Wars in Brazil: The First Vargas Regime, 1930–1945*. Durham: Duke University Press, 2001.

Sights

Bahia: Africa in the America. 1988 (UCMEC).
Black Orpheus. 1958. Directed by Marcel Camus (Facets Multimedia).
Carmen Miranda: Bananas Is My Business. 1995. Directed by Helena Solberg (Facets Multimedia).
Carmen Miranda: the South American Way. 1996. A&E Home Video.
Carmen Miranda Collection, The. 2008. Twentieth Century Fox Film Corporation.
Quilombo. 1984. Directed by Carlos Diegues (Facets Multimedia).
Samba: Reflections of Africa in Brazilian Culture. 2007. Directed by Eduardo Montes-Bradley (Filmakers Library).
Samba da Criação do Mundo. 1978. Directed by Vera de Figueiredo (Cinema Guild).
Spirit of Samba: Black Music of Brazil. 1982. Directed by Richard Bedford (Facets Multimedia).

Sounds

Danzón, The Original Soundtrack. 1992. DRG Records.
Hot Music from Cuba, 1907–1936. 1993. Harlequin compact disc no. 23.

12

Oil, Race, and Calypso in Trinidad and Tobago, 1909–1990

Graham E. L. Holton

All political issues, such as defining national identity, rest in a gray area open to contending views, susceptible to alternative voices, and marked by cranky negotiations. Historically, ruling elites have attempted, with varying degrees of success, to control the process and the terms of such re-creations, either by ignoring or by suppressing the counterrhetoric produced by the marginal and lower classes. Political satire has long been a means by which marginalized groups have responded to their subordination. In Puerto Rico, for example, singers of reggaeton record songs called tiraeras *as direct attacks in lyrics against opponents and institutions that threaten them and in Trinidad and Tobago, black workers have used calypso to respond to elite control of cultural discourse and to resist socioeconomic oppression. Rooted in African musical traditions of spontaneous rhyming, calypso became home to a vibrant and powerful satire that, despite commodification and global popularity, has proved to be a powerful tool of protest. Graham Holton chronicles the development of calypso as a political counter to the economic exploitation of domestic workers by international oil interests and the local elite, and he demonstrates how the music provided an alternative view of national identity.*

Calypso—popular satirical ballads from the West Indies—evolved from the oppression, exploitation, and racism of the former British colony of Trinidad and Tobago. Roaring Lion, one of the great singer-songwriters of twentieth-century calypso, considered calypsonians to be oral historians: "The whole history of Trinidad is in calypso voices," he said. Mighty Chalkdust, another lyricist, described the calypsonian as "a font of public opinion. He is the mouthpiece of the people."[1] While some calypsos were sung for entertainment, others were intensely political, attacking the colonial government and the British companies, especially those that exploited the colony's oil reserves.

This study examines the oil industry's impact on the development of calypsos in Trinidad. The oil companies, by taking away workers' dignity and human rights, gave calypso singers their material: segregation, racism, and insufferable work conditions. The industry gave steel bands used oil drums, which they cut and beat to bring out the desired tones. The industry had a great influence over government policy because of the military and strategic importance of oil for the British during the First and Second World Wars. After 1909, British oil companies poured millions of pounds into developing Trinidad's oil industry, making it the largest production and refinery center in the British empire. "Petro-calypsos" reached their zenith during the oil field riots of 1937.

Afro-Caribbean people historically have been renowned for their distinctive public speaking and word usage in debate, which culminated in a well-developed art form.[2] Rhyming as a type of word interplay has two types, performed by what Richard D. Abrahams calls "men-of-words."[3] The first type is conversation that develops into a contest of wits, giving rise to a person adept at repartee, known as a "broad talker." The second type of rhymer is the "good talker," who holds forth at more formal functions needing an articulate speaker as master of ceremonies. Word usage and verbal invective also served as the primary constituents of the lyrics of work-gang leaders, called chantwells, and calypsonians.

Calypso is a unique Afro-European synthesis that evolved out of a mixture of African, Hispanic, French, and British influences blended to represent the Creole experience of Trinidad. The etymology of *calypso* is uncertain. Some argue that it originated from the word *kaiso* or *kaito*, a word used by the Huasa people of northern Nigeria and meaning a cry of satisfaction akin to "bravo," or "serves him right." The expression "*kaiso*" is still used in Trinidad and Tobago to describe a particularly fine performance. Other historians see the word *calypso* as a corruption of the old French colonial word *griot* (festivity), used for professional musicians in West Africa, who combined the roles of town crier and public jester. *Griots* sang, declaimed news and gossip, or lampooned the political elite. Their music, improvisatory skill, and quick wit were the stew from which emerged the songs of political and social intent of modern West Indian calypso and reggae and North American rap music. Coincidentally, the name of the Greek goddess Calypso means "she who conceals," suggesting the shrouded meaning of many Calypso lyrics.[4]

Calypso resembles the samba musically. The double meter gives it a Caribbean jump style of dancing enjoyed in Carnival road marches. Its lyrical origin derived from the *gayup*, a communal work song of Nigeria. The slaves brought by French plantation owners to Trinidad in the 1780s carried with them a tradition of improvised song that formed the base for calypso. The lead singer of each slave gang, called the chantwell, improvised songs of praise to inspire his work gang and songs of derision to condemn the inadequacies of the other gangs. The chantwell sang one line, to which the group would respond in chorus as they worked. These songs gave rise to the *picong* tradition of improvised verbal dueling.[5] The call-and-response format in competitions, a form of verbal dueling, was an essential part of the music accompanying the *kalenda*, an acrobatic dance with sticks popular with Trinidadian slaves as a thinly disguised African form of stick fighting.

Because slaves could not take part in the French pre-Lenten celebrations and masquerade balls leading up to Ash Wednesday, they set up their own *canboulay* (from the French *cannes brulées*, burning cane) procession in which the marchers carried burning sticks in a preharvest celebration of the burning of the sugarcane fields. These processions were based on West African harvest celebrations. With emancipation in 1838, the two celebrations—French and African—merged. While the French masquerades became satirical street pantomimes, the procession of torches became the great opening procession of Carnival. The *canboulay* procession became the J'Ouvert (from the French *jour ouvert*, daybreak), the 6 A.M. procession into town on Monday morning.

During the nineteenth century, Trinidad's calypsonians were the news bearers, rendering the history and political figures of the island into calypso lyrics. These lyrics were characteristically topical, with biting satirical comment. Song texts were set to a corpus of some fifty melodies, most of European origin. During this time the majority of the composers were anonymous, and only a few of the nineteenth-century lyrics that sought to comment, debate, attack, praise, satirize, or repeat bawdy stories have survived. Among the exceptions are the lyrics of Hannibal and Boadicea, which deal with topical events in the Port of Spain underworld or strike at the repressive policies of the colonial government.

Trinidadian slave society developed its own underground world, complete with secret hierarchies and rituals. Most early calypsos were sung in French Creole dialects, with the singers switching from one dialect to another to conceal the true meaning of the song. *Kaiso* surfaced in the 1840s in communal "tents" (large halls) of bamboo and thatch that functioned as rudimentary *mas'* (derived from *masquerade*) camps, complete with drumming and drum dances, singing, and entertainment. These candle-lit sanctuaries were often presided over by a Carnival king and queen selected by the community. The chantwell led the community through the streets on Carnival days. Out of this practice evolved some of Carnival's traditional figures, such as "Dame Lorraine," a cartoon figure that mocked the white planters. Others included the "jab-jabs" and "jab mollassies," the devils and bats, the "pierrots" and tall-stilted "Imoko-jumbies," and the "Midnight Robber" with his convoluted oratory.

From these Carnival celebrations the singing of *kaiso* by the *kalindas* developed into calypso, an integral part of the cultural and social life of Trinidad. Each calypso band played in tents (halls), where singers were led by a big name, such as Mighty Sparrow. Their repertoire ranged from traditional styles, heavy on lyrics with sharp political and social criticism, to modern dance party numbers.

Today calypsonians begin their training in January for performances at midnight on Shrove Tuesday, preceding Ash Wednesday that begins Lent. During the weeks preceding Carnival, they perform each night, with eight to ten calypsonians in four or five tents. The best singers are selected for the Dimanche Gras show on the Sunday before Lent, at which the Calypso Monarch is crowned for the best calypso of the year, chosen by a panel of judges. The Road March is the people's choice for the most played calypso; the reward is cash and fame for the winning song.[6]

The names used by calypsonians reflect the music's competitive origins and its use as a political weapon. Singers became folk heroes, figures full of swagger with names usually preceded by "Mighty" or "Lord." The most internationally famous calypso musicians include Lord Executor, Lord Invader, Lord Kitchener, Mighty Sparrow, Mighty Spoiler, Attila the Hun, and Roaring Lion. The first woman to win the Calypso Monarch competition was Calypso Rose, in 1978, but female performers have so far failed to gain an international reputation.

Calypso was first recorded in 1912 on 78 rpm disks.[7] It entered a golden age in the 1930s, created a rage in the United States in the 1950s, outselling the recordings of Elvis Presley, and today remains as popular with Trinidadian youth as with their grandparents. Calypso bands appear on the stamps of Trinidad and Tobago (the first band so recognized, the Calypso Kings, appeared in 1968) and perform daily on national television. Their songs are played at full volume from every maxi-taxi (minibus) in Trinidad and even are heard at the U.S. embassy in Port of Spain during July 4 celebrations.

Race is a primary factor in calypso, foremost because the music is primarily derived from African origins but also because calypso bands excluded East Indians. Hindi calypsos have become a curious exception to the history of Trinidadian musical development, and they have appeared only since the 1970s. Traditional calypso lyrics made virtually no reference to East Indians, even in a derogatory way. Exclusion was total, a consequence of the separation imposed on the East Indians by the colonial government. The syncretism of African and European musical styles excluded East Indian music.

This racial differentiation in Trinidad originated with slavery on the sugar estates, which made a sharp distinction between white overseers, the black gangs and factory workers, and the East Indian field hands. Between 1845 and 1917 more than 144,000 indentured laborers and their families were brought to Trinidad from India. Creoles and East Indians were separated socially and spatially, initially by white design but later through mutual consent. Both groups internalized white racial stereotypes. Creoles denigrated East Indians as "coolies" and scorned them as scabs who depressed rural wages and lowered working conditions. East Indians retaliated with racial insults learned from the white overseers. The economic and political dominance of whites remained intact into independence, as did the system of institutionalized racism.[8] Blacks, for example, were not allowed into the Hilton Hotel in Port of Spain until the 1960s. Independence in 1962 and the election of a Creole prime minister, Eric Williams, brought fears of a racial war (which fortunately did not eventuate). The postcolonial two-party system divided power between the two major racially defined social segments, Creole and East Indian.[9] It was not until the 1986 election that East Indians won major representation in Trinidadian electoral results.

Social stratification in colonial Trinidad and Tobago evolved out of legislation and the practice of slavery, which divided society by ethnicity and color. Skin color and physical attributes, dependent on phenotypical or somatic characteristics, were graded into sixteen levels, of which white was the highest and dark black the lowest. Class in colonial Trinidad was of tertiary significance as a social differentiator; distinctions were not primarily ordained by occupational stratification but by institutionalized ethnicity. Even at present the upper class is dominated by persons of white and light brown skin color and the lower classes are predominantly dark brown to black, especially blue-collar workers.[10] Race was a major factor up to the 1950s in Trinidad's oil sector. Whites operated the industry. Blacks did the low-skilled manual work, and Indians were rarely employed by the industry. It was a world of strict segregation and bigotry.

Commercial oil production began in the colony of Trinidad and Tobago in 1909. Oil soon caught the attention of the British Admiralty, which established contracts with British oil companies operating in Trinidad to supply fuel oil for the Atlantic fleet. In 1913, Trinidad Leaseholds Ltd., a subsidiary of Central Mining and Investment Corporation of Johannesburg, South Africa (Cecil Rhodes's estate), secured a petroleum exploration concession in exchange for the company's setting up a bunkering station to refuel the admiralty's Caribbean fleet. The massive British and South African investment that followed soon made Trinidad one of the most important petroleum centers under British control in the Western Hemisphere.[11] By 1918 Trinidad had the second largest annual oil production in South America, exceeded only by Peru.[12] This influx of money brought few benefits to the ordinary people of the colony.

The oil companies made sizable profits during the 1920s and the Great Depression. Even so, they put into place work practices such as the "Red

Book" system and Trinidad Leasehold's triplicate "discharge ticket" system in 1935. These became the source of widespread worker militancy, victimizing workers by recording the holder's history and performance. The "Red Book" had to be presented each time someone applied for employment at any work camp. This ensured that if the worker had been fired for political activities, he would find no further employment in the oil industry.

Working conditions were dangerous, with no occupational health and safety legislation provided by the colonial government or compensation for injuries. Mortality rates from fatal oil rig accidents, natural gas blowouts, and disease were high. Manual workers (roughnecks and roustabouts) were not issued safety helmets and worked barefoot on wet, slippery derrick floors while moving tons of drilling pipe and operating heavy equipment.

The social life of the oil field and refinery camps was rigidly segregated, divided by color and class and controlled by regulations governing dress, behavior, and where one ate and relaxed. White employees and their families were expected to maintain a certain "form," and an employee's contract could be terminated if he failed to live up to expectations. Such policies of exclusion and enforced inferiority generated great tensions in the camps.[13] Many blacks left to work in Venezuela and the Netherlands Antilles rather than continue suffering under such a system of racial injustice.[14]

Political calypsos protested the workers' plight in this racist society and attacked the British and colonial government policies and British oil companies that forced them to work in intolerable conditions. The oil industry that gave steel bands their oil drums also provided calypsonians with their material: segregation, blatant racism, and dangerous working conditions.

Discontent finally exploded in the oil fields on June 19, 1937. As riots broke out across Trinidad, the British sent in 2,200 troops, backed by the heavy guns of the HMS *Ajax* and HMS *Exeter*. Workers faced the machine guns and rifles of the Royal Marines. When it ended, fourteen Trinidadians lay dead and fifty-nine injured; several hundred were arrested. Calypsonians attacked the government's brutality with a barrage of deep-biting song. Attila the Hun (Raymond Quevedo) described the scene in his "The Strike":

> I wanted material for calypso
> So I took a bus to San Fernando
> But I wouldn't tell you friends all I saw
> For I'm afraid of the sedition law
> Fyzabad was like a battlefiel'
> Police surrounded by a ring of steel
> With blood an' carnage litterin' the scene
> An' pandemonium reigning supreme.[15]

He then criticized the Forster Commission's inquiry into the riots, in the "Commission's Report":

> Through the unrest that we had recently
> A commission was sent from the mother country
> To investigate an' probe carefully
> The cause of the riots in this colony
> They accumulated a bulk of evidence
> I cannot speak of their competence
> But, I can say independently
> The report was a revelation to me . . .
> The only time they found the police was wrong
> Was when they stay too long to shoot people down
> A peculiar thing this Commission
> In that ninety-two lines of dissertation
> Is there no talk of exploitation
> of the worker or his tragic condition
> Read through the pages, there is no mention
> Of capitalistic oppression
> Which leads one to entertain a thought
> And wonder if it's a one-sided report.[16]

The colonial government retaliated by tightening censorship and increasing police intimidation. The Theatre and Dance Halls Ordinance of 1934 had given the police the power to censor songs, the colonial secretary the right to ban recordings, and bureaucrats the authority to require a license for calypsonians to sing in tents. These regulations were used to control any music, either recorded or played in public, considered in the slightest way seditious. King Radio (Norman Span) attacked the government censorship:

> They want to licen' me foot,
> They no want me to walk.
> They want to licen' me mouth
> They no want me to talk . . . [17]

The outpouring of music following the troubles of 1937 created a golden age in which calypso achieved its greatest musical accomplishments and international fame. Attila the Hun and Mighty Lion appeared on the prestigious American record label Decca. Their early U.S. hits included "Dynamite," in 1934, followed by "Don't Le' Me Mother Know," in 1935. The U.S. crooner Bing Crosby heard their music and arranged for them to make a guest appearance on *The Rudy Vallee Show* in New York in March 1938. Calypso became the rage in the United States. Record executives dictated they appeal to white, middle-class American tastes, and as a result most of the songs lacked any overt political message. Instead, these calypsos spoke of relationships and romance, and sometimes were a little risqué.[18]

The military and strategic importance of oil meant that the colonial government could not tolerate any disruption to the industry during the 1930s. The *Port of Spain Gazette* summed up its importance: "[O]il is an imperial asset. It is very much more so when Britain is rearming with feverish haste: and this necessarily gives oil producers of the Empire a much more favourable position for stipulating their own terms than they would normally have enjoyed."[19] In World War II the colony of Trinidad was the largest oil producer in the British empire, the nearest source of colonial oil supply to the United Kingdom, and a major supplier of 100-octane aviation fuel. The 100-octane refineries gave an edge to Britain's Spitfires and Hurricanes in the Battle of Britain (1940–1941) against the Luftwaffe's Messerschmitts and Junkers. Trinidad's oil refineries had to be defended at all costs. Between 1942 and 1943 the greatest concentration of shipping losses experienced during World War II occurred within a 250-kilometer radius of Trinidad and Tobago. German U-boats in the area sank 24,750,000 tonnes of shipping, of which oil tankers accounted for one-fourth.[20]

The colonial government signed a ninety-nine-year lend-lease agreement in 1941 to set up three U.S. bases, including a major naval base at Chaguaramas. The arrival of American troops with their money and racist attitudes had a significant impact on the people of Trinidad, inspiring a new wave of political calypsos. The songs of local girls chasing the American dollar expressed a thinly veiled invective against the American presence in the colony. Even so, the songs and rhythms of calypso were adopted by American bandleaders and singers and became big hits with American audiences. In 1943, Lord Invader's "Rum and Coca Cola," based on the Cuban "Son de la loma," came to symbolize the impact the American presence had on Trinidadian women:

> Since the Yankees come to Trinidad,
> They have the young girls going mad.
> The girls say they treat them nice,
> And they give them a better price.
> They buy rum and Coca Cola.
> Go down Point Cumana.
> Both mother and daughter
> Working for the Yankee dollar.[21]

The song became one of calypso's greatest successes. Its lyricist, Lord Invader (Rupert Grant), was forced to litigate in U.S. courts before he received any financial rewards. In 1944 the Andrews Sisters released a cover version that sold more than four million copies around the world. Part of its success came from being banned by the four major radio networks for providing Coca-Cola with free advertising and, more important, for portraying unfavorably the U.S. armed forces in Trinidad. Rupert Grant was paid nothing, since the Andrews Sisters believed that he held no copyright to the song. Grant sued in the U.S. courts, because Mighty Lion and Attila the Hun had included his lyrics to the song in a copyrighted calypso booklet before the Andrews Sisters released their version. It took many years before Grant was compensated. That the Andrews Sisters tried to steal the song gave its words an added irony.[22]

By the 1950s, calypso and steel bands had changed their image to appeal to Trinidad's middle-class values. Audiences were now packed with local whites and tourists, and recording companies were on the lookout for new talent for international recordings. The American recording company RCA-Victor signed Mighty Sparrow in 1950. Harry Belafonte released his album *Harry Belafonte—Calypso* at the end of 1956, selling more than a million and a half copies, more than any single-artist album ever had before. The album remained on the charts for a year and a half, outselling Elvis Presley and Frank Sinatra. Belafonte was named the "King of Calypso." His was the first long-playing record to sell more than a million copies in America, going platinum in 1957. His great success was resented by Trinidad calypsonians, who saw his standard American English and the apparent lack of any political message in his music as selling out to white America.[23] His number one hit, "The Banana Boat Song," written by Lord Melody and memorable for its haunting "Daaay-o!," was actually a portrayal of the harsh daily life of the banana loaders exploited by the United Fruit Company. Belafonte, born in New York in 1927 to a Jamaican mother and a Martinique father, worked for radical politics and was a friend of Martin Luther King, Jr., and other civil rights activists.[24] But he deliberately kept politics out of his songs because otherwise they might well have been relegated to the category of "race records" aimed at the nonwhite market.

In 1956 the Texas Oil Company (later Texaco) purchased Trinidad Leaseholds and turned Trinidad into the hub of its international empire. British and Dutch oil companies began to pour millions into Trinidad, setting up the world's largest refinery transshipment complexes in the Caribbean in the wake of the Suez crisis in 1956.[25] Mighty Sparrow attacked the purchase in his "The Yankees Back":

> Well, the day of slavery back again!
> Ah hope it ain't reach in Po'rt of Spain.
> Since the Yankees come back over here
> They buy out the whole of Pointe-&-Pierre.[26]

By the 1980s Trinidad was supplying nearly 50 percent of Caribbean oil exports to the United States. Williams had said of the 1970s oil boom, "Money is no problem," which Mighty Bomber satirized as "Oil don't spoil." The reliance on oil revenues to develop the local economy created growing hardship, which Derek Walcott attacked in "The Spoiler's Return":

as, like a sailor on a spending spree,
we blow our oil-bloated economy
on projects from here to eternity,
and Lord, the sunlit streets break Spoiler's heart,
to have natural gas and not give a fart.[27]

Trinidad's oil boom collapsed with the fall of international oil prices in 1986, causing great social and economic hardship. Lord Gypsy's "The Sinking Ship" caught the mood of the nation and was credited with helping to bring down the government:

But sadly Eric Williams passed away
The ship hit rough water that day
And someone turned the bridge over
To a captain called Chambers
Made blood crawl, things start to fall
Hold me head when a sailor fall.
Captain, the ship is sinking.[28]

Reduced oil receipts led to a debt crisis, which in turn led to the attempted coup by the Jamaat-al-Muslimeen on July 27, 1990. Calypsonians made fun of Prime Minister A. N. R. Robinson's being forced to strip off his pants while being held hostage in parliament. Calypso attacked the government with a vengeance. When the regime lost office, calypso proved once again that it was the voice of the people of Trinidad and Tobago. Calypso offered an important political tool that could be used to remove unwanted political parties from government in this turbulent West Indian republic.

SUGGESTED READINGS

Abrahams, Roger D. *The Man-of-Words in the West Indies: Performance and the Emergence of Creole Culture*. Baltimore: Johns Hopkins University Press, 1983.

Boggs, Vernon F. *Salsiology: Afro-Cuban Music and the Evolution of Salsa in New York City*. New York: Excelsior Music Publishing Co., 1992.

Cohen, Abner. *Masquerade Politics: Exploration in the Structure of Urban Cultural Movements*. Berkeley: University of California Press, 1993.

Cowley, John. *Carnival, Canboulay, and Calypso: Traditions in the Making*. New York: Cambridge University Press, 1996.

Dudley, Shannon. *Music from behind the Bridge: Steelband Aesthetics and Politics in Trinidad and Tobago*. New York: Oxford University Press, 2007.

Green, Garth, and Philip W. Scher. *Trinidad Carnival: The Cultural Politics of a Transnational Festival*. Bloomington: Indiana University Press, 2007.

Guilbault, Jocelyne. *Governing Sound: Cultural Politics of Trinidad's Carnival Musics*. Chicago: University of Chicago Press, 2007.

Harney, Stefano. *Nationalism and Identity: Culture and the Imagination in a Caribbean Diaspora*. Kingston: University of the West Indies, 1996.
Hill, Donald R. *Calypso and Calaloo: Early Carnival Music in Trinidad*. Gainesville: University Press of Florida, 1993. Includes CD.
Liber, Michael. *Street Life: Afro-American Culture in Urban Trinidad*. Boston: Schenkman Publishers, 1981.
Manuel, Peter. "Trinidad, Calypso, and Carnival." Pp. 183–211 in *Caribbean Currents: Music from Rumba to Reggae*. Philadelphia: Temple University Press, 1995.
Mason, Peter. *Bacchanal! The Carnival Culture of Trinidad*. Philadelphia: Temple University Press, 1998. Includes CD.
Neptune, Harvey R. *Caliban and the Yankees: Trinidad and the United States Occupation*. Chapel Hill: University of North Carolina Press, 2007.
Ryan, Selwyn D. *The Muslimeen Grab for Power: Race, Religion, and Revolution in Trinidad and Tobago*. Port of Spain: Imprint Caribbean, 1991.
Warner, Keith. *Kaiso! The Trinidad Calypso: A Study of the Calypso as Oral Literature*. WDC: Three Continents Press, 1982.

Sights

Calypso Music History: One Hand Don't Clap. 1991. Directed by Davery Dutta.
Celebration! A Caribbean Festival. 1998. Filmakers Library.
Chutney in Yuh Soca: A Multicultural Mix. 1993. (Three short features). Directed by Karen Martinez (Filmakers Library).
The Insatiable Season: Making Carnival in Trinidad and Tobago. 2008. Directed by Brian MacFarlane.
Kantik'i Maishi: Songs of Sorghum. 1992. Directed by Joan Kaufman (UCEMC).
Mas Fever: Inside Trinidad Carnival. 1989. Directed by Larry Johnson (UCEMC).
Recycled, Re-Seen: Folk Art from the Global Scrap Heap. 1997. (Video documentary from the International Folk Art Museum of New Mexico; includes a section on the "pans"—steel drums—of Trinidad and Tobago).
The Toured: The Other Side of Tourism in Barbados. 1991. Directed by Julie Pritchard Wright and Ellen Frankenstein (University of California Extension Center for Media).

Sounds

For compact discs from the Caribbean, a starting place is the Descarga Catalog, 328 Flatbush Ave., Ste. 180, Brooklyn, NY 11238.

Calypso Breakaway: 1927–1941. Rounder 104.
Calypso Calaloo: Early Calypso Music in Trinidad. Rounder.
Calypso Carnival: 1936–1941. Rounder 1077.
Calypso Ladies: 1926–1941. Interstate Music, Crawley, England, 1991.
Calypsos from Trinidad: Politics, Intrigue & Violence in the 1930s. Arhoolie Productions, 1991.
Calypso War: 1956–1958. Selquel NE 232.

Carnival in Trinidad, 2009.
Fall of Man: Calypsos on the Human Condition, 1935–1941. Rounder.
History of Carnival: 1914–1939. 2 vols. Matchbox 90-90.
Neville Marcano: The Growling Tiger of Calypso. Recorded by Ian Loma in 1962 and at the 1966 Newport Folk Festival. Rounder 1717.
Roosevelt in Trinidad: Calypsos of Events, Places and Personalities, 1933–1939. Rounder.
Sir Lancelot. Flyright 942.
Steel Drums. Steel Drums of Trinidad, 2009.

13

The Dictator's Seduction

Gender and State Spectacle during the Trujillo Regime

Lauren H. Derby

The search for and the maintenance of legitimacy have been behind much of the government's sponsorship of great spectacles, whether in ancient Rome or mid-twentieth-century Latin America. Always at issue is the most effective manner in which to represent the goals, the policies, and the identity of the nation. To achieve these ends, government officials typically have appealed to the average citizen through evocations of patriotism or community, often a community re-created or conveniently reinterpreted for the occasion at hand. With the advent of popular consumerism and mass media, other legitimizing forces could be marshaled for purposes of the state in ways never before possible. Popular culture itself became fertile soil as leaders could enter into and manipulate cultural patterns for their own purposes. Gender relations, specifically machismo, provided one such pattern. Civic spectacle presented official female figures whose presence manifested the power of their male counterpart (the ruler), who in turn received the admiration of the masses. Lauren Derby discusses one such case involving the Dominican dictator Trujillo, who presented to his public the official romantic intrigues of himself and his children. Through this discourse of amorous exploits the dictator was humanized; spectacle became a medium for sentimental investment in the regime.

In 1955 a Free World's Fair of Peace and Confraternity was held in the Dominican Republic to celebrate the twenty-fifth anniversary of the Trujillo regime. A full year of trade fairs, exhibits, dances, and performances culminated in a "floral promenade" that showcased the dictator's daughter, sixteen-year-old María de los Angeles del Corazón de Jesús Trujillo Martínez, better known as Angelita, who was crowned queen during the central Carnival parade. One-third of the nation's annual budget was spent on this gala affair, a good portion of which was invested in Italian designer Fontana gowns for chic Angelita and her entourage of 150 princesses. Queen Angelita's white silk satin gown was beyond fantasy proportions: it had a 75-foot train and was decorated with 150 feet of snow-white Russian ermine—the skins of 600 animals—as well as with real pearls, rubies, and diamonds. The total cost of the gown was U.S. $80,000, a significant fortune at the time. In full regalia, her costume replicated that of Queen Elizabeth I, replete with erect collar and adorned with a brooch and scepter that cost another $75,000.[1] For $1,000, two imperial hairdressers were flown in from New York to set the royal coiffure. A full army of street sweepers scrubbed by hand the main boardwalk of the capital city where Angelita's float would process, to protect Her Majesty's snow-white robe. Her royal entry was made on a mile of red carpet and in the company of hundreds of courtiers. A new western extension of the city was even built for the fair that became municipal office space after the event. This national extravaganza surpassed all other events of the regime in its excesses of magisterial pomp and spending. The fair framed the dictator's daughter as a charismatic center of national value and the luminous totem of the regime, the nation, and even the "free" world (as the name of the fair announced).[2]

The symbolic climax of the "Year of the Benefactor," dedicated to Trujillo, the fair was intended to highlight the achievements of the regime by placing them on display. In this nationalist mythology, signs of progress equaled the regime, which equaled the man himself. As Trujillo stated, the Free World's Fair of Peace and Confraternity was "the patriotic achievement of the Era which national gratitude has baptized with my name. There it is, objectively materialized in each one of the exhibitions of this Fair, the period that I have presided over and that I offer today, at the end of twenty-five years, to the judgment of the people who entrusted their destiny to me in 1930 in a gesture of deep faith in my patriotism and in my acts, that rewards my long vigils and my fever for work during these twenty-five years in which was forged this prodigious reality. That work is my only crown, and with it I submit myself today to history."[3]

The fair was convened not merely to represent the "prodigious reality" of Trujillo's rule. Filtered through Angelita's aura of perfection, the event was a particularly grandiloquent manifestation of the larger-than-life ceremonial regime that was the era of Trujillo, the Trujillato. On the cusp of an epoch in which nations were judged by their ability to represent their virtues at trade exhibits and world fairs,[4] *la Feria* was proof that a man with a big vision could make even a small country look great. But why was it not the figure of the dictator that came to stand for the regime? Why was the dictator's daughter the emblematic icon of the regime and the chosen medium for its consecration?

This study explores two representations of women in official spectacles during the Trujillo regime. Like Marie Antoinette, Trujillo had many bodies, which were variously represented through the women of the regime.[5] The feminine imagery functioned as a foil for the dictator's multiple masculine identities; each female relationship revealed a different facet of his power. One could say that the display of women, particularly those of high social status, was a means of accumulation in Trujillo's drive for symbolic capital, although this symbolic capital had to be constantly renewed.[6] Trujillo drew on a traditional genre of masculinity in which his self-aggrandizement was based on the sheer number of women he could lay claim to—women who highlighted his prowess as lover, father, husband, as well as defender of his female liaisons and extended family. His *macho* stature grew especially through the acquisition of women of superior social status. Trujillo was the quintessential Latin American "big man" whose authority was based on dramatic acts that drew loyal followers. As Parker has argued for Brazil, the good *macho* expresses the values of activity, dominance, and violence, penetrating and metaphorically consuming by possessing both clients and women.[7] Trujillo's power was based as much on the consumption of women through sexual conquest as it was on the consumption of enemies of state through violence. His charisma was founded as much on the concrete numbers of women he acquired (and their class status) as it was on violence and the near-mythological fear he inspired by eliminating men. And whereas his insatiable sexual cupidity incited ignominy, it also brought him respect and was a key to his legitimacy as a *caudillo*-turned-statesman.

THE DICTATOR'S TWO BODIES

Scholars exploring the issue of gender representation and politics have focused on the identity of first ladies, female regents, and queens, and particularly on how they often become magnets for negative commentary and abuse. In an apparently transnational and transhistorical paradigm, public women from countries as diverse as Argentina (Eva Perón) to Nigeria (Maryam Babangida) and from periods ranging from *ancien régime* France (Marie Antoinette) to post–Cold War United States (Nancy Reagan) have borne the brunt of popular disaffection for their husbands. Scholars have explained this recurrent negative imagery surrounding women in the public sphere in several ways. Historians have argued that the transfer of political life out of regal households and courts, and the growing divergence of public and private domains, banished women from politics. Women then became the focus of loathing and resentment when they ventured onto terrain that was no longer their own.[8] Other scholars have taken an alternative culturalist approach, pointing to a cross-cultural bifurcation of power in which men inhabit the controlled, ordered, and hierarchical while their female counterparts inhabit the uncontained, dangerously protean spiritual power of the feminine. This paradigm stresses the complementarity of feminine and masculine powers and is in line with other theories that explain dualistic gender ideologies in terms of constructions of nature and culture, or power and authority.[9]

The Trujillo regime did not fit either of these paradigms. The prevalence of feminine iconography did not engender popular loathing of women in the public sphere or an obsessive concern with their sexual exploits during the Trujillato. Rather, stories of hyperactive sexual antics were a stock feature of popular mythmaking concerning all of the Trujillo family, primarily the men but including the women. Even today, popular books charting the lascivious exploits of Trujillo and his inner court are the most popular form of literature about the regime.[10] Stories also abound of Trujillo's abduction of virginal girls during his provincial travels, of his beautiful victims spied and romanced during official balls and functions. Indeed, to have been chosen as an object of Trujillo's desire elicited a certain pride, even among the highly sheltered but rebellious adolescent daughters of the elite, who snuck off to official functions. As a result, parents went to great lengths to prevent their daughters from being noticed by the dictator, since refusing his attentions carried a high price and could even cost a girl's father his job.[11]

Nor was power in the Dominican popular imagination configured in the binary conjugal fashion. Indeed, Trujillo's wives played little or no role in either state iconography or popular mythmaking. His several legal consorts were dowdy and unassuming, taking little or no public role in regime affairs. His first wife, Aminta Ledesma, was of simple peasant stock from Trujillo's provincial hometown; he divorced her to marry "a more socially suitable wife," Bienvenida Ricardo, a "poor blueblood" from a provincial aristocratic family.[12] Although the official party, the Partido Dominicano, established a women's branch in 1940, the first lady did not actively participate, outside of the occasional cameo appearance as hostess for Party parties.[13] Doña María Martínez, Trujillo's third wife, the daughter of Spanish immigrants, was guarded and reclusive, keeping to a tiny coterie of confidants and insiders. She focused her attention on raising the children and on business affairs; she was less interested in her public profile than in concrete material returns for her efforts. In fact, during her tenure as first lady, Doña María succeeded in amassing one of the largest personal fortunes of the era. Toward the end of the regime, when she began to take an active interest in urban planning and architectural affairs, she did so entirely behind the scenes. Doña María founded a social welfare organization after 1953. However, she never cultivated an active maternal hands-on approach to the masses. Rather, her reputation was one of cool distance, reserve, and sporadic outbursts of impetuous ire that some allege was due to rancor stemming from her earlier social exclusion as Trujillo's mistress.[14] Doña María's most significant venture into the public was as author of an etiquette booklet entitled *Moral Meditations,*[15] a chiding, schoolmarmish mixture of popular philosophy and manners for Dominican mothers. The book disappeared without a ripple.

The Trujillo regime stands out because it was not the dictator's wife who took center stage in regime iconography. Nor was the connubial couple the basis of the nuclear family. Instead, it was Trujillo's other women who provided erotic imagery for the body politic,[16] most especially his young lover Lina Lovatón, through her participation in the 1937 Carnival, and his two daughters—Angelita, who was queen of the 1955 World's Fair, and Flor de Oro, who served as cultural ambassador in New York, where she became doyenne of the Hollywood jet set by virtue of her one-time marriage to Dominican playboy Porfirio Rubirosa. Although the passions of heterosexual courtship among the Trujillos became an important idiom of legitimacy for the regime, this romance of state was based not on the binomial couple but rather on several family triangles. The intricacy of this imagery in part derives from the complex and contradictory structure of the Dominican family, which is characterized by concubinage, serial unions, female-headed households, de facto polygyny, and a rigid set of unattainable gender-role expectations. For the majority of rural and urban poor, a family headed by a stable male wage-earner is an ideal but unreachable goal. For example, although women ideally should not work, most find they have to: either they are the sole wage-earners in their family or their husband's income is insufficient. Indeed, some have argued that the economic emasculation of the lower-class urban and rural male has taken its toll on gender roles and driven men to exhibit their masculine prowess, machismo, in alternative arenas of daily life.[17] The Dominican male is expected to be an honorable father to his public family, which shares his *apellido* (surname), as well as secretly to maintain his unofficial wives and offspring, his *casa chica* (small house). The Dominican family, then, provides several "triangles of dramatizations" through which "unconscious images of a familial order" are defined, an obvious example being the husband-wife-mistress triangle.[18]

Stories of the erotic adventures of the Trujillo family brought the regime down to earth by translating the apparently superhuman first family's sexual activities into sexual exploits described by the language and mode of expression drawn from everyday life. In the arena of popular rumor, official romance offered a medium for sentimental investment in the regime while also providing grist for moral criticism of the excesses of statecraft and male philandering run amok. The public recognized a form of legitimation based on lust, not love, since adulation of the daughter and lover did not invoke the promise of "natural" childbearing.[19] The parading of Trujillo's women involved a performance of masculinity that drew on the figure of the popular antihero from the *barrio* (marginal neighborhood) who achieves status, money, women, and position from nothing but the result of his own efforts. Trujillo embodied the *tigre* (tiger), the quintessential Dominican underdog who gains power, prestige, and social status through a combination of wits, will, sartorial style, and *cojones* (balls).[20] The *tigre* seduces through impeccable attire, implacable charm, irresistible sexuality, and a touch of violence. His defining feature is his daring, audacious willingness to go after whatever he wants—money, commodities, or women, particularly those beyond his social reach.[21]

The daughters and wives of the state elite created by the Trujillato merely represented their husbands in official pageants and reenacted the exchange of gifts and favors that was part and parcel of politics under the regime. But staging affairs of state through a rhetoric of female corporeality had its own particular effects. First, it created a public of voyeurs convened to gaze upon, assess, appreciate, and above all admire the mythic dimensions of Trujillo's masculinity: as exemplary father, husband, *caudillo, patrón,* and lover. Second, Trujillo's women as objects of value were crucial tropes for the construction of his power. They accrued to the person of the dictator through their evaluation and exchange. Rejected by the traditional white elite as a ruthless mulatto arriviste with Haitian (that is, black) lineage, Trujillo sought out the daughters of the bourgeoisie in his erotic forays as a means of insinuating himself into elite circles. Not only did he seek to defy the aristocracy by stealing their daughters, but, in true *tigre* fashion, he also legitimated himself through the conquest of women of superior status. Romantic conquest, then, became a means both of subjugating the bourgeoisie and of entering their ranks. Scholars have focused on Trujillo's accumulation of land, commerce, and capital while neglecting perhaps the most important economy of male personal status in the Dominican Republic. Through the display of his women, Trujillo amassed prestige.

LINA LOVATÓN: "I, THE QUEEN"

In 1937, Trujillo was taking one of his daily strolls in tree-shaded Gazcue, a scenic neighborhood in Santo Domingo. During his outing that balmy late afternoon, he came upon the young Lina Lovatón Pittaluga, tall and lithe and looking ravishing in a dreamy tulle dress. She was the sole daughter of Ramón Lovatón, a prominent lawyer from one of the most exclusive Santo Domingo families who was known for his elegant attire. Lina, one of the most eligible debutantes at the time, was a contestant for Carnival queen. She was facing stiff competition from the beautiful Blanquita Logroño, sister of an esteemed jurist and close ally of Trujillo. But, as the legend goes, Trujillo was smitten, and proceeded to arrange things in her favor.[22] And, it seems, Trujillo knew that giving Lina the queenship would create a large debt that would have to be repaid.

Trujillo at this point had recently divorced his second wife, Bienvenida Ricardo, to marry María Martínez. Nonetheless, in 1937 he was to have a daughter by his former spouse. Doña María, having just married Trujillo, did not take well to Lina or to what rapidly became a quite public challenge to their marriage. The challenge was multifaceted. First, Lina, as a member of the old aristocracy of the capital, had social class, something Trujillo craved. She was described as "young, beautiful, cultivated, virtuous, distinguished, aristocratic, while being simple and generous."[23] Stories abound that Trujillo had become vengeful toward the traditional elite when he was denied admittance to a prominent social club. In this context, possessing Lina implied social acceptance; it also signified domination of the new Trujillista state elite over the traditional culture brokers. Lina became the ultimate accouterment and sign of Trujillo's unfulfilled bourgeois ambitions. To make matters worse, Trujillo fell passionately in love with Lina. Much to Doña María's chagrin, Lina indeed became Carnival queen, and a much-loved one at that. The sole recourse in Doña María's arsenal, it seems, was to pressure the papers into refraining from publishing any further pictures of Lina, and indeed they did not. As a result, 1937 stood out as the year in which no photographs of Carnival festivities appeared in the newspapers.

Although Lina was the centerpiece of the 1937 Carnival, it was clear from the outset that the event was not about her but about Trujillo, to whom she owed her title. Indeed, entitlement, or empowering individuals to speak in the name of the state, was a common strategy under the regime, one that proved useful because it spread responsibility by implicating the citizenry in an otherwise highly centralized political system. But this case was rather more extreme. The 1937 Carnival re-created the state in ritual form through its women, using as a pretext a two-month-long feudal masquerade ball. Her Majesty Queen Lina stood at the apex, with a court of princesses of her choosing, nearly all of whom were the daughters of state functionaries. Next in line came the ladies of honor and the ambassadors to Lina's court, each of whom represented a province; each princess also had her own court. The Departments of Public Administration, the (official Trujillista) Dominican Party, social clubs, and organizations also sent representatives to Queen Lina. There was even a Princess of Meritorious Firemen. Needless to say, these women were authorized to represent the regime by Trujillo. Lest they forget, they were reminded often. For instance, Queen Lina sent a letter to Lourdes García Trujillo praising her as the greatest of princesses "because in your veins runs the same blood as the Maximum Hero."[24] Queen Lina also named honorary titles, yet in recognition for efforts made on behalf of Trujillo, not for Lina herself. In the end, she was unquestionably Trujillo's vassal.

Carnival's monarchical theme underscored the "courtly" aspects of the regime. Carnival's simulation of statecraft also extended to the practice of official prestation, a form of ritual tribute and fealty required of insiders during the regime. During her two months in office, Lina not only issued decrees (which constituted, in a sense, symbolic gifts—she named Trujillo's wife and mother "great and unique protectors of my kingdom," probably much to Doña María's consternation), she also participated in the exchange of favors, an important expression of reciprocity and recognition during the regime. She gave a ball for the municipal government, the *barrio* princesses held a dance for Trujillo, the secretaries of state offered Lina a reception, and Lina gave a champagne toast in gratitude for both the "protectors" of her fiefdom and the allegiance of her vassals. Nor were these activities to be scoffed at by officials. Trujillo arrived at the *barrio* dance, honoring princesses from lowly working-class neighborhoods such as Villa Duarte and Villa Francisca, in formal military dress attire, in a "smoking" (a tuxedo) arrayed with a full display of military decorations.[25] If it was not already crystal clear that Lina was but a simulacrum of the true monarch, Trujillo, it was when she designated "Military Maneuvers of Dajabón" one of the "preferred sonnets" of her kingdom.[26] Lina was an elegant feminine mascot for a regime that relied primarily on military iconography. Her Highness even posed for photographs with personnel of the Ministries of the Interior, Police, War, and Marines.

Although the 1937 Carnival did invert the social order, its choreography had far more in common with a military parade than with a typical carnival procession.[27] The opening reception took place in the National Palace on January 9, and Lina received Trujillo as a president would a visiting dignitary. The queen was given symbolic keys to the city to the accompaniment of a twenty-one-gun salute before making her triumphal march; she then proceeded to traverse the principal capital thoroughfares in a cavalcade. The climax of Carnival thus replicated the form of a presidential rally. The result was an intricate celebration of hierarchy and a dramatization of the glories of entitlement.

Previously, Dominican Carnival had coincided with the Independence Day celebrations of February 27, marking the day the country achieved freedom from Haitian rule (1822–1844) and rendering it a day commemorating and fêting popular sovereignty. However, the overall plan of the proceedings made it quite clear that the 1937 Carnival was not intended to be a licentious, popular affair, nor was it intended to have been touched by a "feminine" perspective. Rather, it was a civic tribute to "the populator"[28] Trujillo, "savior of the nation." In fact, the central events occurred on February 23, the anniversary of Trujillo's ascendence to power in 1930. Only a concluding dance remained for Independence Day, since by then the crowning activities were all over. Moreover, a new event was scripted in that became the culminating moment of the festivities: the unveiling of a forty-meter obelisk to pay homage to Trujillo's seemingly miraculous reconstruction of the city after the devastating 1930 hurricane and to mark the name change of the capital city from Santo Domingo to Ciudad Trujillo in 1936. Although Carnival was entrusted to women this year, they were called on to sing collective praises to this great phallic token of Trujillo's fecund and promiscuous dominion. If anyone missed the sexual allusion, it was clarified in the inaugural speeches. Head of the Pro-Erection Committee and Dominican vice president Jacinto Peynado declared the obelisk a fitting tribute to a man "of superior natural gifts." Municipal government chief Alvarez Pina remarked, "[T]he allegory of this monument has close similarity with the man it glorifies. Its base firm, its lines severe. . . . This obelisk, a gigantic needle of time in space, will stand out forever."[29] The obelisk, luminescent with marble dust and laced with gold-leaf aphorisms at its base, stood contrapuntally in relation to Queen Lina herself. Both were symbolic reminders of the force of Trujillo's masculine powers, of the dictator as sexual conquistador, or, in Lina's words, of Trujillo as "inexhaustible sower."[30] Queen Lina and her court were seated at the dignitaries' pavilion on the *malecón*, where they first viewed the obelisk's inauguration rites, and then Trujillo, Lina, and her courtiers were serenaded by the Army Band.

Although 1937 was a carnival of women, it was by no means a protofeminist affair. The prevailing mood was romantic and highly sentimental. The female image espoused by the regime was ornamental, baroque, and saintly. This angelic aura was enhanced by the fact that Trujillo's wife invariably appeared accompanied by his mother—never alone. Additionally, the patron saint of the Dominican Republic, the Virgin of Altagracia, was championed as embodying the Dominican nation so perfectly that she even shared the very substance of *dominicanidad*. Even nonreligious Dominicans were said to feel a "congenital impulse" of reverence and respect toward her.[31] This official version of femininity, however, did resonate with middle-class women's values. Bourgeois Dominican women argued for a woman's place in the public sphere, but one sharply delineated from the world of men, which they saw as corrupting. For example, one group, called the Feminine Creed of Culture, argued that male culture—objective and materialist—had reached its decadence and that female culture, embodying subjectivity and the emotions, must be cultivated for renovation. Women would be the sentinels of the spiritual renewal of the West: not to substitute for men but to complement them, to remind humanity of the "correct" path of real human sentiment.[32]

In this sense, the official choreography of womanhood in the 1937 Carnival resonated with one strand of women's thought that advocated an honor-shame morality and a cult of "good womanhood." This elite vision championed women as representatives of a larger collectivity and stood firmly against a liberal "Americanized" female prototype, the "modern woman," which they saw as antithetical to the values of family and nation. In the 1930s the image of the "new woman" propagated by "Hollywood" was received with some ambivalence and not a small measure of fear in the Dominican Republic, a country just emerging from a direct U.S. military regime and the 1929 world depression. Certainly there was coy support for the "modern woman" who need not merely be a good mother or wife but who could pursue a career. But there was also anxiety that secretly men were not pleased by this encroachment on their terrain or by the thought of sharing privileges with this "masculinized" woman.[33] The debate as articulated was not really over whether women could or should aspire to a professional identity; instead, it focused on the politics of self-fashioning, the right of young women to aspire to a new, glamorous image through dress and adornment. At issue was whether a girl should feel free to dress and make up in an alluring fashion and whether the male attention she received as a result rendered her a woman of ill repute. At stake in this debate was whether women should aspire to new public identities that recognized them as individuals and not as members of their family lineages (and thus as part of a particular race and class). This was probably most salient to the new middle sectors of urban professionals, a group that had developed as a result of rapid economic development of the sugar sector in the 1920s and that was still fighting for "social space" in the 1930s.

Thus the 1937 Carnival, planned and executed entirely by the regime, did articulate with a new reactionary woman's voice that vilified American culture, feminism, modernity, and consumer capitalism in one fell swoop. Elite tirades against the "new woman" as quintessential emblem of modernity and North American culture (that is, Hollywood) had commenced in the 1920s but became more uniformly negative in the 1930s. Clearly, many Dominican middle-class women were captivated by the new fashion and hairstyles brought to them through the silver screen, as evidenced by the newspaper fashion column "Hollywood Secrets." Articles focused on whether mulatta ("*trigueña*") women's hair would take to the new styles as they became vogue, such as the gently bobbed "China style" popularized by the film *The Good Earth*.[34] Nor was this debate relegated to the politics of style; U.S. norms of etiquette became a highly charged issue as well. Some women complained about the relinquishing of respectful social distance in public that resulted from North American influence. One writer linked the expanding use of the familiar *tú* form of address to U.S. influence. The use of *tú* previously had divided honorable from disreputable girls, and the loose use of *tú* by "modern" girls was causing "disequilibrium." As D'Erzell stated, "A man addressed as '*tú*' feels authorized to solicit. The woman using '*tú*' feels disposed to concede."[35] Concern over adequate social space here clearly indexed a set of class and moral markers elites felt were disintegrating through a U.S.-propagated mass culture.

In the end, the message of the 1937 Carnival was that Trujillo, the great father, had forged a nation by providing its citizens with an identity. As one editorial writer put it, "Trujillo has taught us who we are and has taught us to be it with satisfaction and dignity."[36] Or, perhaps more accurately, he made *la nación* great by making it masculine. In the words of Pérez Alfonseca, "We have a president who is a Repúblico [male republic]. . . . The Repúblico makes a Republic, just as a King makes a Queen."[37] Yet even if it was Trujillo who made the nation great, it was Lina and others who ultimately gave it value.

ANGELITA AT THE FAMILY FAIR

From one of the first major spectacles of the regime we now turn to the last, the twenty-fifth anniversary of Trujillo's coming to power in 1955.[38] In only eight short months the artists, architects, and urban planners of the Free World's Fair choreographed a year's worth of shows, spectacles, and music, and drew up and built from scratch a new western extension of the capital city totaling some 8,000 cubic meters and encompassing seventy-one buildings. The event was intended to achieve several objectives. First, it was conceived of as a money-making enterprise. Unlike most public entertainments under the regime, tickets were sold. This was not an event for the masses but rather for the expanding bourgeoisie, the new industrial and landowning class fostered by the expanding internal market of the postwar period. Much like the New York World's Fair of 1940, which served as template for the Dominican version, *la Feria* was intended to have a strong trade component—the English-language brochures even called it an international trade fair.[39] It was intended both to promote the Dominican Republic as a site for foreign investment and to publicize the country's natural resources, political stability, and national products. However, while the century-of-progress expositions used the fair as a medium for expanding commerce and promoting consumer capitalism, *la Feria* was essentially what Robert Rydell has called a "theater of power" to legitimate the Trujillo regime.[40] The fair was also intended to render the Dominican Republic a U.S. ally by situating it squarely in the Western anticommunist bloc. It was a reminder to the United States that even if it objected to Trujillo's lack of political liberties at home, the Dominican Republic served as an essential hemispheric anticommunist bulwark.

A crucial precondition to the fair was the postwar expansion of the Dominican economy. The country embarked on a program of import substitution industrialization during World War II, as global prices for many of the nation's primary commodities soared, especially sugar. Although historians may debate to what extent Trujillo's economic policy was nationalist or not, the net effect of the postwar scarcities was both an expanded production of essential staples and light industry items and the encouragement of foreign direct investment—as long as it stayed away from Trujillo's personal fiefdoms. By the mid-1950s, domestic demand had expanded dramatically as a result of growth in population, per capita income, and urbanization. During the Korean War, Trujillo established highly favorable terms of investment, for example by eliminating tariffs on raw material imports. In this context, a U.S. $25 million expenditure on a world's fair was only part lavish showmanship; it also had a strong advertising and public relations component.[41]

One objective of *la Feria* was to bring the world physically to the Dominican Republic. Trujillo had tried to encourage tourism from the early days of the regime. In 1937 the first major luxury tourist vessels had arrived from Canada, bringing hundreds of visitors to explore Santo Domingo. In dock, visitors lunched at the exclusive "Country Club." Their arrival caused tremendous excitement, particularly the arrival of one British lord who traveled with an entourage of fifteen servants. One editorial proclaimed that Ciudad Trujillo had finally become "a Mecca of curiosity and universal interest."[42] But it was not until the early 1950s that the regime endeavored to cultivate tourism in earnest, erecting "sparkling and new" beach hotels under American management and persuading Pan American Airlines to establish direct bargain flights from New York. An esteemed historical archaeologist was commissioned to write a walking tour of the colonial city in English for visitors, and pamphlets extolling the virtues of the country were distributed overseas. The regime built several luxurious new hotels in anticipation of scores of tourists, although few actually came. However, the regime's intended message was not lost on those few visitors who did attend, who enthusiastically commended Trujillo's achievement in transforming the capital from the "dirty, pestilential and unattractive city known as Santo Domingo," "a disease-ridden pest hole . . . loaded with foreign debt and infested with bandits," to the "sophisticated modernity of Ciudad Trujillo." They proclaimed the country "the most modern of all our Latin-American neighbors," "the Switzerland of the tropics," and Dominicans "the Yankees of Latin America"—in sum, an island of familiarity in a sea of difference.[43]

If few foreigners were inspired by *la Feria* to visit the Dominican Republic, Dominicans were nonetheless thrilled at the exotic global cultures *la Feria* brought to them. The Trujillo regime had created a virtually closed society, sealing off Dominican access to passports and foreign travel and establishing tight control over the flow of information into the country. The vacuum was partially filled by what had become by the 1950s one of the largest and most technologically advanced state-owned radio and television networks in Latin America.[44] Nonetheless, Dominicans craved news of the outside, particularly the steamy cosmopolitan glamour flourishing in neighboring Cuba and the United States, which they consumed vicariously through Cuban rumba albums and Hollywood films. In this context, through revealing glimpses of fantastic faraway dreamscapes and situating Dominicans as the subjects of the gaze, *la Feria* provided enticing entertainment to a public starved for high style and things foreign. Each country had its own day at the fair, when its national pavilion was unveiled and its own cultural program and exhibit took center stage. Some of the local favorites were the Chinese pavilion, with its intricately carved porcelain and wooden objects, delicately painted fans, and luxurious silks, and the futuristic Atoms for Peace exhibition, which was later reassembled in Geneva by the United States after its presentation at the fair. France sent a helicopter, and Japan and Mexico sponsored weeklong film festivals. Overall, Western nations emphasized themes of scientific and industrial progress, while other nations focused on traditional artisanry or culture. Women figured prominently in all of the displays as the quintessential sign of nationhood: from Indonesia, which sent a Javanese woman in traditional batik, to Guatemala, which provided a living display of the country's rich, hand-woven textiles. Even Holland, the Dominican Republic's third largest export market, selected tulip and gladiola bulbs and girls in traditional maidens' outfits as conveyors of Dutchness. But Latin American nations more commonly intended their female exhibitors to represent modernity. Such was the case for Venezuela, which flew in the *compatriota Miss Mundo* (Miss World) from London for the occasion, and Mexico, which held a weeklong fashion parade of Mexican designer outfits in honor of Queen Angelita that featured ball gowns with tulle skirts *à la haute couture Parisian*. Mexico also courted the ladies, however, by erecting a tortilla provision stand and handing out free bags of corn flour to housewives.

The national displays provided a means of legitimation that Trujillo capitalized on heavily. Whenever possible they were transformed into emblems of commendation and tribute for Trujillo's virtues as a statesman. The letters of praise and thanks from participating countries were reproduced and publicized widely, such as the French delegate's note declaring the progress of the country was "miraculous" and that he "felt honored to be Trujillo's friend." Not surprisingly, the most effusive praises came from strongmen Somoza and Franco, but Japan called Trujillo an "organizational genius" and characterized the Trujillisto era as "splendorous." Brazilian president Kubitschek was the highest-level political figure to attend, and photographs of him embracing Trujillo or standing with Trujillo family members and the regime's inner circle were legion. Somoza even sent a military decoration for Trujillo's elder son Ramfis, the Order of Ruben Darío, in frank recognition that Trujillo, like Somoza, was grooming his son to take over the position, in Somoza's words, of "permanent sentinel of national greatness." The note from the U.S. ambassador strained to praise not Trujillo but the anticommunist significance of the fair and the "marvelous" energy that went into constructing the fair in such a short period of time.

Ultimately the central pedestal of *la Feria* was reserved for the Trujillo regime. As one visitor observed, "the government itself is the principal exhibitor, displaying evidence of political, economic, social, and cultural progress during the past quarter-century—'The Era of Trujillo.'"[45] In fact, most of the pavilions and floats in the central parade were put on by state agencies, ministries, provincial governments, and the central bank, although local and foreign industries and banks participated as well. The ubiquitous image of Trujillo, El Benefactor, loomed large in all of the government pavilions, here smiling, there bending down or signing a document, such as the all-important Hull-Trujillo treaty of 1940, which canceled the U.S. administration of customs, in place since 1924, and established the first national Dominican currency and central bank (and, not coincidentally, also allowed Trujillo much closer surveillance over the national coffers). The armed forces had a prominent part in *la Feria* as well, since Rafael Trujillo at that time was serving as its head, with his brother Héctor "Negro" Trujillo reigning as chief of state. Indeed, this explains the predominance of military iconography at the event, in conjunction with growing opposition to the regime overseas. Not only did the armed forces pavilion house an impressive collection of tanks, jeeps, and advanced artillery, they also were displayed in a military parade staged for the occasion, which included elegantly uniformed battalions in procession. Over the years, Trujillo had created one of the strongest militaries in Latin America, tripling its size and creating a full-fledged professional air force. Needless to say, this amount of military preparedness exceeded the country's actual defense needs, which were minimal.[46]

The World's Fair did present a family model of state authority in which obedience to the patriarchal father was "naturalized."[47] The Carnival parade, which took place on April 1 in tribute to Queen Angelita's birthday, enacted the "family romance" of the regime. The familial model of authority was laid out in allegorical form as Trujillo, "Father of the New Fatherland" (Padre de la Patria Nueva), was represented at the head of the parade in the form of an enormous bronze bust. In the rest of the floats women figured prominently, as contestants representing provinces and parastatal organizations competed for a ranked series of prizes. Some of the most popular themes were drawn from classical Greece, such as the display of the Dominican Party, which featured a bevy of women representing the muses of Zeus, swathed in Greek togas and adorning a huge lute. In the contribution of the Dominican Electrical Corporation, allegorical women workers dressed in black-and-white men's uniforms waved from atop an oversize electrical plant; a model of the technically sophisticated Rhadamés bridge was similarly decorated with "professional girls" in the Ministry of Public Works float. Drawing on the iconography of women in World War II cinema, the air force paraded a two-seater airplane amply decorated with uniformed female "pilots." A high school, the Colegio San Luis, featured a boy's choir that sang praises to a queen bee centerpiece amid lush floral garlands. Another popular theme was a folkloric pastoral scene. Incorporating a *bricolage* of Mexican peasant dress and Hollywood's Carmen Miranda, this style was represented by young peasant boys in wide-brimmed straw sombreros accompanying ruffled-sleeved and hoop-skirted women with slightly risqué off-the-shoulder peasant gowns who lacked only the fruit-bowl turban. The province of Samaná, an isolated Atlantic coastal zone, won first prize for best costume with a group of lithe mermaids crowned by a large conch shell in gentle pastel colors. However, this parade of European queens, folkloric fantasies, and fables was a congeries of imported dreams. The fact that the bulk of these costumes were imported from overseas added to *la Feria*'s otherworldly feel. It also drew the ire of local dressmakers, who protested vociferously over the loss of work and questioned just how "nationalist" the fair really was.

While *la Feria* privileged women in the floats, as signs they stood in relationship to emblems of manhood, namely cattle. Both cattle and women were media for extending the male self into the world—for dominating and mobilizing clients, territory, and familial networks. Cattle also served as currency in the domain of the traditional *caudillo*, a figure that accumulated cattle, women, and money, through which he established ties of patronage and alliance. This was clear in the International Cattle Fair, a popular component of the fair that showcased purebred horses, cattle, and pigs from Cuba, the United States, and Puerto Rico. *La Feria* elided cattle as a traditional symbol of national value with money, the sign of postcolonial nationhood, and the iconography of the fair linked them both through the person of Trujillo. Indeed, money was perhaps the most trumpeted symbol at the fair. Not only were commemorative bronze coins, embossed with Trujillo's profile (hard and stern) minted for the event, but the Finance Ministry set up an entire pavilion with a historical money exhibit, one that placed U.S. and Dominican money side by side, as if rendering commensurable the economies of the two nations.[48] The Spanish painter Vela Zanetti also created an allegorical mural in one of the new ministry buildings that depicted sweating futuristic laborers struggling to prop upright an enormous gold coin. This depicted the Hull-Trujillo treaty, which in Trujillista ideology established full fiscal autonomy and, more important, the symbolic sovereignty of the Dominican nation.[49] Trujillo, then, became the mediator of national conversion: one who transformed cattle into money and colony into nation. At *la Feria,* the dictator himself became the principal sign of national sovereignty and value.

More than 250,000 people turned out to see the crowning glory of the fair, however—Her Majesty First Daughter Angelita's float, which was named "The Reign of Love." The float featured an oversize baroque carriage decorated with gold leaf and adorned with rubenesque angels floating atop a cloud. The women all wore white, with red hearts on their busts and smaller hearts appliquèd on their expansive skirts. Additionally, Angelita wore a Dominican national emblem on her chest. Cascading downward from Angelita's pedestal was her court. Angelita's "reign" had actually begun in August, when, at the tender age of sweet sixteen, she was handed the symbolic keys to the city and greeted with the pomp and circumstance afforded a foreign dignitary, with full military observances, as combat planes and naval ships came out in her honor. Wearing a naval jacket with a captain's stripes (perhaps an allusion to her brother, Ramfis, who was made army colonel at age three and brigadier general at age nine), Angelita's *quinceñera* (coming-out party) was not to be forgotten, either by her or by the nation.

If the dictator's daughter was intended to provide a lovable face to the regime, however, she was never as successful as Lina. Partly this was due to her age; at sixteen she was essentially a *tabula rasa,* a mute mirror for national fantasy. And partly it was because of Angelita's personality. Cool, distant, and reserved, Angelita had grown up as the coddled younger daughter, showered from the first with national attention and sequestered by her jealous father, for whom no suitor was good enough. An unhappy person, she suffered from a strange back malady for which she was frequently hospitalized. Unlike Queen Lina, she was neither gracious nor grateful. Nor was she legitimate in class terms. Lina had been born into a traditional aristocratic family; lily-white, she was born to rule. Angelita, on the other hand, lacked both the achieved status of her father or the ascribed social prestige of the Lovatón family. Worse still, she was considered neither especially beautiful nor warm and generous by the general public. Finally, she was the central icon of a festival that lacked the populist trappings and participatory élan of other rituals of state. This event was aimed primarily at impressing the world, not Dominicans, in a context in which a combination of state monopolies and postwar affluence had created unprecedented social distance between the elite and the masses. In the end, *la Feria* was magnificent but not inclusive; it inspired reverence, not love. The fair reflected what Trujillo wanted his country to be, not what it was. With *la Feria,* Trujillo stretched too far.

This consideration may account for the fact that one of the most dramatic protests of the entire regime occurred over the selection of Miss Dominican Republic at the fair, when the beauty contestants' favorite was overlooked for the daughter of a Trujillista insider (apparently at the behest of First Lady Doña María). When the announcement was made, the contestants (all daughters of public functionaries) angrily threw rum-and-soda bottles and chairs and marched out in disgust.[50] Like all state rituals during the Trujillato, from elections to rallies to civic parades, the fair was choreographed from above; nonetheless, within those confines, state pageants such as this one included an important participatory space. No one objected to the election of Angelita as queen, because that was nonnegotiable, but the remaining winners were seen as the choice of the contestants, as within the realm of their "democratic" freedom to choose. Doña María was perceived as interfering with the populist component of the state rite, an arena regarded as outside her jurisdiction. If Angelita represented the state at *la Feria*, Miss Dominican Republic represented the nation, and the Trujillo family had no moral claim on who embodied this popular emblem of nationhood.

Angelita symbolized a particular genre of feminine participation in the public realm, a vertical as opposed to a lateral principle.[51] Trujillista ideology was highly authoritarian, embodying hierarchy, order, and the sacred. The role of the mystical body of the regime, the ideal, invisible, and immortal body politic, was played by Trujillo's youngest daughter, Angelita.[52] Authority, in abstract, ideal, and transcendent form, was ascribed to Angelita, who, like her namesake, came to represent rarified purity itself, a kind of living embodiment of the Virgin of Altagracia, patron saint of the Dominican Republic. Hierarchy was also expressed through establishing the daughter as the ultimate emblem of the regime, and one thoroughly disciplined by the unquestioned authority of her father.

TRUJILLO, *EL TIGRE*

This study has explored the culture of a particular kind of "theater state"[53] and its impact on the logic of class, gender, and race marking. As events surrounding the 1937 Carnival and the 1955 Fair during the Trujillato demonstrate, spectacles of women can exhibit masculinity and gender representations can convey messages about social class. Indeed, in the Dominican Republic, a nation of predominantly mixed race, where race and class are deeply interpenetrated, Queen Lina conveyed an important message about social distinction. Many elites feared that Trujillo was "resentful" (*resentido*) as a poor mulatto who rose up from the dregs of society, and dreaded he would wage war against the society from which he felt excluded (ironically, though, in popular terms, the revenge of the underdog after his arrival is part of the heroic mythos of *tigueraje*). Trujillo's success in seducing and displaying the crème de la crème of Dominican society demonstrated that it was power and wealth, not race and background, that ultimately counted.

In the end, to some extent the Trujillo regime did "culturally democratize"[54] the elite, by transforming the logic of status accumulation of high society. The coronations of Queen Lina and Queen Angelita had a small part to play in that process. However, state rituals such as these were effective less as "encapsulations" or even "approximations."[55] They worked through their creation of what Timothy Mitchell has called a "reality effect," in which people come to inhabit the world they see represented.[56]

Trujillo himself had little personal charisma to speak of. Portly in his later years, he was fiery, enigmatic, and had a notoriously squeaky voice. What made him a hero was the fact that he put the Dominican Republic on the map both by extending the country into the world, and bringing the world to the Dominican Republic. In part this was achieved by his staging the nation through larger-than-life, world-class festivals. But most important, Trujillo became a popular hero in the Dominican Republic through his ability to achieve absolute power and wealth from a socially marginal, mulatto, provincial background. He was "every man," while he became a member of the global ultrarich. The part-*flaneur*, part-*tigre*, part-Horatio Alger myth of the regime was achieved in part through Trujillo's monopolization of the commanding heights of the economy, which some have proposed reached as high as 60 percent of all arable land, and 80 percent of all business. And yet—as I have argued here—an important component of this myth was how he accumulated symbolic capital through the seduction and display of women of value.[57]

In this context, it is ironic that the opera *Aïda* was for Trujillo a privileged allegory of the family romance of empire after which he named his two sons. Written to mark the opening of the Suez Canal in 1871, the plot explores the dilemma between patriotism and romantic love in the saga of an Egyptian hero who rejects marriage to a princess (and therefore the legacy of her father's kingdom) for the love of a slave. Set against the lavish and exotic backdrop of the Egyptian empire at the time of the pharaohs, the story ends in tragedy, as Rhadames and Aïda die in tandem, the victims of jealousy and patriotism. The story was an ironic nationalist fantasy for Trujillo, since it celebrated precisely the opposite dynamic from that revealed by his own family romance. Trujillo himself was not a man to die for reasons of pure romantic fulfillment; he was not one to give up the hand of the king's daughter for his perfect love of an abject slave. Nor was he likely to sacrifice love of nationhood for a love supreme. Yet one strand of *Aïda* does ring true to Trujillo. In the opera, nationhood is defined by fatherhood. And ultimately, no one can successfully escape the bonds of family or national allegiance except through the ultimate exit, death.

It is the centrality of the father-daughter bond in this iconography of state, however, that distinguishes the Trujillo regime from other Latin American family romances. It is the father who ultimately represents the nation, through whom the nation derives its name and lineage and public identity. Yet the father here is represented by the daughter. Of course, father-daughter symbolism offers an even sharper hierarchical relation than the couple, invoking both rankings of age and gender. Furthermore, this allegory makes sense, given the real Dominican family. Outside of the Europeanized elite strata, the father tends to be a distant figure, one who is often absent from the actual raising of children. In the serial marriage system, in which children are raised primarily by their mothers and other female kin, the father is a distant and problematic figure who often conjures up feelings of resentment and abandonment. In this context, the daughter analogy presents a more tender, and desirable, face for the state. Finally, as we have seen, Trujillo's parading of his lover and daughter reverted to a subaltern model of male authority, one based on virility, fecundity, and control over women. The daughter substituted for the wife, but invoked the mistress.[58] Even while seeking status ascendence though the production and consumption of bourgeois femininity, Trujillo at the same time invoked a very *barrio* style of male self-fashioning—in Bourdieu's words, "the outcast's aristocratism"—that deliberately broke the rules of elite sexual comportment.[59]

Trujillo fulfilled the ultimate dream of the *tigre*, the mythic paragon of *barrio* masculinity who gains power—riches, women, control over others—apparently from nothing; he was thus the ultimate transgressor of the rules of the game both for race and for class. The *tigre* is the classic dissimulator, someone who gains access to a station above his own through dressing the part, through the appropriate style and women, but also through being bold, daring, and a smooth talker. There are several substyles of *tigueraje*, however. Trujillo gained power largely through political control and a large dose of violence. His bravery, manliness (*hombria*), athletic build, and especially his capacity for ruthlessness qualified him as a *tigre gallo* (a tiger-cock). While the *tigre* as a mythic figure always appears alone, there was a larger sociological transformation at work behind these individual rogue-hero success stories. Trujillo, Angelita, and Lina expressed a logic of social prestige in which distinction was accorded those in Geertz's terms "near the center of things," those at the center of the social gaze. The message of the Trujillista state elite was that "blood" lineage was meaningless; what counted was being on the national stage and having style and cash to burn. This had become a world in which social capital was based less on who you were, but on being there and looking the part. And while access to those spaces of prestige depended on plenty of capital, money, it seems, could make race and other symbols of origin melt away.

Unlike other Latin American dictators, Trujillo did not privilege the bourgeois family as a metonym of moral nationhood. In fact, he actually innovated laws aimed at loosening family bonds. For example, he passed one law allowing children to be disinherited and another enabling divorce after five years of childless marriage. Early on, the Dominican Republic had some of the most liberal divorce laws in the Western Hemisphere as a result of Trujillo's maneuvers, in large part to accommodate his own *tigre* ambitions. A discourse of family values would have appealed to a middle-class and elite audience, for whom marriage was a stable union of social equals. However, Trujillo chose instead an idiom of authority with more mass appeal, one based on social mobility through the conquest of superior women who were more frequently lovers than wives, and one that made sense to the rural and urban poor who usually lived in concubinage, not formal unions. Trujillo was the *tigre,* the liminal figure who shares power with no one, especially not his wife.

The historical roots of *tigueraje* lay in the relatively open social order of the Dominican Republic. Slave imports were terminated as early as the seventeenth century because of colonial poverty, and many former slaves were able to escape the plantations and mines and found their own *hatos* (small cattle farms) or lived outside the market economy through subsistence agricultural production. The social category of *tigre* in the twentieth century was the *criollo* of the sixteenth, the freed slave of the seventeenth, and the mulatto of the eighteenth century—all figures of difference that threatened the social hierarchy through their status as strangers. Unlike the rigid social order of colonial Haiti or Cuba, the Dominican Republic developed maximal racial mixture and minimal class differentiation, in large part because cattle ranching, logging, and coffee and tobacco cultivation, not sugar and plantation slavery, formed the backbone of the economy until the nineteenth century. Slave escape in this context was relatively easy owing to the low population density. Indeed, by the eighteenth century, the Dominican peasantry was primarily composed of free blacks and mulattoes, who subsisted on the margins of the social order through shifting cultivation, hunting, and only occasionally wage labor.

Yet while this social and economic fluidity created multiple opportunities for individual achievement, it also generated strong anxieties over the boundaries defining class and racial strata. The other side of the logic of "passing" in a mestizo culture is anxiety over lineage. Because everyone has a potential claim to whiteness, the white minority must struggle to create and maintain a bulwark against penetration of the racial frontier from below. As a result, the free mulatto in the Dominican Republic became a locus of fear and revulsion, a figure representing the antithesis of the "civilized" colonial order. In 1780, these fears were confirmed by a bandit known as "the Unknown Black" (*el Negro Incognito*) or "the Cannibal" (*el Comegente*), a mulatto who killed, injured, and pillaged, preying almost exclusively on sugar plantations and their property—slaves, harvests, and farm animals.

As a result of this wave of terror, colonial authorities suggested an imposed relocation scheme whereby rural blacks and mulattoes would be forced to reside within townships. The objective was to eliminate the black rural subculture that evaded subjection by the colonial state and that stood outside the community of "citizens."

It is not coincidental that the dangers of the mulatto were spatialized, seen as deriving from rootlessness and vagrancy, and that the prescribed antidote was forced residence in a township. The danger of the mulatto lay precisely in his ability to move throughout the social hierarchy, and particularly his ability to pass for white. This may explain a colonial injunction punishing free blacks who dressed above their rank, an effort aimed at circumscribing a love of finery and elegance that poor *criollo* colonists had difficulty matching.[60]

The same historical openness that created multiple opportunities for individual achievement for the mulatto underclasses also produced the culture of *tigueraje*, the popular valorization of those who fashioned themselves as "big men" through accumulating the comportment and accouterments of status—the women, attire, bravado—without the ascribed criteria, the *apellido*, or family, class, or racial identity. The *tigre* is a charmer who talks his way into places he doesn't belong through "verbosity, charlatanism [and] . . . a false lyricism."[61] The *tigre* is not given prestige, he steals it. "Born like rats"[62] in revolt against a bourgeois morality that sees them as "matter out of place,"[63] as social filth that should remain at the margins where it belongs, the *tigre* is a man of the public sphere, who frequents the café, the hotel, the theater. He is without a fixed home or official identity (save to the police); he ridicules the status economy of society, snubbing education or "culture" as modes of advancement. The *tigre* can operate outside the rules of society because he seeks respect and approval only from his *barrio*, from *la gente*, the people. Whereas the mulatto trickster had been popular throughout Dominican history, it was only during the Trujillo period that the figure of the *tigre* became generalized as the paradigmatic Dominican hero, the man of the people, the "typical Dominican character par excellence."[64] This was largely due to the elevation and prestige ascribed to the figure of the *tigre* within the Trujillo regime.

To Dominican elites, the classic *tigre* is a dissimulator; he inspires fear as a stranger whose identity resides solely in his appearance. Elites perceive the importance of clothes in *tigre* self-fashioning as a ruse and at times a threat to conventional standards of masculinity. The *tigre* constructs himself as a self-conscious object of the gaze, a position appropriate only to women. Thus, when the insular aristocracy of the 1930s closed ranks against Trujillo, it was apt that a sartorial metaphor was deployed; as one observer put it, "[I]t was the military dress that was accepted, not the man wearing it."[65]

Elite ambivalence became clear at Trujillo's wedding in 1929 to the patrician Bienvenida Ricardo, from a *familia de primera* (society family). Trujillo is remembered as having an alluring, enigmatic, even disconcerting air about him and a reputation as a covetous adventurer—a man not averse to taking risks. He was described as elegant, "impeccably dressed, with a sensual mouth and the look of a 'film star more than a military.'" While loved by the girls (nicknamed not coincidentally "las Correa," the belts, for their attraction to men in uniform), Trujillo was rejected by the girls' parents as a trickster, with his "incommensurable vanity" and his "false and cunning" airs. His identity as an imposter was unmasked at the wedding in a gesture that became emblematic of Trujillo's outsider status. Refusing the cake cutter, he pulled his sword (of solid gold) to cut the first slice of wedding cake, and inadvertently sent the finely decorated wedding cake, an elaborate affair replete with delicate hand-crafted sugar flowers and baroquely adorned with lace, angels, and figurines, crashing down, smashing even the mirror serving as base for the cake.[66] This event embodied for the guests his thinly submerged cruelty while revealing his status as a stranger to the rules of Dominican high society.

By the 1950s, the *tigre* was no longer a focus of elite angst. How then did the *tigre*-cum-*flaneur* achieve respectability? The answer lies in part in the culture of spectacle of the Trujillato. As Benjamin states, "his [the *flaneur*'s] leisurely appearance as a personality is his protest against the division of labour which makes people into specialists. It is also his protest against their industriousness. . . . The intoxication to which the flaneur surrenders is the intoxication of the commodity around which surges the stream of customers." Commodity culture under the Trujillo regime did not enter through the arcade and the department store. Rather, it entered through state pageants that ultimately linked the magic of the commodity to the magic of the regime. This was particularly the case by the 1950s, when the Trujillo family had bought up the commanding heights of the economy and Trujillo himself was one of the richest men in the world. State ceremonies like *la Feria* and the 1937 Carnival were shrines to the great fetish of state that was Trujillo in their sensory overload of goods, fashion, women, money, all of which were ultimately claimed by *El Benefactor*. These rituals of state were hardly window-dressing. Far from it: they were an essential part of making the carnivalesque excess that was the era of Trujillo believable.

SUGGESTED READINGS

Austerliz, Paul. *Merengue: Dominican Music and Dominican Identity*. Philadelphia: Temple University Press, 1995.

Ballerino Cohen, Colleen, Richard Wilk, and Beverly Stoeltje, eds. *Beauty Queens on the Global Stage: Gender, Contests, and Power*. New York: Routledge, 1996.

Callaghan, Karen A., ed. *Ideals of Feminine Beauty: Philosophical, Social and Cultural Dimensions*. Westport, CT: Greenwood Press, 1994.

Deford, Frank. *There She Is: The Life and Times of Miss America*. New York: Viking Books, 1971.

Dewey, Susan. *Making Miss India Miss World: Constructing Gender, Power and the Nation in Postliberalization India*. Syracuse, NY: Syracuse University, 2008.

French, William E., and Katherine Elaine Bliss, eds. *Gender, Sexuality, and Power in Latin America Since Independence*. Lanham, MD: Rowman & Littlefield, 2007.

Galindez, Jesús. *The Era of Trujillo: Dominican Dictator*. Tucson: University of Arizona Press, 1973.

Gregory, Steven. *The Devil behind the Mirror: Globalization and Politics in the Dominican Republic*. Berkeley: University of California Press, 2007.

Hartlyn, Jonathan. *The Struggle for Democratic Politics in the Dominican Republic*. Chapel Hill: University of North Carolina Press, 1998.

Hernandez, Deborah Pacini. *Bachata: A Social History of a Dominican Popular Music*. Philadelphia: Temple University Press, 1995.

Krohn-Hansen, Christian. "Masculinity and the Political Among Dominicans: 'The Dominican Tiger.'" In *Machos, Mistresses, Madonnas: Contesting the Power of Latin American Gender Imagery*, edited by Marit and Kristi Anne Stolen Melhuus. New York: Verso, 1996.

López-Springfield, Consuelo, ed. *Daughters of Caliban: Caribbean Women in the Twentieth Century*. Bloomington: Indiana University Press, 1997.

Pequero, Valentina. *The Militarization of Culture in the Dominican Republic, from Captains Generals to General Trujillo*. Lincoln: University of Nebraska Press, 2000.

Rutter-Jensen, Chloe, ed. *Pasarela paralela: escenarios de la estética y el poder de los reinados de la belleza*. Bogota: Universidad Javeriana, 2005.

Trancer, Shoshana B. "Las Quisqueyana: The Dominican Women, 1940–1970," in *Female and Male in Latin America*, edited by Ann Pescatello, 209–29. Pittsburgh: University of Pittsburgh Press, 1973.

Taylor, Julie. *Eva Perón: The Myths of a Woman*. Chicago: University of Chicago Press, 1979.

Wirarda, Howard. *The Dominican Republic: Nation in Transition*. New York: Frederick A. Praeger, 1969.

Sights

Dominican Republic: Cradle of the Americas. (OAS).
Dominican Women. Directed by Carmen Sarmiento García (FHS).
La Fiesta del Chivo. 2005. Directed by Luis Llosa.
In the Time of the Butterflies. 2000. Directed by Mariano Barroso.
Miss Universe in Peru. 1986. Directed by Grupo Chaski.
Nueba Yol. 1996. Directed by Angel Muniz (Facets Multimedia).

El Poder del Jefe, Nos. 1, 2, 3. 1995–99. Directed by René Fortunato.
Santo Domingo Blues. 2007. Directed by Alex Wolfe.

Sounds

Merengue: Dominican Music and Dominican Identity. Compact disc to accompany the book cited above. Rounder Records, recording no. O2U5, 1997.

14

En el corazón del pueblo

Pedro Infante's Funeral, the *Pueblo* Motif, and the Contest over His Legacy

Sal Acosta

Funerals of government leaders, athletic champions, recognized intellectuals, and entertainment celebrities offer an opportunity to mourn for grief-stricken family, friends, and followers. At the same moment these public events provide an x-ray of society when individuals and communities are most unselfconscious, and they often reveal essential, national characteristics. For Argentina, the funeral of Evita Perón in 1952 exemplified her role in creating the Peronista regime; for Brazil, the funeral of Carmen Miranda in 1955 celebrated her role in creating national awareness of the nation and its culture.[1] *For Mexico, several funerals of the same era could be considered: Pedro Infante, during his lifetime, gleamed in the galaxy of Mexican singers, composers, actors, and radio stars who together formed the face of the nation's golden age of entertainment. Among the celebrated masters of popular music, Pedro Infante, Jorge Negrete, and José Alfredo Jímenez each had substantial followings of fans. Each of them wrote, sang, and recorded songs that still can be heard today on radio and television, and in performances that still incite partisan discussions about which was the greatest of them all. Even in death, the funerals of all three served as expressions of their popularity and their enduring legacy in Mexican and Mexican-American culture.*

Pedro Infante, flying his airplane from Veracruz to Mexico City, crashed and died the morning of Monday, April 15, 1957. By that evening, radio, television, and newspapers had spread the news to a dismayed public.[2] The accident initiated a series of events that sustained a high level of expectation and sorrow over a period of three days. His remains arrived at Mexico City's airport the next day, and thousands of people waited and then followed the hearse through the streets. The funeral vigil took place over the next twenty-four hours, and approximately one hundred thousand people attended.[3] The funeral procession marched through historic avenues—Paseo de la Reforma, Avenida Revolución, and Avenida Tacubaya—as crowds of people lined the streets and thousands of others followed on bicycles and on foot.[4] An estimated one hundred thousand people including family, friends, actors, and fans attended the burial at the Panteón Jardín, hearing and singing Infante's songs. The casket descended as a mariachi played "Las golondrinas," Mexico's heartrending farewell song. People cried, several women fainted, and the police made a few arrests. Infante was laid to rest next to his father and near his fellow actors and friends Blanca Estela Pavón and Jorge Negrete. The family's choice of that site prevailed over the suggestion of National Actors' Guild of a plot closer to the statue of the Ariel (the Mexican equivalent of the Oscar that the actor won only once—for the drama *La vida no vale nada* [1954]—and which, according to Irma Dorantes, he refused to pick up in person to protest against the customary bias against comedies and melodramas).[5] Mexicans had bid goodbye to their beloved Pedro Infante, barely forty-eight hours after learning of his death. The massive turnout clearly illustrated his enormous popularity among the masses.

Newspaper coverage of the death and burial of Infante conveyed the idea that the actor had a genuine connection with the common people. Mentions of *el pueblo* appeared frequently, and references to his life emphasized his modest origins and his humble character. *Excelsior* reported Infante's death and made references to his rise from mere carpenter to fan favorite and to his kindness and devoutness, reminding people of the twenty-seven straight hours he spent on television to raise over one million pesos for the expansion of the Basílica de Guadalupe.[6] *El Universal* mentioned his ascent from baker's apprentice, carpenter, and unemployed singer to one of the richest performers in the country. The paper also called him a symbol of *mexicanidad* (Mexicanness).[7] The reaction from his fans illustrated their affection for the movie star, and newspaper reports informed of the desire of *el pueblo* to be near him and their determination when their efforts met resistance. Disturbances occurred at the vigil and at the funeral when the police unsuccessfully attempted to keep people out.[8] The press emphasized the lower-class position of the people who attended the services. According to these accounts, a woman from *el pueblo* and a laborer spoke of Infante's connection to the people; a girl of humble origins knelt in front of the casket and prayed for hours; people of the lower class filed through during the vigil; members of *el pueblo* stood guard throughout the night; the women of *el pueblo* cried; *el pueblo* bid farewell with tears and song. Photographs from these events reinforced the ubiquitous presence of working-class people and their love for Infante, and *Excelsior* reported that modest composers had already written eight *corridos* to recount his life and death.[9]

Few could have predicted when Pedro Infante (1917–1957) died at the pinnacle of his career that his legacy would actually surpass the great success he enjoyed during the last two decades of his life. He perished two months before receiving international recognition by winning the best-actor award at the 1957 Berlin International Film Festival for his leading role in *Tizoc* and after agreeing to a lucrative contract to perform in Spain for over one million pesos (90,000 U.S. dollars).[10] The celebrations surrounding the fiftieth anniversary of his death in 2007 underscored the immense popularity and commercial appeal he still commands as well as the continuing struggle over who can claim ownership of his legacy and thus shape it. Televisa, Mexico's major television network, used its acquisition of exclusive rights to the anniversary of his death and its monopoly of his films to augment the commemoration it offers every April. It labeled its programming "Pedro Infante Vive," which included a concert by the same name where current artists associated with the network performed some of his most famous songs and a series of brief spots that ran throughout the month where clips of his films appeared as an announcer conveyed a nostalgic and self-promoting message: "Pedro Infante, *ésta es tu casa.*" Televisa also supplemented its traditional showing of *Así era Pedro Infante,* the most popular documentary on the actor's filmography and funeral, with eleven movies over the five Sundays of the month. Cable subscribers enjoyed an eight-movie marathon on April 15 on De Película, a channel owned by the network that also appears as a mirror channel in the United States, where Spanish networks Univisión and Telemundo featured Infante movies on April 15.[11]

The 2007 celebration illustrated the contestation over Infante's legacy and patrimony. It featured masses at the national cathedral and the Basílica de Guadalaupe, which Televisa broadcast; a photographic tribute in the Chamber of Deputies; and the annual pilgrimage to his gravesite in the Panteón Jardín, where as many as fifty thousand people gathered to pray and to sing some of his songs.[12] It featured the Warner Brothers release in the United States of twenty-three of his movies on DVD, titles that had already sold over two million copies in Mexico, and the sale of a commemorative box set with all his music recordings. Infante's legacy thus lives on, and the seemingly impossible will reportedly take place soon: he will appear in the upcoming film *Tequila,* in which a special-effects team will superimpose his face on an actor and thus Infante, more than fifty years after his death, will play the supporting role of a gravedigger.[13]

For this anniversy, Irma Dorantes, his last love interest, abandoned her reticence and positioned herself as heir to his everlasting love. She published a personal account of their life, *Así fue nuestro amor,* which completed the biographical trilogy of Infante's most famous companions: Maria Luisa León's account appeared in 1961 as *Pedro Infante en la intimidad conmigo,* which eventually became the movie *La vida de Pedro Infante,* and Lupita Torrentera published *Un gran amor: La verdad en la vida de Lupita Torrentera y Pedro Infante* in 1991, in which she recounts their relationship and dedicates a few pages to her reaction to the news of his death and her experiences at the funeral. Dorantes, like León and Torrentera, claims sole possession of his true love. All three have unique claims: León was Infante's only legitimate wife but was unable to have children; Torrentera bore him three children—two survived—but did not live with him for any substantial amount of time; and Dorantes lived with him during the last five years of his life, although, as she painfully admits in her book, the annulment of their marriage caused her emotional and financial problems. She, nonetheless, cleverly narrates the other two women into literary inconsequentiality and ignobility, barely mentioning Torrentera and depicting León as heartless and avaricious. She asserts that Maria Luisa followed Infante to Mexico City in 1939 where a radio station had sent him, and not, as Maria Luisa claims, that they moved to the city together to seek his fortune. She also insists that Maria Luisa agreed to divorce Infante in exchange for a generous settlement that included one million pesos and 50 percent of his future earnings, but later continued to harass him to renegotiate.[14] After all, Infante died as he was making an emergency trip to Mexico City, at Dorantes's insistence, because a judge had ruled their marriage invalid since he had not legally divorced León.

Current disputes center almost entirely on financial issues and claims of control, and they involve two camps that one might label the *cousins* (Infante's surviving children and the two women who bore them) and the *siblings* (Infante's surviving siblings and their children). Thus, only the siblings attended the tribute at the Chamber of Deputies and the mass at the cathedral, and the cousins, associated with Televisa, participated in the televised morning mass at the Basílica and in the much-publicized ceremony at the Panteón Jardín. Dorantes continued her dissociation with public events by organizing a private evening mass at the Basílica. Only the cousins have direct access to his image to use, for example, in the current plan to develop a tequila brand bearing his name, and other sources of income. This occasionally threatens the business affiliation with Televisa, typically over royalty disputes.[15] The siblings, therefore, profit by association, and often accuse the cousins of exploitation and negligence. The latest dispute occurred when the siblings accused one of the cousins of attempting to auction the actor's gravestone, to which Lupita Infante asserted that the proceeds would go to charity, and she threatened to exhume the remains of her father and move them to another cemetery.[16]

Over the fifty years, conflict has continued over the story of Infante's life and career, and it has resulted in the emphasis on the films that Infante made with the director Ismael Rodríguez. Examining the issue helps explain why Infante, who had neither the best voice nor the greatest acting skills, enjoys such an enduring legacy, securing his position as the nation's most beloved entertainer and tragic figure. In part, his representation as a common man, a man of *el pueblo* (the people), cemented a popularity that was already unparalleled during his lifetime. His films and songs, his humble beginnings and his charisma, but also his death and funeral, the novelization of his life through documentaries, and the programming decisions of Televisa, all have combined to sustain him as Mexico's most popular icon of cinema and music. This interpretation revolves around his funeral to illustrate his popularity at the time of his sudden death, the public response to his tragic end, including its effect on the Mexican community in the United States, the role that images of his burial have acquired through the documentary *Así era Pedro Infante,* and the effect the documentary has produced in the almost inevitable association of Infante with Rodríguez. Infante's funeral marked the convergence of two Infantes—the end of his role as an actor and singer and his birth as a cultural and symbolic figure that have reverberated among old and new generations of fans. The connection between the two Infantes and his longevity and growing popularity lie in the events surrounding his death, including the self-serving editing of Rodríguez and the marketing tactics of Televisa.

Infante's death and funeral have had a significant impact on his legacy and lasting popularity. One can compare his death to that of Elvis Presley. Both died young (Presley at forty-two and Infante at thirty-nine) after exceptionally successful careers, and reports of their purported sightings have become common. Infante's death in a plane crash is also reminiscent of the assassination of president John F. Kennedy, as both were violent events that produced shock and disbelief in their respective countries. Hundreds of thousands of people attended Infante's public wake and funeral, illustrating the magnitude of his popularity and helping to secure his image as a caring and humble person, as a man of the people and the deep adoration of his fans, but the funerals of other Mexican entertainers have produced similar crowds and reactions. Infante himself had experience great anguish in 1953 when his friend and mentor Jorge Negrete (b. 1911) died of hepatitis complications in Los Angeles. An estimated two hundred thousand people followed the funeral procession through Mexico City, and his fellow actors openly mourned the death of the leader of their guild. Infante demonstrated tremendous grief as he stood guard during the vigil and in fact rode his motorcycle at the front of the caravan that took his friend to the same Panteón Jardín that would welcome him four years later. Newspapers, furthermore, have repeatedly used impressive descriptions of *thousands, multitudes,* and *el pueblo,* among others, as estimates of the crowds that attended Negrete's funeral and those of Javier Solís (1931–1966), Mario Moreno "Cantinflas" (1911–1993), Lola Beltrán

(1932–1996), Paco Stanley (1942–1999), and María Félix (1914–2002). None of these deaths and funerals could truly match the reaction to Infante in the collective memory of Mexicans and Mexican Americans that no other entertainer can rival.[17]

These celebrities had a strong fan base that inevitably grieved the loss of its luminaries. Solís died of postoperative complications, but he had become famous fairly recently and mostly for his singing ability—as his looks and acting did not compare favorably to either Infante or Negrete; "Cantinflas" died at the age of eighty-one, and he had not made a movie for more than a decade; Beltrán had been hospitalized recently, and her funeral took place outside of Mexico City; the murder of Stanley outside a restaurant outraged the population, but as he neither sang nor acted to any significant extent, his fame did not extent beyond daytime television; María Félix did indeed achieve great acclaim and admiration, but she died at the age of eighty-eight, and had not acted in more than thirty years. Their vigils and funerals certainly attracted thousands of people and, as in the case of Infante's funeral, famous entertainers and common people visibly grieved, prayed, and bid a musical farewell. Newspapers repeatedly referred to the massive turnout and outpour of emotions of *el pueblo* and *la gente popular*. Only Infante combined the acting and singing career, the good looks and charisma, and the public intrigue and tragic death that distinguished his death. Perhaps only Negrete could have achieved the lasting legacy Infante has attained, but unlike the latter, Negrete did not have the strong connection with Ismael Rodríguez nor would he have the marketing support of Televisa that eventually led to Infante's enshrinement as the unquestioned icon of the golden age of Mexican cinema and the most beloved and mourned entertainer the nation has known.[18]

Ismael Rodríguez, who directed sixteen of Infante's movies (among the most popular for both), released the documentary *Así era Pedro Infante* in 1963, reinforcing the connection between the actor and the populace.[19] The director in fact opens the film by commenting that he hopes the story will reverberate faithfully in the heart of *el pueblo*. Contemporaneous publicity for the film promised that the *ídolo del pueblo* had not really died and that the tribute Rodríguez offered was the story of Infante as told by *el pueblo*.[20] The documentary combines images from the funeral and excerpts from movies. The *pueblo* motif appears from the outset: a truck driver goes about his daily routine and turns up the volume on his radio to hear Infante sing "Que me toquen 'Las golondrinas'"; more images of ordinary men and women appear.[21] The narrator interrupts with the succinct and dramatic announcement of Infante's death.[22] He makes numerous references to the link between Infante and the working class, underscoring his humble beginning as a laborer from the countryside, a man who knew how to sing, laugh, and cry like the *pueblo* that now mourns his death. The film explains that the commotion of the people stemmed from their intimate sense of loss. They lined up in the streets and followed the caravan, crying and holding his picture.

The documentary immortalized the sorrow not only of family members but also of common people and famous actors. A mariachi plays "Las golondrinas," and the camera focuses on the dejected face of Mexico's best comedic actor, Cantinflas, who stood guard during the vigil and served as pallbearer at the funeral. Other famous actors—the Soler brothers, Eulalio González "Piporro," Luis Aguilar, Emilio Fernández, and Sara García—stood near the family, surrounding the grave. Viewers, furthermore, could contrast the memorably funny scenes of Fernando Soto "Mantequilla" as Infante's sidekick with a gloomy look on his face at the funeral as he unsuccessfully struggles to contain his tears. The film leaves no doubt that an extraordinary event has taken place, but it also reveals the talent of Rodríguez at its very best. *Así era Pedro Infante* remains the unrivaled authority on Infante's career and funeral.

Rodríguez has overcome several visual and literary challenges over who gets to shape the legacy of Pedro Infante. Not counting the revised version of *Así era Pedro Infante*—a mediocre film that Rodríguez's son released in 1994 and that makes no substantial contribution while deleting important parts of the original documentary[23]—three major efforts have attempted to appropriate the story of Infante's life. Rodríguez first envisaged making *Así era Pedro Infante* during the immediate aftermath of Infante's death, but he did not complete the film until 1963.[24] The same year, Miguel Zacarías, director of three of Infante's most successful movies, adapted a biography by Infante's widow, María Luisa León, to create a fictionalized version of the artist's life, ambitiously and misleadingly titled *La vida de Pedro Infante*.[25] Filming wrapped up in July 1963, four months before the Rodríguez documentary premiered, but Zacarías decided not to release the movie until 1966, thus avoiding direct competition.[26] Publicity for the movie, nonetheless, sought to draw a distinction with *Así era Pedro Infante*, promoting it as the genuine, human, and intimate cinematic version of Infante's life, not a mere documentary.[27] Both Zacarías and León, furthermore, must have understood that a contest over the legacy of Infante was taking place and thus underscored their role in his life: Zacarías included actual clips of the movies he directed as part of a plot that insinuates that Infante achieved success only after entering into an exclusive contract with him, while entirely ignoring the work of Rodríguez and other directors;[28] León similarly takes credit for skillfully guiding Infante to success even as his ascent to fame coincided with an increasing infidelity that she withstood with anguish and self-sacrifice. The plot revolves as much around Infante's career as it does around the effect his every move had on León. In real life, Infante had abandoned León and attempted to marry Irma Dorantes, but the latter only appears in a movie clip that precedes a scene where he tells León that he was only pretending to get divorced, presumably to fool Dorantes.[29] Infante, the movie repeatedly claims, saw León as his true love and was flying back to reunite with her on the day he died. *La vida de Pedro Infante* depicts a playful, naïve, and mischievous Infante for whom the women around him shaped and determined his triumphs and setbacks. The accident that took his life, the movie implies, might not have occurred had he carried with him the religious images León insisted he always take with him when he flew.[30]

The biographical representation of Infante received an important contribution in 1996 with the appearance of *Cine gloria: Pedro Infante*, a documentary made for an independent television station in Mexico City.[31] The film, illustrating its journalistic and academic approach, proves superior to *Así era Pedro Infante* and *La vida de Pedro Infante* in its treatment of the actor's childhood, family, early career as a singer and actor, and rise to fame. Thus, it includes scenes from movies by various directors to exemplify the most memorable traits—playfulness, bravery, charisma, and singing ability of his characters—and to show him in important moments of his career. For example, his first appearance on film, first leading role, and first film for Rodríguez appeared in no other documentary. It includes his first cinematic incursion as an extra in *En un burro tres baturros* (1939) and his role as a Spaniard—dubbed by a Spanish actor—in *La razón de la culpa* (1942). The film indeed begins with a balanced account of his life and career, but it eventually devolves into a tribute to Rodríguez, who appears holding a list of the movies he directed and discusses each film and explains how he transformed Infante from talented but raw actor and singer into such a popular performer. The film accentuates that by the 1990s the legacies of Infante and Rodríguez had become inseparable.

Jaime Kuri's *No me parezco a nadie: La vida de Pedro Infante*, the best documentary to date, appeared in the Televisa series México Siglo XX in 1998.[32] It contains numerous photographs and videos to recount Infante's life: his birth, childhood, family, early days as a singer in Culiacán, move to Mexico City, and ascent to national and international prominence. Unlike previous cinematic efforts, Kuri underscores Infante's professional and personal lives equally efficiently. The film follows his increasing singing and acting triumphs but also his unstable love life and his personal anguish as he copes with the deaths of his friend and mentor Jorge Negrete, his cinematic love interest and personal friend Blanca Estela Pavón, and his father. Scenes from his most important movies appear mostly in chronological order and include all of Rodríguez's films but also eighteen other films by various directors. Such a diverse compilation grants the viewer access, for instance, to the memorable scene of a duet with Pedro Vargas, one of Mexico's most renowned singers, that could not have appeared in the self-promoting Rodríguez and Zacarías films since it comes from *También de dolor se canta*, directed by René Cardona.[33] The documentary does contain some problems, nonetheless. It, for example, promotes the primacy of the Rodríguez films by incorrectly asserting that the tremendous box-office success of *Nosotros los pobres* (1948) convinced the director of filming a sequel. The movie did not play for months, as the narrator avers. In fact, its first run lasted only five weeks as the lead of a double feature and later returned for a mere nine days in discounted theaters.[34] Nor, as one movie critic argues, was Rodríguez a marketing genius for selecting a plebeian neighborhood for its premiere.[35] As late as 1957, during the aftermath of Infante's death, the movie played only sparingly, remaining in theaters far less time than some of the films the actor did for other directors. Its relative success, nonetheless, might have indeed influenced Rodríguez since it represented his biggest attainment to date and a feat he would not surpass until *Tizoc*, which premiered after Infante's death and ran for seven weeks. Kuri's documentary, its minor flaws notwithstanding, offers the most balanced account of Infante's life.

One would assume then that Televisa and the Spanish-language networks in the United States would favor Kuri's documentary instead of *Así era Pedro Infante*, but the latter conveys the emotional elements that resonate more acutely among Infante's fans. Rodríguez did not make the best documentary, but he did produce the most dramatic story. As a director of melodramas, he created one more fictional story for his beloved actor: this tale suggests that these are his greatest films and that only Rodríguez could have assisted in their creation; only Rodríguez could have related such a story, because, at the time, only he saw Infante's career so firmly tied to his. His tale eventually became reality. No one can tell the extent to which his documentary and the constant playing of his movies by Televisa have shaped the preferences of Infante's fans, but there does a exist a clear divergence between the films his fans preferred before and after Rodríguez, in effect, announced that Infante's greatest movies came under his direction. He skillfully captured the drama that surrounded Infante's death, a phenomenon that the death of other Mexican celebrities also produced, and injected his cinematic touch to help to prolong the legacies of both actor and director.

The documentary effectively captures Rodríguez´s ability to create some of the most memorable moments in the history of Mexican cinema. An assortment of clips presents Infante in both dramatic and comedic moments, demonstrating that his characters experienced both pain and happiness to their fullest. Rodríguez exhibited a particular talent in combining Infante's acting, charisma, and singing ability to create emotionally charged scenes. The documentary thus contains a wide range of emotional moments, such as Infante singing "Mi cariñito" while drunk at a cantina, unable to cope with the death of his adored grandmother, who loved the song; a singing duel between Infante and Jorge Negrete, one of his biggest contemporary cinematic rivals—although, contrary to popular belief, a good friend and mentor to Infante, who admired Negrete's superior singing ability and his altruistic endeavors;[36] one of the most romantic scenes in Mexican cinema as Infante, playing the role of a carpenter, sings "Amorcito Corazón" to his dear Chorreada across the hallway of their tenement; a heartfelt rendition of "¿Qué te ha dado esa mujer?" accompanied by a choir of fellow police officers as he laments the estrangement with his best friend; and the simple but meaningful serenade "Te quiero más que a mis ojos" that Infante as the Indian Tizoc sings to the white-complexioned María, played by María Félix.[37] These Infante songs, along with many others, have become virtually inseparable from the cinematic moments that accompany them. Listening to "Amorcito Corazón," for instance, immediately conjures up images of Infante and Blanca Estela Pavón, deeply in love and tragically connected in film by the death of their child and in real life by their deaths in separate plane accidents, though eternally reunited in their neighboring burial plots at the Panteón Jardín and in the collective memory of Infante fans across the Hispanic world. The documentary has helped to convince the public that these scenes and movies best represent the immortal Infante.

The documentary in fact cemented not only Infante's immortality but also ensured Rodríguez's fame as one of the eminent directors of the golden age of Mexican cinema. It opens with a written statement where Rodríguez announces that the film contains Infante's favorite scenes. The compilation clearly sought to highlight the best work Infante did for Rodríguez, since, far from offering a representative assemblage of the actor's filmography, Rodríguez only included movies that he directed.[38] It even includes a brief clip from an interview that took place one year before Infante's death and in which Infante praises and thanks Rodríguez for his vision and commitment. The conclusion becomes inescapable: Infante owed his legacy to Rodríguez. The director stated in an interview he gave a few months before his own death in 2004, that he did not create Pedro Infante, as the interviewer suggested, that he simply found the characters that made him who he was.[39] Thus, Rodríguez tones down the statement. Yet, as he did in his documentary, he still circumscribes Infante within the realm of the movies he directed. Such a declaration does not entirely lack merit, for the two indeed collaborated in some of the most popular films of the era, and their legacies deservedly became intertwined. The primacy of the Rodríguez films in Infante's career, nevertheless, only emerged after the actor's death and the appearance of *Así era Pedro Infante*.

The preeminence of Rodríguez's productions among the most popular films in Infante's career, in fact in the history of Mexican cinema, finds a strong corroboration in recent proclamations by television programmers and movie critics. The magazine *Somos uno* polled twenty-five movie experts in 1994 and published a list of the one hundred greatest Mexican films. Seven of Infante's films appeared in the list—only surpassed by Pedro Armendáriz (eight) among actors—and Rodríguez placed in a tie for second with eight films among directors—only behind Emilio Fernández (ten).[40] Infante and Rodríguez collaborated in six of these movies, and, remarkably, two of the films in which they did not work together—*Escuela de vagabundos*, for Infante, and *La cucaracha*, for Rodríguez—fell outside the first eighty-nine films that received enough votes to qualify for a ranking.[41] A 2007 interview lends even more credence to the popularity of the Infante-Rodríguez movies fifty years after the actor's death. Luis Terán, director of movie programming for Televisa, compiled a list of the twenty most popular Infante movies based on viewer demand, ratings, and sales at video stores. Rodríguez's movies occupied the top six spots, ten of the first twelve, and accounted for thirteen of the twenty films. In other words, only three Rodríguez films failed to make the list.[42]

One might incorrectly surmise, as indeed does the journalist who interviewed Luis Terán, that the documentary offers a representative assemblage of Infante's best work or most memorable cinematic moments. Such a conclusion may simply illustrate the effect that the documentary and Televisa's programmers have had on public perception. Namely, the emotional depiction of Infante's death, the montage of clips from Rodríguez's movies, the reiteration by Televisa that those films indeed represent the actor's best work—all have combined to create a self-fulfilling prophecy. The viewing public and movie critics alike may truly perceive these films as the best of Infante's career, but insistence and repetition might have prompted their seemingly personal preferences. Of course, Rodríguez could have included clips from movies by other directors. Other producers, in particular Antonio Matouk, who, fully or partially, financed all Infante movies after 1953, would have certainly permitted the use of his films. Antonio Matouk and Rodríguez in fact traveled to Germany together to pick up Infante's posthumous award at the Berlin International Film Festival, and Producciones Matouk even collaborated in the documentary.[43] Limiting the montage to his movies meant that Rodríguez neglected to include powerful scenes that perfectly fit the tone of his film, particularly its musical motif: in *Cuidado con el amor* Infante sings "Cien años," one of his most popular songs, to Elsa Aguirre; he romances Miroslava with "Grito prisionero" in *Escuela de vagabundos*; in *El inocente* he and Silvia Pinal playfully sing a potpourri of children's songs, and he passionately sings "No volveré" when distraught over their relationship; he teasingly sings "Ella" to Libertad Lamarque in *Escuela de música* and serenades Irasema Dilián with "Te amaré, vida mía" in *Pablo y Carolina*. These scenes could have justifiably figured in the documentary as representative Infante performances. The films, furthermore, have indeed received public and critical acclaim. *Escuela de vagabundos* and *El inocente* placed seventh and eighth in Terán's list, and the former was the only non-Rodríguez film to make the *Somos uno* list. All of these films achieved excellent box-office success during their original runs in Mexico City, yet Rodríguez excluded them from the documentary simply because he did not direct them.[44]

Box-office data from the original releases in Mexico City also offer a noteworthy revelation: Rodríguez's films consistently underperformed relative to the films of other directors and producers. In fact, Antonio Matouk, who also served as Infante's manager, guided the actor to feats that Rodríguez never matched. Only two of Rodríguez's films played for five weeks or more during their original release: *Nosotros los pobres* (1948), which ran for five weeks, and *Tizoc* (1957), which premiered after Infante's death and played for seven weeks but was in fact a Matouk-Infante production. The Rodríguez films typically played for an average of three weeks and later appeared, as most Infante films, as part of double features in discounted theaters.[45] Even the movies that eventually made the lists as best or most popular films fared only slightly better. The six films that appear on both lists, for instance, played for an average of only 3.5 weeks. Matouk, on the other hand, produced or coproduced the last thirteen films of Infante's career in a three-year period after *Pepe el Toro*, during which Rodríguez and Infante worked together only on *Tizoc*. Not counting *Tizoc*, those twelve movies played for an average of almost seven weeks in their first run, or twice as long as the Rodríguez films. Seven Matouk films actually matched or surpassed the seven-week *Tizoc* run, Rodríguez's longest, and *Escuela de música* and *Escuela de rateros* played for twelve weeks each. Finally, films like *Pablo y Carolina* and *La tercera palabra*, which failed to make any list, originally played for nine and ten weeks, respectively. Matouk had clearly discovered what audiences wanted out of Infante.

The weeks that followed the death of Infante also attest to the relative inconsequentiality of the Rodríguez films in the 1950s. Infante films were making their typical rounds in the discounted theaters even before news of his death appeared. Movie listings for April 15, 1957, illustrate that one Infante movie was playing in Mexico City and three more were already scheduled for the next few days. The next thirty days witnessed a return of most of his films, as forty-eight of the fifty-three movies he had released appeared mainly as matinees in both discounted and first-run theaters.[46] The only premiere, *Pablo y Carolina*, played as a single feature for nine weeks, but some of his older films also had long runs during April and May of that year: *Pueblo, Canto y Esperanza*, *El inocente*, and *La tercera palabra* played for many days, and on May 2, two weeks after his death, six theaters began Infante double features of *Escuela de música* and *Cuidado con el amor*, both of which had enjoyed great success during their original release more than two years earlier.[47] Rodríguez did not direct any of these films, and while his Infante movies did play during this period, all of them had brief runs, typically of one or two days. In fact, some films that eventually became classics and made the Terán and *Somos uno* lists and play frequently on Televisa returned to theaters more than three weeks after Infante's death and played only briefly: *A toda máquina*—which Terán listed as Infante's most popular movie—*Los tres huastecos*, and *No desearás la mujer de tu hijo* arrived in theaters almost four weeks after his death and only for short stints.[48]

One might argue that in spite of the original lack of success, the quality of the Rodríguez films eventually triumphed among the public, but the Rodríguez documentary and the programming decisions of Televisa with its exclusive rights to Infante's movies have undoubtedly influenced public perception and preferences. Rodríguez fully understood the momentous opportunity the Infante funeral presented. He coordinated the filming of the footage that eventually served as the basis for the documentary, focusing particular attention on the displays of affection and grief, not only on the part of the general public, but also, and especially, on the faces of members of the movie industry, including images of Rodríguez himself as he attends the vigil and the funeral. The narrator Arturo de Córdova, one of Mexico's greatest actors, repeatedly reminds the viewer that Pedro Infante has died, interweaving his comments between images of Rodríguez's films and the sorrowful faces of fellow actors, most of whom, perhaps not by coincidence, appeared in those productions. The message seems clear: these are Infante's greatest movies, the scenes he loved the most according to the opening credits, and these actors accompanied him as he achieved his best work.

The documentary clearly had Mexicans as its primary audience, but Infante's death also reverberated outside of Mexico, particularly in the United States southwest. The Mexican press reported on extensive media coverage from Colombia and Venezuela.[49] One can assume that the same occurred in other countries where his movies and songs played and where he performed. His death also made news in English-language newspapers in Chicago, New York, and, especially, Los Angeles, where not only the Spanish-language *La Opinión* covered the story, but also the *Los Angeles Times*,[50] which frequently had reported on Infante's movies and live performances in local theaters during the previous thirteen years.[51] Spanish-language newspapers throughout the Southwest most likely responded in similar fashion, like the examples of *El Tucsonense* (Tucson) and *La Prensa* (San Antonio) illustrate.[52] Theaters where Infante had performed—the Mayan, the Million Dollar, and the California—played his movies, gave away photographs, and broadcast news bulletins that included photographs of the accident and his burial.[53]

Hispanics in the United States embraced Mexican movies as early as the 1920s, a penchant that increased and caused an expansion in the number of Spanish-language theaters during the 1940s and 1950s. Mexican films became a regular feature in approximately 300 theaters by 1945, and by their peak in 1951, they played in as many as 653 screens in 443 cities, most prominently in Texas, California, Colorado, New Mexico, and Arizona, and to a lesser extent in agricultural and industrial areas in states like Kansas, Nebraska, and Michigan, and in urban areas like Chicago and New York City. Such growth coincided with the golden age of Mexican cinema, but also with the increase in Mexican immigration due to the Bracero Program and clandestine crossings that responded to wartime industrial and agricultural necessities and to the postwar boom. Mexican films played in English-language theaters in many states but provided the main source of income for a number of theaters in cities with high concentrations of Spanish speakers, like El Paso, San Antonio, and Los Angeles. Armando del Moral, a refugee of the Spanish Civil War, capitalized on the rising interest of the public by creating *La Novela Cine-Gráfica* (1949–1964), a Los Angeles magazine that published novelized versions of the latest Mexican films and, later, articles and pictures of the most famous Spanish-speaking entertainers.[54]

Infante enjoyed unparalleled popularity among the Mexican community in the United States. Theater owners relied on Infante movies to perform particularly well at the box office, playing them frequently as double features with new films that might not excel on their own. The popularity of his films became even more apparent after his death, when many of his old movies played for several weeks and his three final films far outsold movies by other actors. Infante films played continuously in Los Angeles theaters for approximately two months after his death. Theaters in the United States represented such an important market that Infante's last two films—*Tizoc* and *Escuela de rateros*—premiered in San Antonio months before they opened in Mexico.[55] Readers of *La Novela Cine-Gráfica* expressed their overwhelming preference for Infante as early as 1950. The magazine conducted a poll to determine what entertainers should appear as Personality of the Month in forthcoming issues. The first monthly distinction went to Infante when fans selected him by more than a two-to-one margin over Jorge Negrete. He won again the following month, then again, and continued to win until the editors understood the flaw of their feature: unless they made Infante ineligible, he would win every month. Indeed, Infante remained on top of every poll, and his margin of victory only increased. The contest eventually ended after repeated attempts to encourage readers to support other celebrities. The final results placed Infante as the clear winner, receiving more votes than the next five entertainers combined.[56] *La Novela* regularly included features on Infante, and its June 1957 issue illustrated the impact his death caused in Los Angeles. In fact, the editors had to skip the May issue and omit regular pieces in June so they could provide extensive coverage of Infante's life and death. Del Moral, chief editor and friend of Infante, wrote a biographical sketch in which he underscored the strong connections Infante had with the Mexican community in the United States, including his recent tour in California and Arizona in 1955 and the humble origins of the Rodríguez brothers, who left their bakery business in Los Angeles and eventually produced many of his films.[57] (Ismael Rodríguez spent two long periods in Los Angeles: he attended elementary and junior high school, worked in his parents' bakery between 1926 and 1930, and attended the Radio-Television Institute of California while working as busboy and shoe repairman between 1935 and 1937.[58]) *La Novela* marked the first anniversary of Infante's death by putting him on the cover—with the plain and telling caption "El ídolo del pueblo"—and offering a pictorial tribute that included images of Infante's visits to the Million Dollar Theater in Los Angeles.[59]

La Opinión probably offered the most extensive coverage of any major newspaper in Mexico and the United States, illustrating the popularity Infante enjoyed among Los Angeles's Mexican community and, most likely, in other southwestern towns and in Chicago. Coverage of his death appeared on the front page of *La Opinión* from April 16 to 21, and on April 22 the paper began the weeklong column "El Pedro Infante que conocí," where Armando del Moral recounted the performer's life, particularly his connections to Los Angeles. The paper underscored his humble origins and his appeal among all social classes, often printing reports from Mexico City's *El Universal*.[60] "Pedro Infante es una fuerza," a similar series, ran in *El Tucsonense*, Tucson's Spanish-language newspaper, from August 16 to December 20, 1957. The feature appeared almost entirely on the front page and included a large headline that invited readers to learn about his life. The editors of these newspapers clearly understood the marketing power Infante commanded even after death, and their coverage remained a major feature long after Mexico City newspapers had moved on to other news.[61] Del Moral characterized Infante as humble, generous, and sincere, as a performer of *el pueblo* who always remained true to his people, even claiming that his performances in Texas, California, and Arizona took place at a crucial moment in his career. Infante, del Moral posited, would have remained unnoticed had he not triumphed in *el Mexico de afuera*.[62]

Novelist Denise Chávez effectively captures Infante's significance to the Mexican community in *Loving Pedro Infante*. Infante and his movies influence the lives of the protagonist and all the other members of the Pedro Infante Club de Admiradores Norteamericano #256. The author infuses a complex intertextual relationship between her novel and the life, songs, and movies of the Mexican icon. The constant citations of Pedro Infante films and music enhance the understanding and appreciation of *Loving Pedro Infante*. Characters frequently make comparisons between his films and their lives, making social commentary and drawing conclusions about morality, patriarchy, and personal conduct.[63] Tere, the protagonist, whose most salient characteristic is her love, bordering on obsession, of Pedro Infante and his movies, continues an unhealthy love affair with Lucio, hoping that he will turn out to be as caring as the Infante characters—for instance, as the womanizer in *La vida no vale nada*. Tere continually expects that Lucio will complete her film fantasy and keeps waiting for a dramatic twist in which he will walk through the door, admit his wrongdoing, and pledge his eternal love as an Infante character would. In another example, *Angelitos negros* triggers an animated discussion among club members on race, and one club member bluntly says, "Black, gay, it's all the same thing. A sin against God, nature and Pedro Infante."[64] These comments serve a dual purpose: they inform the reader about the opinions of these characters, and they criticize those members of the Mexican American community who hold racist and homophobic viewpoints. The infusion of Infante references reaches such an extent that readers most familiar with his films and music will undoubtedly make intertextual connections that will provide greater character development and more insightful conclusions. In fact, the turning point in the novel offers such an example of intertextuality: while looking into a mirror, Tere notices that she feels like Cruz, Pedro Infante's father in *No desearás la mujer de tu hijo*. Tere realizes that her love affair will never bring her happiness and that she, unlike Cruz, must accept her reality. Readers familiar with the film know that Cruz refuses to accept that he has aged, gets on his son's horse, and falls while attempting to prove he can still jump over a gate. Cruz eventually dies from his injuries. Symbolically, however, he dies because he cannot cope with a reality in which he is not a revered macho.[65] Tere, on the other hand, perceives an authentic, impartial reality and accepts its implications. She proves that, unlike Cruz and other Pedro Infante characters, her life does not have to follow a script. The new Tere differentiates between the idylls of film and the struggles and shortcomings of romance and real men including the real Pedro Infante. The title of the novel thus refers both to Tere's adoration for Pedro Infante and specifically to the loving Infante she saw, not to the decadent, irredeemable, and chauvinist men like Lucio.

One cannot dismiss the connection between Infante and *el pueblo* as mere media fabrication.[66] Common people understandably related to his characters and to his background. He, like hundreds of thousands of other working-class Mexicans, migrated to Mexico City in search of economic opportunities. Thus, as the populations of small villages steadily declined and that of the capital almost tripled between 1940 and 1960, more people shared the plight of the rural and urban characters of his movies.[67] Infante and his films and songs also resonated strongly among the residents of Mexican ancestry who lived in the United States and the millions of immigrants, mostly laborers from rural areas of central Mexico, who arrived between 1940 and 1960, either as temporary workers under the Bracero Program or as legal or undocumented immigrants. This surging population resided primarily in places Infante visited as a performer in Arizona, California, Illinois, New Mexico, and Texas.[68] These audiences could thus catch a glimpse of the life they or their ancestors left behind. His songs, furthermore, told stories of pain and misery, of loves lost, of drinking to forget one's suffering, but he also recorded "Las mañanitas," Mexico's most popular birthday song, which instantly became his label's biggest-selling record and, according to a recent estimate, reigns as the country's biggest-selling album of all time.[69] Some authors focus exclusively on the patriarchal and despairing messages in his songs and movies, overlooking the redeeming qualities that his characters invariably possessed. Infante, in other words, reminded poor people of who they were or wanted to be. His triumphs and plight were vicariously theirs and so was his death.

Several factors distinguish Infante's funeral from those of other famous performers: his death came suddenly and violently when he was at the pinnacle of his career; *el pueblo* greatly identified with his persona and his fictional characters; and coverage of his funeral further helped to perpetuate his image as a humble and honest person. *Así era Pedro Infante* served a dual purpose: it helped to dramatize his life even more—further endearing him with his fans—and to create the perception that Rodríguez directed his best and most popular films, an appreciation that contemporaneous audiences did not express at the box office. Television stations in Mexico and the United States often broadcast this documentary, especially on the anniversary of his death, a date faithfully observed by the fans who visit his grave every year.

The Infante legacy endures, and the vicarious existences of family, companions, and directors alike illustrate not that each of them was particularly central in shaping his life, but on the contrary, that he was the most important person who ever entered their lives. Unlike the continuing family contest over his image and patrimony and the rivalry among three women for recognition as his true love, the competition over the cinematic Infante has indeed produced an undisputed victor: Rodríguez encapsulated an enduring characterization that other films—of lesser and greater quality—have been unable to match; actor and director have become inseparable. The documentary might thus rank as Rodriguez's greatest directorial feat. Infante's image as a man of the people has remained particularly popular in Mexico and the United States greatly due to his connection to the type of person who most frequently migrates north:

poor and until recently rural. Hispanics in Los Angeles convinced a local city council to name a street after him in 1983, and he has a star on the Hollywood Walk of Fame.[70] For Denise Chavez's protagonist, he represents the only reliable constancy in her life and a strong reminder of her heritage. He had flaws, but like her people, he also had redeeming qualities. She sees the eternally young and handsome Pedro Infante that Mexicans and Latin Americans have seen since he first appeared on the movie screen in 1939. *Así era Pedro Infante* and *La vida de Pedro Infante* end in strikingly similar fashion: Infante is dead, the narrators remind the viewer, yet he is still alive; he emerged from *el pueblo* and he will continue living and singing *en el corazón del pueblo*.[71] Such statements continue to prove correct more than fifty years after his death.

SUGGESTED READINGS

Amezcua Castillo, Jesús. *Pedro Infante: Medio Siglo de Idolatría*. Mexico: Ediciones B, Grupo Zeta, 2007.

Monsiváis, Carlos. *Pedro Infante: Las leyes del querer*. Mexico City: Aguilar, 2009.

Mora, Carl J. *Mexican Cinema: Reflections of a Society, 1896–2004*. London: McFarland and Company, 2005.

Mora, Sergio de la. *Cinemachismo: Masculinities and Sexuality in Mexican Cinema*. Austin: University of Texas Press, 2006.

Nobel, Andrea. *Mexican National Cinema*. New York: Routledge, 2005.

Sights

Así Era Pedro Infante. 2007. Directed by Ismael Rodríguez. Warner Home Video/ Madera CineVideo.

Colección Pedro Infante: La triología de Pepe El Toro. 2009. Directed by Ismael Rodríguez.

Los Tres Huastecos. 1948. Directed by Ismael Rodríguez.

Nosotros los Pobres. 1947. Directed by Ismael Rodríguez.

Tizoc. 1957. Directed by Ismael Rodríguez.

Sounds

Homenaje a Pedro Infante: 50 Aniversario. (EM Music Mexico, Miami Beach, FL)

15

Nostalgia for the Future: The New Song Movement in Nicaragua

Janet L. Sturman

Music serves as the sounds, lyrics, and rhythms of political revolutions, social changes, military repressions, and most other milestones that shape individual, community, and national lives. Later the same music acts as a mnemonic, inspiring memories of these events or creating associations with them. For example, events such as the French revolution, Colombian wars for independence, U.S. intervention in Central America, Mexican Revolution, or Latin American student movements are associated with La Marseillaise, La Guaneña, Alexander's Ragtime Band, la Cucaracha, and Venceremos. The riptide of social insurrection and student demonstrations inspired musicians in the fervid belief that songs, especially in the genre of nueva canción *with its folk music base, could remake society in the 1960s and early 1970s. Not even the discovery of Soviet missiles in Cuba (1963) and the military overthrow of Salvador Allende in Chile (1973), causing doubts about Castro's revolutionary independence and resulting in repression, imprisonment, and death for Chilean Leftists, could diminish the belief in the dynamic role of music. While studies have focused on Chilean* nueva canción *with its personification in Victor Jara, a victim of Pinochet's death camp, or Cuban* nueva trova, *other studies have begun to examine this music in Venezuela and other locations. Here Janet Sturman examines* nueva canción *and its relation to revolution in Nicaragua.*

Volcanto! The word explodes with its joint reference to song (*canto*) and to the volcanoes (*volcanes*) that comprise a distinctive element of the Central American landscape. Surfacing as an album title with the subtitle ¡Aquí no se rinde nadie! (Here, no one gives up!), it became Nicaragua's catchy signature label for socially conscious song. As a genre, *volcanto* represents a practice rooted in the relatively recent and far from homogenous Latin

American tradition of new song: *nueva canción*. Few scholars, with notable exceptions such as Jan Fairley, T. M. Scruggs, and Greg Landau, have paid much attention to *nueva canción* in Central America.[1] Yet the trajectory of the genre in this volatile region provides some of the clearest examples of the continuing belief of musicians and their listeners that song has the power to point the way toward a new future. This chapter will focus on the work of Nicaraguan artists representing different generations and connecting in different ways to the history of the new song movement in Latin America. While creating new song to address local concerns, Central American artists drew inspiration from a larger movement of popular song that swept Latin America after its emergence in the 1950s. Although styles differed significantly, a common thread linking these artists, despite generational and regional differences, is their shared view that music serves as a tool for influencing the present, reclaiming the past, and most important, creating the future. This perspective gives rise to the distinctive directions of the last group of performers examined in this chapter, Duo Guardabarranco, with their ecological songs that link past and future. By challenging histories and social policies that emerged from colonial legacies and global commerce, the leaders of the new song movement reviewed the past with selective nostalgia for its yet unfulfilled promise of the future.

FRAMING CONCEPTS: RECOLLECTION, PROTEST, POPULARITY

In looking back, the singers of new song sought to reclaim the past as well as critique it, and although many of the leaders of the movement came from the among the intelligentsia and were of comfortable economic status, they eschewed elite expression and chose popular music as their medium.[2] An opening example from the Central American nation of El Salvador offers a point of departure for a more general introduction to the new song movement.

In 1975 four Salvadoran teenagers, brothers Franklin and Roberto Quezada along with Paulino Espinoza and Manuel Gómez, formed the musical group Yolocamba I Ta. The name mixes two languages of people indigenous to El Salvador, the Lenca and the Chorti, and literally means "rebellion in the sowing season," a reference to the crowds of antigovernment demonstrators that had assembled in San Salvador only to be fired upon and massacred by the military. Singing and performing on guitar, mandolin, flute and drum, Yolocambi I Ta used the sounds of *música popular* to bear witness to the events of this brutal repression and continued to support antigovernment reformists during the tumultuous era that ensued. Franklin Quezada states, "El artista, y sobre todo el trovador, es un cronista de su tiempo. Uno no puede quedarse callado ante la injusticia." (The artist, and above all the singer, is a chronicler of his time. One cannot stay quiet in the face of injustice.)[3] The group's sense of responsibility and its overt recognition of indigenous residents and workers denied recognition, land, and rights by official government policies represented concerns shared by many of the creators of new song across Latin America.

Yolocambi I Ta's[4] first recording was called *Basta Ya!* (Enough Already!).[5] While directed in this case at specific Salvadoran experience, the phrase might easily serve as a slogan encapsulating a fundamental sentiment that gave rise to *nueva canción* as a musical movement. As early as the 1950s and continuing into the next three decades, musicians, singers, and songwriters across Latin America felt they had enough of repressive leaders, debilitating traditions of social hierarchy, lack of concern for working class people, limited access to education, and the choking residual cultural patrimony of colonizing powers. They turned to song to convey their exasperation, support rebel forces, and point the way to social change.

The musicians of Yolocambi I Ta, like many across Latin America, had also enough of the encroachment of foreign music, whether popular, classical, or elite. Radio and the increasingly international recording and film industry brought commercial music, including jazz and rock from the United States, as well as European pop, especially the Beatles. The threat of encroachment and displacement was not limited to the influence of American and British rock and pop. Cuban dance music as well as Mexican boleros and mariachi enjoyed wide circulation in Central and Latin American.[6] Listeners enthusiastically embraced this imported music as evidence of their cosmopolitan taste, frequently at the expense of homegrown popular or traditional music styles. The Latin American new song movement began in part to address this encroachment. Individual artists developed their own responses, and trends differed from one country to the next, but even as individual national traditions of new song developed, the simultaneous rejection and adoption of practices from borrowed popular music became a defining quality of *nueva canción*. In addition to this inherently contradictory stance, new song artists have also had to contend with the popularity (or nonpopularity) of their own work. While *nueva canción* became popular in limited, well-defined circles, and certain artists have achieved star or hero status, in general, artists in the new song movement addressed popularity with ambiguity and caution. Indeed the growing pan-Latin community of new song artists tended to reject performers who achieved too much commercial recognition; no matter how outspoken they were regarding matters of social reform. Landau offers the example of singers and songwriters present at the 1981 UNESCO meetings dedicated to Nueva Canción Latinoamericana arguing that Panamanian salsa performer Ruben Blades was too mainstream and therefore too distant from the core of the movement to be considered a new song *trovador*. This view held sway despite Blades's probing, poetic, and socially conscious song lyrics. For those critics, the commercial success of his recordings, which had become global hits in the international marketplace, overshadowed his social conscience.[7]

Central American and Nicaraguan new song artists allied with each other and with *nueva canción* artists representing other Latin American nations. To better define this pan–Latin American song tradition, and to frame the later discussion of developments in Central America, a brief exploration of the complicated and varied stances of new song proponents in Chile, Argentina, Cuba, and Puerto Rico will follow.

DEFINING *NUEVA CANCIÓN*: CHILEAN ACTIVISTS

Most histories of Latin American *nueva canción* begin with activity in Chile. Chilean new song epitomizes the power inherent in the movement and its combination of nostalgia with visions of a new future. The pioneer of Chilean *nueva canción* was Violeta Parra (1917–1967), a singer-songwriter who initiated a series of investigations into Chilean folk music in the 1950s. In the 1960s, her efforts to transform society with music gained new support by activist singer-composer Victor Jara and socially conscious musicians who followed in Parra's footsteps, including the ensembles Quilapayún and Inti Illimani, as well as her own children Angel and Isabel.[8] Victor Jara became a legend in his own right because of his artistry, influence, and tragic death. He used music structure, in particular national dance rhythms, such as the *cueca*, and evocative melodic contours to underscore his poetic texts. His singing and guitar playing painted musical pictures of verbal imagery and the messages of his lyrics. He sang tributes to underrecognized local heroes representing farmers, craftsmen, and laborers, and people paid attention. The intelligentsia rallied around Jara and other singers of new songs celebrating local people and values. Café-style social clubs, especially at universities and in city centers, provided supportive environments for the new song movement by hosting *peñas* (literally clubs) where young, educated listeners drank wine, shared poetry, and sang along with the presenters. Chilean new song in the 1970s helped secure popular support for the election of the socialist reformer Salvador Allende to the presidency.[9] Allende's rise to power inspired social reformists throughout Latin America, including Central America, but it alarmed the political right and worried political allies, including the United States, who feared the encroaching influence of communism in the region. Allende's presidency was short-lived; he died on September 11, 1973, in the coup led by General Agusto Pinochet to overthrow his government.[10] Chilling evidence of the power imputed to new song in Chile was the subsequent murder of Victor Jara only six days later and the exile of sympathetic musicians after the overthrow of President Allende by General Pinochet.[11]

DEFINING *NUEVA CANCIÓN*: ARGENTINEAN SONG COLLECTORS

Musicians in Argentina were equally important in launching the *nueva canción* movement; indeed some scholars claim the new song movement begins with Argentine efforts.[12] The indomitable singer Mercedes Sosa (b. 1935) began compiling her *cancionero argentino* in the 1950s. Her efforts to collect music representing the folk and historic traditions of the many different Argentine regions provided source material for new songs that merged traditional sounds with contemporary concerns. Her work initiated an early and crucial theme of the new song movement, that of revitalization, even resuscitation, of local culture. Her compatriot, Atahualpa Yupanqui (1908–1992), a skilled guitarist, achieved renown for his newly created folk songs championing the causes of the poor, particularly the Andean campesino, and for weaving Andean styles into his music.[13] One of the successes was to convince Argentine national radio stations to include local music as part of the daily programming. Most importantly for this chapter, their efforts underscore one of the principal goals of the new song movement: to celebrate local, regional culture and bring it to the attention of urban listeners and international audiences. The time-honored traditions they promoted, the *canto nativo* (native song), as Yupanqui referred to his music, became the base for a music of a new future.

DEFINING *NUEVA CANCIÓN*: CUBAN REVOLUTIONARY IDEALS

The Cuban revolution in 1959 had a tremendous influence across Latin America in a way that might be difficult to appreciate for readers from the United States, where official trade and political boycott of Cuba's Communist state continues. For many Latin Americans Castro's success in reforming society indicated that dramatic change, and resistance to the regulations influenced by foreign commerce, was indeed possible. Thus singers of new song from Cuba served as spokesmen for revolutionary ideals.

In Cuba the new song movement was called *nueva trova*, to emphasize its affiliation with a distinguished heritage of poetic song. Castro's revolutionary government provided official support for singer-songwriters who might serve as the voice of the people, and the new government. Such support facilitated the circulation of the anthem-like ballads of the movement's signature artists, the most famous of which was Silvio Rodriguez (b. 1946). Rodriguez believed that music should have a goal beyond protest and should present a new vision of a just society, and his perspective inspired many of his contemporaries as well as artists to follow. So well known were the songs of Rodriguez that young Cuban listeners well into the 1980s would join together en masse, singing along to sanctioned broadcasts of his songs over public address systems at large civic gatherings. Government support of this kind was uncommon in other Latin American countries where the *trovadores* more often operated in opposition to the political mainstream.

Rodriguez became a popular hero and spiritual leader in Cuba and abroad. His work also illustrates the stylistic diversity inherent in the pan-American new song movement. In contrast with the new singer-songwriters in Chile and Argentina, initially, Rodriguez did *not* customarily incorporate local folk or traditional music into his songs. Cuban rhythms such as the habanera, rumba, mambo, or forms like *son* do not shape his songs.[14] Instead, he set his commanding poetry to more international ballad-like melodies and accompanied himself by playing the acoustic guitar with a rock-inflected rhythm. He was more influenced by the Beatles than by Pete Seeger, and he wanted to create music that had not yet been heard. Like American or Latino pop singers, many of Rodriguez's verses address matters of love and romantic relationships and do not seem overtly political. He adroitly mixes love and political commentary in songs like "Te doy una canción" from *Mujeres* (1974), with lyrics like "Te doy una canción como un disparo/como un libro, una palabra, una guerrilla/como doy el amor" (I give you a song like a shot/like a book, a word, a rebel soldier/like I give love). In his song, discerning listeners might hear parallel messages and elegantly coded critiques of revolutionary government couched in language of love, such as "Como esperando Abril" (As I wait for April) from *Dias y Flores* (1974/5): "Mucho más allá de mi ventana . . . /Un reloj se transforma en espejo . . . /Mucho más allá de mi ventana . . . /Mucho más allá de mi ventana/mi esperanza jugaba a una flor/a un jardín como esperando abril" (Far from my window, a watch transforms into a mirror/much farther away from my window/my hope plays with a flower/in a garden where I am waiting for April). The glorious, yet purposeful ambiguity of his poetry enhanced his popularity with young listeners. Even as he enjoyed direct support from Castro's administration to produce recordings, sing at public gatherings, and represent his country at international festivals, he retained his right to voice concern publicly and defended the right of other singers to do the same.[15]

BEYOND PROTEST, PLACE, AND TIME

Although performers of Latin American *nueva canción* in the 1960s and '70s were indeed influenced by protest singers from the United States, it would be incorrect to simply equate the two trends. In Latin America open political dialogue carried risks so great that many performing artists and groups, including Quilapayún (Chile), Mercedes Sosa (Argentina), Danilo Viglietti (Uruguay), Inti Illimani (Chile), Gilberto Gil (Brazil), Carlos Meijia Godoy (Nicaragua), and Yolocambi I Ta (El Salvador), found themselves forced to work in exile when political tides turned against them.[16]

In general, the sustaining energies for Latin American new song primarily came from young intellectuals, particularly university students, and left-leaning countercultural activists. This base of support accounts for many aspects of the tradition. Not only were young intellectuals and college-educated devotees the most visible creators and performers of new song, they also formed, and continue to form, the core audience for this reform-minded music. Young intellectuals created the avenues for circulation and support of new song in university concert halls, coffeehouses, and formal festivals.[17] The message-oriented *nueva canción* was not the music of nightclubs, discos, or dance halls. Beyond that, it is difficult to define a shared sound. The self-conscious blending of genres and practices at the heart of the new song movement is also connected to its academic support base.[18] In many ways, the movement draws upon the sensibilities of classical music practice in addition to folk and popular practice. While many songs are clearly rooted in specific historical moments, some transcend their time, such as "El Pueblo Unido Jamás Será Vencido" by Sergio Ortega of Quilapayún, or Violeta Parra's "Gracias a la Vida," and may be interpreted as lasting classics of the tradition.[19]

Supporters of new song today continue to look to these artists and to their songs with nostalgia and with regard for their continuing potential to shape the future. The Spanish psychoanalyst Gabriel O. Alvarez links the music and poetry of the *nueva canción* tradition to that of the resistance fighters in the Spanish Civil War[20] and turns to them for inspiration and to help clients understand the multidimensional nature of memory and its role in shaping future-oriented action. "Memory," Alvarez writes, "is the place where utopias are possible" (La Memoria: El lugar donde las Utopias son posibles), and he cites Uruguayan singer Daniel Vigiletti: "Por detrás de mi voz, escucha, escucha, otra voz canta. Viene de atrás de lejos . . . " (From behind my voice, listen, listen, another voice sings. It comes from behind, from afar . . .).[21] Vigiletti was reminding his listeners to listen for the voices of the peasants who sang and struggled before he began his own singing for revolutionary causes in the 1970s.

NUEVA CANCIÓN IN NICARAGUA

The position of *nueva canción* in Central America, and in particular in Nicaragua, invites consideration of the future of the local relevance of this now international movement. Although Nicaragua's revolutionary period is past, interest in the new song tradition of topical songs of social consciousness continues. Recent encounters with *nueva canción* through the Nicaraguan singers Katia and Salvador Cardenal, better known as Duo Guardabarranco, indicates that performers are finding ways to build on the traditions of the movements that marked the last half of the previous century and are finding ways to adapt the performance tradition to contemporary concerns. Their work confirms the ongoing importance of the new song movement and contrasts with the impression Landau gives when he speaks of the "short life" of *nueva canción* in a manner that seems to imply its days of influence are over.[22] To facilitate a richer understanding of contemporary Nicaraguan new song efforts and the direction they appear to be charting, a brief review of the history of *nueva canción* in Nicaragua follows. The work of Carlos and Luis E. Mejia Godoy is then examined before exploring the work of the younger artists Duo Guardabarranco in order to highlight local trends of the new song movement and show its integration with local politics. The chapter concludes by focusing on the latest work of the Duo Guardabarranco and on the independent work of Katia and Salvador Cardenal, showing their vision and nostalgia for Nicaragua's promised, but yet to be realized, future.

NUEVA CANCIÓN AND NICARAGUAN POLITICAL HISTORY

The Duo Guardabarranco did not begin working until 1980, and thus they represent a new wave of a movement that began at least two decades earlier in their country. It is impossible to understand their work or the work of their predecessors without a brief foray into Nicaraguan political history.

Although Nicaragua officially achieved status as an independent nation free from the colonial rule of Spain in 1821, the century that followed that move was fraught with political instability and an uneasy relationship with its Central American neighbors as well as foreign powers, and it was not until 1945 that Nicaragua established a national government of its own. Even then, the United States maintained a presence in the country.[23] As the twentieth century progressed, the United States supported selected Nicaraguan leaders who might advance U.S. interests in Nicaraguan exports as well as U.S. strategic concerns. In 1925, the Conservative leader Emilio Chamorro took the Nicaraguan presidency in a coup d'etat aided by the Espino Negro pact with the United States. In protest, General Augusto César Sandino (1893–1934) departed for the mountains, initiating a sequence of events that would establish him as a controversial, but legendary, national icon and, as we shall see, the subject of many revolutionary songs.[24]

In 1933 the United States–created National Guard handed power over to General Anastasio Somoza Garcia and President Sacasa. Just as he had opposed Chamorro, the renegade general Sandino opposed Somoza's authority, Sacasa's presidency, and the U.S. imperialism that made it possible. He was equally opposed to Nicaragua's complacent, insensitive middle class who allowed, even welcomed, such interventions. While camped in the mountains, Sandino led a struggle against imperialism, initiating a new practice of guerrilla warfare. He and his followers attacked U.S. marine camps as well as mining and lumber companies. He was also a union organizer of sorts, forming local cooperatives among agricultural laborers and landless peasants while "taxing" rich landowners. In 1934 Anastasio Somoza's forces tracked down Sandino, tricked him into a compromising position, and shot him.

In 1937 Somoza seized the presidency and began a family reign of more than forty-two consecutive years. Although five puppet leaders officially held government office at various stages during those years, the Somoza dynasty continued to control actual operations. The Somozas became known for their policies of extortion, their control of all sources of production, and for the resulting increase in the number of landless farmers.

In 1964 a young student of Marxist theory named Carlos Fonseca Amador, inspired by Castro's revolution in the 1950s, resurrected Sandino's image and used it as inspiration for a new force to reform Nicaraguan government and rid it of the Somozas and their influence. Drawing on his romanticized vision of the gritty general, he called this movement the Frente Sandinisa por la Liberación Nacional, better known as the FSLN. In 1967 the nascent FSLN movement stepped up its attacks just as Anastasio Somoza Debaye assumed the presidency. The formation of the FSLN, and insurrection that it led, marked the beginning stages of a revolutionary war that would last until 1979. It was during this war that the story of Nicaraguan *nueva canción* really gets started.

During the long fight throughout the 1970s, the leading musical voice of the revolution and the most visible Nicaraguan proponent of the new song movement was Carlos Mejia Godoy. Mejia Godoy came to Nicaragua's capital city, Managua, in 1962 from the rural town Somoto. His father, Don Carlos Mejia Fajardo, was a customs agent, a marimba player, and a tango singer who championed the music of Argentina's king of tango, Carlos Gardel. He shared his musical passions and the legacy of Nicaraguan folk music with his children. Young Carlos studied to be a journalist, but his work as a musician has been most influential. One of his tools for influencing his listeners was the radio. Radio, not television, was the most important mode of international communication for Nicaragua in the 1960s. Carlos Mejia Godoy began his own show with the National Radio Corporation in 1963. He created his own radio personality, an alias named Coporito, an elderly gentleman and a *trovador* of the new and old wave, who arranged old folk songs, tangos, and corridos and gave them new words to critique government policy, especially alliances that favored international commerce at the expense of local people.[25] Predictably, this bold movement brought reprobation, and in 1965 Mejia Godoy had to leave the program, at which time he went to Germany to study radio and film. When he returned to Nicaragua, the revolution was under way, and he took his smooth baritone to the streets and countryside, visiting local folk and *campesino* (peasant) communities. Some of the new songs he created included bold lyrics cheering on the rebel fighters. His travels and performances gave him a firsthand knowledge of Nicaraguan customs and local music traditions. In 1972, he returned to radio and hosted a broadcast called "El Son Nuestro de Cada Día" (our song for each day), created expressly to rescue Nicaraguan culture, and again used music and traditional antiauthoritarian folk tales to satirize and critique the Nicaraguan government. In this same year Columbia Records released a recording of Carlos's brother, Luis Enrique Godoy, called *Hilachas de Sol* (Ragged Rays of Sun).

During the decade of revolution in the 1970s, Carlos Mejia Godoy and his compatriots turned to music as an aggressive tool for aiding the revolutionary cause. Artists organized themselves into brigades modeled on the guerrilla revolutionary strategy. Mejia Godoy formed a Brigade for the Salvation of Nicaraguan Song (Brigada de Salvación del Canto Nicaragüense), and along with his Popular Sound Workshop, his work provided an important model for the engagement of musicians with social reform. Greg Landau, who participated in brigade operations during this time, observed that artists became "ideological combatants." Their work was dangerous; the young musicians often traveled into the heart of combat zones and into remote rural regions where their personal safety was at risk. They used their new songs to raise consciousness about the Sandinista cause and to inspire action.[26]

Dramatic examples of such songs can be found on the recording *Guitarra Armada.* The catalog includes songs sung by Carlos Mejía Godoy y Los Palacagüina such as "¿Qué Es el Fal?" (What is the FAL—the Fuerza Armada de Liberación—the Armed Forces of Liberation), "Las Municiones" (Weapons), "Carabina M1" (with lyrics about how to load and shoot using this firearm), and "Los Explosivos" (Explosives). Other musicians who contributed to the album included Carlos's brother Luis Enrique Godoy, Liliana Felipe, Jorge González, Claudia Christiasen, Eduardo Bejarano, Hely Orsini, Carlos Díaz "Caito," Amparo Ochoa, Lili Bug, Los Integrantes de la Camerata Punta del Este, Délfor Sombra, Delia Caffieri, Hebe Rosell, Leticia Flores, Ricardo Rud, Guadalupe Pineda, and Nora Zaga. The collection became a guidebook for action, providing instructions for fighting aggressive guerrilla warfare as well as for developing the peace that should follow. Even with less aggressive songs, the *trovadores* aided the revolution, and in so doing they established a tradition of expectation for *nueva canción*. Long after the war had ended, the ideological potential of new song would continue to motivate singers and composers of social conscience.

It was also during the 1970s that Carlos Mejia Godoy and his Sound Workshop created a major composition, the *Misa Campesina*. This work, created in the spirit of *nueva canción*, was much more ambitious than a single song. Mejia Godoy's mass was a collection of songs and music that commemorated the struggles of simple people and the revolutionary fighters who gave their lives for a vision of a better society. He drew upon the liberation theology of Ernesto Cardenal[27] and equated these revolutionaries with saints. Cardenal's theology thus provided the framework for linking revolutionary concepts of political order to revolutionary views of spirituality. While highlighting the dignity of the peasant, Mejia Godoy also celebrated the retention of indigenous elements in Nicaraguan Catholicism. In an interview with Zayda García Zeledón, Mejia Godoy states that in the music of the mass he tried to include rhythms representative of all of Nicaragua: the songs of the Miskito Indians from the Atlantic Coast, the mazurkas of Segovia, bullfight songs, festival music, marimba music, and Easter songs, "for Easter," he said, "is the day of poor."[28] The powerful *Misa Campesina* premiered in 1975 in the modest church on Solentiname. Later attempts to present it in public in Managua were quashed; presenters were forced to stop, and the archbishop issued a ban on its performance. Shortly thereafter Carlos Mejia Godoy took refuge in Spain.[29]

In 1979 the Sandinistas overthrew the Somoza government and began a project of massive social reform and land redistribution. The year 1980 was named the "year of literacy," and the new government recruited college students to travel to rural regions to teach reading, writing, and basic math. A secondary goal was to create a map of the nation. The literacy campaign brought the people of rural regions and their culture (including music) to the attention of those residing in urban areas. According to musicologist and expert on Nicaraguan music T. M. Scruggs, some of the volunteers were charged with documenting folk music of the regions they visited, in part with the intention of "rescuing it." Scruggs also reminds us that the culture of Nicaragua is far from homogenous: ethnic and linguistic differences, geographic conditions, inadequate routes of transportation, and economic realities kept people and their cultural expressions largely isolated from each other. People on one coast had very little contact with people on the other, and those in interior rural communities were isolated not just from each other, but also from the cities where national policies were determined.

The year 1980 was also the year of "Plan 80," a new government-sponsored effort to establish more equitable balance between private ownership and state control—an effort vigorously resisted by some longtime landowners and those in commercial sectors. The difficulties that emerged in implementing this plan foreshadowed the struggle the Sandinista government was to face in building a new, stable order. It was not long before formal resistance to the Sandinistas emerged, and in 1981 U.S. president Ronald Reagan began funding the so-called Contras, the resisters whom the Sandinistas knew as *contra-revolucionarios* (i.e., sympathizers of the former Guardia Somocista, or National Guard, now operating as counterrevolutionaries). The FSLN further antagonized the United States by building ties with Cuba and Russia and backing the FMLN (Frente Farabundo Martí para la Liberación Nacional), the revolutionary group that opposed the U.S.-backed president in El Salvador. In response, the United States stopped sending aid to Nicaragua.

DUO GUARDABARRANCO: A NEW WAVE OF NEW SONG

It was during this volatile period that Salvador Cardenal Barquero (b. 1960) began performing with his sister Katia (b. 1963) and formed the group Duo Guardabarranco.[30] They developed their own approach to performance by drawing on many influences. Their grandfather, musicologist Salvador Cardenal, collected a wide variety of Nicaraguan folk music in the 1950s and 1960s representing the country's folk traditions and documented how much of it represented the hybrid blending of Spanish and indigenous traditions. He also ran the country's classical music radio program, and some describe him as the Leonard Bernstein of Nicaragua because of his efforts to introduce audiences to a mix of classical, folkloric, and popular music. Though the influence of their grandfather was not directly evident in their music, Salvador and Katia were also attracted to a wide array of musical traditions. In addition to being mentored by family members, the duo was well acquainted with the music of Carlos Mejia Godoy, who helped them with their first recordings, as well as the more dance-oriented sound of his brother Luis Enrique Godoy and others who started their work in the revolutionary period of *trova Nicaragüense*. They were also especially influenced by the music and poetry of Cuban *trovador* Silvio Rodriguez. As the decade of the Nicaraguan Civil War began, there was still work for *trovadores*, and the Cardenal siblings quickly developed their own sound and their own way of responding.

Salvador, a student of philosophy, religion, and ecology, wrote most of the songs' poetic lyrics and melodies and played guitar. Katia, an ecology student who later earned a degree in music education, performed as lead singer. By the time of their first recording, *Un Trago de Horizante* (A Drink of Horizon), they began appearing as the Duo Guardabarranco, using the name of the Nicaraguan "cliff guard," the national bird that makes its nests in ravines to protect itself from danger. The guardabarranco has a guttural song (certainly in no way reflective of Katia's silky voice) and long, brilliant tail feathers. It cannot live in captivity because, according to Katia, it will die of sadness. Apparently the guardabarranco refuses to recognize the restraints of captivity and if caged will often kill itself by repeatedly flying into the bars of the cage. Clearly the bird became a symbol for the duo. Respect for nature and the importance of freedom have remained central values in their work.

Another reason for choosing the guardabarranco is the appearance of this bird as a witness in one of Carlos Mejia Godoy's famous songs "El Zezontle pregunta por Arlen" (The Mockingbird asks Arlen). In the song two birds, a mockingbird and a guardabarranco, converse about a female guerrilla fighter whose brave death resulted in sainthood achieved by her soul residing "undercover" as a butterfly. Landau offers this lovely translation: "Brother guardabarranco, brother of the wind, song, and light/Tell me if in your travels you have seen a girl named Arlen Siu?/I saw her friend mockingbird/a sweet star in the cane field, dressed in a thousand colors/among the cornstalks."[31] The spiritual and testimonial role of the guardabarranco embodies the aspect of Nicaraguan new song that most attracted the Cardenal siblings.

While Carlos Mejia Godoy's music consciously reflects the national musical heritage of Nicaragua, this is not the case with the sound of Duo Guardabarranco. They are influenced by another generation of pop music. Their friend, the Tucson-based folk singer and concert promoter Ted Warmbrand, remembers Katia telling him how much she liked the Bee Gees and jokingly observing that the two groups share the same initials, only in reverse.[32] The sound of DG (or Deedgies, as Ted pronounced it to emphasize the shared vowel sounds) is not the disco sound of the Bee Gees, but it does share the immediate appeal associated with an international pop sound. The delivery and their messages are, however, more compelling, as author Barbara Kingsolver wrote: Guardabarranco's risky, tender songs about love and human purpose make it impossible to see the world as "us" and "them."[33] Rather like the music of another musician they admire, Silvio Rodriguez, it has an international pop character. Their signature is not distinctly Nicaraguan, but instead relies on ballad-style melodies that suit Katia's velvety voice, most often in 4/4 meter, supported by Salvador's folk rock–style guitar harmonies. Despite this cosmopolitan quality, certain signature songs, such as "Si Buscabas" (If you were looking) and "Mi Luna," incorporate Latin American metric shifts, and the guitar work includes rhythmic accents and patterns that distinguish it from more generic rock/pop practice.

The duo's general resistance to incorporating signature rhythms or forms of Nicaraguan folk and traditional music corresponds to their desire to speak to a global audience. Their message is meant to reach beyond Nicaraguan borders, but on their own terms. In no way would a listener be able to interpret their music as nationalistic, and certainly not as touristy or clichéd. Their resistance to any such expectations bears some resemblance to observations of the Peruvian scholar Raul Romero in his exasperated reflections on outsider expectations of Latin American Scholars. Tired of having to justify projects of local importance that do not reflect a suitably colorful character to American and European scholars, he writes, "We [Latin American Scholars] are instantly categorized as 'others,' as insiders, OBLIGED to be different, to develop novel methods, new approaches, and original perspectives to Western Scholarship."[34] Similarly Katia and Salvador have little interest in meeting obligations imposed by the tastes of others, including those of nationalist musicology. Neither are they interested in newness for its own sake; they have a message to relate, and they work for the sound that best serves their talents, tastes, and purpose. In short, if anything is to be rescued via their new songs, it is not a repertory of Nicaraguan music but is instead humanity and their proposed vision for a new way of living. The closing verse to "Hacer Amanecer" (Making Dawn) speaks to this vision: A pesar de todo/tierra sangre y todo/creceremos todos/para hallar el modo de vencer/y hacer nacer amanaecer/un nuevo ser (in spite of everything/bloody earth and all/we will all grow/to recognize a way of winning/and to give birth to the dawn/of a new way of being).[35]

While the music of Carlos Mejia Godoy embodies his messages, for the Duo Guardabarranco, the music is the servant, an attractive bearer, for their powerful lyrics. Yet the words of Duo Guardabarranco's songs rarely indicate directly their political affiliations. Several songs, some of them expressly commissioned for a specific cause, refer to their political proclivities, such as "Ya Era Santo de Nombre" ("He Was of Sainted Name")—from *Sandino, General de Hombres Libres* (Sandino, General of Free Men), a compilation album recorded in the early 1980s. Even when addressing specific political issues, the duo wanted to resist creating "pamphlet songs." Another example is Katia's composition, "El Salvador," ostensibly concerning the Savior, but inescapably calling to mind the nation and struggle of El Salvador. The lyrics expressly address the love that may be born at the center of struggle and its search for harmony. The majority of their songs address more general themes such as solidarity with the poor, love for humanity, love for peace, love for liberty, and an expanded vision for the future.

Both Katia and Salvador participated in the famed national literacy brigade of 1980 and went to remote regions of Nicaragua to teach children how to read, write, and learn mathematics.[36] The Nicaraguan cultural ministry, led at the time by their father's uncle Ernesto Cardenal, recognized that songs were useful tools in this mission, even though the struggling people of the countryside did not necessarily take to the new music. In 1982, shortly after completing their commitment, Katia and Salvador released their first album, produced by Luis Enrique Mejia Godoy (brother of Carlos Mejia Godoy). The recording shared its title with of one of Salvador's songs "Un Trago de Horizonte" (A Drink of Horizon), and the collection made clear the duo's interest in expanding awareness and their advocacy for developing a wider, socially conscious vision for the future.

Even before that first recording, the Duo Guardabarranco had begun touring, and they quickly made alliances with established artists of the Latin American new song movement as well as politically minded singers from around the world. They became regular participants in the International Festival of Latin American New Song (beginning with the third festival in 1982) and came to the attention of several prominent U.S. singer-songwriters, in particular Jackson Browne, who helped them produce their second recorded album. This album, *Si Buscabas* (If You Were Looking), was released by Browne's label, Redwood Records, in 1985 and sold ten thousand copies in United States.[37] In that same year the duo appeared at the Twelfth Festival of Political Song in Berlin, where they shared the program with Atahualpa Yupanqui, Quilapayún, and Miriam Makeba.

In 1986 Salvador won first prize as singer-songwriter for "Dias de Amar" in the national OTI (Organización de la Televisión Iberoamericana)[38] festival; however, he was not permitted by the Sandinista government to go to Chile for the finals, since Nicaragua opposed the dictatorial rule of then–Chilean president Augusto Pinochet. The OTI festivals were extremely important to the national stature of Katia and Salvador. In 1984 Katia sang at the festival OTI, interpreting a song by fellow Nicaraguan Pablo Buitrago, and won third prize. Both Salvador and Katia returned to the OTI festival in 1986, where they performed as a duo singing "Vengo como la lluvia" (I come like the rain) and were among the six finalists. In 1986 "Días de amar" won first prize for Salvador as composer and Katia as singer in the national Organizatión de Televisión Iberoamericana (OTI) festival. She won second place at the OTI International festival in Las Vegas in 1990 singing "Dame tu Corazon," where they faced artists from twenty-two different countries. They were only the second artists from Nicaragua, following Carlos Mejia Godoy, to win such recognition in the OTI. The international significance of these awards raised the status of Katia and Salvador in Nicaragua, where even people with little interest in new song expressed pride in having them represent Nicaragua in a global context.

Duo Guardabarranco's work during the 1980s established them as one of the most important performing groups representing Nicaragua. They toured the globe giving concerts, participating in festivals and workshops, and making recordings. Artists of like mind and international stature such as Roy Brown (Puerto Rico), Silvio Rodriguez (Cuba), Jackson Browne

(United States), as well as Luis and Carlos Mejia Godoy befriended and inspired the duo, and the brother-sister team quickly became favorite singers in their home country of Nicaragua.

NEW SONG TODAY, NOSTALGIA FOR THE FUTURE

Today, as we begin the twenty-first century, Katia and Salvador have reached middle age and are raising their children. They have developed separate interests, and each has recorded independently. Katia has been the more successful in this regard; she has seven solo albums to her name, many of them recorded in Norway, where she made a temporary second home after her marriage to Parvez Kapoor, a Hindu Norwegian in 1994.[39] Her popularity in Scandinavia has enlarged the scope of her influence.

Brother and sister continue to collaborate, and in addition to new tours (twenty-five of them between 2000 and 2001), retrospective concerts, commemorative engagements (such as their 2001 performance for the opening of the new Teatro Nacional Rubén Darío), and recording reissues (in 2002 Nicaraguan label Mantica Waid reissued all the recordings of Duo Guardabarranco),[40] they have new projects with a decidedly educational focus. In 2001 the duo worked on two collections of children's songs with their older sister Violeta's daughter Cristina and Katia's daughter Alfonsina. Creating music for children has become a priority and is in many ways an extension of their longstanding aim to raise consciousness and educate the public regarding their vision of a humane society. In keeping with the duo's legacy of broad purpose, these songs, while inspired by and intended for their children, are not necessarily children's songs in the traditional sense. Just as the love songs of their youth also carried messages for social transformation and peace in a time of war, their new songs for educating youth address issues such as stewardship of the earth and equality among humans. Salvador notes that young people represent the majority in Nicaraguan society; these young people are destined to construct the future Nicaragua, and they must address persistent problems of social violence, lack of education, lack of health care, general poverty, inadequate employment, and the degradation of the environment. Art, they argue, has a role to play; the *trovadores* must turn now to these issues.[41]

In 2002, Salvador secured foundation support for a new set of recordings devoted primarily to achieving ecological stewardship as a linchpin of a just society. This is hardly a new concern for him. Images of nature as a guiding force for humanity pervade the music of the 1980s and '90s. Songs such as "Guardabosques" ("Guardian of the Forest," in which the gamekeeper of the tiger, deer, ax, wind, and fruit tree reside inside him) and "Colibrí" ("Hummingbird," in which the hummingbird seeks the flower of heaven, the flower of peace, only to find it in his little heart) come immediately to mind. Others bear less obvious titles but also link liberty and justice to nature. His "Dias de Amar" ("Days of Love") tells of the days of love that are yet to come, when respect for nature and equality will guide humanity; the song begins, *Vienen ya/dias de amar la casas que habitas/la tierra vegetal flor y animal vienen ya/rios con agua sin envenenar/agua que beben los que tienen sed/igual que usted.* (They are coming/days to love the houses you live in/ the earth of vegetable, flower, and animal, they are coming/rivers with unpolluted water/water to drink for those who thirst/like you). In this song, a kind of nostalgia for the future appears, a nostalgia for a time of peace and justice that once characterized natural order and that we must regain.

Drawing on the words of a 1992 United Nations Report on the 1992 Conference on Environment and Development, Salvador presents a need for an education that "affirms the values and actions that contribute to the human and social transformation with the preservation of natural resources and the environment."[42] His interest in using art (he is also an accomplished visual artist) and music to stimulate social justice, promote ecological equilibrium, and conserve diversity reflects a perspective that is as much Central American as it is personal.[43]

Nicaragua's neighbor to the south, Costa Rica, has achieved notable success, beginning in the 1980s, with various programs of sustainable development that promote economic growth while taking care to preserve ecological resources and diversity. Indeed ecological resources are positioned at the core of many development projects such as the burgeoning ecotourism industry and preservation efforts linked to new pharmacological research and development of rain forest vegetation. In this context, the ecological direction of *nueva canción* sung by Salvador Cardenal has new significance and potential.

The volcanoes that provide the signature image for the Central American *volcanto* movement also provide rich soil for local agriculture. Central American nations are beginning to take control of agricultural production and resist soil-depleting cash crops like cotton and bananas; they respond to the poisoning of their waters from pesticides and poisons resulting from farming and processing methods. Collectives of Costa Rican farmers are gaining support from their government for rejecting methods promoted by multinational agribusinesses and developing instead local techniques of farming that sustain local populations and replenish the local land. Nicaragua, like other Central American nations, is still recovering from years of strife and has yet to effectively address the problems resulting from what scholar Daniel Faber calls the functional dualism of ecological impoverishment and the proletarianization of the peasantry.[44] Furthermore, while Costa Rica has led the way for Central America in its attempts to use tourist dollars to help support national parks, promote care of endangered species, and fund rain forest conservation, these efforts have not met with unqualified success.[45] Salvador's interest in ecological preservation thus points toward a critical, and still new, direction not just for Nicaragua, but also for the world at large.

As ambitious as such a claim is, the scope is characteristic of the new song movement in general. The nostalgia for an imagined past, one that promised a better future, has become an increasingly significant part of the latest wave of new song production, especially in Central America. Indeed, artists such as the Duo Guardabarranco exhibit nostalgia not just for an untapped future but also for the first wave of the new song movement. The songbook and autobiography that Katia prepared for Duo Guardabarranco[46] in 2002 bears the stamp of nostalgia for a time when the two artists were at their peak and when they were soaring on the wings of a song movement that seemed powerful enough to change the world. That incipient power continues to inspire them as they carry forward the tradition today.

While the first wave of *nueva canción* was class conscious and challenged imperialist governmental practices, the second wave of Latin American new song, as exemplified by Silvio and Katia Cardenal, is more earth conscious. Even with this focus on the earth, their work appears to transcend mundane concerns by emphasizing the dawn of a new spirit, a new perspective that rises above the struggles of existence. This perspective calls to mind the observations of anthropologist June Nash, who has written about how workers in Mexico, Bolivia, and the United States respond to debilitating economic policies by forming semisubsistence collectives in order to redress the imbalance of power resulting from transnational, global economic policies. She concludes that in case after case, the protest is moving from "the workplace, to the streets and fields . . . and the appeal is founded in morality and the right to survive rather than in economic rationality and the end of exploitation."[47] It is on a parallel level of collective organization, also spurred by moral imperatives, that the new song movement has operated. Songwriters like Salvador Cardenal do not directly address the complicated economic forces that create dependency and exploitation. However, he and his sister Katia know the power of marginalized forces to mobilize collective action. Like other performers of new song, they were not afraid to set themselves apart as artists working in their own collectives to speak for the rights of the socially and economically marginalized. Certainly the history of the new song movement is inseparably linked to the power of song to organize people. And the realization of where new song has been most effective corresponds to Nash's observation that collective action is more prevalent in marginal developing economies than in the economically ravaged areas of core industrial economies.

The next wave of *nueva canción*, the *eco-canciones* of Salvador Cardenal, may indeed point to a saving path. Will enough ears hear and will enough people organize in response to the call? These are questions that test the power of any song. History has shown that *nueva canción* has the power to mobilize people; if in their efforts to operate as independent artists they do not forget the importance of collective operation, Salvador and Katia may indeed be able to promote the future with their nostalgia. The lyrics from the *volcanto*-era song "El Salvador" (The Savior)[48] by Katia Cardenal speak of this promise and seem as relevant today as they were more than a decade ago.

Un beso de polvo sobre el agua	A kiss of dust on the water
enciende volcanes con su amor	ignites volcanoes with its love
alzando el invierno que esperamos	raising up the winter we expected
Nace del centro de estos días	From the center of these days is born
vida buscando la armonia	life in search of harmony
nace del centro de este abismo	from the center of this abyss is born
vida para salvar al Itsmo	life to save the Isthmus

SUGGESTED READINGS

Borland, Katherine. *Unmasking Class, Gender, and Sexuality in Nicaraguan Festival.* Tucson: University of Arizona Press, 2006.

Diaz, Clara. *La nueva trova*. Havana: Letras Cubanas Editorial, 1997.

Fairley, Jan. "Annotated bibliography of Latin American popular music with particular reference to Chile and to *nueva canción*," *Popular music* (1985) 5:305–56.

Reyes Matta, Fernando. "The New Song and Its Confrontation in Latin America." In *Marxism and the Interpretation of Culture*, ed. Cary Nelson and Lawrence Grossberg. Urbana: University of Illinois Press, 1988, pp. 447–60.

Schechter, John M., editor. *Music in Latin American Culture.* New York: Schirmer Books (Thompson Learning), 1999.

Staten, Clifford L. *The History of Nicaragua*, Santa Barbara, CA: Greenwood, 2010.

Whisnant, David. E. *Rascally Signs in Sacred Places: The Politics of Culture in Nicaragua.* Chapel Hill: University of North Carolina Press, 2009.

Sounds (in addition to those listed in the notes)

Duo Guardabarranco. *Un Trago de Horizonte* (1982 Enrigrac, Nicaragua; reissued as a CD in 2001).

———. *Si Buscabas* (1984; 1985 Redwood Records, USA; reissued as a CD in 1991).

———. *Dias de Amar* (1991 Redwood Records, USA).

———. *Casa Abierta* (1994 Redwood Records, USA).

———. *Antología* (1995, Nicaragua).

——. *Una Noche con Guardbarranco* (2001 Mantica Waid, Nicaragua).

Godo, Luis, y Grupo Mancotal. *Un son para mi pueblo: Songs from the New Nicaragua*, 2009.

Mejia Godoy, Carlos, and Luis Enrique Godoy. *Guitarra Armada*. Compact disc version of cassette recording made in 1976. Ediciones Pentagrama, CP 016.

Sights

American/Sandinista. 2008. Directed by Jason Blalock.

Carla's Song, film starring Robert Carlyle, inspired by and featuring Duo Guardabarranco's performance of *Guerrero de Amor*. London; Fox Lorber, 1996; released as DVD in 2001. Ken Loach, director.

La Historia de la Nueva Trova Cubana. 2005. Dynamo.

Mecate: A New Song. 1994. Directed by Felix Zurita de Higes (Icarus Films).

Nicaragua from Red to Violet. Produced and Directed by Carmen Santiago, 2004 (FHS).

Rebel Music: Americas. 2007 (FHS).

Silvio Rodríguez: Nueva Trova Cubana. 1985.

Notes

REVISED INTRODUCTION

1. See William E. French, "Living the Vida Local: Contours of Everyday Life," in William H. Beezley, ed., *The Companion to Mexican History and Culture* (Malden, MA: Wiley Blackwells, 2011), pp. 13–33.

2. Examples of Indians from the Upper Tarahumara area mocking, slandering, or threatening priests can be found in reports by Jesuits Joseph Tarda and Tómas de Guadalajara to Francisco Ximénez in 1676. See Archivum Romanum Scietatis Iesu, Mexicana 17, 355–92v, dated August 15, no place. Also see Archivo General de la Nación (Mexico), Misiones 26, fols. 366 and 370v.

3. Ricardo Palma, *Tradiciones Peruanas* (Lima, 1870–1915), 3:154.

4. Linda A. Curcio-Nagy, "The Pious City: Describing Corpus Christi in Colonial Mexico," paper delivered at Conference on Latin American History, Washington, D.C., American Historical Association, 9 January 1999; "Giants and Gypsies: Corpus Christi in Colonial Mexico City," in *Rituals of Rule, Rituals of Resistance: Public Celebrations and Popular Culture in Mexico*, ed. William H. Beezley, Cheryl English Martin, and William E. French (Wilmington, DE: SR Books, 1994): 1–26; William H. Beezley, ed., "Mexican Puppets as Popular and Pedagogical Diversions," Special issue of *The Americas*, 67, no. 3 (Jan. 2011).

5. See Francisca Miranda and William H. Beezley, ed., "Puppets." For Villoldo, see the entries about him at the website http://www.todotango.com.

6. Rosario Manzanos, "Una verdadera 'salinasmania,' de objectos con la imagen del expresidente," Proceso (25 December 1995): 50–57; Vicenge Razo, *Museo Salinas* (Santa Monica, CA: Smart Art Press, 2002).

7. Adriana Williams, *Covarrubias* (Austin: University of Texas Press, 1994).

8. Miguel Rojas Mix, "Los héroes están fatigados: El comic cien años después," *Casa de las Americas* 207 (Abril–Junio 1997): 9–10.

9. Consuela Medina uses her Sonora grandmother's recipe at El Mezon de Cobre. Suzanne Myal, *Tucson's Mexican Restaurants: Repasts, Recipes and Remembrances* (Tucson, AZ: Fiesta Publishing, 1997): 36.

10. Alma Guillermoprieto, "Cuban Hit Parade," *New York Review of Books* (14 January 1999): 34; "Vive para contar el nacimiento del Mambo," *El Imparcial* (Oaxaca de Juárez, Oaxaca, Mexico), 14 March 1999, 3e.

11. For an introduction to theories of popular culture, see Chandra Mukerji and Michael Schudson, eds., *Rethinking Popular Culture: Contemporary Perspectives in Cultural Studies* (Berkeley: University of California Press, 1991).

12. Readers interested in this topic should begin with Alma Guillermoprieto, *Samba* (New York: Vintage Departures, 1991).

13. Alison Rafael, "Samba and Social Control: Popular Culture and Racial Democracy in Rio de Janeiro" (Ph.D. diss., Columbia University, 1980): 19–81.

14. Kevin Stayton, "Converging Cultures in Viceregal Peru," *Antiques* (April 1996): 584–93; Diana Fane, *Converging Cultures: Art and Identity in Spanish America* (New York: Henry N. Abrams, 1996).

15. See Eric Hobsbawm and Terence Ranger, eds., *The Invention of Tradition* (Cambridge: Cambridge University Press, 1983).

16. Benjamin Orlove, *The Allure of the Foreign: Imported Goods in Postcolonial Latin America* (Ann Arbor: University of Michigan Press, 1997).

17. William H. Beezley, editor of the special issue of *Studies in Latin American Popular Culture*, 28 (2010) on world fairs.

18. Carlos Monsiváis, "La tradición de la memoria de religiosa: el catecismo del Padre Ripalda," *Imágenes de la tradición viva* (México: Fondo de Cultural Económica, 2006; 2a ed.), pp. 123–38.

19. This concept comes from Benedict Anderson, *Imagined Communities: Reflections on the Origin and Spread of Nationalism*, rev. ed. (London: Verso, 1991).

20. José Saramago, *The Year of the Death of Ricardo Reis* (San Diego: Harcourt Brace, 1992): 11.

CHAPTER 1

1. See June E. Hahner, ed., *Women through Women's Eyes: Latin American Women in Nineteenth-Century Travel Accounts* (Wilmington, DE: SR Books, 1998): 19–20.

2. For other works on death and cemeteries in eighteenth- and nineteenth-century Mexico, see Anne Staples, "La lucha por los muertos," *Diálogos* 13, no. 5 (September–October 1977): 15–20; Juan Pedro Viqueira Albán, "El sentimiento de la muerte en el México ilustrado del siglo XVIII através de dos textos de la época," *Relaciones* 2, no. 5 (winter 1981): 27–63; María Dolores Morales, "Cambios en las prácticas funerarias: Los lugares de sepultura en la Ciudad de México, 1784–1857," *Historias* 27 (October 1991–March 1992): 97–105; and Francisco de la Maza, *Las piras funerarias en la historia y en el arte de México: Grabados, litografías y documentos del siglo xvi al xix* (Mexico: Anales del Instituto de Investigaciones Estéticas, 1946).

3. This information comes from four hundred Veracruz burial records, from 1720 to 1810, and 2,100 Mexico City wills, from 1640 to 1850.

4. *Concilios provinciales primero, y segundo, celebrados en la muy noble, y muy leal Ciudad de México. Presidiendo el Illmo. Y Rmo. Señor D. Fr. Alonso de Montúfar, en los años de 1555, 1565. Dados a luz por el Illmo. Sr. D. Francisco Antonio Lorenzana* (Mexico: Antonio de Hogal, 1769): 78–79.

5. Gregorio M. de Guijo, *Diario, 1648–1664*, 2d ed. (Mexico: Editorial Porrúa, 1986): 183, 212.

6. Archivo General de la Nación (hereinafter A.G.N.), Gobernación 3a, legajo 2154, caja 2630, exp. 2, cuaderno 10, fol. 135. On the prices of parish tombs, see A.G.N., Veracruz Defunciones. On the wages of urban artisans in Mexico City, see Michael C. Scardaville, "Crime and the Urban Poor: Mexico City in the Late Colonial Period" (Ph.D. diss., University of Florida, Gainesville, 1977): 88.

7. A.G.N., Gobernación 3a, legajo 2154, caja 2630, exp. 2, cuaderno 10, fols. 78–83.

8. Conde de Revillagigedo, *Informe sobre las misiones e instrucción reservada al Marqués de Branciforte* (Mexico: Editorial Jus, 1966): 162, and A.G.N., Correspondencia de Virreyes 2a, vol. 30, letter no. 69, fol. 82.

9. A.G.N., Gobernación 3a, legajo 2154, caja 2630, exp. 2, cuaderno 10, fols. 132–132v.

10. A.G.N., Gobernación 3a, legajo 2154, caja 2630, exp. 2, cuaderno 10, fols. 132–132v.

11. A.G.N., Gobernación 3a, legajo 2154, caja 2630, exp. 2, cuaderno 10, fol. 149, 189.

12. A.G.N., Gobernación 3a, legajo 2154, caja 2630, exp. 2, cuaderno 10, fol. 227, 229.

13. After Corral's death, his widow petitioned the city council for a pension, arguing that he had supported his six children and donated funds to the city's water project with his only income. See Instituto Nacional de Antropología e Historia (hereinafter I.N.A.H.), Veracruz microfilm, rollo 16, libro 87, fol. 197.

14. Burial record of Barbara Bauza, April 30, 1790, A.G.N., Veracruz Defunciones, rollo 2367, no. 42720. Her husband's genealogy is found in A.G.N., Inquisición, vol. 1174, exp. 3, fol. 20.

15. Archivo General de Indias (hereinafter A.G.I.), Estado, vol. 21, no. 4, fol. 5v.; Archivo Histórico de la ciudad de Veracruz (herafter A.H.C.V.), caja 30, vol. 31, fol. 229v.; A.G.N., Gobernación 3a, legajo 2154, caja 2630, exp. 2, cuaderno 10, fol. 191, and legajo 2154, caja 2630, exp. 2, cuaderno 10, fol. 196.

16. A.G.N., Gobernación 3a, legajo 2154, caja 2630, exp. 2, cuaderno 10, fol. 62.

17. A.H.C.V., caja 30, vol. 31, fols. 330–331v.

18. A.G.N., Correspondencía de Virreyes, ser. 2a, vol. 30, letter no. 69, fol. 182. The Dominicans had argued that one of the prime reasons for burying Cabeza de Vaca in their convent was that the group had no designated space in the cemetery. See A.G.N., Gobernación 3a, legajo 2154, caja 2630, exp. 2, cuaderno 10, fol. 252.

19. A.G.N., Reales Cédulas Duplicadas, vol. 188, exp. 1, fol. 130; and Gobernación 3a, legajo 2154–2155, caja 2630, exp. 1, fol. 52. On the regular religious orders receiving the order from Revillagigedo, see A.G.N., Gobernación 3a, legajo 2154, caja 2630, exp. 1, fols. 263–269.

20. A.G.N., Reales Cédulas Duplicadas, vol. 188, exp. 1, fols. 127–131. On the move to request masses only from the regular orders, see A.G.N., Gobernación 3a, legajo 2154, exp. 2, cuaderno 10, fol. 235.

21. A.G.N., Ayuntamientos, vol. 1, exp. 3, fol. 61.

22. A.H.C.V., caja 30, vol. 31, fols. 229–331v.

23. I.N.A.H., Veracruz Microfilm Collection, rollo 13, libro 83, fols. 259v–260.

24. A.H.C.V., caja 30, vol. 31, fols. 229–231v.

25. A.H.C.V., caja 37, vol. 39, fol. 276.

26. A.G.N., Gobernación 3a, legajo 2154, caja 2630, exp. 2, cuaderno 10, fol. 23.

27. On the Veracruz city council's advocate in Madrid, see I.N.A.H., Veracruz Microfilm Collection, rollo 16, libro 87, fol. 60.

28. Burial record of Miguel Laso de la Vega, November 1791, A.G.N., Veracruz Defunciones, rollo 2367, no. 42720. Burial record of Doña Josepha Britto, July 17, 1770, A.G.N., Veracruz Defunciones, rollo 2366, 342719. For the pasquinade, see A.G.N., Gobernación 3a, legajo 2154, caja 2630, exp. 2, cuaderno 10, fol. 294v.

29. On the cemetery debate in Spain, see Council of Castile, *Memorial ajustado del expediente seguido en el Consejo, en virtud del orden de S.M. de 24 de marzo de 1781 sobre establecimiento general de cementerios* (Madrid: Ibarra, 1781).

30. A.G.N., Reales Cédulas Originales, vol. 150, exp. 190, fol. and vol. 150, exp. 84, fols. 133–137, and Correspondencia de Virreyes, ser. 1a, vol. 168, exp. 371, fol. 17v. Also see A.G.N., Correspondencia de Virreyes, ser. 1a, vol. 164, exp. 422, fols. 59–59v, and A.G.I., Estado, vol. 21, no. 4, fols. 1–2.

31. A.G.N., Correspondencia de Virreyes, ser. 1a, vol. 168, exp. 384, fol. 27, and Gobernación, legajo 2154–2155, caja 2630, exp. 12, fols. 15–17.

32. Burial record of Juan José de Echeverría, May 13, 1791, A.G.N., Veracruz Defunciones, rollo 2367, no. 42720.

33. I.N.A.H., Veracruz Microfilm Collection, rollo 14, libro 85, fols. 38v–40v.

34. A.H.C.V., caja 37, vol. 39, fol. 272.

35. A.G.N., Gobernación 3a, legajo 2154, vol. 2630, exp. 4, fol. 11v.

36. A.G.N., Gobernación 3a, legajo 2154, vol. 2630, exp. 4, fol. 123, 14v.

37. Jean Delumeau, *Catholicism Between Luther and Voltaire: A New View of the Catholic Reformation* (London: Burns and Oates, 1977): 360–74.

38. Pedro Rodríquez, Conde de Campomanes, *Discurso sobre el fomento de la industria popular* (Madrid: Fábrica Nacional de Moneda y Timbre, 1975): 91.

39. A.G.N., Cofradías y Archicofradías, vol. 18, exp. 1, fols.1–2, and Reales Cédulas Originales, vol. 228, exp. 133, fol. 301. David A. Brading, *Una Iglesia asediada: El obispado de Michoacán, 1749–1810* (Mexico: Fondo de Cultura Económica, 1994): 150–51. On receipt of the order in Veracruz, see Veracruz, Governor of Veracruz, Aug. 31, 1791, A.G.N., *Correspondencia de Diversas Autoridades*, vol. 45, exp. 60, fol. 145. Cofradías y Archicofradías, vol. 18, exp. 7, fols. 160 and 309v. "Tridentine Catholicism and Enlightened Despotism in Bourbon Mexico," *Journal of Latin American Studies* 15 (May 1983): 12.

40. A.G.N., Reales Cédulas Originales, vol. 228, exp. 133, fol. 301.

41. A.G.N., Correspondencia de Virreyes, ser. 2a, vol. 27, letter no. 368, fols. 213–214; Correspondencia de Diversas Autoridades, vol. 46, exp. 66, fol. 1; and Reales Cédulas Originales, vol. 190, letter no. 8, fols. 13–14.

42. Antonio López Matoso, "Viaje de perico ligero al país de los moros," in *Cien Viajeros en Veracruz: Crónicas y relatos. Tomo II, 1755–1816*, edited by Martha Poblett Miranda, 204 (Veracruz: Gobierno del Estado de Veracruz, 1992).

43. For the Tertiaries' petition, see A.G.N., Gobernación 3a, legajo 2154, caja 2630, exp. 1, fol. 11. For the response of the governor, bishop, and viceroy, see A.G.N., Gobernación 3a, legajo 2154, caja 2630, exp. 1, fols. 13, 15, and 17, respectively.

44. Bishop of Teruel to Council of Castile, "Informes de los MM.RR Arzobispos, RR. Obispos, y vicarios capitulares, sede-vacante. Colocados por el orden de sus metrópolis y Diócesis," in Council of Castile, Memorial Ajustado, 204.

45. See, for example, the comments of the bishops of Canarias, Palencia, Cartagena, and Vich in Council of Castile, *Memorial Ajustado*, 32–33, 58–61, 139, 166–167.

46. As cited in Jean Sarrailh, *La España ilustrada de la segunda mitad del siglo XVIII* (Mexico: Fondo de Cultura Económica, 1957): 685.

47. María Giovanna Tomsich, *El jansenismo en España: Estudio sobre ideas religiosas en la segunda mitad del siglo XVIII* (Madrid: Siglo Veintiuno, 1972): 21. William J. Callahan, *Church, Politics, and Society in Spain, 1750–1874* (Cambridge: Harvard University Press, 1984): 70.

48. As quoted in Sarrailh, *La España ilustrada*, 673.

49. A.G.N., Gobernación 3a, legajo 2154, vol. 2630, exp. 4, fols. 60v–62, 79v, 119, 100v–103v.

50. A.G.I., Estado, vol. 21, no. 4, fols. 3, 9., and A.G.N., Gobernación 3a, legajo 2154, caja 2630, exp. 4, fol. 124.

51. José María Laso de la Vega, *Oración panegírica, que en la festividad de N.S de Guadalupe, celebrada el día doce de deciembre del año de 1793, en la paroquia de la Nueva Veracruz, dixó su párroco Dr. D. Joséph María Laso de la Vega, quien la dedica al muy ilustre ayuntmiento de aquella ciudad* (Puebla: Seminario Palafoxiano, 1794): 1–2.

52. For a discussion of Saint Augustine as a precursor of modern identity, see Charles Taylor, *Sources of the Self: The Making of Modern Identity* (Cambridge: Harvard University Press, 1989): 129–135. Also see John McManners, *Death and the Enlightenment. Changing Attitudes to Death Among Christians and Unbelievers in Eighteenth-Century France* (New York: Oxford University Press, 1981), and Gaspar Melchor de Jovellanos, "Informe sobre la disciplina ecclesiástica antigua y moderna relativo al lugar de las sepulturas (1783)," in *Biblioteca de Autores Españoles desde la formación del lenguaje hasta nuestros días: Obras publicadas e ineditas de don Gaspar de Jovellanos* (Madrid: Ediciones Atlas, 1956), vol. 5:83.

53. José María Laso de la Vega, *Oración panegyrica del gran padre y doctor de la iglesia sr. S. Augustín que en el convento de San Francisco Xavier el Real de Veracruz, del mismo orden dixó (el día 28 de aug del año de 1780) don Joséph María Loazo de la Vega, clerigo presbytero del obispado de la Puebla de los Angeles, colegial que fue por beca real por opposición del Colegio de San Ildefonso, de la misma ciudad, doctor por la Real y Pontífica Universidad de México, opositor a la canongía lectoral de la santa iglesia de Puebla , y a la magistral de la de Oaxaca, calificador del Santo Oficio, y su comisario en la Ciudad de Veracruz, cura interino,y juez ecclesiástico de la real fortaleza de San Juan de Ullua* (Mexico: Felipe de Zúñiga y Ontiveros, 1781): xii–4.

54. I.N.A.H., Veracruz Microfilm Collection, rollo 12, libro 83, fol. 170v. Also see Condumex, Miscelánea, Cartas Pastorales, Puebla, no. 1, foleto 8, fol. 57.

55. As cited in Sarrailh, *La España ilustrada*, 684.

56. *Martin Luther: Selections from His Writings*, ed. John Dillenberger (New York: Anchor Press–Doubleday, 1961): 498–99.

57. A.G.N, Veracruz Defunciones, rollo 2367, no. 42720.

58. A.G.N., Veracruz Defunciones, rollo 2366, no. 42719. For other examples of testators who insisted on modest funerals, see, for example, A.G.N., Veracruz Defunciones, rollo 2367, no. 42720, rollo 2367, no. 42720, and rollo 2367, no. 42720.

59. A.G.N., Ayuntamientos, vol. 1, exp. 8, fol. 262, and A.G.I., Estado 21, no. 4, fol. 13.

60. The 1791 Veracruz census reported 3,990 residents inside the city's walls; see Veracruz, Veracruz census, 1791, A.H.C.V, caja 40, vol. 42; Romeo Cruz Velásquez, "Los hospitales," 116–21. Alexander Von Humbolt, *Ensayo Político sobre el reino de la Nueva España* (Mexico: Mariano Galván Rivera, 1839), vol. 4, 131; Jackie R. Booker, *Veracruz Merchants, 1770–1829: A Mercantile Elite in Late Bourbon and Early Independent Mexico* (Boulder, CO: Westview Press, 1993): 7; and Ralph Widemer, "La ciudad de Veracruz en el último siglo colonial (1680–1820): Algunos aspecto de la historia demográfica de una ciudad portuaria," *La palabra y el hombre 73* (1992): 121–34. Robert Sydney Smith argues that the population merely doubled between 1791 and the 1818 census, which registered 8,934 residents; see his "Shipping in the Port of Veracruz, 1790–1821," *Hispanic American Historical Review* 23 (February 1943): 5. Pierre Chanu reports figures similar to those of Smith; see his "Veracruz en la segunda mitad del siglo XVI y primera del XVII," *Historia Mexicana* 36 no. 9 (April–June 1960): 543. See also Richard E. Boyer and Keith A. Davies, *Urbanization in 19th Century Latin America: Statistics and Sources* (Los Angeles: University of California Press, 1973): 48.

61. Matilde Souto Mantecón, "El consulado de comerciantes de Veracruz" (master's thesis, Universidad Naciónal Autónoma de México, Departamento de Filosofía y Letras, 1989): 61.

62. A.G.N., Gobernación 3a, legajo 2154, caja 2630, exp. 2, cuaderno 10, fols. 227, 229, and exp. 3, fol. 48.

63. I.N.A.H., Veracruz Microfilm Collection, rollo 29, libro 95, fols. 445–446.

64. On the royal order of 1804, see Juan M. Rodríquez, ed., *Pandectas Hispano-Mexicanas ó sea codigo general comprensivo de las leyes generales, útiles, y vivas*, 1:114; and *Novísima Recopilación* (1854), tomo 1, tit. 3, ley 1, pp. 209–10. On the Ayuntamiento's pledge, see A.G.N., Ayuntamientos, vol. 1, exp. 3, fol. 58.

65. Alejandro de Humbolt, *Ensayo político sobre el reino de la Nueva España* (Mexico: Editorial Pedro Robredo, 1941), vol. 4:158.

66. Rolf Widemer explains that beginning in 1780 and peaking in 1800, an agricultural crisis hit the area around Veracruz. Unable to obtain the money to pay taxes, peasants fled to the city in search of work (Widemer, "La ciudad de Veracruz," 133).

67. Thomas Gage, *A New Survey of the West Indies: or, The English American his Travail by Sea and Land* (London: E. Corte, 1915): 23; Francisco de Ajofrín, *Diario del viaje que hizo a la América en el siglo XVIII el padre Francisco de Ajofrín* (Mexico: Instituto Cultural Hispano Mexicano, 1964), vol. 1:35; Henry George Ward, México

en 1827 (Mexico: Fondo de Cultura Económica, 1985): 67; and Antonio de Ulloa, "Descripción geográfico física de una parte de la Nueva España, 1777," in *Cien viajeros en Veracruz*, 76.

68. Widemer, "La ciudad de Veracruz," 133.

69. Veracruz Census, 1791, A.H.C.V., caja 40, vol. 42. The census data are confirmed by the parish marriage records for 1798 and 1804, which reveal that 49 percent of Spanish and mestizo males originated in Europe (the two were grouped together), with only 43.7 percent from New Spain and 10.4 percent from Veracruz. In contrast, none of the brides came from Europe and 80 percent had been born in New Spain, particularly in Veracruz (46.7 percent). See Widemer, "La ciudad de Veracruz," 133.

70. I.N.A.H., Veracruz Microfilm Collection, rollo 20, libro 19, fols. 43, 45–45v.

71. I.N.A.H., Veracruz Microfilm Collection, rollo 20, libro 19, fol. 45v.

72. For the Puertas comments, see I.N.A.H., Veracruz Microfilm Collection, rollo 20, libro 19, fols. 48v and 52v, respectively.

73. I.N.A.H., Veracruz Microfilm Collection, rollo 20, libro 19, fol. 57.

74. I.N.A.H., Veracruz Microfilm Collection, rollo 20, libro 19, fols. 50 and 32, respectively.

75. I.N.A.H., Veracruz Microfilm Collection, rollo 12, libro 83, fol. 169, and Antonio de Ulloa, "Descripción geográfico," 76.

76. Antonio Gramsci, *Selections from the Prison Notebooks* (London: Lawrence & Wishart, 1971): 123–209. As he points out, a dominant class not only must impose its rule via the state, it must also demonstrate its capacity for intellectual and moral leadership.

77. I.N.A.H., rollo 12, libro 83, fols. 169–175.

78. For the society, see Miguel Lerdo de Tejada, *Apuntes históricos*, 1:378; Manuel B. Trens, *Historia de la H. Ciudad de Veracruz y de su Ayuntamiento* (Mexico: Ayuntamiento de Veracruz, 1955): 54; Jackie R. Booker, *Veracruz Merchants*, 111; and I.N.A.H., rollo 21, libro 90, fol. 21v. For the Junta de Policia, see I.N.A.H., rollo 17, libro 88, fol. 73; rollo 16, libro 87, fol. 110; rollo 12, libro 83, fol. 176v; and rollo 14, libro 84, fols. 693–695v. Bishop Biempico y Sotomayor relied on the expert testimony of several Junta members to discredit city councilman Echeverría's anti-cemetery allegations. See A.G.N., Gobernación 3a, legajo 2154, caja 2630, exp. 4, fols. 66–66v, and legajo 2154, caja 2630, exp. 4, fol. 95v. For the poorhouses, see Manuel B. Trens, *Historia de la H. Ciudad de Veracruz*, 55; I.N.A.H., rollo 27, libro 94, fol. 362; and Cruz Velasquez, "Los Hospitales," 143.

79. Cruz Velásquez, "Los hospitales," especially 110–26; Joséfina Muriel, *Los Hospitales*, vol. 2:26–28; and Miguel Lerdo de Tejada, *Apuntes históricos*, 404–05.

80. I.N.A.H., Veracruz Microfilm Collection, rollo 21, libro 90, fols. 123–126, rollo 24, libro 92, fols. 338–340, 363, rollo 22, libro 91, fol. 206, rollo 27, libro 94, fol. 261–261v. A.H.C.V., caja 82, vol. 93, fols. 574–616; Manuel B. Trens, *Historia de la H. Ciudad de Veracruz*, 47; I.N.A.H., rollo 22, libro 91, fol. 203; and *Veracruz y Oaxaca en 1798* (Mexico: Editorial Vargas Reas, 1946): 12.

81. For the Alcaldes de Barrio of the capital, see Eduardo Báez Macías, "Ordenanzas para el establecimiento de Alcaldes de Barrio en la Nueva Espana: Ciudades de Mexico y San Luis Potosí," *Boletín del Archivo General de la Nación*, 10, nos. 1–2 (1969). For the city council discussion, see A.H.C.V., caja 58, vol. 67, fols.

115–121v; and I.N.A.H., Veracruz Microfilm Collection, rollo 27, libro 94, fol. 332. It is not clear when the Alcaldes de Barrio were established in Veracruz or when the Veracruz city council divided the city into wards; by 1810, however, both measures were in practice. See A.H.C.V., caja 93, vol. 108, fols. 253–253v, and A.H.C.V., caja 87, vol. 98, fol. 438. State officials did, of course, play a role in establishing the Alcaldes de Barrio in Veracruz. Viceroy Branciforte suggested the measure, and in 1787 the city council decided to implement it as a tribute to him; see A.H.C.V., caja 58, vol. 67, fol. 115.

82. Francois-Xavier Guerra, *Modernidad e Independencias: Ensayos sobre las revoluciónes hispánicas* (Mexico: Fondo de Cultura Económica, 1993): 13, 85, 89, 101, 290, 338.

83. Nineteenth-century Mexican liberalism is amply detailed in Jesús Reyes Heroles, *El liberalismo mexicano*, 3 vols. (Mexico: Fondo de Cultura Económica, 1974). Also see José Miranda, "El liberalismo mexicano y el liberalismo europeo," *Historia Mexicana* 8, no. 4 (1959): 502–23.

84. José María Luis Mora, Obras sueltas de José Luis Mora, ciudadano Mexicano (1837) (Mexico: Editorial Porrúa, 1963): 57.

85. See, for example, Pedro Gringoire, "El 'Protestantismo' del doctor Mora," in *Lecturas de "Historia Mexicana" 5. Iglesia y religiosidad, intro.* Pilar Gonzalbo Aizpura (Mexico: Colegio de México, 1992): 115, 117, 121.

86. Octavio Paz, *Sor Juana Ines de la Cruz o las trampas de la fe*, 3d ed. (Mexico: Fondo de Cultura Económica, 1983): 45.

CHAPTER 2

1. See Franklin Kelly's essay in the Smithsonian volume for a discussion of the uncertainty surrounding the circumstances of the first exhibition of *Heart of the Andes*.

2. Gerald L. Carr, *Frederic Edwin Church: The Icebergs* [exh. cat., Dallas Museum of Fine Arts] (Dallas, 1980), 8.

3. Frederic E. Church to Bayard Taylor, 9 May 1859, Bayard Taylor Correspondence, Cornell Regional Archives.

4. I thank Franklin Kelly, curator of collections at the Corcoran Gallery of Art, for supplying me with so much information about Church. The relationship between Church and Humboldt is discussed in Edmunds V. Bunkse, "Humboldt and the Aesthetic Tradition in Geography," *The Geographical Review* 7 (April 1981): 127–46; Albert Ten Eyck Gardner, "Scientific Sources of the Full-Length Landscape: 1850," Metropolitan Museum of Art Bulletin 4 (October 1945): 59–65; David C. Huntington, "Landscape and Diaries: The South American Trips of F. E. Church," Brooklyn Museum Annual 5 (1963–64): 65–98, Franklin Kelly, "Frederic Church in the Tropics," Arts in Virginia 27 (1987): 16–33, and Frederic Edwin Church and the National Landscape (Washington, D.C., 1988); Katherine

Manthorne, *Creation and Renewal: Views of Cotopaxi by Frederic Edwin Church* [exh. cat., National Museum of American Art] (Washington, D.C., 1985); and Barbara Novak, *Nature and Culture: American Landscape and Painting: 1825–1875* (New York, 1980).

5. All references to Humboldt in this paper are from the following English edition of *Cosmos*, an edition owned by Frederic Church: Alexander von Humboldt, *Cosmos: A Sketch of a Physical Description of the Universe*, translated by E. C. Otte (New York, 1852).

6. Manthorne, *Creation and Renewal*.

7. Richard S. Fiske and Elizabeth Nielsen, "Church's Cotopaxi: a Modern Volcanological Perspective," in Katherine Manthorne, *Creation and Renewal*, 1–6.

8. All references to Darwin's *The Beagle Diary* and letters will be found in R. D. Keynes, *The Beagle Record* (Cambridge, England, 1979).

9. Howard Gruber, *Darwin on Man* (New York, 1974) and Stephen J. Gould, *Ever Since Darwin* (New York, 1977).

10. Charles Darwin, *On the Origin of Species* (London, 1859), 62.

11. Gerald L. Carr, "Frederic Edwin Church as a Public Figure," in Franklin Kelly and Gerald L. Carr, *The Early Landscapes of Frederic Edwin Church, 1845–1854* (Fort Worth, 1987), 1–30.

12. I thank Franklin Kelly for sending me the list of Church's library.

CHAPTER 3

1. Roberto Da Matta, *Carnival, Rogues and Heroes* (Notre Dame: University of Notre Dame Press, 1991); Jose Saramago, *The Year of the Death of Ricardo Reis* (San Diego: Harcourt Brace & Co., 1984), 133–38; Peter Abrahams, *Tell Freedom* (New York: Macmillan, 1970).

2. William Rowe and Vivian Schelling, *Memory and Modernity: Popular Culture in Latin America* (New York: Verso, 1991), 34.

3. On the tango's twentieth-century history, see Marta E. Savigliano, *Tango and the Political Economy of Passion* (Boulder, CO: Westview Press, 1995); Donna J. Guy, *Sex and Danger in Buenos Aires: Prostitution, Family, and Nation in Argentina* (Lincoln: University of Nebraska Press, 1991), 141–74.

4. See George Reid Andrews, *The Afro-Argentines of Buenos Aires, 1800–1900* (Madison: University of Wisconsin Press, 1980).

5. Ventura R. Lynch, *La Provincia de Buenos Aires hasta la definición de la cuestión Capital de la República* (1883), cited by Fernando O. Assunçao in *El tango y sus circunstancias 1880–1920* (Buenos Aires: Libraría "El Ateneo" Editorial, 1984), 133–34.

6. Archivo General de la Nación, Buenos Aires (hereafter cited as AGN): Bandos, 8-10-3.

7. AGN: IX, 36-4-3.

8. Teodoro Klein, "Cultura negra y tangos: Las academias de baile," *Desmemoria* 2, no. 6 (1995): 111.

9. Quoted in Ricardo Rodríguez Molas, *La música y la danza de los negros en el Buenos Aires de los siglos XVIII y XIX* (Buenos Aires: Clío, 1957), 9.

10. Cited by Lauro Ayestarán, *La música en el Uruguay* (Montevideo: Servicio Oficial de Difusión Radio Eléctrica, 1953), 70.

11. Néstor R. Ortiz Oderigo, *Calunga: Croquis del Candombe* (Buenos Aires: Editorial Universitaria de Buenos Aires, 1969): 126–27; and Ayestarán, *La música en el Uruguay*, 52.

12. Acuerdos del cabildo de Montevideo, in *La revista del archivo general administrativo* (1887) 3:151.

13. AGN Argentina: Bandos, 8-10-3 (1770–71).

14. In Buenos Aires, blacks were 26 percent of the population in 1778, 30 percent in 1810 (Oscar Natale, *Buenos Aires, negros, y tango* [Buenos Aires: Peña Lillo Editor, 1984]), 34; in Montevideo, blacks were 27 percent of the population in 1769, 35 percent in 1810 (Ayestarán, *La música en el Uruguay*, 61).

15. AGN: IX 36.4.3 (January 23, 1787), IX 19.7.2 (January 25, 1791).

16. Alcide d'Orbigny, Voyage dans l'Amérique Méridionale (Paris, 1835), 1:5.

17. Descripción de las fiestas cívicas celebradas en la capital de los pueblos orientales el veinte y cinco de mayo de 1816 [anonymous pamphlet] (Montevideo, 1816), 11.

18. Natale, *Buenos Aires, negros, y tango*, 19.

19. *El Nacional*, June 11, 1856, quoted in Klein, "Cultura negra y tangos," 112.

20. Andrews, *The Afro-Argentines of Buenos Aires*, 97.

21. "Representación del Síndico Procurador General sobre los bailes de negros," *Actas del Cabildo de Buenos Aires*, Libro XLIX, 628; Rodríguez Molas, *La música y la danza de los negros*, 12.

22. Isidoro de María, *Montevideo antiguo* (Montevideo: Sociedad Amigos del Libro Rioplatense, 1938), 82–86.

23. "Los reyes magos," *La Tribuna* (Buenos Aires), January 10, 1862.

24. AGN: IX 32.8.5 ("Información sobre los Vayles de Máscara," 1773).

25. "Juego de carnaval," *La Tribuna*, February 24, 1854.

26. "Carnaval," *El Nacional*, February 22, 1855.

27. "A nuestros lectores," *Los negros: Periódico semanal redactado por jóvenes de la sociedad de ese nombre*, March 21, 1869.

28. "Los negros," *El Nacional*, February 26, 1873.

29. Natale, *Buenos Aires, negros, y tango*, 135.

30. Ortiz Oderigo, *Calunga*, 64–67.

31. "Arte dramático popular americano," *El Nacional*, July 12, 1869.

32. Enrique H. Puccia, *Breve historia del carnaval porteño* (Buenos Aires: Municipalidad de la Ciudad de Buenos Aires, 1974), 49, 75–76.

33. "Nuestras sociedades carnivalescas," *La Broma*, March 3, 1882; "Sobre el mismo tema," La Broma, March 9, 1882.

34. Cited in Klein, "Cultura negra y tangos," 118.

35. Cited in Klein, "Cultura negra y tangos," 116.

36. Assunçao, *El tango y sus circunstancias*, 81–82.

37. "Doble esperanza," *La Broma*, February 7, 1880.

38. "Tango La Broma," *La Broma*, February 7, 1880.

39. "Canciones carnavalescas," *La Broma*, March 6, 1881.

40. "El tango," *La Ilustración Argentina*, November 30, 1882. Reproduced in Rodríguez Molas, *La música y la danza de los negros*, 19.

41. Eva Canél, *De América* (Madrid, 1899), 56–58.

42. Ayestarán, La música en el Uruguay, 81; *La Broma*, 1880–1882, passim.

43. Blas Matamoros, "Orígenes musicales," in *La historia del tango* (Buenos Aires: Ediciones Corregidor, 1976), 81–94.

44. Natale, *Buenos Aires, negros, y tango*, 294.

45. Lynch, *La Provincia de Buenos Aires* (1883), cited by Assunçao, *El tango y sus circunstancias*, 133–34.

46. "Escenas callejeras," *Caras y Caretas*, December 3, 1898.

47. Andrés M. Carretero, *Tango: Testigo social* (Buenos Aires: Editorial Librería General de Tomás Pardo, 1995), 36 and passim.

48. Vicente Rossi, *Cosas de negros*, 2d ed. (Buenos Aires: Librería Hachette, 1958), 135–36.

49. *La Tribuna*, February 11, 1903, cited in *Antología del tango rioplatense* (Buenos Aires: Instituto de Musicología "Carlos Vega," 1986), 1:19.

50. "Bailes de carnaval," *Caras y Caretas*, February 20, 1904.

CHAPTER 4

Some of the arguments made in this chapter were clarified or emerged in discussions with a number of people who were kind enough to put up with my enthusiasm for *Los bandidos*. I thank Eddie Wright-Rios for accompanying me around Oaxaca City one day in July as I bent his ear about my interpretation of the novel. I also thank Rita De Grandis for encouraging a historian to engage with the novel and for allowing me to assign and discuss a few chapters of it with students in Latin American Studies 201, a class we co-teach. I also wish to thank William Beezley, Ann Blum, Monica Rankin, and other faculty and students participating in the Oaxaca seminar for their comments and for helping to create such a wonderful venue for such discussion.

1. For a study of love letters written by everyday people during the Porfiriato and Revolution, see William E. French, *The Lettered Countryside: Love Letters, the Anatomy of Sentiment, and the Law in Porfirian and Revolutionary Chihuahua* (forthcoming). Some preliminary discussion of this topic can be found in William E. French, "'Te amo muncho:' The Love Letters of Pedro and Enriqueta," in Jeffrey M. Pilcher (ed.), *The Human Tradition in Mexico* (Wilmington, DE: Scholarly Resources, 2003), pp. 123–35.

2. Some have indeed argued that the novel serves as a useful source for the writing of history; see: Anne Staples "*Los bandidos de Río Frío* como fuente primaria para la historia de México," in Rafael Oleo Franco (ed.), *Literatura mexicana de otro fin de siglo* (México: El Colegio de México, 2001).

3. I use the term "literacies" deliberately, in order to stress that people participated in many different forms of literacy. Scholars such as Niko Besnier and David Barton propose an "event-centered" approach to literacy, focusing analysis on one particular social setting or context, such as personal letter writing, to ask how such a literacy derives its meanings from the broader contexts in which it is practiced and opening up the possibility of the existence of many "literacies," each associated, potentially, with different domains of life, different social groups, different

institutions, different genders, and each shaped by and helping to shape power in different ways. See Niko Besnier, *Literacy, Emotion and Authority: Reading and Writing on a Polynesian Atoll* (Cambridge: Cambridge University Press, 1995) and David Barton and Mary Hamilton, *Local Literacies: Reading and Writing in One Community* (Routledge, 1998).

4. Manuel Payno. *Los bandidos de Río Frío*, 2 vols. (México: Promociones Editoriales Mexicanas, 1979). An English translation has recently been published; see Manuel Payno, *The Bandits from Río Frío: A Naturalistic and Humorous Novel of Customs, Crimes and Horrors*, translated by Alan Fluckey (San Francisco: Heliographica Press, 2005) and Manuel Payno, *The Bandits from Río Frío: A Naturalistic and Humorous Novel of Customs, Crimes and Horrors, Part 2*, translated by Alan Fluckey (Tucson: Wheatmark Press, 2007).

5. Angel Rama's work has been particularly important in thinking about both the novelistic production of the lettered city as well as the letters of its less well known inhabitants; see Angel Rama, *The Lettered City*, translated by John Charles Chasteen (Durham: Duke University Press, 1996).

6. *The Bandits from Río Frío*, p. 211. The Spanish reads, " . . . y Juan muy aplicado escribiendo y leyendo la gramática castellana en la biblioteca."

7. As are you—for a recent study of this institution, please see Silvia Marina Arrom, *Containing the Poor: The Mexico City Poor House, 1774–1871* (Durham: Duke University Press, 2000).

8. *The Bandits from Río Frío*, p. 246.

9. The work of Doris Sommer was pioneering and continues to inform studies in this field; see Doris Sommer, *Foundational Fictions: The National Romances of Latin America* (Berkeley: University of California Press, 1993). On the role of reading in this process of imagining, see Fernando Unzueta, "Scenes of Reading: Imagining Nations/Romancing History in Spanish America," in Sara Castro-Klarén and John Charles Chasteen (eds.), *Beyond Imagined Communities: Reading and Writing the Nation in Nineteenth-Century Latin America* (Washington, D.C.: Woodrow Wilson Center Press, 2003).

10. *The Bandits from Río Frío*, p. 207.

11. *The Bandits from Río Frío*, pp. 148–49; in Spanish the line reads, " . . . sin que lograse ni leer con puntuación ni escribir con ortografía una mala letra." (p. 130)

12. *The Bandits from Río Frío*, p. 240.

13. *The Bandits from Río Frío*, p. 198.

14. *The Bandits from Río Frío, Part 2*, p. 561.

15. *The Bandits from Río Frío*, pp. 63, 89, and especially p. 94: "But I do not write novels that can be compared in interest with other French, English, and Spanish novels. Those have a literary value that I am very far from intending; I write these scenes of the actual and positive life of my country, portraits, badly made perhaps, of customs that are disappearing, of people who have died, of buildings that have tumbled down; they are a type of sketch of what actually happened which link the past, more or less, to the present. If a novel succeeds in doing this, so much the better. ['Si asi sale una novela, tanto major' or *If a novel comes out of it, so much the better*] If the reader appreciates this novel, that is my great desire, and that of my good friend and editor; and if through this novel the reader gets to know me better, he will understand that I would be remiss and

indifferent if I did not leave my children something of a moral inheritance, in that I was born into a life of labor and sorrow, not in the 'basket of Eagle pesos and ounces of gold.'"

16. When I was discussing the literary genre of *costumbrismo* with him, Miguel Angel Avilés Galán, a student completing his doctorate in Mexican history at University of British Columbia, remembered that his grandmother had read *Los bandidos* to him when he was a child of five or six years of age (conversation with author, May 22, 2009, Vancouver). In 1995, Carlos Monsiváis quoted long passages from the novel in his address to the Canadian Association of Latin American Studies, held in Vancouver, in order to make apparent the close links between the prose and the rhythms, cadences and expressions of the Spanish spoken at the time.

17. *The Bandits from Río Frío*, p. 29.

18. *The Bandits from Río Frío*, pp. 326–27.

19. *The Bandits from Río Frío*, pp. 84 and 89.

20. *The Bandits from Río Frío*, p. 216.

21. *Los bandidos de Río Frío*, pp. 240–42.

22. *Los bandidos de Río Frío*, p. 242.

23. *Los bandidos de Río Frío*, p. 243. On middle-class discourse, see William E. French, "Prostitutes and Guardian Angels: Women, Work and the Family in Porfirian Mexico," *Hispanic American Historical Review* 72:4 (1992).

24. *Los bandidos de Río Frío*, pp. 244–45.

25. Ibid, p. 245.

26. *The Bandits from Río Frío*, pp. 268–69.

27. Ricardo Pérez Montfort has extensively explored the development of such regional types or stereotypes in his writing. He is especially interested in tracing the history of the emergence of the charro and the china poblana as the dominant representations of Mexicanness from among a great many regional figures; see Ricardo Pérez Montfort, *Estampas de nacionalismo popular mexicano: Diez ensayos sobre cultura popular y nacionalismo*, segunda edición (México y Cuernavaca: Centro de Investigaciones y Estudios Superiores en Antropología Social y Centro de Investigación y Docencia en Humanidades del Estado de Morelos, 2003).

28. *The Bandits from Río Frío, Part 2*, p. 345.

29. *The Bandits from Río Frío, Part 2*, see chapter XXXIV, pp. 349–50.

30. Collapsing the distinction between state and criminal organization, Juan Pablo Dabove argues that it is precisely "Order and progress" and modern bureaucratic organization that the bandit state run by Relumbrón in *Los bandidos* bring to Porfirian Mexico. Dabove thus reads the novel as a critique of Porfirian modernity as well as of the presuppositions that underpinned the Mexican nation-state in the making. See his chapter entitled "Los bandidos de Río Frío: Banditry, the Criminal State, and the Critique of Porfirian Illusions," in Juan Pablo Dabove, *Nightmares of the Lettered City: Banditry and Literature in Latin America 1816–1929* (Pittsburgh: University of Pittsburgh Press, 2007). Perhaps it is too much of a stretch to compare Relumbrón's manipulation of the technology of the written word to the ways that businesses of today hope to harness social networking sites (social media) to target their advertising in a highly specialized manner. Readers will have to come to their own conclusions as to whether this is something to be desired or another "nightmare" of the digital world.

31. I adopt a broader definition of "educación" here than the one often used in translations, one that includes not only "education," but education in the sense of upbringing, manners, and morals. See also *Bandits from Río Frío*, p. 226.

32. *The Bandits from Río Frío*, p. 212.

33. *The Bandits from Río Frío, Part 2*, p. 425.

34. For this and other reasons, Evelia Trejo and Alvaro Matute have referred to the novel as a "parahistoria." They are cited in Staples, "Los Bandidos de Río Frío como fuente primaria para la historia de México," note 8, p. 352.

CHAPTER 5

Research for this chapter was made possible by a fellowship from the Department of History at the University of California, Los Angeles, and a small grant from the Latin American Center, also at the University of California, Los Angeles. Earlier versions were presented at the Southwest Social Science Conference (1995), the UCLA Latin American Center (1994), and the Conference on Latin American History (1997). I thank Robert Rydell, William Beezley, and Leticia Prislei for their comments and assistance.

1. J. M. Hammerton, *The Argentine through English Eyes* (London: Hodder & Stoughton, 1916), 81.

2. Argentina had participated in the Philadelphia and Santiago de Chile expositions in 1878. Moreover, the Sociedad Rural regularly held agricultural expositions in Argentina. In 1882, Argentina hosted a continental exposition in Buenos Aires. Susana I. Rato de Sambucetti, "Del 'Boom' a la crisis: Las presidencias de Juárez Celman y Carlos Pellegrini," *Revista de Historia de América* 71 (January–June 1971): 81; Ezequiel N. Paz, *Compte-Rendu de l'Exposition Continental de la République Argentine uverte en 1882 dans Buenos Aires* (Buenos Aires: Typographie de la "Pampa," 1882).

3. Argentines, like other Latin Americans, celebrated the centenary of the French Revolution as if it were their own national holiday. During the festivities, Argentines drew explicit parallels between their own nation's independence movement and the historical events and personages from the French Revolution. Leticia Prislei and Patricio Geli, "La Fiesta de la Revolución: Una celebración a dos voces," in *Imagen y recepción de la Revolución Francesa en la Argentina: Jornadas nacionales* (Buenos Aires: Grupo Editor Latinoamericano, 1990), 320–21.

4. The literature on expositions is expanding rapidly. The exposition studies that have most influenced my work have included Debora L. Silverman, "The 1889 Exhibition: The Crisis of Bourgeois Individualism," *Oppositions* 8 (1977): 71–91, and idem, *Art Nouveau in Fin-de-Siècle France: Politics, Psychology, and Style* (Berkeley: University of California Press, 1989); Mauricio Tenorio-Trillo, "Crafting the Modern Mexico: Mexico's Presence at World's Fairs, 1880s–1920s" (Ph.D. diss., Stanford University, 1994); Robert Rydell, *World of Fairs: The Century of Progress Expositions* (Chicago: University of Chicago Press, 1993); Warren Susman, "Ritual Fairs," *Chicago History* 12 (fall 1983): 4–7.

5. First published in 1845, this text is commonly viewed as one of the major expressions of nineteenth-century elite thought in Argentina. An example of the duality that Argentine elites perceived in their society appears in the following passage: "Before 1810, two distinct, rival, and incompatible forms of society, two differing kinds of civilization existed in the Argentine Republic: one being Spanish, European, and cultivated, the other barbarous, American, and almost wholly of native growth. The revolution which occurred acted as the cause . . . which set these two distinct forms of national existence face to face. . . ." Domingo Faustino Sarmiento, *Life in the Argentine Republic in the Days of the Tyrants, or Civilization and Barbarism* (New York: Hafner Press, 1968), 54.

6. "Provincial cosmopolitanism" is a term used by Michael Johns in "The Antinomies of Ruling Class Culture: The Buenos Aires Elite, 1880–1910," *Journal of Historical Sociology* 6, no. 11 (1993): 74–101. It refers to the Argentine elite's tendency to adopt modern, cosmopolitan trends within a traditional, patriarchal framework. Prislei and Geli use the term "cosmopolitan nationalism" in "La Fiesta de la Revolución." This term points to the efforts of Argentines to create images of their nation that would be successful within a cosmopolitan setting while enhancing those images with selective nationalist flourishes.

7. David Rock, *Argentina 1516–1987: From Spanish Colonization to Alfonsín* (Berkeley: University of California Press, 1987), 153.

8. Session of August 5, 1887, *Diario de Sesiones de la Cámara de Diputados*, vol. 2 (Buenos Aires: Imprenta La Universidad de J. N. Klingelfuss, 1887), 469.

9. Ibid., 470.

10. General Julio Roca to Antonino Cambaceres, Lucerne, August 13, 1887, Archivo General de la Nación (Argentina), Sala VII, 12-5-4 (hereafter cited as AGN).

11. Decree ordering the formation of an Argentine exposition commission, reprinted in *Catalogue spécial officiel de l'Exposición de la République Argentine* (Lille: Imprimerie L. Danel, 1889), 5. The simultaneous rise of world fairs and museums has been noted by Rydell, *World of Fairs*, 18–19, 32–33.

12. Santiago Alcorta, *La República Argentina en la Exposición de París de 1889 (Colección de informes reunidos por el delegado del gobierno D. Santiago Alcorta, publicación oficial)* (Paris: P. Mouillot, 1890), 3.

13. Francisco Latzina, *L'Agriculture et l'elevage dans la République Argentine d'après le recensement de la première quinzaine d'octobre de 1888* (Fait sous les auspices de la commission chargée des travaux de la section argentine a l'Exposition de Paris) (Paris: P. Mouillot, 1889), ix.

14. The ad hoc committee also included Romualdo Alais, Juan LeLong, N. Maillart, Gustavo Manigot, Ricardo Lezica, and Pablo Mathey. Later the following men were added: Alejandro Astoul, Pedro Christopherson, Adriano Penard, Manuel J. Güiraldez, and Rafael Igarzabal. Alcorta, *República Argentina en la Exposición de París*, 4. When Eduardo Cambaceres had to leave Paris suddenly on the eve of the exposition's opening owing to a terminal illness, he was temporarily replaced by Ricardo Lezica, who presided over the pavilion's inauguration. Santiago Alcorta later became the permanent head of the exposition commission. Luís Bravo, *América y España en la Exposición Universal de París de 1889* (Paris: Imprimerie Administrative Paul Dupont, 1890), 25.

15. María Luisa Bastos, introducción, in Eugenio Cambaceres, *Sin Rumbo* (Madrid: Anaya, 1971), 12–13.

16. David William Foster, *The Argentine Generation of 1880: Ideology and Cultural Texts* (Columbia: University of Missouri Press, 1990), 139.

17. By the late 1880s the Argentine government had launched an unprecedented drive to promote European immigration. In 1886 a network of immigration offices was established throughout Europe under the aegis of Pedro Lamas, a Uruguayan publicist living in Paris. These offices were charged with giving free passage to potential immigrants and ensuring their actual travel to Argentina. Lamas viewed part of his mission as counteracting the "Italianization" of the republic by promoting French, Belgian, and Swiss immigration. For more information on the work of Lamas in Paris, see Ingrid Fey, "First Tango in Paris: Latin Americans in Turn-of-the-Century France, 1880–1920" (Ph.D. diss., University of California at Los Angeles, 1996).

18. Alcorta, *República Argentina en la Exposición de París,* 4–5. The exact reasons for which Ballu's plan was chosen over the others remain unclear. Practical considerations—especially financial concerns—seem to have weeded out a number of plans, but the specific reasons why the commission chose Ballu's designs were not recorded in the minutes of the meetings held to discuss the selection of a plan.

19. Ibid., 6.

20. Gabriel Carrasco, "Exposición de Paris," *La Prensa,* June 11, 1889.

21. After some debate within the Argentine colony in Paris, the pavilion was opened "unofficially" on May 6, when the Universal Exposition was inaugurated. Nevertheless, the Argentine pavilion—and the pavilions of most other nations, for that matter—was not close to being completed. Argentina's early opening met with mixed reviews from Argentine participants, many of whom felt it would have been much better to have waited to open the pavilion.

22. Alcorta, *República Argentina en la Exposición de París,* 9.

23. *Europa y América,* June 1, 1889. Ricardo Lezica was a descendant of one of Argentina's most illustrious families. He had been a member of the ad hoc exposition commission in Paris for some time when he replaced Eugenio Cambaceres, who died not long before the exposition opened.

24. Copies of the new Argentine score were sent to bands all over France and other European countries. Alcorta, *República Argentina en la Exposición de París,* 22.

25. Enrique Ortega, "Desde París, 26 de Mayo de 1889," *La Prensa,* June 27, 1889.

26. Alcorta, *República Argentina en la Exposición de París,* 9. Blue and white were the colors of the Argentine flag. F. Simmonet, "L'Exposition de Paris. Septième lettre. L'Inauguration du Pavillon Argentin," *Courrier de la Plata,* June 26, 1889.

27. Ortega, "Desde París," June 27, 1889.

28. Alcorta, *La República Argentina en la Exposición de París,* 65–66.

29. According to a French dictionary, the term *rastaquouère* (*rastacuero* in Spanish) entered into French usage around 1880. Although a number of explanations have been offered for the term's usage, it apparently derived from the Spanish *raspa-cuero,* a derogatory term used to describe people involved in the trade of hides. Parisians liberally applied the word to the ever-increasing numbers of Latin Americans who traveled to or lived for long periods of time in Paris at the end of

the nineteenth century. For more information on the *rastaquouère,* see Fey, "First Tango in Paris," 84–87.

30. Eugenio Cambaceres to Antonino Cambaceres, Paris, January 20, 1889, AGN (Argentina), Sala VII, 12-5-4.

31. *The Paris Universal Exposition Album* (New York: Published under the patronage of the American Commission, 1889), LXXVIII.

32. "Miscelánea," *Europa y América,* May 15, 1889, 6.

33. Pedro S. Lamas, *Objetivos y resultados de mis trabajos en Europa en favor de la República Argentina (1882–1890)* (Paris: V. Groupy y Jourdan, 1890), 413.

34. *Paris Universal Exposition Album,* LXXIV.

35. Walter Benjamin has observed the connections between the appearance of iron in architecture and the development of the railroad, a potent symbol of nineteenth-century progress. Walter Benjamin, "Paris, Capital of the Nineteenth Century," in *Reflections: Essays, Aphorisms, Autobiographical Writings* (New York: Harcourt Brace, 1978), 147.

36. V. R., "La République Argentine à l'Exposition Universelle," *Revue Illustré du Rio de la Plata* 2 (1889): 4.

37. *Paris Universal Exposition Album,* LXXVIII.

38. C. de Varigny, "Les pavillons de l'Amérique," *L'Exposition de Paris 31* (August 31, 1889): 248.

39. Varigny wrote, "To say that the architecture is in perfect taste would be nevertheless exaggerated" ("Les pavillons de l'Amerique," 248). Ortega noted that the exterior of the upper gallery was a perfect example of *rastacuerismo* ("Desde París," June 27, 1889). A Spanish journalist explained the reception to the pavilion this way: "There is not much agreement among opinions with respect to the architectural taste that must have led to the construction of the palace. Some maintain that, like Mexico, the Argentine Republic has not in any way accommodated itself to what life's realities teach the other countries; and as regards the future, it is true that there is imagination so powerful that it can reach these unlimited horizons that like a reward to the love of work and progress Argentines hold dear" (F. Rivas Moreno, "Exposición de París," *Europa y América,* July 1, 1889, 3).

40. El Dorado is the name of a mythic place in Latin America where the streets are supposedly paved with gold and riches are free for the taking.

41. Quoted in Agustín Rivero Astengo, *Pellegrini 1846–1906,* vol. 2, Obras (Buenos Aires: Imprenta y Casa Editora "Coni," 1941), 213.

42. Silverman describes the light show on the Eiffel Tower as the most magnificent display at the exhibition: "Not only did it [the Eiffel Tower] direct glowing multicolored light beams into the night, but the tower's own structure was an iridescent vision. It was graced by thousands of colored light bulbs, and the surface of its iron lacework was coated by different shades of colored enamel paint" ("The 1889 Exhibition," 74).

43. Moreno, "Exposición de París," 3.

44. In the absence of any good pictures of the front entrance I have relied here on the description of Enrique Ortega ("Desde París," June 27, 1889).

45. Ortega, "Desde París," June 27, 1889.

46. Moreno, "Exposición de París," 3.

47. Alcorta, *Républica Argentina en la Exposición de París,* 13. In 1888 the Argentine government decided to devote a sum of 550,000 pesos a year to the promotion of frozen-meat exports. Rato de Sambuccetti, "Del 'Boom' a la crisis," 85. Uruguay also highlighted its meat industry in its pavilion's entrance. As one entered the main salon, the primary exhibit was a sarcophagus-like structure from which the life-size heads of four cattle emerged, among huge canisters of conserved beef. Aníbal Latino, "Sud-América en la Esposición de Paris," Reprinted from *La Nación in El Mercurio,* August 23, 1889.

48. A photograph of the coin appears in Alcorta's report. It matches Ortega's description of the stained-glass window; therefore, I am assuming that the two designs were nearly identical.

49. *Paris Universal Exhibition Album,* LXXIV.

50. Five gold medals were cast and given to the presidents of Argentina and France and other top French officials. Three hundred ten bronze medals were cast and were distributed to members of the exposition commission, employees, and delegates of other countries. Alcorta, *La Républica Argentina en la Exposición de París,* 22.

51. The French creators of these artworks had relied on sources sent from the Museo de la Plata for their models. Bravo, *América y España en la Exposic*ión, 6.

52. La Pêche à Buenos-Aires, La Vendange. Tony Robert-Fleury was an influential painter in Paris who served as a tutor at the Julian Academy and on the Salon jury. V. R., "La République Argentine à l'Exposition Universelle," *Revue Illustrée du Rio de la Plata* 2 (1889): 5.

53. *L'Architecture, Sculpture.* Jules Lefèbvre was an important academic painter in the second half of the nineteenth century. After the exposition he became a member of the Academie des Beaux-Arts. V. R., "La République Argentine à l'Exposition Universelle," 5.

54. Ibid. Gervex, Cormon, Lefèbvre, and Robert-Fleury had all contributed paintings to the Paris Opera House, built in the second half of the nineteenth century. Besnard was also an artist with experience in decorative arts. Gervex was one of the best known painters in Paris during the 1880s. John Milner, *The Studios of Paris: The Capital of Art in the Late Nineteenth Century* (New Haven: Yale University Press, 1988), 91, 105.

55. These sculptures were executed by Ch. Gautier, Turcan, Lefèbvre, and Pépin. V. R., "La République Argentine à l'Exposition Universelle," 5.

56. The Museo de La Plata. Bravo, *América y España en la Exposición,* 6.

57. Enrique Nelson to Eduardo Olivera, Paris, August 16, 1889, AGN (Argentina), Sala X, 43-9-6.

58. *Paris Universal Exhibition Album,* LXXVIII-IX; Alcorta, República Argentina en la Exposición de París, 13.

59. *Paris Exhibition Album,* LXXVIII-IX.

60. *Paris Exhibition Album,* LXXVIII-IX; Alcorta, República Argentina en la Exposición de París, 14.

61. Alcorta, *Républica Argentina en la Exposición de París,* 15.

62. Silverman, "The 1889 Exhibition," 78–80.

63. Robert Rydell has summed up these aspirations well: "The international exhibitions that shaped the cultural geography of the modern world were arenas for making ideas about progress visible. For the designers of international fairs,

progress was a universal force that active human intervention could direct toward national benefit." Robert Rydell, *The Books of the Fairs: Materials about World's Fairs 1834–1916* in the Smithsonian Institution Libraries (Chicago: American Library Association, 1992), 9.

64. C. de Varigny, "L'Exposition des Trois Amériques," *L'Exposition de Paris* 74 (January 29, 1890): 267–68.

65. Quoted in Rivero Astengo, *Pellegrini*, 213–14. Ironically, while most city dwellers in Buenos Aires were of European descent, the army and police were made up nearly entirely of mestizos from Salta, in northwestern Argentina.

66. José Paz to Dr. Norberto Quirno Costa, Paris, February 12, 1889, AGN (Argentina), Sala VII, Leg. 12-5-1.

67. Enrique Ortega, "Desde París, 9 de Junio de 1889," *La Prensa*, July 13, 1889.

68. Julio Victorica to Governor Acha, draft, Buenos Aires, March, 1888, AGN (Argentina), Sala VII, Leg. 12-5-3.

69. Roberto Cortés Conde, "The Growth of the Argentine Economy, c. 1870–1914," in *Argentina Since Independence* (Cambridge: Cambridge University Press, 1993), 56.

70. Enrique Nelson to Eduardo Olivera, Paris, August 16, 1889, AGN (Argentina), Sala X, Leg. 43-9-6.

71. Alcorta, *República Argentina en la Exposición de París*, 72.

72. Ibid., 65–69.

73. Session of August 26, 1891. *Diario de Sesiones de la Cámara de Diputados*, 1891, vol. 1 (Buenos Aires: Compañía Sud-Americana, 1891), 585–86.

74. Ibid., 586–87.

75. Pellegrini notes the pavilion's score in a letter to his brother Ernesto, then a deputy in the national government. Rivero Astengo, *Pellegrini*, 225.

76. "Echos," *Revue du Rio de la Plata* I, no. 6 (February 1890): 91; *Diario de Sesiones de la Cámara de Diputados*, 1892, vol. 1 (Buenos Aires: Imprenta "General Belgrano," 1892), 959–61; Albert B. Martínez, *Baedaker de la République Argentine*, 3d ed. (Barcelona: A. López Robert, 1907), 204–05; *Diario de Sesiones de la Cámara de Diputados*, 1895, vol. 1 (Buenos Aires: Compañía Sud-Americana de Billetes de Banco, 1895), 113–15.

77. Olga Vitali, "1889: La Argentina en la Exposición Mundial de París," *Todo es Historia* 243 (September 1987): 34.

CHAPTER 6

1. Matthew D. Esposito, "Memorializing Modern Mexico: The State Funerals of the Porfirian Era, 1876–1911" (Ph.D. diss., Texas Christian University, 1998).

2. Mexico City's municipal cemetery of Dolores, inaugurated by Díaz in 1877, served as the usual burial site for the city's population. The low average life expectancy and high infant mortality made death, funeral processions, and grave site patronage conspicuous aspects of everyday life of the era. Between 1876 and 1910, the average life expectancy rose from twenty-five years to thirty-one years. The infant mortality rate was extremely high even among the upper classes. Half of all infants died within their first year. *Historia moderna de Mexico*, vol. 4, *El porfiriato: La vida*

social, ed. Moises González Navarro (Mexico: Editorial Hermes, 1957), xviii, 52, 464; Moises González Navarro, *Sociedad y cultura en el porfiriato* (Mexico: Consejo Nacional para la Cultura y las Artes, 1994), 35. For Day of the Dead, see *Historia moderna de México,* vol. 3, *La república restaurada: La vida social,* ed. Luis González y González, Emma Cosío Villegas, and Guadalupe Monroy (Mexico: Editorial Hermes, 1956), 517.

3. Esposito, "Memorializing Modern Mexico," chap. 2; Barbara A. Tenenbaum, "Streetwise History: The Paseo de la Reforma and the Porfirian State, 1876–1910," in *Rituals of Rule, Rituals of Resistance: Public Celebrations and Popular Culture in Mexico,* ed. William H. Beezley, Cheryl English Martin, and William E. French (Wilmington, DE: SR Books, 1994), 127–50.

4. The population of the Federal District increased from 327,000 in 1877 to 720,753 in 1910. Moises González Navarro, *Estatísticas sociales del porfiriato,* 1877–1910 (Mexico: Dirección General de Estadísticas, 1956), 7–8.

5. Mona Ozouf, *Festivals of the French Revolution,* trans. Alan Sheridan (Cambridge: Harvard University Press, 1988), chaps. 6 and 7; Avner Ben-Amos, "The Sacred Center of Power: Paris and Republican State Funerals," *Journal of Interdisciplinary History* 22, no. 1 (summer 1991): 27–48.

6. For the coronation ceremony of the Virgin of Guadalupe, see William H. Beezley, *Judas at the Jockey Club and Other Episodes of Porfirian Mexico* (Lincoln: University of Nebraska Press, 1987), 9, and his unpublished paper, "Dining with the Dictator and Crowning the Virgin."

7. François Xavier Guerra, *Mexico: Del antigua régimen a la revolución,* trans. Sergio Fernández Bravo (Mexico: Fondo de Cultura Económica, 1995), I:84.

8. Guerra, *Antigua régimen a la revolución,* 79.

9. José Y. Limantour, *Apuntes sobre mi vida política* (Mexico, 1965), 15; Charles A. Hale, *Transformation of Liberalism in Late Nineteenth-Century Mexico* (Princeton: Princeton University Press, 1989), 107.

10. Daniel Cosío Villegas, *Historia moderna de México,* vol. 5, *El Porfirito: La Politica Exterior, Part One* (Mexico: Editorial Hermes, 1960), 76, 81; Hale, *Transformation of Liberalism,* 107.

11. Andrés Clemente Vázquez, *Entre brumas: Reminiscencias americanas y europeas* (Havana: Tip. Del Avisador Comercial, 1899), 28–29; *Mexican Herald,* October 9, 1895; *El Municipio Libre,* October 4, 1895; *El Noticioso,* October 4, 1895; Hale, *Transformation of Liberalism,* 59, 102–38; González Navarro, *La vida social,* 85, 102–03, 125.

12. Guerra, *Antigua régimen a la revolución,* 84.

13. Hale, *Transformation of Liberalism,* 106n, 107; Ricardo García Granados, *Historia de México desde la restauración de la república en 1867, hasta la caída de Porfirio Díaz,* 4 vols. (Mexico: 1923–1928), II:118–29.

14. Cosío Villegas, *La politíca exterior, Part One,* 5:757; Vázquez, *Reminiscencias americanas,* 29; González Navarro, *La vida social,* 8:499; Benedict Anderson, *Imagined Communities: Reflections on the Origin and Spread of Nationalism,* rev. ed. (London: Verso, 1991), 163–65.

15. *El Mundo Semanario Ilustrado, Suplemento,* October 6, 1895; *La Voz de México,* October 4, 5, 1895; *Mexican Herald,* October 4, 1895; *El Universal,* October 4, 1895; *El Tiempo,* October 4, 1895; *Two Republics,* October 4, 1895; *El Siglo XIX,* October 3, 1895.

16. "Manuel Romero Rubio, su expediente personal," Archivo Histórico "Génaro Estrada," Secretaría de Relaciones Exteriores, I/131/2863, docs. 111–117. This folder also contains letters of condolence from foreign legations in Mexico.

17. Rosendo Piñeda to Bernardo Reyes, October 3, 1895, Archivo del General Bernardo Reyes, Centro de Estudios de Historia de México Condumex (hereafter cited as CEHMC) 24/4610/1-2; [Reyes] to [Ignacio M. Escudero], October 1895, CEHMC Reyes 24/4608/1.

18. *Diario del Hogar*, October 4, 1895; *Mexican Herald*, October 4, 1895.

19. *Actas de Cabildo del Ayuntamiento Constitucional de México, Julio a Diciembre de 1895*, Edición de El Municipio Libre (Mexico: Imprenta de la Escuela Correcional, 1898), 174–75; *Discurso del C. Ingeniero Sebastián Camacho, Presidente del Ayuntamiento de 1895, al instalarse el Presidente de 1896. Contestación del C. Gobernador del Distrito Federal Gral. Pedro Rincon Gallardo y Memorias Documentada de los Trabajos Municipales de 1895* (Mexico: Imprenta y Litereria "La Europea," 1896), 32–35.

20. *Diario del Hogar*, October 4, 1895; *Mexican Herald*, October 4, 1895; *La Voz de México*, October 5, 6, 1895; *Two Republics*, October 4, 1895; *El Siglo XIX*, October 4, 1895; *El Partido Liberal*, October 5, 1895; *El Tiempo*, October 3, 5, 1895.

21. *El Siglo XIX*, October 4, 1895.

22. *El Tiempo*, October 4, 1895; *La Voz de México*, October 4, 1895; *Diario del Hogar*, October 6, 1895.

23. *El Nacional*, October 4, 1895; *El Tiempo*, October 4, 1895; *Two Republics*, October 5, 1895; *Diario del Hogar*; April 30, 1889; Francisco Sosa, *Las estatuas de la Reforma* (Mexico City: Secretaría de Fomento, 1900).

24. *El Tiempo*, October 5, 1895; *Mexican Herald*, October 4, 5, 1895; *La Voz de México*, October 4, 5, 1895; *El Noticioso*, October 4, 1895.

25. *La Patria Ilustrada*, October 7, 1895; *El Siglo Diez y Nueve*, August 17, 1895.

26. *La Voz de México*, October 6, 1895. The paper published a list of government officials who participated.

27. *El Mundo Semanario Ilustrado, Suplemento*, September 6, 1895.

28. *La Voz de México*, October 6, 1895.

29. *La Voz de México*, October 5, 1895.

30. *Mexican Herald*, October 5, 1895; *El Siglo XIX*, October 5, 1895; *El Tiempo*, October 5, 1895; Esposito, "Memorializing Modern Mexico," chap. 7.

31. *El Partido Liberal*, October 8, 1895.

32. *El Diario Oficial*, October 5, 1895.

33. *Mexican Herald*, October 5, 1895; *El Tiempo*, October 5, 1895; *El Noticioso*, October 5, 1895; *El Nacional*, October 4, 1895; *El Mundo Semanario Ilustrado, Suplemento*, October 6, 1895.

34. *El Noticioso*, October 5, 1895; *Two Republics*, October 5, 1895.

35. *Two Republics*, October 5, 1895; *Mexican Herald*, October 5, 1895.

36. *La Federación*, October 5, 1895. The population of Mexico City was 476,473. Three-fourths, or 357,000 people, would have been a high figure by any stretch of the imagination.

37. *La Voz de México*, October 6, 1895; *Two Republics*, October 5, 1895; *El Mundo Semanario Ilustrado, Suplemento*, October 6, 1895; *La Patria Ilustrada*, October 7, 1895.

38. *Mexican Herald*, October 5, 1895; *La Voz de México*, October 6, 1895.

39. *Two Republics*, October 5, 1895; *Mexican Herald*, October 5, 1895; *El Tiempo*, October 5, 6, 1895; *El Siglo XIX*, October 5, 1895; *El Gil Blas*, October 6, 1895.

40. *El Noticioso*, October 4, 5, 1895.

41. *Mexican Herald*, October 5, 1895; *Two Republics*, October 5, 1895; *El Noticioso*, October 5, 1895; *El Siglo XIX*, October 5, 1895; *El Mundo Semanario Ilustrado, Suplemento*, October 6, 1895.

42. Colin M. MacLachlan and William H. Beezley, *El Gran Pueblo: A History of Greater Mexico* (Englewood Cliffs, NJ: Prentice Hall, 1994), 138.

43. *La Federación*, October 5, 1895. The speech was later printed in *El Partido Liberal*, October 8, 1895.

44. *El Mundo Semanario Ilustrado, Suplemento*, October 6, 1895; *El Noticioso*, October 5, 1895; *Mexican Herald*, October 5, 1895.

45. *Diario del Hogar*, October 4, 6, 11, 1895; *El Monitor Republicano*, October 10, 11, 1895; and the militant Catholic newspaper *La Tribuna*, October 6, 1895. After the furor died down, *El Tiempo* admitted that the Romero Rubio confession was false (October 13, 1895).

46. Colección General Porfirio Díaz, Legajo 20, numeros 3963–3979, docs. 13931–14839.

47. *Siglo XIX*, October 5, 1895; *El Monitor Republicano*, October 15, 1895.

48. *El Nacional*, November 4, 5, 1895; *El Tiempo*, November 3, 1895; *El Monitor Republicano*, October 15, November 7, 1895; *El Siglo XIX*, November 4, 6, 1895; *El Mundo Semanario Ilustrado*, November 10, 1895.

49. *Discursos y poesías pronunciados en honor del Señor Licenciado Manuel Romero Rubio en el Panteón Frances el día de 1896 y en el Teatro Nacional el 14 del mismo mes y año* (Mexico: Imp. y Lit. de F. Díaz de Leon, 1896), 2–3, 8–9.

50. Joaquín D. Casasus, *En honor de los muertos* (Mexico: 1910; 2d ed.: Consejo Editorial del Gobierno del Estado de Tabasco, 1981), 9–25.

CHAPTER 7

1. *El Comercio*, March 29, 1992, July 19, 1992, and July 12, 1992, respectively.

2. See for example, Hans-Joachim König, "Símbolos nacionales y retórica política en la independencia: El caso de la Nueva Granada," in *Problemas de la formación del estado y la nación en Hispanoamérica*, ed. I. Buisson and G. Kahle (Cologne: Lateinamericanische Forschungen, 1984), 13:389–405; Carlos R. Espinoza Fernández de Córdoba, "La máscara del Inca: Una investigación acerca del teatro político de la colonia," *Miscelánea Histórica Ecuatoriana* 2, no. 2 (1989): 7–39; Georges Lomnê, "La revolución francesa y lo simbólico en la liturgia política bolivariana," *Miscelánea Histórica Ecuatoriana* 2, no. 2 (1989): 41–67.

3. König, "Símbolos nacionales," 389–90.

4. *Hoy*, August 11, 1992.

5. Jonathan Friedman, "Narcissism, Roots, and Postmodernity: The Constitution of Selfhood in the Global Crisis," in *Modernity and Identity*, ed. Scott Lash and Jonathan Friedman (Oxford: Blackwell, 1991), 331–36.

6. Thomas Abercrombie, "To Be Indian, to Be Bolivian: 'Ethnic' and 'National' Discourses of Identity," in *Nation-States and Indians in Latin America*, ed. Greg Urban and Joel Scherzer (Austin: University of Texas Press, 1991), 95–130.

7. Tristán Platt, "Simón Bolívar, the Sun of Justice, and the Amerindian Virgin: Andean Conceptions of the Patria in Nineteenth-Century Potosí," *Journal of Latin American Studies* 25 (1993): 159–83; Blanca Muratorio, *The Life and Times of Grandfather Alonso: Culture and History of the Upper Amazon* (New Brunswick: Rutgers University Press, 1991); Steve J. Stern, ed., *Resistance, Rebellion, and Consciousness in the Andean Peasant World, 18th and 20th Centuries* (Madison: University of Wisconsin Press, 1987).

8. Terry Goldie, *Fear and Temptation: The Image of the Indigene in Canadian, Australian, and New Zealand Literatures* (Kingston: McGill-Queen's University Press, 1989), 5.

9. Bernard S. Cohn and Nicholas B. Dirks, "Beyond the Fringe: The Nation-state, Colonialism, and the Technologies of Power," *Journal of Historical Sociology* 1, no. 2 (1988): 227.

10. "Informe Junta Central del 4º Centenario del Descubrimiento de América. Informe del Ministro del Interior y Relaciones Exteriores al Congreso ordinario 1892" (Quito: Archivo-Biblioteca de la Función Legislativa), p. 3.

11. Eric Hobsbawm, Introduction, in *The Invention of Tradition*, ed. Eric Hobsbawn and Terrence Ranger (Cambridge: Cambridge University Press, 1983), 10.

12. Carol A. Breckenbridge, "The Aesthetic and Politics of Colonial Collecting: India at World Fairs," *Comparative Studies in Society and History* 31, no. 3 (1989): 196.

13. Robert W. Rydell, *All the World's a Fair: Visions of Empire at American International Expositions, 1876–1916* (Chicago: University of Chicago Press, 1984), 3.

14. Breckenridge, "The Aesthetic," 196; Benedict Anderson, *The Imagined Communities: Reflections on the Origin and Spread of Nationalism* (London: Verso, 1983).

15. "Informe Junta Central del 4º Centenario del Descubrimiento de América. Informe del Ministro del Interior y Relaciones Exteriores al Congreso ordinario 1892" (Quito: Archivo-Biblioteca de la Función Legislativa), p. 3.

16. *Catálogo general de la exposición histórico-americana de Madrid 1892, 1983*, vol. I (located in the Department of Special Collections, Henry Madden Library, California State University, Fresno, CA).

17. John Murra, "The Historic Tribes of Ecuador," in *The Handbook of South American Indians*, ed. Julian H. Steward (New York: Cooper Square Publishers, 1963), 2:792.

18. *Catálogo General*, 3–43.

19. L. F. Carbo, *El Ecuador en Chicago: Por el "Diario de avisos de Guayaquil, Ecuador"* (New York: A. E. Chasmar & Co., 1894).

20. *Catálogo General*, 3–43.

21. Blanca Muratorio, "Protestantism and Capitalism Revisited in the Rural Highlands of Ecuador," *The Journal of Peasant Studies* 8, no. 1 (1980): 37–60.

22. Hugh Honour, *The New Golden Land: European Images of America from the Discovery to the Present Time* (New York: Pantheon Books, 1975), 183.

23. David Harvey, *The Condition of Postmodernity: An Inquiry into the Origins of Cultural Change* (Oxford: Basil Blackwood, 1989), 273.

24. Quoted in Henri Favre, "Bolívar et les Indiens," in *Simón Bolívar*, ed. Laurence Tacou (Paris: Cahiers de l'Herne, 1986), 283, n. 12.

25. Ibid.

26. In contemporary Ecuador, the Otavaleños are still the preferred group represented on tourist postcards and made to symbolize Ecuador. It is evident in the

best-seller postcard depicting an Otavaleño family displaying its popular folk art and crafts, with the background of the other "universal" symbol of Ecuador, the rather distasteful-looking monument erected in La Mitad del Mundo, the "must-see" destination for all foreign and national tourists.

27. Breckenbridge, "The Aesthestic," 200–201.

28. Edmund Swinglehurst, *Cook's Tours: The Story of Popular Travel* (Poole, Dorset, U.K.: Blandford Press, 1982).

29. Rydell, 40–41.

30. See, for example, Frank Salomon, "Weavers of Otavalo," in *Cultural Transformations and Ethnicity in Modern Ecuador*, ed. Norman E. Whitten, Jr. (Urbana: University of Illinois Press, 1981).

31. Michael T. Ryan, "Assimilating New Worlds in the Sixteenth and Seventeenth Centuries," *Comparative Studies in Society and History* 23, no. 4 (1981): 537.

32. Robert F. Berkhofer, Jr., *The White Man's Indian: Images of the American Indian from Columbus to the Present* (New York: Alfred A. Knopf, 1978), 59.

33. Blanca Muratorio, "The Gaze of the Other," in *Retrato de la Amazonía: Ecuador 1880–1945*, edited by Lucía Chiriboga and Soledad Cruz (Quito: Ediciones Libri Mundi, 1992), 181–93.

34. Anne-Christine Taylor, "La invención del Jívaro: Notas etnográficas sobre un fantasma occidental," in *Memorias del primer simposio europeo sobre antropología del Ecuador* (Quito: Ediciones Abya-Yala, 1985), 255–67.

35. See Marjorie Munsterberg, "The World Viewed: Works in Nineteenth-Century Realism," *Studies in Visual Anthropology* 8, no. 3 (1982): 55–69.

36. José Maria Vargas, "El arte ecuatoriano en el siglo XIX," *Cultura 7*, no. 19 (1984): 428.

37. Vargas, "El arte ecuatoriano," 376, 428; Juan Castro y Velázquez, "Un importante momento en la pintura ecuatoriana: El Costumbrismo," in *Libro del Sesquicentenario*. Vol. 2. *Arte y cultura: Ecuador: 1830–1980* (Quito: Corporación Editora Nacional, 1980), 471.

38. Vargas, "El arte ecuatoriano," 405.

39. Castro y Velázquez, "Un importante momento," 470; Fileoto Samaniego Salazar, "El retrato en el Ecuador," in *Libro del Sesquicentenario*. Vol. 2. *Arte y cultura: Ecuador: 1830–1980* (Quito: Corporación Editora Nacional, 1980), 457–65.

40. Magdalena Gallegos de Donoso, "Juan León Mera y Joaquín Pinto: Testigos de su tiempo," in *Juan León Mera: Cantares de publo ecuatoriano* (Quito: Museo del Banco Central del Ecuador, n.d.), 11–15.

41. Vargas, "El arte ecuatoriano," 403.

42. Johannes Fabian, *Time and the Other: How Anthropology Makes Its Object* (New York: Columbia University Press, 1983).

43. Eric J. Hobsbawm, *Nations and Nationalism Since 1780: Programme, Myth, Reality* (Cambridge: Cambridge University Press, 1990), 12.

44. Juan León Mera, *La Estatua de Sucre* (Ambato: Imprenta de Salvador S. Porras), 2.

45. Gerald Sider, "When Parrots Learn to Talk, and Why They Can't: Domination, Deception, and Self-Deception in Indian-White Relations," *Comparative Studies in Society and History* 29, no. 1 (1987): 7.

46. Goldie, *Fear and Temptation*, 10.

47. Clifford Geertz, "Centers, Kings, and Charisma: Reflections on the Symbolics of Power," in *Rites of Power: Symbolism, Ritual and Politics since the Middle Ages*, ed. Sean Wilentz (Philadelphia: University of Pennsylvania Press, 1985), 13–38.

48. Peter Mason, *Deconstructing America: Representations of the Other* (London: Routledge, 1990), 163.

49. *Diario Hoy*, August 21, 1992.

50. Stephen William Foster, "The Exotic as a Symbolic System," *Dialectical Anthropology* 7 (1982): 21–30.

CHAPTER 8

1. Jorge Stanburg Aguirre, *La gran cocina peruana* (Lima: Peru Reporting E.I.R.L., 1995), 225.

2. Patricia Quintana with Carol Haralson, *Mexico's Feasts of Life* (Tulsa: Council Oaks Books, 1989).

3. Guadalupe Rivera and Marie-Pierre Colle, *Frida's Fiestas: Recipes and Reminiscences of Life with Frida Kahlo* (New York: Clarkson N. Potter, 1994), 49.

4. Dianna Kennedy, *My Mexico: A Culinary Odyssey with More Than 300 Recipes* (New York: Clarkson N. Potter, 1998), 10.

5. "Lima Gastronómica," I, in *Lima: Paseos por la ciudad y su historia* (Lima: Banco Sudamericano–Guías Expreso, n.d.), 299.

6. Ibid., 296, 312; Kennedy, *My Mexico*, 254–57.

7. Laura Esquivel, *Like Water for Chocolate: A Novel in Monthly Installments, with Recipes, Romances, and Home Remedies*, trans. Carol Christensen and Thomas Christensen (New York: Doubleday, 1992).

8. *El cocinero mexicano*, 3 vols. (Mexico City: Imprenta de Galván a cargo de Mariano Arévalo, 1931), preface and 1:77.

9. *Nuevo cocinero mejicano en forma de diccionario* (Paris and Mexico City: Librería de Rosa y Bouret, 1868), x.

10. *Nuevo y sencillo arte de cocina* (Mexico City: Imprenta de Santiago Pérez, 1836), iv. See also *Libro de cocina: Arreglado a los usos y costumbres nacionales* (Mexico City: Imprenta de I. Guerrero, n.d.).

11. Narciso Bassols, *La cocinero poblana y el libro de las familias: Novísimo manual práctico de cocina española, francesa, inglesa, y mexicana*, 2 vols. (Puebla, Mexico: Narciso Bassols, 1877), 1:3.

12. Vicenta Torres de Rubio, *Cocina michoacana* (Zamora, Michoacán, Mexico: Imprenta Moderna, 1896), iii–iv.

13. *Recetas prácticas para la señora de casa sobre cocina, repostería, pasteles, nevería, etc.* (Guadalajara: Imprenta del Orfanatorio del Sagrado Corazón de Jesús, 1892), 3.

14. *Nuevo cocinero mejicano*, 62, 158, 264; Bassols, *La cocinera poblana*, 1:37; Torres, *Cocina michoacana*, 28, 36, 224, 409; *El Siglo XIX*, February 2, 1853. Donato Guerra, a hero of the French intervention, may have tasted his namesake cod, but Moctezuma never ate the dessert named in his honor, which was made of candied sugar, ground almonds, and bread rolls.

15. Guillermo Prieto, *Memorias de mis tiempos, 1828 á 1840* (Mexico City: Librería de la Vda. de C. Bouret, 1906), 287; *Nuevo cocinero mejicano*, preface, 940; *Diario del Hogar*, February 9, 1886; *La Patria*, December 2, 1898.

16. For a comprehensive listing of cookbooks published in Mexico since 1821, see the appendix in Jeffrey M. Pilcher, "¡Vivan Tamales! The Creation of a Mexican National Cuisine" (Ph.D. diss., Texas Christian University, 1993).

17. Miguel Angel Peral, *Diccionario biográfico mexicano* (Mexico City: Editorial PAC, 1944), 292; *Diccionario Porrúa de historia, biografía y geografía de México*, 3d ed., 2 vols. (Mexico City: Editorial Porrúa, 1970), 1:833, 2:1434, 2:1593.

18. *El cocinero mejicano refundido y considerable aumentado en esta segunda edición*, 3 vols. (Mexico City: Imprenta de Galván a cargo de Mariano Arevalo, 1834), 1:391.

19. Dolores Avila Hernández, "Región centro norte," in *Atlas cultural de México: Gastronomía*, ed. Dolores Avila Hernández, et al. (Mexico City: Grupo Editorial Planeta, 1988), 67–78. This discussion draws on insights from Claudio Lomnitz-Adler, *Exits from the Labyrinth: Culture and Ideology in the Mexican National Space* (Berkeley: University of California Press, 1992), 51–56.

20. *Nuevo y sencillo arte*.

21. *Nuevo cocinero mejicano*, 879.

22. *El cocinero mexicano*, 1:178–88.

23. *Nuevo cocinero mejicano*, 44.

24. Mariano Galván Rivera, *Diccionario de cocina o el nuevo cocinero mexicano en forma de diccionario* (Mexico City: Imprenta Ignacio Cumplido, 1845), quoted in Diana Kennedy, *The Art of Mexican Cooking: Traditional Mexican Cooking for Aficionados* (New York: Bantam, 1989), 84.

25. Juan Pedro Viqueira Albán, *¿Relajados o reprimidos? Diversiones públicas y vida social en la ciudad de México durante el Siglo de las Luces* (Mexico City: Fondo de Cultura Económica, 1987), 132–35 (an English translation of this volume by Sonya Lipsett-Rivera and Sergio Rivera Ayala is available from SR Books); Ignacio González-Polo, ed., *Reflexiones y apuntes sobre la ciudad de México (fines de la colonia)* (Mexico City: Departamento del Distrito Federal, 1984), 61.

26. Fanny Calderón de la Barca, *Life in Mexico: The Letters of Fanny Calderón de la Barca*, ed. Howard T. Fisher and Marion Hall Fisher (Garden City, NY: Doubleday, 1966), 156, 194–99, 541–42; William Bullock, *Six Months Residence and Travels in Mexico* (Port Washington, NY: Kennikat Press, 1971 [1824]), 431; John G. Bourke, "The Folk-Foods of the Rio Grande Valley and of Northern Mexico," *Journal of American Folk-Lore* (1895): 41–71; Fanny Chambers Gooch [Iglehart], *Face to Face with the Mexicans* (New York: Fords, Howard, & Hulbert, 1887), 62–64, 285, 438; Viqueira Albán, *¿Relajados o reprimidos?*, 160–62; Martín González de la Vara, *La historia del helado en México* (Mexico City: Maas y Asociados, 1989), 41.

27. Archivo Histórico de la Secretaría de Salud (hereafter AHSS), Inspección, box 1, exp. 4, proclamation dated June 19, 1854; Archivo Histórico de la Ciudad de México, vol. 3668, exp. 93, Cayetano Teller to Cipriano Robert, September 13, 1870. See also Anne Staples, "Orden y Buen Policía: Nineteenth-Century Efforts to Regulate Public Behavior (Tlacotlalpan, Veracruz, and Mexico City at Mid-Century)," in *Rituals of Rule, Rituals of Resistance: Public Celebrations and Popular Culture in Mexico*, ed. by William H. Beezley, Cheryl English Martin, and William E. French (Wilmington, DE: SR Books, 1994), 115–26.

28. Francisco Bulnes, *El porvenir de las naciones Hispano Americanas ante las conquistas recientes de Europa y los Estados Unidos* (Mexico City: Imprenta de Mariano

Nava, 1899), 7, 17, 30; Julio Guerrero, *La génesis del crimen en México: Estudio de psiquiatría social* (Mexico City: Librería de la Vda. de Ch. Bouret, 1901), 148.

29. *El Imparcial*, August 29, 1897.

30. *La Mujer*, April 15, 1881; *El Imparcial*, July 2, November 30, December 2, 1898.

31. Jacinto Anduiza, *El libro del hogar* (Pachuco, Hidalgo: Imprenta "La Europea," 1893), 6.

32. Calderón de la Barca, *Life in Mexico*, 55, 129, 170, 614.

33. Stephen Mennell, *All Manners of Food: Eating and Taste in England and France from the Middle Ages to the Present* (Oxford: Basil Blackwell, 1985), 134–65; Rebecca Spang, "A Confusion of Appetites: The Emergence of Paris Restaurant Culture, 1740–1848" (Ph.D. diss., Cornell University, 1993), 77–83; Piero Camporesi, *Exotic Brew: The Art of Living in the Age of Enlightenment*, trans. Christopher Woodall (Cambridge, U.K.: Polity Press, 1994), 27–35; T. Sarah Peterson, *Acquired Taste: The French Origins of Modern Cooking* (Ithaca: Cornell University Press, 1994), 183–208.

34. José Luis Juárez, "La lenta emergencia de la comida mexicana, ambigüedades criollas 1750–1800" (Lic. thesis, Escuela Nacional de Antropología e Historia, 1993), 103–05.

35. William H. Beezley, "The Porfirian Smart Set Anticipates Thorstein Veblen in Guadalajara," in *Rituals of Rule, Rituals of Resistance: Public Celebrations and Popular Culture in Mexico*, ed. William H. Beezley, Cheryl English Martin, and William E. French (Wilmington, DE: SR Books, 1994), 178.

36. See, for example, *Manual del cocinero y cocinera, tomada del periódico literario La Risa* (Puebla: Imprenta de José María Macías, 1849), 70; *Novísimo arte de cocina*, 30; María Antonio Gutiérrez, *El ama de casa* (Mexico City: Librería de la Vda. de Ch. Bouret, 1899), 352–54; *Semana de las Señoritas*, 1851, 1:75; *La Semana en el Hogar*, August 12, 1895; *El Heraldo del Hogar*, July 20, 1910.

37. AHSS, Inspección, box 1, exp. 5, report of sanitary inspector Ildefonso Velasco, August 26, 1872. See also the advertisements.

38. Jean Anthelme Brillat-Savarín, *Fisiología del gusto*, trans. Eufemio Romero (Mexico City: Imprenta de Juan R. Navarro, 1852); *El libro de cocina de Jules Gouffé, antiguo jefe de cocina del Jockey Club de Paris*, 2 vols. (Mexico City: Editorial Rodríguez y Co., 1893).

39. Antonio García Cubas, *El libro de mis recuerdos* (Mexico City: Secretaría de Educación Pública, 1946), 50–53; Luis González y González, Emma Cosío Villegas, and Guadalupe Monroy, *La República Resturada: La vida social*, vol. 3 of *Historia moderna de México*, ed. Daniel Cosío Villegas (Mexico City: Editorial Hermes, 1956), 492–93.

40. *Salvador Novo, Cocina mexicana o Historia gastronómica de la Ciudad de México* (Mexico City: Editorial Porrúa, 1993), 125–35; *El Imparcial*, June 3, 1898; *Monterey News*, September 18, 1903.

41. Novo, *Cocina mexicana*, 135–37; *Recuerdo gastronómico del centenario, 1810–1910* (Mexico: n.p., 1910); Beezley, "Porfirian Smart Set," 180; *Monterey News*, September 18, 1903; Harvey A. Levenstein, *Revolution at the Table: The Transformation of the American Diet* (New York: Oxford University Press, 1988), 96.

42. García Cubas, *El libro de mis recuerdos*, 52–53.

43. Camporesi, *Exotic Brew*, 49.

44. Compare *La Mujer*, April 15, 1881, with *El cocinero mexicano*, 1:178.

45. See, for example, *El cocinero mexicano*, vol. 2; *Manual del cocinero y cocinera*, 80–312; *Nuevo y sencillo arte*, 32–134, 162–72, 195–217.

46. Gooch, *Face to Face*, 498.

47. Calderón de la Barca, *Life in Mexico*, 55, 156.

48. Bullock, *Six Months Residence in Mexico*, 253.

49. *Nuevo y sencillo arte*, iv; *Manual del cocinero y cocinera*, 92; Hortensia Rendón de García, *Antiguo manual de cocina yucateca; fórmulas para condimentar los platos más usuales en la península*, 7th ed., 3 vols. (Mérida: Librería Burrel, 1938 [first edition, 1898]), 1:55.

50. Benedict Anderson, *Imagined Communities: Reflections on the Origin and Spread of Nationalism*, rev. ed. (London: Verso, 1991).

51. Silvia Marina Arrom, *The Women of Mexico City, 1790–1957* (Stanford: Stanford University Press, 1985), 231–38.

52. Anduiza, *El ama de casa*, 1.

53. Anduiza, *El libro del hogar*, 6.

54. Jean Franco, *Plotting Women: Gender and Representation in* Mexico (New York: Columbia University Press, 1988), 23–54.

55. Gooch, *Face to Face*, 494.

56. Simone Beck, *Food and Friends: Recipes and Memories from Simca's Cuisine* (New York: Viking, 1991), 35.

57. José L. Cossío, ed., *Recetario de cocina mexicana escrito por Doña María Luísa Soto Murguindo de Cossío* (Mexico City: Vargas Rea, 1968), 7, 46–47; compare with *Recetas prácticas*, 95–97. Dessert recipes attributed to Maxiana and Jesús María appeared in the manuscript by Marianita Vázquez de Celis, "Cuaderno de cosina," 1874, Centro de Estudios de Historia de México, Condumex, Fondo 71–72, 1891. Carmen Cabrera cooked artichokes using Pachita's recipe in Eugenio del Hoyo Cabrera, ed., *La cocina jerezana en tiempos de López Velarde* (Mexico City: Fondo de Cultura Económica, 1988), 48. See also Patricia Preciado Martín, *Songs My Mother Sang to Me: An Oral History of Mexican American Women* (Tucson: University of Arizona Press, 1992), 56.

58. *Recetas prácticas*, 3; Diana Kennedy, *Recipes from the Regional Cooks of Mexico* (New York: Harper & Row, 1978), 138.

59. Torres, *Cocina michoacana*, 39, 58, 74, 102.

60. Ibid., 62; *Recetas prácticas*, 103; *Recetas de cocina*, quoted in Kennedy, *Regional Cooks of Mexico*, 138.

61. See the recipes for chiles fritos, sopa de bolitas, lomo frito, and lengua rellena in Cossio, *Recetario de cocina mexicana*, 24, 25, 49; and *Recetas prácticas*, 144, 13, 32, 55.

62. *Manual del cocinero*, 175.

63. Torres, *Cocina michoacana*, 193, 340–50, 752. On Guadalupine devotion, see Jacques Lafaye, *Quetzalcoatl and Guadalupe: The Formation of Mexican National Consciousness* (Chicago: University of Chicago Press, 1982). For a description of the 1895 crowning ceremony, see Beezley, "Porfirian Smart Set," 181.

64. *La Libertad*, December 23, 1883; Wilhelmine Weber, "The Winter Festivals of Mexico: A Christmas That Combines Aztec and Christian Legends," *Craftsman* 23, no. 3 (December 1912): 266–74; *Excelsior*, December 11, 1926.

65. *Recetas prácticas*, 172; *Nuestro libro*, 40–44.

66. Torres, *Cocina michoacana*, v.

67. *Restaurante*, January 1963.

68. Faustina Lavalle de Hernández M., *La exquisita cocina de Campeche: 400 recetas experimentadas* (Mexico City: Imprenta "Londres," 1939), 19.

69. Jeffrey M. Pilcher, "¡Que vivan los Tamales!" *Food and the Making of Mexican Identity* (Albuquerque: University of New Mexico Press, 1998), chap. 6.

CHAPTER 9

1. Peter Klaren, "The Origins of Modern Peru, 1880–1930," in *The Cambridge History of Latin America*, vol. 5, 1870–1930, ed. Leslie Bethell (New York: Cambridge University Press, 1986), 596.

2. Recent studies examining state modernization programs include Natalia Majluf, *Escultura y espacio público: Lima, 1850–1879*, Documento de Trajo no. 67, Serie "Historia del Arte" no. 2 (Lima: IEP, 1994); Alicia del Aguila, "Callejones y mansiones: Espacios de opinión pública y formas de acción política en Lima: El funcionamiento de una democracia restringida (1895–1919)" (tesis para optar el grado de Maestría en Ciencias Sociales, Facultad Latinoamericana de Ciencias Sociales, Mexico, 1994); Felipe Portocarrero, *El Imperio Prado: 1890–1950* (Lima: Universidad del Pacífico, Centro de Investigación, 1995); Francesca Denegri, *El abanico y la cigarrera: La primera generación de mujeres ilustradas en el Perú* (Lima: Flora Tristan Centro de la Mujer Peruana, Instituto de Estudios Peruanas, 1996); Carlos Aguirre, "La penitenciaria de Lima y la modernización de la justicia penal en el siglo XIX," in *Mundos interiores: Lima 1850–1950*, ed. Aldo Panfichi and Felipe Portocarrero (Lima: Universidad del Pacífico, 1996); and María Emma Mannarelli, "Cuerpo femenino y discurso médico," in *Margenes, encuentro y debate* (Lima: Sur [Casa de Estudios del Socialismo], 1997), IX, no. 15.

3. This study focuses on the elites rather than the oligarchy because this term allows for a better understanding of internal heterogeneity of the managerial class. Studies shaping my understanding of this group include Anthony Giddens, *Elites in the British Class Structure* (Cambridge: Cambridge University, Department of Applied Economics, 1972); Carlos Franco and Hugo Neira, *El problema de las elites y el pensamiento: Los novecentristas peruanos, 1895–1930* (Lima: Central de Estudios para el Desarrollo y la Participación, 1986); and Alfonso Quiroz, "Grupos económicos y decisiones financieras en el Perú, 1884–1930," *Apuntes: Revista de Ciencias Sociales* 19 (1986): 72–95.

4. Atanasio Fuentes, *Estadística general de Lima* (Lima: Tipografía Nacional M. N. Corpancho, 1858).

5. At the end of the eighteenth century Lima encompassed 456 hectares; in 1908 it occupied 1,292 hectares. Manuel Burga and Alberto Flores Galindo, *Apogeo y crisis de la república aristocrática* (Lima: Ediciones Rikchay, 1980), 31.

6. Natalia Majluf in *Escultura y espacio público*, a study of public space and ornamentation, examines the efforts to remove all traces of the colonial past to institute the new republican order at midcentury.

7. Doctoral thesis in medicine by Enrique León, 1908, cited by Burga and Flores Galindo, *Apogeo*, 31.

8. Abelardo Garmarra, Lima: *Unos cuantos barrios y unos cuantos tipos (al comensar el siglo XIX)* (Lima: Editor Pedro Berrio, Litografía y Tipografía Nacional Pedro Berrio, 1903), 4.

9. The 1908 census identified mestizos as anyone not of pure white, black, Asian, or indigenous racial stock. See p. 94 of the census.

10. Garmarra, *Lima*, 5.

11. The Regulation of Municipalities is found in *Ordenanzas de la Ciudad de Lima, Coleción de reglamentos, decretos, resoluciones y órdenes* (Lima: Imp. De Torres Aguirre, 1888), p. 58.

12. Estuardo Núñez, comp., *Colección documental de la independencia del Perú: Relaciones de viajeros* (Lima: Comisión Nacional del Sesquicentenario de la Independencia del Perú, 1971). The editor quoted the French traveler Gabriel Lafond de Lurcy. Others who expressed the same opinion were Charles Wiener, Robert Proctor, Eugene de Sartiges, Von Tschusdi, and Gustavo Otero.

13. *El Comercio*, July 21, 1862.

14. Eugene de Sartiges and Adolfo de Botmilau, *Dos viajeros franceses en el Perú republicano: Colección de viajeros en el Perú dirigida por Raul Porras Barrenechea* (Lima: Editorial Cultura Antártica, 1947), 195.

15. Juan Carlos Estensorro, "Modernismo, estética, música y fiesta: Elites y cambio de actitud frente a la cultura popular, Perú, 1750–1850," in *Tradición y modernidad en los Andes*, ed. Henrique Urbano (Cusco: Centro de Estudios Regionales Andinos "Bartolomé de las Casas," 1992), 181–95; Juan Pedro Viqueira Albán, *Relajados o reprimidos? Diversiones públicas y vida social en la ciudad de México durante el siglo de las luces* (Mexico: Fondo de Cultura Económica, 1987), 161.

16. Francisco García Calderón, *El Perú contemporáneo* (Lima: Banco Internacional del Perú, 1981), 50.

17. Burga and Flores Galindo, *Apogeo*, 148–73.

18. *El Amigo del Pueblo*, February 27, 1892.

19. Robert Malcolmson discusses the campaign by the English bourgeoisie to eliminate violent amusements, the blood sports (bull-, bear-, and cockfights), and replace them with diversions that inculcated good work habits and labor discipline in *Popular Recreations in English Society, 1700–1850* (Cambridge: Cambridge University Press, 1973), 46–94.

20. Archivo Municipal de Lima, Ramo de Espectáculos, December 10, 1891, and October 28, 1892 (hereafter cited as AML).

21. Fuentes, *Estadística*, 58.

22. Robert Proctor, cited in *Colección documental de la independencia*, 2:255.

23. *El Peruano*, February 27, 1864.

24. *Memoria del Congreso Ordinario de 1900* (Lima: El Imprinta El País, 1900), 15.

25. Ibid., 22, 303.

26. The documents do not contain explicit descriptions of the plays, but the records indicate they were regarded as obscene. An indication of the nature of the performances comes from a study of the *sicalípticas* in San José, Costa Rica. Patricia Fumero reports that theaters hosting these plays presented ballerinas with light dresses that "permitted one to see the exquisite forms of the sculpted and perfect women through the transparent muslin" (*Teatro, público y estado en San José (1895–1919)* [San José: Editorial de la Universidad de Costa Rica, Colección Nueva Historia, 1996], 68).

27. See *El Comercio*, November 30, 1859, for example.

28. Aldo Panfichi and Felipe Portocarrero, eds., *Mundos interiores: Lima 1850–1950* (Lima: Universidad del Pacífico, Centro de Investigación, 1995), 220–56.

29. Donald Lowe, *Historia de la percepción burguesa* (Mexico: Fondo de Cultura Económica, 1986), 186–87.

30. For similar developments in Mexico, see William H. Beezley, "El estilo porfiriano: Deportes y diversiones de fin de siglo," in *Cultura, ideas y mentalidades: Lecturas de "Historia Mexicana"* (México: El Colegio de Mexico, 1992), 219–38.

31. *El Comercio*, May 20, 1897.

32. *El Comercio*, May 20, 1897; special centennial supplement, May 4, 1939; Steve Stein, *Lima obrera, 1919–1930* (Lima: Editores El Virrey, 1986), passim; José Gálvez, *Nuestra pequeña historia* (Lima: Universidad Nacional Mayor de San Marcos, 1966), 213.

33. Nicolás de Pierola, *Mensaje del Presidente de la República en la instalación del Congreso Ordinario de 1897* (Lima: Imprenta El País, 1897), xvi.

34. Lowe, *Historia de la percepción burguesa*, 186.

35. Luis Antonio Eguiguren, *La holgazanería en el Perú* (Lima: Imprenta de E. Moreno, 1915), 25–26.

36. Denegri, *El abanico y la cigarrera*, 50–53.

37. Manuel Moncloa y Covarrubias, *El teatro en Lima: Apuntes históricos* (Lima: Librería e Imprenta Gil, 1909), 120.

38. *Ordenanzas de Lima*, 1888, articles 19 and 22, pp. 366–68.

39. *Boletín Municipal no. 662* (May 19, 1891) and no. 773 (February 27, 1892).

40. Isabel Cruz de Amenabar, *La fiesta metamorfosis de lo cotidiano* (Santiago: Ediciones Universidad Católica de Chile, 1995), 19.

41. See Ernest Middendorf, *Observaciones y estudios del país y sus habitantes durante una permanencia de 25 años* (Lima: Dirección Universitaria de Biblioteca y Publicaciones de la Universidad Nacional Mayor de San Marcos, 1973).

42. Reglamento de Policía para la Ciudad de Lima de 1872, in *Ordenanzas de la Ciudad de Lima*, 1888, p. 88. Before this restriction, the Paseo de Descalzos and the Nueva Alameda or Alameda de Acho had been important locations for public meetings.

43. AML, Ramo de Espectáculos, November 5, 1891. The fine was established in the municipal ordinance of February 20, 1890; see ibid., November 29, 1890.

44. The solicitation for the revocation of the ordinance of February 1890 and the 1863 theater curfew law, and the call for new regulations governing theaters, can be found in AML, Ramo de Espectáculos, November 29, 1890.

45. *Ordenanzas de la Ciudad de Lima*, 1888, p. 96.

46. Pedro Dávalos y Lissón, *Lima en 1907: colección de artículos publicados en "El Comercio" con el epígrafe de "Lo que fué ayer Lima, lo que es hoy, y lo que será mañana* (Lima: Gil, 1908), 79–83.

CHAPTER 10

1. Francoise Choay, "Alberti: The Invention of Monumentality and Memory," *The Harvard Architecture Review* 4 (1984): 99–105; David Lowenthal, *The Past Is a Foreign Country* (Cambridge: Cambridge University Press, 1985), 321–24.

2. Murray Edelman, *The Symbolic Uses of Politics* (Urbana: University of Illinois Press, 1985), 95–113.

3. David Glassberg, "Monuments and Memories," *American Quarterly* 43, no. 1 (March 1991): 143–56.

4. This theme is developed more fully in Thomas Benjamin, "Social Memory and the Origins of Official Revolutionary History," *Mexican Studies/Estudios Mexicanos*, forthcoming.

5. Neil Asher Silberman, "Fallen Idols," *Archaeology* (January–February 1992): 88.

6. Carlos Monsiváis, "On Civic Monuments and Their Spectators," in *Mexican Monuments: Strange Encounters*, ed. Helen Escobedo (New York: Abbeville Press, 1989), 110. Originally published as "Va mi estatua en prendas," *Nexos* 84 (December 1984): 29–35.

7. Monsiváis, "On Civic Monuments," 118. Ida Rodríguez Pampolini writes, "a partir de 1880, aproximademente, se despierta al clamor de un exaltado nacionalismo patriótico, un afán de levantar monumentos públicos, estatuas de nuestros hombres celebres." *La critica de arte en México en el siglo XIX* (Mexico: Imprenta Universitaria, 1964), I:127.

8. Charles A. Hale, *The Transformation of Liberalism in Late Nineteenth-Century Mexico* (Princeton: Princeton University Press, 1989), 104–06, 245.

9. Francisco Sosa, *Las estatuas de la Reforma* (Mexico: Colección Metropolitana, 1974), 1:11–18.

10. "Monumento a la Revolución?" *El Universal*, February 21, 1923.

11. According to John Bodnar, "Official culture relies on 'dogmatic formalism' and the restatement of reality in ideal rather than complex or ambiguous terms. . . . Vernacular culture, on the other hand, represents an array of specialized interests that are grounded in parts of the whole. . . . Defenders of such cultures are numerous and intent on protecting values and restating views of reality derived from firsthand experience in small-scale communities." John Bodnar, *Remaking America: Public Memory, Commemoration and Patriotism in the Twentieth Century* (Princeton: Princeton University Press, 1992). See especially chapter 1, "The Memory Debate: An Introduction," and pages 13–14.

12. "Excitativa," broadside in the Colección Instituto Nacional de Estudios Históricos de la Revolucíon Mexicana (hereinafter cited as INEHRM), Caja 11, Expediente 2, of the Archivo General de la Nación (hereafter cited as AGN).

13. AGN, Archivo G. Narváez, Colección INEHRM, Caja 1, Folio 56, Exp. 6/2, and Folio 12, Exp. 6/11.

14. See, for example, "En Puebla se celebró el aniversario de la iniciación de la Revolución de 1910," *El Demócrata*, November 22, 1915; "Conmemoración del 50 aniversario de la firma del Plan de Guadalupe," *El Demócrata*, March 26, 1918; "Se declara día de fiesta nacional el décimo aniversario de la Revolución," *El Demócrata*, November 13, 1920; and "Un grupo de constituyentes celebró ayer el aniversario de la Constitución," *El Demócrata*, February 6, 1923.

15. *Primer Congreso de Unificación de las Organizaciones Campesinas de la República. Celebrado en la ciudad de México, D.F., del 15 al 20 Noviembre de 1926* (Puebla, 1927), 72.

16. *Monumento al General Alvaro Obregón: Homenaje nacional en el lugar de su sacrificio* (Mexico: Departamento del Distrito Federal, 1934).

17. Federico Medrano, head of the Bloc Obregonista of the Camera de Diputados, referred to "nuestra madre común: La Revolución." See "Consolidación de la unidad revolucionaria," *El Nacional Revolucionaria*, September 27, 1929. "The state is invisible," writes Michael Walzer, "it must be personified before it can be seen, symbolized before it can be loved, imagined before it can be conceived" ("On the Role of Symbolism in Political Thought," *Political Science Quarterly* 57, no. 2 [June 1967]: 194).

18. Michael Walzer writes that "politics is an art of unification; from many, it makes one. And symbolic activity is perhaps our most important means of bringing things together. . . . In a sense, the union of men can only be symbolized; it has no palpable shape or substance" ("On the Role of Symbolism in Political Thought," 194).

19. See, for example, Tranquinino Torres, "La unidad política de la revolución," *El Nacional Revolucionario*, September 26, 1929. Torres wrote that over the years, in the epoch of violence and reorganization, "la Revolución ha mantenido su unidad ideológica."

20. "El Monumento a Zapata," *El Nacional Revolucionario*, January 2, 1930.

21. "Monumento a la Revolución," *El Nacional*, April 15, 1932.

22. Carlos Obregón Santacilia, *50 años de arquitectura mexicana (1900–1950)* (Mexico: Editorial Patria, 1952), 30.

23. Enrique X. de Anda Alanis, *La arquitectura de la Revolución Mexicana: Corrientes estilos de la década de los veintes* (Mexico: Universidad Nacional Autónoma de Mexico, 1990), 102–06.

24. Carlos Obregón Santacilia, *El monumento a la Revolución. Simbolismo e historia* (Mexico: Secretaría de Educación Pública, 1960), 35–36.

25. *El monumento a la Revolución: Texto de la iniciativa presentada al ciudadano Presidente de la República por los ciudadanos Gral. Plutarco Elías Calles e Ing. Alberto J. Pani y del Acuerdo Presidencial Recaído sobre la Misma* (Mexico: Editorial "Cultura," 1933).

26. In 1936 Obregón Santacilia drew up plans for a Museum of the Revolution, to be located in the chambers beneath the monument. It took more than four decades to make this museum a reality.

27. Graciela de Garay Arellano, *La obra de Carlos Obregón Santacilia, architecto* (Mexico: SEP/INBA, 1979), 54; Obregón Santacilia, *50 años de arquitectura mexicana*, 84–87; idem, *El monumento a la Revolución*, 42–43.

28. Justino Fernández, *El arte moderno en México: Breve historia—Siglos IXI y XX* (Mexico: Antigua Librería Robredo, José Porrua e Hijos, 1937), 330; Obregón Santacilia, *El monumento a la Revolución*, 49–50.

29. Obregón Santacilia, *El monumento a la Revolución*, 8.

30. Ibid., 73.

31. Ibid., 7.

32. Ibid., 8.

33. Gustavo de Anda, "La tumba de la Revolución," *Impacto*, February 1, 1967.

34. Obregón Santacilia, *El monumento a la Revolución*, 8–9.

35. Ibid., 9.

36. Ibid., 8.

37. J. H. Plenn, *Mexico Marches* (Indianapolis: Bobbs-Merrill Co., 1939), 142.

38. Obregón Santacilia, *El monumento a la Revolución*, 55, 62; *Catálago de monumentos escultóricos y conmemorativos del Distrito Federal* (Mexico: Oficina de Conservación de Edificos Públicos y Monumentos, 1976).

39. Marianne Doezema, "The Public Monument in Tradition and Transition," in *The Public Monument and Its Audience* (Cleveland: Cleveland Museum of Art, 1977), 14.

40. Obregón Santacilia, *El monumento a la Revolución*, 62.

41. Balmori's woodcut was the cover illustration of *Cárdenas Habla* (Mexico: Partido de la Revolución Mexicana, 1940).

42. Garay Arellano, *La obra de Carlos Obregón Santacilia*, 95.

43. "Reposan en el monumento a la Revolución sus adalides," *El Nacional*, January 10, 1942.

44. *Catálogo de monumentos escultóricos y conmemorativos*, 281; Ilene V. O'Malley, *The Myth of the Revolution: Hero Cults and the Institutionalization of the Mexican State, 1920–1940* (Westport, CT: Greenwood Press, 1940), 69–70.

45. "Severa Recordación de la Muerta de Carranza," *El Nacional*, May 22, 1945.

46. Avner Ben-Amos writes, "ancestors' shrines are sacred sites in most human societies. They are the places where communities get together to communicate with their founding fathers and to celebrate their shared values." See Ben-Amos, "The Sacred Center of Power: Paris and Republican State Funerals," *Journal of Interdisciplinary History* 22, no. 1 (summer 1991): 37.

47. "Sobria sencillez para honrar a D. Venustiano," *El Universal*, May 27, 1951.

48. "Los homenajes a Madero y Pino Suárez," *El Nacional*, November 21, 1960.

49. Garay Arellano, *La obra de Carlos Obregón Santacilia*, 84.

50. Gustavo de Anda, "La tumba de la Revolución," *Impacto*, February 1, 1967.

51. *El poder de la imagen y la imagen del poder* (Mexico: Universidad Autónoma Chapingo, 1985), 132.

CHAPTER 11

1. Emilia Viotti da Costa, *The Brazilian Empire: Myths and Histories* (Belmont, CA: Wadsworth Publishing Co., 1985), 137.

2. Defining black music is a difficult proposition, for it is not necessarily determined by such recognizable stylistic traits as African rhythms or structures. Peter Wade argues that black music is defined within the context of power relations, and thus "blackness" is partly determined by a given community's perceptions. Peter Wade, "Black Music and Cultural Syncretism in Colombia," in *Slavery and Beyond: The African Impact on Latin America and the Caribbean* (Wilmington, DE: SR Books, 1995), 121–46.

3. Franz Fanon, *Black Face, White Mask* (New York: Grove Press, 1967).

4. According to some estimates, 50 percent of the population was illiterate. Rosemary Thorp, *Progress, Poverty, and Exclusion: An Economic History of Latin America in the 20th Century* (Washington, D.C.: InterAmerican Development Bank, 1998), 354.

5. Michael L. Conniff, *Urban Politics in Brazil: The Rise of Populism, 1925–1945* (Pittsburgh: University of Pittsburgh Press, 1981).

6. The New Song Movement was a leftist-motivated Latin American renaissance that aimed to create compositions that were socially meaningful, and that employed Latin American popular rhythms and musical forms in an effort to celebrate local or

national traditions. Musicians such as Silvio Rodríguez and Pablo Milanés in Cuba, Chico Buarque in Brazil, and Violeta Parra in Chile are considered pioneers of the movement.

7. Sigmund Freud, "Jokes and Their Relation to the Unconscious," in *The Standard Edition of the Complete Works of Sigmund Freud* (London: Hogarth Press, 1960), VII:221.

8. Ibid., 220.

9. Carmen Miranda requested a Brazilian passport in 1948, but Brazilian authorities did not grant her one until 1953 so that she could complete a European tour to showcase her music.

10. Carmen Miranda's statement is quoted in Martha Gil Montero, *The Brazilian Bombshell: The Biography of Carmen Miranda* (New York: Donald I. Fine, 1989), 31.

11. Abel Cardoso Junior, *Carmen Miranda, a cantora do Brasil* (São Paulo: Símbolo S.A. Indústrias Gráficas, 1978), 97–100; Gil Montero, *Brazilian Bombshell*, 72.

12. Cardoso Junior, *Carmen*, 19–20.

13. Ibid.

14. José Ramos Tinhorão, *Historia social da música popular brasileira* (Lisbon: Editorial Caminho, 1990), 207.

15. Viotti da Costa, *The Brazilian Empire*, 244.

16. See for example, Jeffrey Needell, "Identity, Race, Gender and Modernity in the Origins of Gilberto Freyre's Oeuvre," *American Historical Review* 100, no. 1 (February 1995): 51–77.

17. Recorded on September 6, 1940.

18. See, for example, J. D. Flugel, "Humor and Laughter," in *Handbook of Social Psychology* (1954), 2:709–16. See also Freud, "Jokes," 200.

19. Dulce Damasceno de Brito, introduction, *O ABC de Carmen Miranda* (São Paulo: Companhia Editora Nacional, 1986). In the original Portuguese quotation, "Sua bossa especial deu a música popular algo que lhe faltava: classe," de Brito inadvertently creates a pun with the use of *classe* (class). The popular class had no class, and it takes someone from the middle class to give their music "class."

20. Alfred da Rocha Vianna, Jr. (1898–1970), better known as Pixiguinha, was one of Brazil's most inspirational and sought-after composers, arrangers, and instrumental performers of the 1930s. He and his orchestra the Velha Guarda (Old Guard) provided the background music for many artists of the era.

21. Carmen starred in the Brazilian film *Banana da Terra* as the *Bahiana* for the first time in February 1939. That same month she recorded the smash hit, "O qué é qué a Bahiana tem," with Dorival Caymmi.

22. *Carmen Miranda: The Brazilian Fireball*, World Record Club, recording no. SH114, side 1, track 5.

23. *Carmen Miranda*, Series Revivendo Músicas, Comercio de Discos, XCD 5719, track 8.

24. Arlindo Marques and Roberto Roberti, "Nova descoberta," released in 1935. Joubert de Carvalho, "Terra morena," released in 1936.

25. The *antropófagos*, led by intellectuals such as Mario and Oswald de Andrade from São Paulo, called for the devouring of all foreign influences in order to create a unique Brazilian nation.

26. Damasceno de Brito, *O ABC*, 69.

27. Quoted in Cardoso Junior, *Carmen*, 101, 177–78.

28. Gilberto Freyre's 1933 work *Casa grande e senzala* is often cited as one of the principal texts that founded the notion of Brazil as a racial democracy. However, intellectuals such as the abolitionist Joaquim Nabuco had already begun to compare Brazil to other slave economies in idyllic terms.

29. Edigar de Alencar, *O carnival carioca através da música* (Rio de Janeiro: Franciso Alves, 1985), 246.

30. Ibid.

31. *Carmen Miranda: The Brazilian Recordings*, Harlequin, recording no. 1XYP, song no. 19. "Sahe da toca Brasil" was written by Joubert de Carvalho and was recorded in 1938.

32. The original recording of May 2, 1939, can be found on the remastered compact disc *Carmen Miranda: The Brazilian Recordings*, by Augusto Vassuer-Marques and Porto Luis Peixoto, Harlequin, recording no. 1XYP, song no. 10. "Preto e branco" was also recorded by Aracy Cortes in 1930.

33. *Carmen Miranda*, Series Revivendo Músicas, Comercio de Discos, XCD 5719, track 18.

34. Written and composed by Ary Barboso-Kid Pepe with the Victor band Diabo do Céo.

35. *Carmen Miranda*, Series Revivendo Músicas, Comercio de Discos, XCD 5719, track 13.

36. *Carmen Miranda: The Brazilian Recordings*, Harlequin Recording No. 1XYP, song no. 13.

37. Waldem M. Da Silva, 1937.

38. Sinval Silva, 1937.

39. Arlindo Marques, Jr., and Roberto Roberts, 1935.

40. *Carmen Miranda: The Brazilian Recordings*, Harlequin, recording no. 1XYP, song no. 12. This song was written by Assis Valente and probably recorded in 1939.

41. Roberto da Matta, *Carnavais, malandros e heróis: Para una sociologia da dilema brasileiro* (Rio de Janeiro: Zahar Editores, 1980).

42. Almir Chediak, *Songbook: Doryval Caymmi* (Rio de Janeiro: Lumiar Editora, 1994), 48. The original recording can be found on the remastered compact disc *Carmen Miranda: The Brazilian Recordings*, Harlequin, recording no. 1XYP.

43. Orson Welles, *It's All True* (Paramount Pictures, 1994). This film is a posthumous product that brings together two unreleased short films (one from Mexico) and documentary footage from Welles's filming expedition in Brazil.

44. Gil Montero, *Brazilian Bombshell*, 33.

45. Mario de Andrade, *Dicionario Musical Brasileiro* (Belo Horizonte: Editora Italiana Limitada, 1989), 53.

46. With few exceptions, Carmen was ever predisposed to satire and even to self-parody, which added a sense of wonder and electricity to her work. She was able to play with her own recordings. In the 1940 recording of "Ginga ginga" (written with Juracy de Araujo-Gomes Filho), for example, Carmen played with the rhythm of "O qué é qué a Bahiana tem," as if to remind the viewers of the black roots of Brazilian popular music, but in a tongue-in-cheek way.

CHAPTER 12

1. *World Music* (London: Rough Guides, 1994), 506, 247.

2. Elizabeth Saft, ed., *Trinidad & Tobago* (Hong Kong: APA Productions, 1987), xv–39.

3. Richard D. Abrahams, *Deep Down in the Jungle: Negro Narrative Folklore from the Streets of Philadelphia* (Hatboro, PA: Folklore Associates, 1964).

4. *Music of the World* (London: Quarto Publications, 1991), 89.

5. This type of verbal contest is called "playing the dozens" in the United States and "rhyming" in the West Indies. Richard D. Abrahams, *The Man-of-Words in the West Indies: Performance and the Emergence of Creole Culture* (Baltimore: Johns Hopkins University Press, 1983), 3.

6. Saft, *Trinidad*, 229–48.

7. In a similar pattern in the United States, the word "jazz" was first used in 1912, and the first jazz recordings were made in 1917 by the Victor and Columbia recording companies.

8. Colin G. Clarke, "Society and Electoral Politics in Trinidad and Tobago," in *Society and Politics in the Caribbean*, ed. C. Clarke (New York: Macmillan, 1991), 48–54.

9. Arthur Napoleon Raymond Robinson, *Patterns of Political and Economic Transformation in Trinidad and Tobago* (Cambridge: Massachusetts Institute of Technology Press, 1971).

10. L. Braithwaithe, *Social Stratification in Trinidad: A Preliminary Analysis* (Mona, Jamaica: Institute of Social and Economic Research, University of the West Indies, 1975). Also see Jeannine M. Purdy, *Common Law and Colonised Peoples: Studies in Trinidad and Western Australia* (Brookfield, VT: Ashgate Publishing Co., 1997).

11. Edgar Wesley Owen, *Trek of the Oil Finders: A History of Exploration for Petroleum*, AAPG Memoir, no. 6 (Tulsa, OK: American Assoc. of Petroleum Geologists, 1975), 1012.

12. Leonard M. Fanning, *American Oil Operations Abroad* (New York: McGraw-Hill, 1947), 256–57, table 43.

13. Selwyn D. Ryan, *Good Innings: The Life and Times of Ray Edwin Dieffenthaller* (Port of Spain, Trinidad: McEnearney Alstons, 1990), 29–30.

14. Venezuela prohibited the entry of foreign-born blacks in 1927. Afro-Caribbean workers then went to the thriving oil refineries of the Netherlands Antilles. A. Garcia, *History of the West Indies* (London: George G. Harrap, 1965), 288.

15. Recording released on Calypsos from Trinidad: *Politics, Intrigue and Violence in the 1930s*, Folk Lyric Records, recording no. 23TA, track 15, 1992.

16. Ibid., track 21.

17. Garcia, *West Indies*, 239.

18. See, for example, recordings released on *Calypso Ladies: 1926–1941*, Interstate Music, Crawley, England, 1991.

19. *Port of Spain Gazette*, December 1, 1937.

20. Fitzroy André Baptiste, *War, Cooperation, and Conflict: The European Possessions in the Caribbean, 1939–1945* (New York, Greenwood, 1988), 144.

21. Lord Invader [Rupert Grant], 1943. The song was recorded by the Andrews Sisters in 1944. For the Andrews Sisters version of the song, see *Rum and Coca Cola*,

Golden Stars Records, recording no. 5MRF, 1993. To hear the original performed by Lord Invader, see *Calypso at Midnight: The 1946 Town Hall*, Uni/Rounder Records, recording no. K2A4, track 5, 1999.

22. Saft, *Trinidad*, 239–40.

23. Rough Guide, 507.

24. Interview with Belafonte by Henry Louis Gates, Jr., *The Age*, December 7, 1996, El-2.

25. Graham E. L. Holton, "State Petroleum Enterprises and the International Oil Industry: The Case of Trinidad and Tobago" (Ph.D. diss., La Trobe University, Bundoora, Australia, 1994).

26. Paula Burnett, ed., *The Penguin Book of Caribbean Verse in English* (London: Penguin Books, 1986), 43.

27. Ibid., 252.

28. Selwyn D. Ryan, *The Muslimeen Grab for Power: Race, Religion and Revolution in Trinidad and Tobago* (Port of Spain: Imprint Caribbean, 1991). The recording was released on "Caribbean Beats," vol. 2, Intuition Music, New York, 1995, track 6, "The Sinking Ship."

CHAPTER 13

1. Robert D. Crassweller, *Trujillo: The Life and Times of a Caribbean Dictator* (New York: MacMillan, 1966), 294; Ramón Alberto Ferreras, *Trujillo y sus mujeres* (Santo Domingo: Editorial de Nordeste, 1990), 80; Germán Ornes, *Trujillo: Little Caesar of the Caribbean* (New York: Thomas Nelson & Sons, 1958), 219. Another version of this essay was published as "La seducción del dictador: Lo masculino y el espectáculo estatal durante la Era de Trujillo," in Ramonina Brea, Rosario Espinal, and Fernando Valerio-Holguín, eds., *La República Dominicana en el Umbral del Siglo XXI: Cultura, Política y Cambio Social* (Santo Domingo: Pontífica Universidad Católica Madre y Maestra, 2000), pp. 195–214. This essay is based upon a chapter of my dissertation, "The Magic of Modernity: Dictatorship and Civic Culture in the Dominican Republic, 1916–1962" (Department of History, University of Chicago, 1998), the fieldwork for which was sponsored by the Social Science Research Council and Fulbright-CIEE. The Newcombe Foundation supported my dissertation write-up. Special thanks to César Herrera and Julio César Santana, who have helped me to understand *tigueraje* as a parable of race and class ascent and masculine self-fashioning.

2. Clifford Geertz, "Centers, Kings, and Charisma: Reflections on the Symbolics of Power," in *Culture and Its Creators: Essays in Honor of Edward Schils*, ed. Joseph Ben-David and Terry Nichols Clark (Chicago: University of Chicago Press, 1977), 150–71.

3. Crassweller, *Trujillo*, 295. All translations were newly prepared by me.

4. For more on world fairs, see Robert W. Rydell, *All the World's a Fair: Visions of Empire at American International Expositions, 1876–1916* (Chicago: University of Chicago Press, 1984), and idem, *World of Fairs: The Century of Progress Expositions* (Chicago: University of Chicago Press, 1993).

5. Lynn Hunt, "The Many Bodies of Marie Antoinette: Political Pornography and the Problem of the Feminine in the French Revolution," in *Eroticism and the*

Body Politic, ed. Lynn Hunt (Baltimore: Johns Hopkins University Press, 1991), 108–30.

6. I am drawing here on the work of Christopher Waterman, who discussed performance as a means of accumulation in a talk entitled "The Production of Celebrity in Yoruba Music Videos," presented by the Department of Anthropology, University of Chicago, November 1994.

7. Marshall Sahlins, "Poor Man, Rich Man, Big-Man, Chief: Political Types in Melanesia and Polynesia," *Comparative Studies in Society and History* 5, no. 1 (1962): 287–303; Richard G. Parker, *Bodies, Pleasures and Passions: Sexual Culture in Contemporary Brazil* (Boston: Beacon Press, 1991), 43.

8. Sarah Maza, *Private Lives and Public Affairs: The Causes Célèbres of Prerevolutionary France* (Berkeley: University of California Press, 1993); Joan Landes, *Women and the Public Sphere in the Age of the French Revolution* (Ithaca: Cornell University Press, 1988); Mary P. Ryan, *Women in Public: Between Banners and Ballots, 1825–1880* (Baltimore: Johns Hopkins University Press, 1990).

9. J. M. Taylor, *Eva Perón: The Myths of a Woman* (Chicago: University of Chicago Press, 1979); Sherry Ortner, "Is Female to Male as Nature Is to Culture?" in *Women, Culture and Society*, ed. M. Z. Rosaldo and L. Lamphere (Stanford: Stanford University Press, 1974), 67–87.

10. See works by Ramón Alberto Ferreras such as *Trujillo y sus mujeres*, op cit., and his *Cuando la Era*, Vols. I–IV (Santo Domingo: Editorial del Nordeste, 1991). Manuel Rueda's *Bienvenida y la noche* (Santo Domingo: Fundación Cultural Dominicana, 1994) covers Trujillo's second marriage. Enriquillo Sánchez's *Musiquito: Anales de un déspota y de un bolerista* (Santo Domingo: Editora Taller, 1993) is a thinly veiled fictional account of a lascivious dictator fond of deflowering virgins; the picture is clearly based on Trujillo. Gilberto de la Rosa's *Petán: Un cacique en la Era de Trujillo* (Santiago: Universidad Católica Madre y Maestra, n.d.) includes a chapter on Trujillo's brother's sexual antics. Marcio Veloz Maggiolo's *Ritos de cabaret* (Novela rítmica) (Santo Domingo: Fundación Cultural Dominicana, 1991) explores Villa Francisca, the underworld barrio of pimps and prostitutes that Trujillo was fond of frequenting. René Fortunato's documentary film *Trujillo: El Poder del Jefe II* (1995) also treats Trujillo's love life.

11. There was a certain pride in having been chosen, although there was definitely shame in consummation. While interviewing in 1992, I heard many stories from Santo Domingo elite women about having been noticed by Trujillo, as well as how parents often withdrew their daughters from the public arena (from ballet classes, society balls, and the like) so as to preempt their possible deflowering by Trujillo.

12. Flor Trujillo as told to Laura Berquist, "My Tormented Life as Trujillo's Daughter," *Look* 29, no. 12 (June 15, 1965): 44–66, esp. 52.

13. See Shoshana B. Tancer, "La Quisqueyana: The Dominican Woman, 1940–1970," in *Female and Male in Latin America*, ed. Ann Pescatello (Pittsburgh: University of Pittsburgh Press, 1973), on official feminism during the Trujillo regime. For more on the Dominican Party, see Ornes, Trujillo, and Crassweller, *Trujillo*.

14. Joaquín Balaguer, *Memorias de un cortesano de la "Era de Trujillo"* (Santo Domingo: Editora Corripio, 1989), 197–98.

15. New York, Caribbean Library, 1954.

16. See Julie Skurski, "The Ambiguities of Authenticity in Latin America: Doña Bárbara and the Construction of National Identity," *Poetics Today* 15, no. 4 (winter 1994): 605–43, esp. 614; and Lynn Hunt, introduction, in *Hunt, Eroticism and the Body Politic*, 1.

17. Tancer, "La Quisqueyana," 215, and Fernándo Ferrán, "La familia nuclear de la subcultura de la pobreza dominicana: Notas introductorias," *Estudios Sociales* 27, no. 3 (1974): 137–85, esp. 163–65. For more on Dominican gender identity, see Peter Grant, "Masculinity and Femininity in the Dominican Republic: Historical Change and Contradiction in Notions of Self" (Ph.D. diss., University of Michigan, 1994).

18. Roberto DaMatta, *Carnivals, Rogues and Heroes: An Interpretation of the Brazilian Dilemma*, trans. John Drury (Notre Dame, Ind.: Notre Dame Press, 1991), esp. 204–06 and 207–09; Lynn Hunt, *The Family Romance of the French Revolution* (Berkeley: University of California Press, 1992), xiii. For a historical discussion of the development of the dual marriage system in the Caribbean, see Raymond T. Smith, "Hierarchy and the Dual Marriage System in West Indian Society," in *Gender and Kinship: Essays Toward a Unified Analysis*, ed. Jane Fishburne Collier and Sylvia Junko Yanagisako (Stanford: Stanford University Press, 1987), 163–96.

19. See Jane Gallop, "The Father's Seduction," in her *The Daughter's Seduction: Feminism and Psychoanalysis* (Ithaca: Cornell University Press, 1982), 56–79, for an exploration of the Electra complex and father-daughter desire.

20. I am drawing on Roberto DaMatta's discussion of the hero figure in Brazil; see his *Carnivals, Rogues and Heroes*, 204–06.

21. Trujillo was a *tigre* until he became president, after which time he ruled less through his wits than through the state—the national army and treasury. When he became *jefe* he transferred his role as regime *tigre* to Porfirio Rubirosa, since neither dynastic first son Rafael (Ramfis) nor second son Leonidas Rhadamés had the personal charisma for the part. Indeed, Rubirosa, who became an affinal "son" of Trujillo's through his marriage to daughter Flor and his close friendship with Trujillo's son Ramfis, became a surrogate for Trujillo, reaching even greater heights of *tigueraje* than Trujillo himself, for which he was rewarded handsomely in diplomatic positions for his unrivaled success in marital conquests. The charming and winsome Rubirosa thus served as Trujillista gigolo and conduit for the symbolic accumulation and display of women—ever richer, more famous, and more beautiful—to the regime. The analysis of Flor and Rubi forms part of a larger study that, due to brevity constraints, I was unable to elaborate in this chapter.

22. Flor Trujillo, however, notes that Trujillo first met Lina as one of Flor's adolescent friends in her "My Tormented Life as Trujillo's Daughter," 15.

23. "Editorial: El gran carnaval de 1937," *Listín Diario*, January 9, 1937.

24. "Ecos del Gran Carnaval," *Listín Diario*, January 12, 1937. See also "Imponente fué la presentación de las princesas a S.M. La Reina del Carnaval de 1937," *Listín Diario*, January 12, 1937.

25. See Eric Roorda, *The Dictator Next Door: The Good Neighbor Policy and the Trujillo Regime in the Dominican Republic, 1930–1945* (Durham, NC: Duke University Press, 1998), 84–87.

26. "Ecos del Gran. . . ." The choice of this poem had special significance: in January the 1937 Haitian massacre was just drawing to a close, and most of the killing

had taken place in the Dajabón area. In selecting this poem, Lina was commending Trujillo's patriotic border reinstatement and ethnic cleansing of the country.

27. I am referring here to the distinction made by Roberto DaMatta in his classic essay, "Carnivals, Military Parades, and Processions," in his *Carnivals, Rogues and Heroes*, 26–60.

28. Trujillo is called *"el poblador"* in Sánchez's *Musiquito*, a rubric that puns on his official title as founder (as in cities, architecture) and his virile fecundity (to people, populate).

29. "Esplendida conmemoración," *Listín Diario*, January 12, 1937.

30. Letter from La Reina, *Listín Diario*, January 9, 1937.

31. "Editorial: Nuestra Señora de Altagracia," *Listín Diario*, January 21, 1937.

32. Claudia Koontz, "The Competition for a Women's Lebensraum, 1928–1934," in *When Biology Became Destiny: Women in Weimar and Nazi Germany*, ed. Renate Bridenthal, Atina Grossmann, and Marion Kaplan (New York: Monthly Review Press, 1984), 199–236; "Credo feminino de cultura," *Listín Diario*, February 22, 1937.

33. "La mujer nueva," *Listín Diario*, February 21, 1937.

34. "Secretos de Hollywood," *Listín Diario*, February 28, 1937.

35. Catalina D'Erzell, "Digo yo como mujer," *Listín Diario*, February 28, 1937. I thank Katherine Bliss for bringing this issue to my attention.

36. "Editorial: El 'Duchess of Richmond' en Ciudad Trujillo," *Listín Diario*, February 21, 1937.

37. Ricardo Pérez Alfonseca, "El repúblico," *Listín Diario*, February 27, 1937.

38. The information in this section was culled from the *Album de oro de la Feria de la Paz y Confraternidad del Mundo Libre* (Ciudad Trujillo, n.p., 1956).

39. "10 Reasons Why You Should Discover the Dominican Republic," Dominican Republic Tourist Office advertisement, *American Magazine* 159 (April 1955): 106.

40. Rydell, *World of Fairs*, 11.

41. This paragraph draws on Frank Moya Pons, *Empresarios en conflicto: Políticas de industrialización y subtitución de importaciones en la República Dominicana* (Santo Domingo: Fondo Para el Avance de las Ciencias Sociales, 1992), 23–72. By contrast, Claudio Vedovato focuses on the economic distortions caused by Trujillo's nationalist economic policy making; see his *Politics, Foreign Trade and Economic Development in the Dominican Republic*, Lund Economic Studies, no. 32 (Lund: Research Policy Institute, University of Lund, 1984).

42. "Editorial: El 'Duchess of Richmond'"; "Llegaron en el transatlántico Inglés 'Duchess of Richmond' numerosos turistas ingleses," *Listín Diario*, February 20, 1937.

43. For all the above descriptions, see respectively Jack Long, "Columbus Landed here!" *American Magazine* 159 (April 1955): 104–08; Erwin Walter Palm, *The Pocket Guide to Ciudad Trujillo* (Ciudad Trujillo: Impresora Dominicana, 1951); "La Feria de la Paz será la mayor atracción invierno en naciones mundo libre," *La Nación*, November 28, 1955; "Rediscovery," *The New Yorker*, January 7, 1956, 14–15. The modernity of the Dominican Republic is also praised in "Mademoiselle Says Let's Go Caribbean Island-Hopping—to the Dominican Republic," *Mademoiselle* 44, no. 50 (December 1956): 6. "El Benefactor Wants to See You," *Harper's*, December 1955, 83–84, gives negative and positive views of the Dominican Republic as a tourist site.

44. In 1952 the Dominican Republic became the fourth country in Latin America to have national television. See Arístides Incháustegui and Blanca Delgado Malagón,

"En el cincuentenario de La Voz Dominicana," *Isla Abierta* 11, no. 572 (August 1, 1992): 1–20, for a brief history of radio and television in the Dominican Republic.

45. "Mademoiselle Says Let's Go," 6.

46. On Trujillo's expansion of the army, see Peguero, "Trujillo and the Military," and Crassweller, *Trujillo*, 263–66. Crassweller treats the Hull-Trujillo treaty on pages 182–83. On the impact of the invasions, see Bernardo Vega, *Trujillo y las fuerzas armadas norteamericanas* (Santo Domingo: Fundación Cultural Dominicana, 1992). Of course, equally important to the heavy military presence at the fair were two attempted exile invasions in 1947 and 1949 and the growing climate of hostility to the regime from abroad, with the formation of the prodemocratic Caribbean Legion and organized anti-Trujillista forces in Haiti and Cuba.

47. Lynn Hunt, "The Family Model of Politics," in her *Family Romance of the French Revolution*, 1–16.

48. See Jean Comaroff and John L. Comaroff, "Goodly Beasts, Beastly Goods: Cattle and Commodities in a South African Context," *American Ethnologist* 17, no. 2 (May 1990): 205. I also treat the symbolics of cattle, money, and gender in "Haitians, Money and Magic: Raza and Society in the Haitian-Dominican Borderlands, 1900–1937," *Comparative Studies in Society and History* 36, no. 3 (July 1994): 488–526. In terms of money and coins, see Andrés L. Mateo, who discusses the "myth of equivalence" in his *Mito y cultura en la Era de Trujillo* (Santo Domingo: Librería la Trinitaria, 1993), 124. For more on the logic of icons and sovereignty, see Louis Marin, *Portrait of the King* (Minneapolis: University of Minnesota Press, 1988).

49. The Dominican display at the 1901 Pan American Exposition had a painting of the first coinage minted on the continent as its centerpiece. (Frederick Starr Collection, Department of Special Collections, University of Chicago Library, Box 29, Pan American Exposition Notebook, September 1–8, 1901). My thanks to William Beezley, who provided me with this citation.

50. This incident was recounted to me by a witness who participated in Queen Angelita's court at *la Feria* but preferred to remain anonymous.

51. Dorinda Outram, *The Body and the French Revolution: Sex, Class and Political Culture* (New Haven: Yale University Press, 1989), 3.

52. Ernst H. Kantorowicz, *The King's Two Bodies: A Study in Mediaeval Political Theology* (Princeton: Princeton University Press, 1957), 409.

53. Clifford Geertz, *Negara: The Theater State in Nineteenth-Century Bali* (Princeton: Princeton University Press, 1980).

54. Mabel Berezin, "Created Constituencies: The Italian Middle Classes and Fascism," in *Splintered Classes: Politics and the Lower Middle Classes in Interwar Europe*, ed. Rudy Koshar (New York: Holmes & Meier, 1990), 142–63.

55. The idea of encapsulation comes from William H. Beezley, "The Porfirian Smart Set Anticipates Thorstein Veblen in Guadalajara," in Beezley et al., eds., *Rituals of Rule*, 179–90; the idea of approximation comes from Eric Van Young, "Conclusion: The State as Vampire—Hegemonic Projects, Public Ritual, and Popular Culture in Mexico, 1600–1990," ibid., 343–69.

56. Timothy Mitchell, "Egypt at the Exhibition," in his *Colonizing Egypt* (New York: Cambridge University Press, 1988), 1–33. For an analysis of the contemporary figure of the tigre, see Christian Krohn-Hansen, "Masculinity and the Political Among Dominicans: 'The Dominican Tiger,'" in *Machos, Mistresses, Madonnas: Con-*

testing the Power of Latin American Gender Imagery, edited by Marit and Kristi Anne Stolen Melhuus (New York: Verso, 1996). I am homing in here on but one aspect of Dominican sentiments toward Trujillo. He was also despised for his ruthless killing, his monopolistic hold on the economy, his iron-clad control, his megalomania, the total absence of civil liberties during the regime, the requisite deference toward him on the part of the elite, and the frequent rituals of submission he forced members of the bourgeoisie to endure. Dominican memories of the Trujillo regime are complex and volatile, and I am focusing in this chapter on only one aspect of popular mythology of the man and his thirty-year rule.

57. Howard Wiarda, *The Dominican Republic: Nation in Transition* (New York: Frederick A. Praeger, 1969), 40.

58. The substitution of the first daughter for the first lady has also taken root in Peru and Argentina; see Calvin Sims, "El Presidente's New First Lady: Take Your Daughter to Work," *The New York Times*, April 23, 1995.

59. Pierre Bourdieu, appendix, "Did You Say Popular?," in his *Language and Symbolic Power* (Cambridge: Harvard University Press, 1991), 90–102, esp. 96.

60. Raymundo González, personal communication.

61. Federico García Godoy, *El derrumbe* (Santo Domingo: Editora del Caribe, 1975 [1916]), 72.

62. Damirón, "El Tigre," *De Soslayo*, 106.

63. Mary Douglas, quoted in Peter Stallybrass and Allon White, *The Politics and Poetics of Transgression* (Ithaca: Cornell University Press, 1986), 23.

64. Lipe Collado, *El tíguere dominicano* (Santo Domingo: El Mundo, 1992), 24. *Tigueraje* as a social phenomenon is also intimately tied to the rise of an urban culture. Other examples of Dominican popular heroes before the ascendance of the urban *tigre* figure are the mountain peasant, Enrique Blanco, killed by Trujillo's army in 1936, and Dios Olivorio. Both Blanco and Olivorio became popular martyrs, in part through their struggle against the state. See Jan Lundius, *The Great Power of God in San Juan Valley: Syncretism and Messianism in the Dominican Republic*, Lund Studies in History of Religions (Lund: University of Lund, 1995); and Luis Arzeno Rodríguez, *Cuentos de Enrique Blanco* (Santo Domingo: Expansion Editorial, 1985). Lewis Hyde stresses the adversarial role of the trickster in his *Trickster Makes This World: Mischief, Myth and Art* (New York: Farrar, Straus & Giroux), 1998.

65. Ornes, *Trujillo*, 41.

66. The elites' perception of Trujillo is well described in Ornes, *Trujillo*, 41; and Rueda, *Bienvenida*, 22–25, 79, and 149–50. For fairs as shrines to commodity fetishism, see Walter Benjamin, *Charles Baudelaire: A Lyric Poet in the Era of High Capitalism* (London: Verso, 1983), 54–55.

CHAPTER 14

1. See the film *Bananas Is My Business* (UK/Brazil, 1995), directed by Helena Solberg.

2. The Mexico City newspaper *Excelsior* reported record sales of over half a million copies of its late edition. *Excelsior*, April 16, 1957, p. 1A.

3. "Interminable Desfile ante los Despojos," *Excelsior*, April 17, 1957, pp. 1A, 8A.

4. *Excelsior*, April 18, 1957, p. 12A.

5. The reference to "Las golondrinas" appeared in *El Universal* April 18, 1957, sec. I, part 2, p. 16. *Excelsior*, April 17, 1957, p. 6B. Irma Dorantes recalls that Infante particularly resented not having received the Ariel for his role as Pepe el Toro in either *Nosotros los pobres* or *Ustedes los ricos*. Dorantes, *Así fue*, 139.

6. The telethon took place in 1954. *Excelsior* April 16, 1957, pp. 1A, 15A, 23A.

7. *El Universal* April 16, 1957, sec. I, part 1, p. 31; sec. I, part 2, p. 1.

8. "DEJAN ENTRAR AL PUEBLO," read a headline that described the vigil. *Excelsior* April 17, 1957, p. 6A. Anne Rubenstein posits that the violent reaction of the crowd at the cemetery—which she classifies as a riot (fifty people received injuries and six graves were damaged)—emanated from three contestations over the meaning of citizenship: (1) a tension between modernity and tradition—the author argues that people reacted violently because they associated Infante's death with technology and attacked the police as representatives of the government that promoted it; (2) poor women impulsively behaved as the desperate female characters of Infante's movies—the author describes them as having no choice; and (3) working-class discontent over its condition. Rubenstein's structural approach thus focuses on the sociopolitical conditions of the time and pays little attention to the funeral as a cultural event. She dismisses the possibility that poor people simply wanted to be near their beloved performer and that their success at gaining entrance to the vigil likely reinforced their sense of entitlement vis-à-vis Infante. Anne Rubenstein, "Bodies, Cities, Cinema: Pedro Infante's Death as Political Spectacle," in Gilbert M. Joseph et al., *Fragments of a Golden Age: The Politics of Culture in Mexico since 1940* (Durham: Duke University Press, 2001), 219, 221, 225–228. On damages, see *El Universal* April 18, 1957, sec. I, part 2, pp. 1, 14, 16. For other interpretations of Infante and his fans, see a personalized reading of his movies and the impact he might have had on the gay community in Sergio de la Mora, *Cinemachismo: Masculinities and Sexuality in Mexican Film* (Austin: University of Texas Press, 2006), and a discussion on the possible connection between his films and songs and alcoholism in Tim Mitchell, *Intoxicated Identities: Alcohol's Power in Mexican History and Culture* (New York: Routledge, 2004).

9. *El Universal*, April 17, 1957, sec. 1, part 2, pp. 1, 18–19; April 18, 1957, sec. I, part 2, pp. 1, 16. *Excelsior*, April 17, 1957, pp. 8A, 6B; April 18, 1957, pp. 10A, 12A.

10. Gustavo García, *No me parezco a nadie: La vida de Pedro Infante*, III (Mexico City: Clío, 1994), 41–42; *Excelsior* 17 April 1957, p. 6B.

11. Ismael Rodríguez directed all eight movies on De Película and nine of the eleven on Televisa. The two channels had seven films in common.

12. Héctor Guerrero, "Diputados rinden homenaje a Pedro Infante," April 10, 2007. http://www.esmas.com/noticierostelevisa/mexico/618079.html [April 13, 2007]. *Excelsior*, April 15, 2007, Función 6–8.

13. Warner Brothers Press Release, March 16, 2007. http://www.fastpitchnetworking.com/pressrelease.cfm?PRID=6584 [April 13, 2007]. "Grabará Pedro Infante una película a 50 años de su muerte," *El Universal*, March 29, 2007 http://www.eluniversal.com.mx/notas/vi_415401. html [April 13, 2007].

14. Irma Dorantes, *Así fue nuestro amor*, coll. Rosa María Villarreal (Mexico City: Planeta, 2007), 52, 79, 149. The book appeared in April 2007, and the magazine

Proceso published an excerpt in "Del rayo te salvas, pero . . .," *Proceso* April 15, 2007: 73–75. See also note 24.

15. The surviving children are Graciela, Pedro, and Guadalupe (from his relationship with Lupe Torrentera) and Irma (his only child with Irma Dorantes). For the ceremony at the House of Representatives, see "Rinden diputados homenaje a Pedro Infante," *El Universal* http://www.el-universal.com.mx/notas/417638.html [September 26, 2007]. For other events the families attended, see *Excelsior*, April 15, 2007, Función pp. 6–8. On the disputes over royalties, see *Excelsior*, Funcion p. 7 and "Los millones póstumos: Su herencia: discos y películas," Univision Online http://www.univision.com/ content/content.jhtml?cid=6488 [September 25, 2007].

16. "Prevén exhumar restos de Pedro Infante para terminar disputa familiar," *Terra* http://www.terra.com.pr/ocio/articulo/html/oci171962.htm [April 28, 2007].

17. *New York Times*, December 9, 1953, p. 11; April 18, 1957, p. 11. *El Universal* estimated the crowd at Infante's funeral at over one hundred thousand. *El Universal*, April 18, 1957, p. 1. Figures in the hundreds of thousands appear as estimates for the funerals of Cantinflas and María Félix. *Los Angeles Times*, April 23, 1993, p. 1; April 10, 2002, p. 1.

18. For coverage of the death and funeral of Jorge Negrete, see *El Universal*, November 6–9, 1953; for Javier Solís, see *Excelsior*, April 20–21, 1966; for Cantinflas, see *Excelsior*, April 24–25, 1993 and *La Opinión*, April 22–24, 1993; for Lola Beltrán, see *Reforma*, March 26–28, 1996 and *La Opinión*, March 26–27; for Paco Stanley, see *Reforma*, June 9, 1999, *La Opinión*, June 8–9, 1999, and *La Jornada*, June 9, 1999, "Una multitud respondió al llamado de televisoras" www.jornada.unam.mx/1999/06/09/funeraria.html [May 2, 2007]; for María Félix, see *El Universal*, April 9–10, 2002, and "Música, aplausos y miles de admiradores en homenaje a María Félix" and "Un adiós a la diva María Félix con fervor popular," both from *Agence France Presse*, April 9, 2002.

19. Rodríguez used three cameras to record the funeral. *Excelsior*, April 17, 1957, p. 8A.

20. *Excelsior*, November 27, 1963, p. 23A; November 28, 1963, p. 23A.

21. In the Tomás Méndez song, Infante requests "Las golondrinas" (a farewell song) because he is going far, far away. The song includes an excerpt of a mariachi solo of "Las golondrinas." Thus, Infante gets his wish. The song plays, just as it did during his funeral in 1957.

22. The narrator says "Pedro Infante ha muerto," which can translate as both "Pedro Infante has died" and "Pedro Infante is dead."

23. Ismael Rodríguez, Jr., directed *Pedro Infante: El hombre cine mexicano*, a documentary that borrows much of its content directly from *Así era Pedro Infante*. This version, like the original, contains no scenes from the films of other directors. It also includes an interview with Ismael Rodríguez in which he takes credit for Infante's singing success and claims that the actor told him that his favorite movies were *Los tres García* and *Vuelven los García*. The documentary does contain the original trailer of *Los tres huastecos*, and it also adds interviews with members of a recording studio where the ghost of Infante supposedly appears.

24. *Testimonios para la historia del cine mexicano* Vol. VI (Mexico City: Cuadernos de la Cineteca Nacional, Secretaría de Gobierno, 1976), 117. Rodríguez states that

he created the documentary without leaving his house, which could in some way explain why he only used clips from his movies and footage he coordinated on the day of the funeral.

25. Zacarías directed Infante in *Ansiedad* (1953), *Cuidado con el amor* (1954), and *Escuela de música* (1955), which played for an average of eights weeks in their original run. The closing credits of the movie fail to mention the title of León's book, but her account of their relationship appeared in 1961 as *Pedro Infante en la intimidad conmigo*.

26. Emilio García Riera, *Historia documental del cine mexicano* Vol. XI (Guadalajara, Mexico: Universidad de Guadalajara, 1992), 311–313. Rodríguez has claimed on at least two occasions that polls named *Nosotros los pobres* as the film with the highest number of screenings in the history of Mexico. I have not been able to verify this claim. *Testimonios*, 120; and Mara Carnaya, "Hace medio siglo inició el rodaje de Nosotros los pobres bajo la dirección de Isamael Rodríguez," Concejo Nacional para la Cultura y las Artes (1997) http://www.cnca.gob.mx/cnca/nuevo/diarias/171097/ismael.html [September 26, 2007].

27. *Excelsior*, April 20, 1966, p. 35A.

28. Zacarías includes numerous clips from his three movies, but even when Infante sings "Amorcito corazón," which famously appeared in Rodríguez's *Nosotros los pobres*, the song appears out of context and not in a scene or clip that connects it to Rodríguez.

29. In the movie Infante calls León on the day of his fatal flight and tells her that they will move back to a decrepit room similar to the one they rented when they first arrived in Mexico City, and there they will find the happiness that fame had eroded. Infante was in fact flying to comfort Dorantes, who was unable to cope with the court ruling that had annulled their marriage. Of course, Lupita Torrentera, the second of Infante's three principal companions, assured in a 2007 interview that he would have returned to her had he not died in 1957. *El Universal*, April 15, 2007 http://www.eluniversal.com.mx/espectaculos/75824.html [September 7, 2007].

30. The theme of the preeminence of women in his life appears early in the movie when the narrator portends that Infante's life, "like that of all men, was shaped by the women who entered his life." The movie also suggests that the 1949 plane accident that uncovered the affair between Infante and Torrentera (nameless in the movie) occurred because Infante had not slept well due to his late-night sexual encounters.

31. The Publicorp documentary was part of the series *Caminantes Sí Hay Camino* for Canal 40 and may also appear under the simpler title, *Pedro Infante*, or as part of a DVD that also features the life of Jorge Negrete.

32. Jaime Kuri directed the documentary based on Gustavo García's three-part minibiographies *No me parezco a nadie* (Mexico City: Editorial Clío, 1994).

33. Infante and Vargas sing "La negra noche" in their only cinematic collaboration.

34. The film opened on March 25, 1948, in the El Colonial theater, which increased its ticket prices from the regular two pesos to three, but still charged less for its double than other theaters that priced their tickets at three or four pesos for a single feature. The film then returned to seven discounted theaters on June 10 for one peso for a double feature. The ambitious second engagement ended abruptly

on June 18. *El Universal,* movie listings from March 17 to June 30, 1948. The documentary also mislabels the award Infante received in the Berlin Film Festival, calling it the Golden Bear—which only the best film receives—instead of the Silver Bear, which is for acting.

35. Emilio García Riera suggests that Rodríguez astutely chose the theater because of its location amid the lower-class people the film depicted, but in fact three Rodríguez-Infante films had recently opened at El Colonial: *Los tres García* (1946), *Vuelven los García* (1947), and *Cuando lloran los valientes* (1947), all with success not far below *Nosotros los pobres.* Furthermore, Rodríguez's decision to premiere the sequel *Ustedes los ricos* in the single-feature, higher-priced Palacio Chino in December of 1948 demonstrates that the location of the theater and a desire for a lower-class audience were not primary concerns. The movie played for only two weeks. García Riera, *Historia documental,* Vol. 4, 161–63.

36. Armando del Moral, "El Pedro Infante que conocí," *La Novela Cine-Gráfica* 96 (June 1957): 10.

37. The songs come from the following films: "Mi cariñito" from *Los Tres García* and *Vuelven los García;* the singing duel with Negrete from *Dos tipos de cuidado;* "Amorcito Corazón" from *Nostoros los pobres,* but serving as background music for this film and for the two sequels, *Ustedes los ricos* and *Pepe el Toro;* "¿Qué te ha dado esa mujer?" from *¿Qué te ha dado esa mujer?;* and "Te quiero más que a mis ojos" from *Tizoc.*

38. Emilio García Riera points out that Rodríguez only left out two of the films Infante did for him, *Escándalo de estrellas* and *Ustedes los ricos,* and even excluded movies that other Rodríguez brothers directed. García Riera, *Historia documental,* Vol. 5, 346.

39. Francisco Cuevas, "Ismael Rodríguez, autor de Pedro Infante: Responsable de la leyenda llamada Pedro," http://www.univision.com/content/content.jhtml;jsessionid=VFFJFLKJ2A1K0CWIAANCFEYKZAABWIWC?cid=7125 [April 17, 2007].

40. Among actresses, Dolores del Río had six films and María Félix had six. Roberto Gavaldón tied with Rodríguez among directors, and Luis Buñuel came in fourth with seven films. *Somos uno: Las 100 mejores películas del cine mexicano* 5:100 (July 1994), 26, 40, 58.

41. The six films they had in common were *La oveja negra* (ranked 24), *Nosotros los pobres* (27), *Dos tipos de cuidado* (34), *Los tres huastecos* (51), *A toda máquina* (55), and *Los tres García* (83). Four of these films (24, 27, 55, and 83) had sequels that did not make the list. One can surmise that either the voters chose not to include more than one film or that they chose one film to represent the other works. Rodríguez's other film, *Los hermanos del Hierro,* placed highest, at number 15, among any of the films in question. The last eleven films on the top-one-hundred list failed to get mentions in at least two of the lists that the voters originally compiled and thus derived from a runoff vote among only three critics. *Somos uno,* 6–7.

42. Luis Terán participated in the *Somos uno* poll, but he clearly did not favor Infante movies in his list of the top twenty-five movies, since he only included one Infante film, *A toda máquina* at number 17. *Somos uno,* 110. Terán listed the top twenty movies in the following order: *A toda máquina, ¿Qué te ha dado esa mujer?, Dos tipos de cuidado, Los tres García, Los tres huastecos, Vuelven los García, Escuela de*

vagabundos, El inocente, La oveja negra, Nosotros los pobres, No desearás la mujer de tu hijo, Ustedes los ricos, Los gavilanes, El mil amores, Pepe el Toro, Tizoc, Cuidado con el amor, Escuela de rateros, Dicen que soy mujeriego, and *Las mujeres de mi general.* The three films that did not make the list are *Escándalo de estrellas, Cuando lloran los valientes,* and *Sobre las olas.* Juan Carlos Castellanos, "Infante genera buen rating a Televisa," in Cine-Notas. http://www.terra.com.mx/formato.aspx?articuloid=263906&paginaid=1& formatoId= 1&canal=cine [May 1, 2007].

43. The opening credits of the Rodríguez documentary refer to those who collaborated in the film, including actors, movie critics, songwriters, and, among others, Producciones Matouk. Dorantes mentions the trip to Berlin in *Así fue nuestro amor.* "Del rayo," 74. http://us.imdb.com/Sections/Awards/Berlin_International_Film_Festival/1957 [August 27, 2007].

44. These movies had average runs of approximately nine weeks.

45. The average first run for all Infante-Rodríguez films was 3.2 weeks; their twelve films on Terán's top-twenty list played for an average of 3.4 weeks; the top six on that list played for an average of 2.8 weeks; and the six films on the *Somos uno* list played for an average of 3.5 weeks All information regarding the first-run box office numbers for individual films comes from García Riera's *Historia documental* in the volumes corresponding to the production year of each movie.

46. Three of his films premiered after his death: *Pablo y Carolina* (April 25, 1957), Tizoc (October 23, 1957), and *Escuela de rateros* (May 9, 1958). Thus, *Pablo y Carolina* was the only film that premiered during the thirty-day period discussed here. The five full-length films with Infante as protagonist that did not appear in theaters during this period were *La vida no vale nada* (1954), *Las Islas Marías* (1950), *El Ametralladora* (1943), *Cuando habla el corazón* (1943), and *Jesusita en Chihuahua* (1942). All information on the films that played between April 15 and May 15, 1957, comes from the movie listings in the Mexico City newspaper *Excelsior.*

47. *Escuela de música* played for twelve weeks in 1955, and *Cuidado con el amor* ran for seven weeks in 1954.

48. Terán listed these three movies as numbers 1, 5, and 11, respectively, and the *Somos* uno list of the one hundred greatest Mexican films ranked Los tres huastecos as number 51 and *A toda máquina* as number 55. The highest Infante film on the *Somos uno* list is *La oveja negra* (24), whose sequel is *No desearás la mujer de tu hijo.* Infante filmed the two movies simultaneously and both shared the same artistic quality. The critics who participated in the poll might have simply decided that only one film should represent movie series, a consistent pattern on the list.

49. *El Universal,* April 17, 1957, sec. I, part 2, pp. 1, 17.

50. *Chicago Daily Tribune,* April 16, 1957, p. 23. *New York Times,* April 18, 1957, p. 11. *Los Angeles Times,* April 16, 1957, p. 2; April 18, 1957, p. 24. Infante had performed in New York, Chicago, and Los Angeles. *Excelsior,* April 16, 1957, p. 15A.

51. For reports on his movies, see *Los Angeles Times,* May 2, 1944, p. A11; August 14, 1944, p. 8; December 23, 1945, p. B3; August 11, 1947, p. A2; December 24, 1947, p. 6; and June 6, 1951, p. B9. For reports on his live performances, see *Los Angeles Times,* May 25, 1945, p. A7; 10 December 1949, p. 13; January 17, 1952, p. B9; January 20, 1952, p. D3; and September 21, 1955, p. 19.

52. Both newspapers treated the death and burial of Infante as the most important event in several issues.

53. The images the theaters played appeared from April 27 to May 5, 1957, for different periods at all three theaters. It is not clear whether the movie listings referred to photographs or to newsreel since they simply used the term *imágenes*, which can have both meanings. Theater publicity for the release of *Así era Pedro Infante* in 1963 announced that the film included video of the funeral never before seen, leading one to believe that only photographs appeared in 1957. His movies remained a regular feature until June 10, 1957. *Excelsior*, November 27, 1963, p. 23A; November 28, 1963, p. 23A.

54. Rogelio Agrasánchez, *Mexican Movies in the United States: A History of the Films, Theaters, and Audiences, 1920–1960* (Jefferson, North Carolina: McFarland and Company, 2006), 8–11, 40–46, 80–83; see also the Appendix in pages 169–86.

55. Agrasánchez, *Mexican Movies*, 40, 100–104, 127–28, 160.

56. The magazine began the poll in April 1949. The first results appeared in November 1949, and had Infante (1,800 votes) ahead of Negrete (801) and María Félix (651). The poll ended in November 1950 with the following results: Infante (5,892 votes), Negrete (1,457), María Félix (1,058), Luis Aguilar (1,042), Libertad Lamarque (887), and Pedro Armendáriz (873). The results listed the top twenty-six places. The magazine repeatedly called on readers to support their celebrity, then arranged the entertainers by category so more of them appeared to be leading—though the ballot did not list any specific artist or category, and Infante appeared under singers—and even listed the order of the results without the number of votes received. All these efforts most likely sought to encourage—or at least not discourage—the fans of other entertainers. *La Novela Cine-Gráfica* April 1949–November 1950. The initial ballot appeared on page 8 of the April 1950 issue, and the final results came on page 30 of the November 1950 issue.

57. Armando del Moral, "El Pedro Infante que conocí," *La Novela Cine-Gráfica* 96 (June 1957): 6–13. Del Moral, as mentioned above, published a column with the same title that ran in *La Opinion* from April 22 to April 28, and the two texts have only slight differences; notably the magazine's version includes many photographs of Infante.

58. *Testimonios para las historia*, 112–14.

59. Mario Hernández, "Recondando a Pedro Infante en su primer aniversario," *La Novela Cine-Gráfica* 104 (April 1958) 6–10.

60. *La Opinión*, April 16, 1957, p. 1; April 17, 1957, p. 1; April 18, 1957, p. 1; April 19, 1957, p. 7.

61. Armando del Moral was a famous entertainment reporter and editor of the Los Angeles entertainment magazine *La Novela Cine-Gráfica*, which published mostly about Latin American entertainers and mostly in Spanish. He appears with Pedro Infante in a picture that ran on the first day of the series.

62. *La Opinión*, April 27, 1957, p. 3; April 28, 1957, p. 3.

63. For instance, in the case of *Arriba las mujeres*, Tere and Irma recognize and praise the blatant feminist message and lament its eventual concessions to a patriarchal system. When discussing the scene in *Ahora soy rico* where Pedro-as-Pedro is drinking with two women, Tere applies the lesson to her current situation and concludes, "I didn't want to be one of those two drunken women with the smeared

lipstick. Neither did I want to be Marga, stuck at home waiting for her man." Also, when she learns that Lucio, her lover, sees yet another woman, Tere feels like Lupe in *Las mujeres de mi general,* whom Pedro-as-Juan Zepeda betrays. Later, Tere adds that Lucio's affair with that woman "was such a betrayal. I knew how the poor Indita felt in *La mujer que yo perdí.*" Denise Chavez, *Loving Pedro Infante* (New York: Washington Square Press, 2002), 122, 191, 240–44.

64. Chavez, *Loving,* 77 and 266.

65. The mirror scene represents the key to the novel. Tere had previously referred to that scene, also while looking in a mirror, but did not pursue the matter further, simply admonishing Cruz for not accepting the fact that he is getting old. Tere proves that she is finally capable and willing to accept evidence that is counterproductive to her desire to be with Lucio. Thus while looking into the mirror, she sees herself when she was nine years old and met her father's mistress. Tere remembers the pain she felt and thinks of the effect her relationship must have on Lucio's daughter. Tere reemerges a "resurrected" phoenix. She resolves to concentrate on her life and forget about Lucio. Chavez, *Loving,* 162, 282–83.

66. Rubenstein deals effectively with this aspect of Infante's appeal.

67. James W. Wilkie, *Statistics and National Policy* (Los Angeles: UCLA Latin American Center, 1974), 41–44. The author explains that to understand the demographic centrality of the capital, one must consider that in 1960 the city accounted for 14 percent of the country's population, whereas in the United States the fifteen most populous cities combined for a total of 13.7 percent. For information on the decline of the populations of small villages and the growth of urban areas, see Richard W. Wilkie and Francis E. Lindsay, "Urbanization versus the Persistence of Small Places in Mexico, 1900–1990," *Statistical Abstract of Latin America* (Los Angeles: UCLA Latin American Studies Publications, Vol. 31, 1995), 1230–1245.

68. Approximately five million Mexican workers participated in the Bracero Program (1942–1964) in addition to the several million legal and undocumented migrants who came during those two decades. Arizona, California, and Texas accounted for over 80 percent of the Mexican-born population between 1940 and 1960, most of whom were farmworkers, laborers, and factory operatives. George J. Borjas and Lawrence F. Katz, "The Evolution of the Mexican-Born Workforce in the United States," NBER Working Paper 11281, April 2005, pp. 3, 53–55. For an explanation of the correlation between the Bracero Program and the surge in legal and undocumented arrivals, see Douglas S. Massey et al., *Beyond Smoke and Mirrors: Mexican Immigration in an Era of Economic Integration* (New York: Russell Sage Foundation, 2002), 32–38.

69. The article, which appeared in online services and Mexican newspapers, came from the news agency EFE and indicated that the album that includes "Las mañanitas" has sold twenty million copies in the last five decades. "Tiene Pedro Infante el disco más vendido de la historia de México," *El Universal,* April 12, 2007 http://www.eluniversal.com.mx/notas/418209.html [August 24, 2007]. The documentary *No me parezco a nadie* asserts that "Las mañanitas" became Peerless Records' biggest selling record in 1950.

70. *Los Angeles Times,* August 7, 1983, p. SE2.

71. The narrator of the documentary combines *nosotros* and *el pueblo* and thus says that Infante will continue singing in *nuestro corazón.* The narrator of the movie,

on the other hand, responds fervently to an actual *Excelsior* headline that reported Infante's death and exclaims, "No! Pedro Infante no ha muerto. Surgió del pueblo y continúa viviendo en el corazón del pueblo." Both films transition into the singing voice of Infante.

CHAPTER 15

1. See Jan Fairley, "The Rebellion and the Song," *Index on Censorship*, 14, No. 2 (March 1985) pp. 46–48, which focuses on the Salvadoran group Yolocamba I Ta; Gregorio Landau's dissertation, "The Role of Music in the Nicaraguan Revolution—Guitarra Armada." (Ph.D. Communications, University of California, San Diego, 1999; and T. M. Scruggs, "Nicaraguan State Cultural Initiative and the "Unseen Made Manifest," *Yearbook for Traditional Music*, 30 (1998) 53–73.

2. In Latin America, *música popular* refers to music of the people and may include folkloric, rural, and regional forms. The term is more inclusive than popular music as used in the United States, where general usage tends to equate popular with commercial success.

3. Carlos Mantica, "Las Memorias de Yolocamba I Ta," *Cuzcatlan* website. Accessed February 25, 2004. http://www.geocities.com/cuzcatlan76/cuzcatlan.html.

4. Yolocambi I Ta, along with Mahu Cutah Nah gui and Tepe gua ni, formed the vanguard of Salvadoran new song or *trova Salvadora* in the late 1970s.

5. Long before the Yolocambi I Ta created their song, "Basta Ya" circulated as the title of a Puerto Rican song credited to Abraham Pena that argues for the island's independence from the United States. The printed version appears along with other songs addressing matters of social justice in *The Second People's Song Book: Lift Every Voice!* edited by Irwin Silber with an introduction by Paul Robeson (New York: The People's Artists, 1953).

6. T. M. Scruggs, "Central American Music: Marimba and Other Musics of Guatemala and Nicaragua," in *Music in Latin America*, edited by John M. Schechter. New York: Schirmer Books (Thompson Learning), 1999:94.

7. Landau, "The Role of Music," 45. Ironically, I can remember salsa fans in New York's Latino clubs in the 1980s arguing that Blades's music was "overly intellectual" and too message oriented.

8. To learn more about *nueva canción chilena*, see John Schechter's overview of the tradition in his book *Music in Latin American Culture* (New York: Schirmer Books, 1999) 424–38 and the chapter on Latin American music by Schechter in the book *Worlds of Music* (New York: Schirmer, 1996) 428–94. Another useful overview that compares Chilean examples with the movement across Latin America appears in Peter Manuel, *Popular Music of the Non-Western World* (London: Oxford U. Press, 1988) 37–38; 68–72. Jan Fairley's comprehensive "Annotated bibliography of Latin American popular music with particular reference to Chile and to nueva canción," *Popular music* (1985) 5:305–56, includes extensive references to the Chilean new song movement, but covers other countries in Latin America as well. Fairley's introduction provides the context for the movement and makes an insightful comparative overview of ideological position and practice across Latin America.

9. In 1948 in the United States, the Peoples' Artists movement led by singers such as Pete Seeger, Alan Lomax, and Paul Robeson also envisioned new uses for traditional song that included articulating political leadership. Their efforts to use song to influence the election campaign of socialist Henry Wallace did not result in the kind of success, short-lived though it was, that Chilean *trovadores* experienced in the case of Allende. See Alan Lomax and Pete Seeger, *The People's Songbook.*

10. Debate rages on regarding the amount of involvement of the United States Central Intelligence Agency in unseating Allende. For insight into the period of the coup, see Edward Boorstein, *Allende's Chile: An Insider's View* (International Publishers, 1977); for a sense of Allende's policies through his own speeches and writings, consult the *Salvador Allende Reader: Chile's Voice of Democracy* by Salvador Allende Gossens, edited by James D. Cockcroft with Jane Canning (Ocean Press, 2000); for a broader view that considers the impact of Pinochet's dictatorship as well see *A Nation of Enemies: Chile under Pinochet* by Pamela Constable (W.W. Norton, 1993).

11. For personal insight offered by Jara's wife on his life and on the impact of his work and death on the *nueva canción* movement see Joan Jara, *An Unfinished Song: The Life of Victor Jara* (Boston: Ticknor and Fields, 1984).

12. See Jan Fairley, "Annotated bibliography of Latin American popular music with particular reference to Chile and to nueva canción," *Popular music* (1985) 5:305–56.

13. See Norberto Felix Galasso, *Atahualpa Yupanqui: El canto de la patria profunda* by (Colihue/Argentina 1992). *Viajes por el Mundo* (The Orchard, 2003) is the title of a recent compact disc recording of Yupanqui's music. Another recent CD audio compilation is *Atahualpa Yupanqui* (Le Chant du Monde, #274750, 1996).

14. There are exceptions especially in recent compositions and even in the early work; for example, the "Canción Urgente" that Rodriguez sang at the Second Festival of New Latin American Song in Managua in 1983 featured a guitar accompaniment with rock-tinged *guajira* rhythms. See *II Festival Nueva Canción Latinoamericana: Managua Nicaragua Libre* (Audio cassette recording, New Song c/o Robin Anderson, 1983). Other important Cuban *trovadores,* including Pablo Milanes, Sarah Gonzalez, and Grupo Mancada, did use or reference *son* in their new songs. Distinct approaches to the new song movement surfaced within national boundaries as well as across them.

15. For a brief discussion of Rodriguez's coded lyrics see Greg Landau, "Guitarra Armada: The Role of Music in the Nicaraguan Revolution," 71. There are other instances of performers in the new song movement receiving official support from their national governments, notably the Mexican singers Amparo Ochoa, Oscar Chavez, and the ensemble knows as Los Folkloristas.

16. Landau, "Guitarra Armada," 58.

17. It is hard not to see this point as one of the significant reasons that *nueva canción* continues to attract attention in academic circles. Although I am arguing in this article that the tradition continues to exert important influence today, it would be misleading to imply that *nueva canción* is at the critical center of Latin American popular music. By and large, the tradition continues to operate outside the commercial mainstream, and while that may be part of its ultimate strength, it does not generate the economic power or the kind of widespread commercial support that accrues to mainstream rock or pop musicians.

18. Academic support for music directed toward grassroots causes is hardly unique to the Latin American new song movement. Academic attention helps sustain interest in this music, as it has with music of the U.S. folk revival such as that of Pete Seeger or Woody Guthrie. On the other hand, the appeal of such artists is not purely academic. Anthony Seeger, former director of Smithsonian/Folkways, reports continued sales of the recordings by these artists. Their recordings certainly overshadow many recordings, including those of world music traditions, in the catalog that were generated for academic purposes (verbal communication, November 2003).

19. Compact disc recordings are now available for signature collections by these artists: Quilapayún, *Pueblo Unido Jamas Sera Vencido* (WEA International, 2003; originally recorded in 1966); Quilapayún, *Antología 1968–1992* (WEA International 2003); Violeta Parra, *Antología* (WEA International, 2003); Mercedes Sosa, *Gracias a la Vida* (Polygram, 1994); Mercedes Sosa, *30 Años* (Polygram, 1994).

20. Nicaraguan *trovadores*, including the Duo Guardabarranco, along with other self-described people's artists such as Arlo Guthrie, Pete Seeger, and John McCutheon, contributed to a recent compact disc singing songs of the Spanish Civil War; see *Spain in My Heart* (West Chester, PA: Appleseed Recordings, 2003).

21. "La Memoría: El lugar donde las Utopias son posibles," (Memory: The place where utopias are possible) Accessed February 25, 2004. http://www.elalmanaque.com/psicologia/memoria/musica.htm.

22. Landau, "Guitarra Armada," 85.

23. U.S. interest in commerce and expansion in Nicaragua, like elsewhere in the Americas, has roots in the Monroe Doctrine of 1823, which prohibited European expansion in the Western hemisphere, predicated on the presumption that the United States held those rights.

24. See *Sandino General de Hombres Libres* (Sandino, General of Free Men) (Enrigrac, Cassette audio tape, n.d.) featuring a collective of musicians including Carlos Mejia Godoy y los de Palacagüina, Grupo Pancasán, Duo Guardabarranco, Grupo Pueblo, Los Soñadores de Sarawasca, Luis Enrique Mejía Godoy, and Mancotal. *Sandino General de Hombres Libres* is also the title of a book written in 1955 by Gregorio Selser (Buenos Aires: Ediciones Pueblos Unidos de América).

25. Walter Fehrmann, "Artists/Entrevistas. Carlos Meijia Godoy (Nicaragua)." *Estación tierra* website, http://www.estaciontierra.com/nt/c_mejiagodoy.htm (accessed February 25, 2004).

26. Landau, "Guitarra Armada," 8; 39.

27. Ernesto Cardenal, the poet and Catholic priest whose work inspired Carlos Mejia Godoy, was the paternal uncle of Duo Guardabarranco's Katia and Salvador Cardenal. In the 1960s, the young priest renounced his wealthy background and retreated to the archipelago of Solentiname. The humble farming people who lived in the simple adobe homes there became the focus of his ministry and the site became, as Landau reports, his "laboratory for a blend of Marxism, liberation theology and Nicaraguan nationalism." In his ministry he encouraged local people to produce their own testimonies in paintings and poetry.

28. *El Nuevo Diario* (Nicaragua) December 2001.

29. He later returned to Nicaragua. For the composer's comments on the mass, see Zayda García Zeledón, "La Misa de Carlos," *El Nuevo Diario*. (Nicaragua,

December 2001) available on the website: Cultura. *La Insignia*, December 16, 2001. http://www.lainsignia.org/2001/diciembre/cul_030.htm.

30. Katia Cardenal Barquero, *20 Canciones con acordes para guitarra: Duo Guardabarranco cancionero*. [Twenty songs with guitar chords: a Duo Guardabarranco Songbook]. Managua: Guardabarranco, 2002.

31. Landau, "Guitarra Armada," 270.

32. Ted Warmbrand, personal communication with the author, Tucson, February 2004.

33. Barbara Kingsolver, *High Tide in Tucson* (New York: Perennial, Harper Collins, 1999). Ted Warmbrand echoes this view when he says, "When I hear Carlos Mejia Godoy, I hear the national music of Nicaragua; when I hear Duo Guardabarranco, I hear myself" (personal communication, March 2003).

34. Raúl R. Romero, "Tragedies and Celebrations: Imagining Foreign and Local Scholarships," *Revista Música Latinoamericana/Latin American Music Review* (2001) 22 no. 1: 50.

35. "Hacer Amanecer" is included on the audiocassette recording *Guardabarranco Días de Amar*, (Redwood Records—RRC9102) 1991. Translation is mine.

36. Salvador Cardenal, *Música y Canto*. (Managua: Disco Juvenil, 1976).

37. Katia Cardenal Barquero, *20 Canciones con acordes para guitarra: Duo Guardabarranco cancionero*, p. 10.

38. The first festival of the Organization of Iberoamerican Television took place in Spain in the auditorium of the Palacio de Congresos y Exposiciones in Madrid in November of 1972 before two thousand spectators. It was broadcast to twenty-one countries with an estimated audience of 100,000,000 viewers. The OTI festival, sponsored by *Billboard* magazine, quickly became one of the most prestigious festivals for Spain and Latin American.

39. Katia and Parvez are now divorced.

40. For information on Mantica-Waid and its catalogue of Nicaragua music, visit http://www.ibw.com.ni/~cmant/discos.html; or http://www.musicanica.com.

41. For Salvador, the issue has added urgency. He has been diagnosed with cryoglobular anemia, a disease with a fatal progression.

42. Salvador Cardenal Barquero, "Production and Publication of a CD of Ecological Music" (grant proposal dated February 22, 2002).

43. Ibid.

44. See Daniel Faber, "Imperialism, Revolution, and the Ecological Crisis of Central America," *Latin American Perspectives* 19:1 (Winter 1992) 17–44.

45. Two contrasting views of ecotourism are Mario A. Boza, "Conservation in Action: Past, Present, and Future of the National Park System of Costa Rica," *Conservation Biology*, Vol. 7, No. 2 (June 1993), pp. 239–47; and J. Robert Hunter, "Is Costa Rica Truly Conservation-Minded?" *Conservation Biology*, Vol. 8, No. 2 (June 1994), pp. 592–95.

46. Katia Cardenal Barquero, *20 Canciones con acordes para guitarra: Duo Guardabarranco cancionero*.

47. June Nash. "Global Integration and Subsistence Insecurity," *American Anthropologist*, Vol. 96:1 (March 1994), 24.

48. Katia Cardenal Barquero. *20 Canciones con acordes para guitarra: Duo Guardabarranco cancionero*.

Video Distributors

Cinema Guild
1697 Broadway, Suite 506
New York, NY 10019
212-246-5522
www.cinemaguild.com

Facets Multimedia, Inc.
1517 W. Fullerton Avenue
Chicago, IL 60614
800-331-6197
www.facets.org

Films for the Humanities and Sciences
P.O. Box 2053
Princeton, NJ 08543-2053
800-257-5126
www.films.com

Filmakers Library
124 E. 40th Street
New York, NY 10016
212-808-4980
www.filmakers.com

International Media Resource Exchange
124 Washington Place
New York, NY 10014
212-463-0108
Fax: 212-243-2007

Madera Cinevideo
525 East Yosemite Avenue
Madera, CA 93638
800-828-8118
Fax: 209-674-3650

Organization of American States (OAS)
Audio Visual Unit
1889 F Street NW
Washington, DC 20006
202-458-6016
Fax: 202-458-6021

PBS Video Sales
1320 Braddock Place
Alexandria, VA 22314
800-344-3337

University of California Extension Media Center (UCEMC)
200 Center Street, 4th Floor
Berkeley, CA 94704
510-643-9271
cmil@uclink.berkeley.edu

World Video
P.O. Box 30469
Knoxville, TN 37930
615-691-9827

Index

About the Editors

William H. Beezley is one of the pioneers of the cultural history of Mexico. He wrote essays in the early 1980s that examined Mexican popular culture and political humor and in 1987 published *Judas at the Jockey Club*, one of the first monographs to consider the efforts at modernization during the regime of Porfirio Díaz (1876–1911) by investigating topics such as sport, public hygiene, fashion, and consumerism. In the same volume, he offered perhaps the first examination of nineteenth-century material culture and national poverty, and in the conclusion he explored the use of public celebrations as opportunities for political resistance and satire. With Colin MacLachlan, he wrote *Latin America: The Peoples and Their History* (2000). He and Michael C. Meyer edited *The Oxford History of Mexico* (2000), now in a second edition (2010), and he edited *A Companion to Mexican History and Culture* (2011). In an effort to understand popular performances and cultural nationality, he wrote *Mexican National Identity: Memory, Innuendo and Popular Culture* (2008).

Linda A. Curcio-Nagy is associate professor of history at the University of Nevada, Reno. She has published articles on popular culture, ritual, and piety in colonial Mexico and has edited a special volume of *The Americas* on colonial ritual and popular culture. Her monograph *The Great Festivals of Colonial Mexico City: Performing Power and Identity* was published in 2004, and she is currently writing a book on sexual desire and popular religion utilizing solicitation in the confessional cases for seventeenth-century Mexico City.

About the Contributors

Sal Acosta specializes in the history of Latinos in the United States as an assistant professor of history at Fordham University. In his work, he has focused on the historical evolution of society in the Southwest and on the social and cultural experiences of Latinos since 1846. His current project examines interethnic marriages in Arizona (1854–1930), using both quantitative and qualitative methods to reevaluate the perception that intermarriages in the nineteenth-century Southwest occurred primarily among enterprising white men and the daughters of Mexican elites. In addition, he is completing a book that uses the funeral of Pedro Infante as a window on post–World War II Mexican and Mexican-American popular culture.

Thomas L. Benjamin, professor of history at Central Michigan University, is best known for his two monographs, *A Rich Land, A Poor People: Politics and Society in Modern Chiapas* (1996) and *La Revolución: Mexico's Great Revolution as Memory, Myth, and History* (2000), but he has also published two significant anthologies dealing with modern Mexican history. With William McNellie he edited *Other Mexicos: Essays on Regional Mexican History, 1876–1911* (1984), and with Mark Wasserman he edited *Provinces of the Revolution* (1989). His current research focuses on more global topics, and he recently published *Atlantic World: Europeans, Africans, Indians and Their Shared History, 1400–1900* (2009).

John Charles Chasteen received his Ph.D. at the University of North Carolina, where he is now professor of history. The author of several books on the border region and peoples of Brazil and Uruguay, he has written the well-known textbook *Born of Fire and Blood* and the outstanding monograph on music and dance in Latin America titled *National Rhythms, African Roots: The Deep History of Latin American Popular Dance* (2004), and translated several important volumes from Spanish, including Angel Rama's *The Lettered City* (1996) and Federico Gamboa's *Santa: A Novel of Mexico City* (2010).

Darién J. Davis, associate professor at Middlebury College, received his Ph.D. from Tulane University. He has published *White Face, Black Mask: Africaneity and the Early Social History of Popular Music in Brazil* (2008) and edited *Slavery and Beyond: The African Impact on Latin America and the Caribbean* (1995), in the Latin American Jaguar Series.

Lauren (Robin) H. Derby, assistant professor at University of California, Los Angeles, examined the cultural history of the Dominican Republic in her dissertation at the University of Chicago, titled "The Magic of Modernity: Dictatorship and Civic Culture in the Dominican Republic, 1916–1962." From this research she published "Haitians, Magic and Money: Raza and Society in the Haitian-Dominican Borderlands, 1900–1937" in *Comparative Studies in Society and History,* which won the 1995 Conference on Latin American History Award, and the monograph *The Dictator's Seduction: Politics and the Popular Imagination in the Era of Trujillo* (2009). Her volume won the 2010 book of the year award from the Conference on Latin American History. In Chicago, she regularly appeared on radio programs on Caribbean popular music.

Matthew D. Esposito received his Ph.D. from Texas Christian University in 1997. His dissertation was recently published as *Funerals, Festivals, and Cultural Politics in Porfirian, Mexico.* It examines, among other topics, the connection between state funerals and the campaign to legitimate the regime of Porfirio Díaz (1876–1911). Currently he is chair of the history department at Drake University in Des Moines, Iowa.

Ingrid E. Fey is adjunct professor at University of California, Los Angeles, where she received her Ph.D. in 1996. In addition to revising her dissertation, titled "First Tango in Paris: Latin Americans in Turn-of-the-Century France, 1880–1920," she and Karen Racine are the editors of the anthology *Strange Pilgrimages: Exile, Travel, and National Identity in Latin America, 1800–1990s* (2000). She has written one of the few studies on Latin American participation in the world fairs.

Stephen Jay Gould (1941–2002), world-renowned paleontologist at Harvard University, published more than fifteen books on a variety of topics in natural history, including *The Mismeasure of Man* (1981), *Bully for Brontosaurus* (1988), *Full House: The Spread of Excellence from Plato to Darwin* (1996), *Leonardo's Mountain of Clams and the Diet of Worms* (1998), and *Rocks of Ages: Science and Religion in the Fullness of Life* (1999). He also wrote a monthly scientific essay for *Nature* magazine. Gould, at the end of his career, held the Alexander Agassiz Professorship of Zoology at Harvard University and the Vincent Astor Professorship of Biology at New York University.

Graham E. L. Holton received the University Medal for his 1995 dissertation, "State Petroleum Enterprises and the International Oil Industry: The Case of Trinidad and Tobago," at LaTrobe University, Bundoora, Australia. His research builds on his two undergraduate degrees in history (LaTrobe) and petroleum geology (Royal Melbourne Institute of Technology). His dissertation will be published as a monograph by the University of the West Indies, Jamaica.

Fanni Muñoz Cabrejo, a native of Lima, Peru, wrote her dissertation on modernization programs and social change in Lima during the Belle Epoque in the doctoral program in the Department of History at El Colegio de México in 1999. She published it with the title *Diversiones públicas en Lima 1890–1920: La experiencia de la modernidad* (2002). Currently a member of the faculty at the Pontificia Universidad Cathólica del Perú, she now focuses her research on issues of education and gender in modern Peru.

Blanca Muratorio, professor emerita of anthropology at the University of British Columbia in Vancouver, has published extensively on a variety of topics dealing with ethnicity and Native Americans, especially in Ecuador. Her works include *Etnicidad, evangelización y protesta en el Ecuador: Una perspectiva antropológica* (1982), *The Life and Times of Grandfather Alonso: Culture and History in the Upper Amazon* (1991), and *Imágenes e imagineros* (1994).

Jeffrey M. Pilcher, beginning with the publication of *¡Que vivan los tamales: Food and the Making of Mexican Identity!* (1998), has established himself as one of the leaders in the history of cuisine, especially in Mexico. His current project examines the globalization of Mexican food. In addition, he has written *Cantinflas and the Chaos of Mexican Modernity* (2000) and edited *The Human Tradition in Mexico* (2002). He is professor of history at the University of Minnesota.

Janet Sturman, an ethnomusicologist and pianist, teaches in the Department of Music at the University of Arizona. She earned a Ph.D. from Columbia University with research that resulted in the book *Zarzuela: Spanish*

Operetta, American Stage (2001). She has also published articles and reviews in *The Garland Encyclopedia of World Music, Current Musicology, The Yearbook for Traditional Music, Ethnomusicology, The World of Music, Interdisciplinary Humanities,* and *Louisiana Folklife*. She served as the editor for *The World of Music Journal* from 1995–2001. Her research centers on the role of music in the maintenance, creation, and projection of ethnic and social identity. Her special interest in American multicultural practice has led to studies of music in the American Southwest as well as Spanish and Latin American expressions. She has produced and directed successful Mexican and Costa Rican zarzuelas at the University of Arizona.

Pamela Voekel, an associate professor at the University of Georgia, currently has a new book project that focuses on the interplay of gender, race, religion, and politics in Mexico and the larger Atlantic world, 1750–1870. She received her Ph.D. from the University of Texas for her dissertation "Scent and Sensibility: Pungency and Piety in the Making of the Veracruz Gente Sensata, 1780–1810," which she published as *Alone before God: The Religious Origins of Modernity in Mexico* (2002). She also published the widely cited article "Peeing on the Palace: Bodily Resistance to Bourbon Reforms" in the *Journal of Historical Sociology*.

CPSIA information can be obtained at www.ICGtesting.com
Printed in the USA
BVOW071008031011

272563BV00001B/5/P

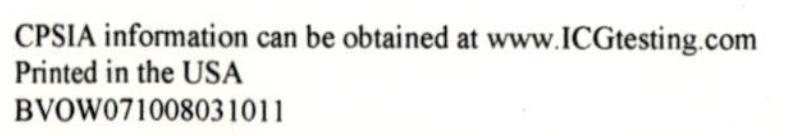

9 781442 212558